FNM

KT-215-840

808.81

...hose to
...he work
...ho have
...the poet
... are, no
...bel, but
...nd their
...ctions to
...ne's own
...mpiled a
...**rdimer**,
...iterature

...ng cries,
...ble rich
...mething
... a robust
...enty-first
...es intent
...nyakaa,
...zer Prize

LANGUAGE FOR A NEW CENTURY

CONTEMPORARY POETRY
from the MIDDLE EAST, ASIA, and BEYOND

EDITED BY

TINA CHANG, NATHALIE HANDAL,
AND RAVI SHANKAR

W. W. NORTON & COMPANY

NEW YORK | LONDON

Since this page cannot legibly accomodate all the copyright notices,
Permissions Acknowledgments constitutes an extension of the copyright page.

Manufacturing by Courier Westford
Book design by JAM Design
Production manager: Julia Druskin

Library of Congress Cataloging-in-Publication Data

Language for a new century : contemporary poetry from the Middle East,
Asia, and beyond / edited by Tina Chang, Nathalie Handal, and Ravi Shankar. — 1st ed.
    p. cm.
  Includes bibliographical references and index.
  ISBN 978-0-393-33238-4 (pbk.)
  1. Poetry—Translations into English. I. Chang, Tina. II. Handal, Nathalie, 1969– III. Shankar,
Ravi, 1975–
    PN6101.L26 2008
    808.81—dc22

                                                                            2007049424

W. W. Norton & Company, Inc., 500 Fifth Avenue, New York, N.Y. 10110
www.wwnorton.com

W. W. Norton & Company Ltd., Castle House, 75/76 Wells Street, London W1T 3QT

1 2 3 4 5 6 7 8 9 0

FOR OUR FAMILIES

AROUND THE WORLD

CONTENTS

Contents

Contents

Contents

Contents

Contents

Contents

Contents

Contents

Contents

Contents

Contents

Contents

Contents

Contents

Contents

Contents

Contents

Contents

FOREWORD

In *Language for a New Century* we are brought into a new *milieu*, or rather into *mille lieux*—a thousand places—in which poetry calls out on the threshold of a perilous future to readers who have, until now, been impoverished by the scarcity of what is found here: an assemblage of poetry silenced or unattended, a symphony of utterance, a mosaic of discreet moments of written art. While traveling, I have carried this collection through Macedonian mountain passes bordering Albania, Greece, and Kosovo, beside roadways collapsed under military convoys, taking the long way around because the bridges gave way beneath the weight of tanks. Accompanying me were poets of Azerbaijan, Turkey, India, and Iran, eager to meet each other, read poems, recite those of others committed to memory, drink a prodigious number of espressos, and smoke an alarming quantity of tobacco. It is only by coincidence that I am here while writing an introduction for this unprecedented collection, but it so happens. In the next days, we will hear the poets on our bus, and also poets of Japan, Palestine (Ramallah, West Bank), Iceland, and the nations of Europe. In a war-torn country, in a "fragile state," at Struga, site of the oldest poetry festival on earth, we will watch a procession by torchlight in honor of our art, fireworks sent into the night air, and later fishing boats, kayaks, and canoes row and paddle toward the bridge over the river Drim where the poets will read, while thousands gather along its banks, the whole of it broadcast live on television. I bear this news to a country where poets have been told that their art doesn't matter, that poetry makes nothing happen—my country—where poetry is almost never news. Take heart. We have entered a different epoch, and this anthology is, let us say, our guide and interpreter.

We know, from the mellifluous litany of poets' names, *who* wrote these poems, but we might also consider *what* wrote them: the urge to sing, pray, cry, announce, and whisper; to write cultures into visibility; to write not *after* events but in their *aftermath*, through collisions in time and space, exile within and without; to walk around in the ruins of wars, awake. What wrote them was a determination to *revolt against silence with a bit of speaking*. What wrote was an upwelling of poetic apprehension of world.

"What the poem translates," wrote Philippe Lacoue-Labarthe, "I propose we call experience, on condition that this word be taken literally—from Latin, *experiri*: the risky crossing . . . and this is why one can refer, strictly speaking, to a poetic existence." The poems of *Language for a New Century*, whether composed originally in English or borne into English from another language, attempt this crossing: from experience to experience, culture to culture, world to world. Those who remain in the countries of their ancestry send their poems out as messages in bottles, as the *Flaschenpost* called for by the poet Paul Celan. These poems float in a sea of hope that one day they will be retrieved and apprehended by the *other*. Those who are by force, or force of circumstance, exiled, at times remain on the bridge, shuttling between realities as messengers and interpreters unable themselves to fully inhabit again the regions of past and future. I call them "bridge people," who live by choice or destiny in a realm suspended over a chasm of incomprehension, tethered neither to their birth countries nor to their adopted lands.

The poets who share this condition are represented in great numbers here, as are the poets who are haunted by memories of events through which they did not live, but which nevertheless marked them through the impress of extremity on their parents and grandparents. There are sections in this symphony of utterance for those who live in cultures still capable of slowing the passage of time, for those connected to their surroundings not by years, decades, or centuries but by millennia, and those who find their cultures hurling toward a vertiginous future. There are voices, light as wind instruments, who are able to sustain contemplation, and those who, as mournfully as violas, attend to human suffering, striking poignant notes of compassion and lament. Many of these poets write with an uncommon and unabashed directness, whether condemning injustice or confessing the passions of the heart.

In what might be an unprecedented move (this is, after all, an unprecedented collection), the editors have included the poets of the diaspora: poets of Asia and the Middle East who have scattered across the world in search of work, reunion, refuge. These poets have amplified the age-old poetic inclination toward longing—the Armenian *garod* of Barouyr Sevag's poem "The Analysis of Yearning." What do the diaspora poets yearn for? Theirs are the voices of exilic being, not always exile itself perhaps but a dislocation, through which passes recollections of the aromas of certain spices carried by cook-smoke, the muezzin's call to prayer, a silken wind having cleansed itself through a particular mountain pass, the silver of olive groves. These poets live toward a future that does not yet beckon to them, in a present that seems empty—a space for economic survival, where they watch their children grow inexorably away from their ancestors. Exilic being can also be an internal condition of inner restlessness or sense of difference experienced by those who have never left their natal country, or recognize within themselves something of the nomadic spirit. They do not feel *at home*, but rather *en route*.

What the poem asks is that we enter into their lyric disclosure as we would cross the threshold of another's dwelling—with curiosity, respect, and a withholding of assumptions. This is especially true of poems that have been written out of rifts between peoples or are the fruit of cultural hybridity, aware that consciousness, out of which the poem arises, is experienced differently by different people, who are variously aware, receptive, curious—who might share affinities at a distance or estrangements close at hand. In entering these poems, we are shown something through the eyes of another. The most vivid memory of this from my own life happened more than twenty years ago, when militia fighters in the Shouf mountains of Lebanon passed me their field glasses, through which I saw my own country's military forces, far below us, dug into their bunkers: my country as seen through the eyes of others.

We are submerged, as all humans are, in what is politically understood as *ideology* and what is humanely called *culture*; these constitute "world" for us—our versions of world, invisibly walled and roofed. This anthology is an invitation to go outside. As the Korean poet Ko Un writes, *everything outside my door / is my teacher*. There is no more powerful passage through the impasse of misunderstanding than through the perceptions of others: we see ourselves through them, perceive our acts through their experience, and glimpse a means by which we might arrive at ethical relation, a modesty of being, an attitude of discretion. By this means we are able to calculate true cost (of economic and political oppression, institutional violence, warfare, environmental destruction) and alter the way our lives are understood at the deepest levels, so as not to allow any possible future to be foreclosed by our unjust and violent past and present. Against the possibility that these thoughts might seem abstract or at a remove from the concerns of literature, I would argue that such radical meeting of the *other*, in various prosodies and forms, is the way poems constellate meaning, and the way poems transmit the life form of language.

From the poems themselves, in a collage of quotation, we find answers to the question of what this poetry *knows*. It knows *centuries of quietude*, and that *poverty leads to desperation*. It knows that *life is filled with errors*, and *regrets change nothing*. It knows *the violence / with which the past is suppressed*, that *killer and killed . . . speak the same language*, and that *whatever rises is a fort, / whatever spreads is a battlefield*. It knows *things that have disappeared, bullet holes in a curtain, the blaze of hunger,* and what it is to be killed but forget to die. Herein is *the first hour of another life*, and a poet who wishes not to eat anything *that's not generally available to mankind.* This poetry knows why it is *crazy to throw yourself headlong into a volcano and sing* and knows, too, *the skydom of migrant birds* and *the solitude of the antelope*.

The human condition, for these poets, cannot be generalized but is intricately faceted, incommensurate, and particular. There is, in the diction of these poets, a richness of association: *winter monsoon, cicada, liana, joss stick,* a fruit called *lansones,* and the trees *changmas, banyan,* and *Juan Tamad.* There is also an edgy inclusion of *toxic rain,* a *dialysis machine, CNN, Toyota.* In these poems we find street sweepers, border guards, barbers, censors, butchers, scavengers, market women, schoolchildren, soldiers, refugees. There are surgeries, orphanages, police stations, libraries, and liquor shops. We learn the *ninety nine names of Exile,* and the language of *fragmen+a+ion grenades* and Claymore mines. We learn, in context, the meanings of *tai-qi-quan, prashad, lalang, amrit, lungi, aazan, bindi, fallah, bhaat, ezan, bailarina.* This is poetry of *pitch smoke, carburetors, / potash alum, fruit husks,* of temples and city dumps. Where else would we find poetry from a two-thousand-year-old Seal script, poetry written in the graphemic style of Sanskrit, as well as English versions of experimental poetry from the Marathi language? In these collisions, poetry for the twenty-first century begins.

In Central America many years ago, a human rights worker pondered the prospect of a new ambassador from the United States to his country in the aftermath of over a decade of revolutionary struggle and civil war. "Why send us your bureaucrats?" he asked. "Send us your poets. Send us the soul of your country." Having spent brief periods of my life in towns and cities that are wellsprings for this anthology, I had to think for a long time about what he meant by this. In Nablus, Ramallah, Nazareth, and

Jersusalem, and in Sidon, Tyre, Beirut, Tripoli, Kyoto, Hiroshima, Naga-saki, and Tokyo, I met those who were at that moment encountering, some for the first time, a citizen of the United States who knew the poetry of her own country but did not know well enough the poetry of theirs. This knowl-edge might have proved as beneficial as proficiency in the language—as poetry *is* a language—held in common by all cultures, and there is noth-ing more familiar, and at the same time more surprising, than the sponta-neous recitation of poems by people thrown together by circumstance or destiny in unexpected places and times, even the most dire: Pablo Neruda in Arabic, whispered in the Shouf mountains on the eve of an impending attack; Mahmoud Darwish sung in a refugee camp by the light of a whirring Coleman lamp; Nâzim Hikmet spoken in the seven-gate lockup of a men's maximum-security prison. These are but a few of the places I have heard poetry spoken.

With deference to the notable exceptions proving the rule, and acknowledged by this volume's editors, there were very few anthologies of international poetry available in the United States even through the 1980s, as astonishing as that may seem. It was just such a dearth that prompted me to assemble one, for the benefit of my students, and since its publication there have been others, but not until now one quite as imaginatively constructed and as sweeping as *Language for a New Cen-tury*, wherein we read through poetry unknown to us one poem at a time, through nine realms of human experience: childhood, selfhood, experi-mentation, oppression, mystery, war, homeland and exile, spiritual life, love and sexuality, from Afghanistan to Yemen. Now, in the words of the Japanese poet Shiraishi Kazuko, *there is a language / for them to talk to one another.*

That language is *poetry*, but it is also often the language of translation. In our country especially, it is necessary for translators to assimilate the poets' labors and, in many of these poems, to construct a vessel in a new language that might resemble the poem shattered by the translator's art, then reassembled to suggest the original, bearing the sensibility of the poem into English but, inevitably, without retaining its original music. *Translation lays open the forbidden*, writes Steve Bradbury, translating from the Chinese of Hung Hung in this collection. Yes, but in the same poem, Hung also calls translation *that peculiar calling so resembling undercover work . . . Its sole injunction, to resist all injunctions.* There are those who claim that the translation of poetry is impossible, but if that supposition had held, we would be denied the sacred texts of the world's spiritual tra-ditions, and also Homer, Ovid, Dante, and our early English-language poets. I prefer to think it not only possible but necessary and salvific to bring poetry from one language to another, with Hans Magnus Enzensberger's caveat: "*kann nicht Übersetzung von Poesie sein*": what is not poetry cannot be a translation of poetry. The editors of this collection have chosen with great care among available translations, and thankfully the number of translators, whether working in isolation or collaboratively, has grown during the past few years, even while the willingness of publishers to take a risk on an "unknown" poet from a foreign language has, to our misfortune, diminished, and therefore *our* language has also suffered— because just as much as we translate poets into English, we translate English into these poets, and the English language is thereby enriched.

When we consider poetry in translation, we consider the transmission of sensibility and the expressivity of content rather than the music, cadence, sound, and wordplay of prosody in a foreign language. But herein are also poems originally written in English: poems that carry no translator's signature but are written (whether in the United States or other English-speaking countries) in English made freshly original by poets who were formed, if not by another language, then by another culture, at least in part. These poets, who are inhabitants and descendents of Asia and the Middle East, guide us by means of poetry toward an understanding necessary to the world's survival. If poetry is, indeed, the natural prayer of the human soul, what better way to approach the *other* than by language elevated beyond the service of diplomacy to the realm of art?

There are among these lyric poems, ghazals, narratives, dramatic monologues, concrete poems, epistolaries, poems of confession and address, odes, elegies, postcards, inventories, haiku, and the less familiar Japanese form *zuihitsu*. There are intimate voicings of erotic experience, spiritual awakening, and praise of domestic life, and also the poetry of testimony, of *témoignage*—poems that confer on us a certain obligation. In poems written under siege and occupation, in the aftermath of wars, in mourning and the bewilderment of unanticipated survival, we read the *cri de coeur*, the song, the saying of the other. There are also poems that instruct us on how to live as a stranger among a hostile or unwelcoming people, on how to take refuge, and where to find, under the most adverse conditions, small moments of joy and respite.

In the late twentieth century, Czeslaw Milosz wrote: "The poetic act changes with the amount of background reality embraced by the poet's consciousness. In our century, that background is, in my opinion, related to the fragility of those things we call civilization or culture. What surrounds us, here and now, is not guaranteed. It could just as well not exist."

Read *Language for a New Century* as you would a field guide to the human condition in our time, a poetic survival manual if you will, for how much more fragile do those things we call *civilization* and *culture* seem now? If, as Milosz also wrote, "posterity will read us in an attempt to comprehend what the twentieth century was like," then this collection will be read to know the beginning of the twenty-first.

— CAROLYN FORCHÉ
MACEDONIA, SEPTEMBER 2007

PREFACE

Following the events of September 11, 2001, two of us, Tina Chang and Ravi Shankar, began asking ourselves with whom did we identify? Though we grew up keenly aware of our respectively Chinese American and Indian American backgrounds, we began to feel an even deeper solidarity between ourselves and others of Eastern descent. How could we respond to the destruction and unjust loss of human lives while protesting the one-sided and flattened view of the East being showcased in the media? What was the vantage point we could arrive at in order to respond on a human level, to generate articulate dialogue, conversations that did not fall into the rhetorical fallacies of *us vs. them*? As poets and editors, we desperately sought to find a solution, though there was no solution. There was, however, a distinct path to choose and that was one of further understanding. What we turned to was what was most innate to us: poetry, which provided the impetus for beginning this project. Rather than focusing on our own personal reactions, we felt that looking outward toward a wide spectrum of poetry would give us the opportunity for discovery and transformative wisdom. Putting together an anthology seemed the necessary path. We sought the expertise of a third editor and found Nathalie Handal, who had just published the groundbreaking anthology *The Poetry of Arab Women* and was herself of Arab descent. After speaking to her, we knew that we had found the right person because the way in which she spoke about the project was similar to our own vision. Together, we set out on a journey to gather voices that add to the ongoing dialogue between East and West.

On September 29, 2001, less than three weeks after 9/11, novelist Arundhati Roy wrote an editorial in the *Guardian* entitled, "The Algebra of Infinite Justice." This prescient essay acknowledged that we were living in a changed moment, where, "box-cutters, penknives and cold anger,"[1] would be "the weapons with which the wars of the new century will be waged." In putting this anthology together we had an alternate vision of the new century in which words, not weapons, could define our civilization. Roy further wrote, "the first step is to acknowledge [that we] share the planet with other nations, with other human beings, who, even if they are not on TV, have loves and griefs and stories and songs and sorrows." The poems collected here are proof of this truth; indeed this anthology includes poets writing in over forty different languages. Yet, while we might traditionally think of language in terms of accent and idiom, the many distinct forms of communication that exist in specific geographic regions, our title, *Language for a New Century*, proposes that these voices converge in the dream of shared utterance.

We next considered how to define the East, a challenging task since there is no general consensus as to what defines the region. Initially, while reflecting on what countries to include, we sat down with an atlas and realized that if we were to be true to our intention of inclusiveness, we had to deal with a much wider region than we might have presupposed. For instance, Central Asia has generally been neglected and left out of most discussions of the East; therefore, it was important for us to include those poets. Other countries are also considered part of two distinct regions, such as Sudan, which is both Middle Eastern and African. We might not have included some countries that readers or critics believe to be part of the East and we might have included others that some might question, but ultimately our intention was to provide as comprehensive a view as possible.

We've gathered a broad selection of established and emerging South Asian, East Asian, Middle Eastern, Central Asian poets as well as poets living in the diaspora—over four hundred diverse voices, native and transplanted, political and apolitical, monastic and erotic, known and unknown, in the hope of providing insights that transcend any narrowly defined strata of Eastern culture. We decided to include the following sixty-one countries and/or territories: Afghanistan, Algeria, Armenia, Azerbaijan, Bahrain, Bangladesh, Bhutan, Burma (Myanmar), Cambodia, China, Egypt, Hong Kong, India, Indonesia, Iran, Iraq, Israel, Japan, Jordan, Kashmir, Korea, Kurdistan, Kuwait, Kyrgyzstan, Laos, Lebanon, Libya, Macau, Malaysia, Maldives, Morocco, Nepal, Oman, Palestine, Pakistan, Philippines, Qatar, Saudi Arabia, Singapore, Sri Lanka, Sudan,

---

[1] http://www.guardian.co.uk/Archive/Article/0,4273,4266289,00.html.

Syria, Taiwan, Tajikistan, Tartarstan, Thailand, Tibet, Tunisia, Turkey, Turkmenistan, United Arab Emirates, Uzbekistan, Vietnam, and Yemen, as well as the diaspora in Australia, Canada, Europe, the United Kingdom, and the United States. We hope that assembling these voices raises awareness of the abundance and variety of poetry produced in these regions. These poems share a vision of humanness and a devotion to the transformative power of art, irrespective of ethnic or geographic background.

The poetic traditions of many of the countries we've included span thousands of years. For instance, Arabic poetry dates from prior to the sixth century and the tradition of oral poetry is earlier, while the roots of Chinese poetry go back even further; however, we've chosen to concentrate on contemporary poetry, which we've defined as post-1946, for a number of reasons. First, the end of the Second World War reshaped the global landscape in many profound ways: India declared its independence from British rule and partition created the nation of Pakistan; the modern state of Israel was created as part of wartime reparations; Burma, a former British colony, achieved independence, saw the end of democratic rule, and the eventual rise of a military junta that changed the country's name to Myanmar; and many countries of Central Asia were splintered from the former Soviet Union at the end of the century. Second, we are particularly interested in how the contemporary literary landscape has changed in the last sixty years; how in some cases there has been a profound break between ancient tradition and modern life; how literary and arts movements proliferated, allowing for innovative poetic styles and more linguistic experimentation; how women writers fashioned their own self-images, delved into subject matter that was previously taboo, and created more publishing opportunities for themselves; and, most importantly, how these poems speak directly and powerfully to us. Third, because there's such a plethora of crucial voices throughout the twentieth century, we had to delimit ourselves by choosing a particular point in history to begin from. For example, though they were hugely influential, we have not included the poems of Rabindranath Tagore, Yi Sang, or Eghishe Charents because they died prior to the defined time period. Finally, over the last sixty years, there has been a gradual yet fitful progression in the dialogue between the countries of the East and West, so that on some levels there seems to be an unbridgeable gulf between the governments of countries but on other levels, underneath the veneer of official culture, there's a burgeoning sense of shared community and mutual concern that's helping to foster a less one-sided conversation.

Our selection process was composed of the following elements: we solicited work from poets whom we admired; we consulted with experts about the literatures of each country; we contacted translators of note; we researched intensively in libraries and arts organizations, and also referenced magazines such as the *Asian Pacific American Journal* and *Softblow*. Invaluable to our process was the assistance we received from journals and institutions, such as *MĀNOA, A Pacific Journal of International Writing, World Literature Today, The Little Magazine*, Sahitya Akademi (India's National Academy of Letters), the Asian American Writers' Workshop, the Asian Canadian Writers' Workshop, PROTA: The Project for the Translation of Arabic, the Center for Literary Translation at Columbia University, among others. In addition, many individuals (including poets, scholars, editors, translators, professors, and arts coordinators) were instrumental in providing us with the names and contacts of some of the poets we've included. We're deeply grateful for their knowledge and generosity.

The criterion for the selection of the work was fulfillment of the premises put forth by the poems themselves; therefore, various schools of poetry from narrative to lyric are represented, as are translations from the more straightforward to the more oblique and experimental. Every single poem that we've included was carefully vetted and approved by all three editors and some of the more spirited and contentious conversations we had encompassed issues of translation, dual/multiple citizenship, identity, equality of national representation, and ideas of dialects and languages. Our goal was to create a healthy balance of emerging and established poets, from various generations and aesthetic sensibilities; therefore, due to the scope of the project, many fine voices could not be included. Also, there are a few regrettable instances where we were unable to reach a poet, their estate, or their press, or where we could not obtain the rights to print the work. Regarding new voices, our minimum requirement was the publication of at least one book, except in those exceptional cases where we were startled by the work and particularly convinced of the potential longevity of the poet's literary output. In an effort to include as many crucial voices as possible, we've chosen one poem per poet. We should stress that it was not our goal to be representative and we're not making any claims that we're including the best or most important voices of a generation, but simply those poets by whose work we were most compelled and moved.

We envision this anthology as a beginning, not as a summation, but as an initial step in the reader's understanding of a small portion of the rich and varied literary traditions coming out of these countries. We only hope that we've instilled a measure of curiosity that will inspire readers to research these regions further and to seek out individual collections from the poets we've included. In turn, we also hope this anthology inspires the translation of new and existing work into English and other languages. Particularly, as we have become more and more aware, a number of poets of exceptionally large stature in their home countries have not yet been translated.

Another aspect of our selection process had to do with the issue of national representation. An understandable question is that of balance; why do certain countries have so many poets represented while others so few? The answer to this varies on a case-by-case basis. For example, one of the countries that has only one poet represented is Cambodia and that fact is directly traceable to the effect of Pol Pot's regime on the country. Culture in general and literature in particular were crushed by the Khmer Rouge. According to some estimates, within days of launching his "Year Zero" campaign, Pol Pot had reduced Phnom Penh's population by 1.75 million, nearly a fifth of Cambodia's population. In the face of such genocide, no literature could possibly survive. Additionally, as U Sam Oeur's translator Ken McCullough has written, "traditional Khmer poetry is usually chanted and invariably the poet accompanies himself on a two-stringed guitar as a drone instrument. . . . Khmer, unlike numerous other languages in Southeast Asia, is nontonal. Khmer words are not ideograms, although they sometimes have characteristics of ideograms. Thus, you can't come up with a clean and consistent scheme of translating the word/picture/concept as you can in Chinese. Also, Khmer has no articles, pronouns, plurals, or possessives, while there are a number of grammatical and syntactical rules peculiar to Khmer. . . . It is difficult, to say the least, to translate Khmer poetry into English and capture its unique qualities—the languages are worlds apart."[2] Therefore we found only very few examples of Khmer poetry that even approached doing justice to the work in English.

One of the countries that has the most poets is India, which is due to a number of reasons as well. Besides having a population of over one billion people, India also has innumerable discrete languages. Apart from English and Hindi, there are a total of twenty-one official languages recognized by the Indian Constitution, not including the official state languages, the Bihari and Rajasthani languages and the other regional dialects that have over a million people who speak them. Many of these languages are, it's worth noting, more fundamentally different to each other than the Romance languages—so the gulf between Assamese and Tamil, or Urdu and Konkani is vaster than the gulf between French and Italian. We have

[2] Ken McCullough, "Translating U Sam Oeur," *Artful Dodge*, Issue #26/27 (1994). http://www.wooster.edu/ArtfulDodge/introductions/2627/mccullough.htm.

included translations from only a handful of these languages, which is not to diminish the fertile literary traditions that they—along with many other Eastern languages from around the world—possess.

In the case of translations, there were just as many complex issues to navigate: can a poem really be translated when the difference between the original language and English is considerable, differing in poetic traditions, ideas, historical references, prosody, lyricism, figurative and rhetorical language? Part of the difficulty lies not only in translating the literal meaning, but in conveying the cultural landscape in which the poems were written. As editors, we respected the integrity of each translator's process; some translators believed in remaining as close to the original meaning of the poem as possible, while others moved further away from the original text to allow the poem to read more colloquially in English, and yet others found alternate methods. While some translators worked independently and were fluent in both languages, others worked in teams where a native speaker collaborated with an English speaker. In some instances, we worked with the author directly and in other instances we worked with translators, providing suggestions that they either integrated or did not. We also commissioned translations and these poems will be appearing in English for the first time. Ultimately, as with poems originally written in English, it was quality that governed our decisions.

Once the poems were chosen, we deliberated on how to organize the collected material. We contemplated a number of traditional organizational schemes—listing poets alphabetically, by region or country, by chronology, by literary movements—many of the modes that other anthologies use to structure their content. However, these categories seemed to us to replicate in an insidious way the very mentality that separates person from person, nation from nation. Our vision of shared dialogue and community dictated a very different form. We were most interested in how these voices engaged one another. In the process of reading the poems we found that irrespective of their linguistic, cultural, and temporal differences, many of the poems shared certain commonalities with respect to notions of home and family, ruminations on mortality, protestations of war and inequity, and recognition of erotic and divine love. After recognizing these similarities, we found that the poems coalesced very organically into nine major sections. This organization allows the poems to speak to each other and to generate a certain productive frisson that is ultimately more illuminating.

Those of the Bahai faith use the nine-pointed star as their symbol; in land divisions for feng shui there are eight exterior squares for cultivation and a final ninth square known as "God's acre" dedicated to Shang-ti, the supreme ruler; the enneagram is alleged to be a two-thousand-year-old Sufi system of the nine primary personality types, codified by Islamic mystics; in South India, a nine-day festival called Navaratri, the Sanksrit word for "nine," is celebrated to commemorate a nine-day battle between a goddess and a demon; in Japan, the number nine, or *ku*, is related to *kurushii*, or suffering; in Judaism, the three letters that make up the word "truth" (*emet*) add up to nine, and are the first, middle, and last letters of the Hebrew alphabet. There are many applications of the number nine, relevant or tangential, and in the case of our anthology, the organization of the poems into nine sections represents an entire cosmology of planets that, when taken together, offers a glimpse into the complex array of voices that make up these regions' poetry.

The title of each section is derived from a poem in that section. A variety of poems constellate around the theme the line encompasses. The book opens with the section *In the Grasp of Childhood Fields*, which embodies Rilke's advice that childhood is that "jewel beyond all price, that treasure house of memories." It continues with *Parsed into Colors,* which shows how the kaleidoscope of identity is defined. *Slips and Atmospherics* stretches the cords of syntax, exploding normative lineation and familiar imageries to present an avant-garde sensibility. *Earth of Drowned Gods* brings together a parliament of poems that reflects the world of politics and social strictures that too often dehumanize and delimit its citizens. *Buffaloes Under Dark Water* contains mysterious, shrouded, *duende*-tinged luminescent bursts of lyric that resist the notion of taxonomy, even as they inhere together like shadows. *Apostrophe in the Scripture* speaks of war, the pervasive condition of discord that has damaged many countries and remains a continuing threat. *This House, My Bones* shows the multiple manifestations of homeland, its comforts and conflicts, departure and ultimate return. *Bowl of Air and Shivers* delves into spirit and mortality, sketching the specter of birth and death, consolation and bliss, the body and beyond. *The Quivering World* maps the terrain of bodies, whether they be loci of pleasure or the spiritual component of love, subverting stereotypes of Eastern sexuality.

Additionally, the sections are introduced with a personal essay written by one of the editors. In conversation with our agent, Sarah Jane Freymann, we came up with the idea of revealing our intimate connections to the poems. We hope the readers of this anthology are not just lovers of poetry but those interested in expanding their notions of the human experience. By writing these introductions, we hope to usher the reader into the work, providing a foundation for the section and illuminating certain aspects of poems that we find provocative or compelling. We also found that embarking upon these short essays allowed us to embrace and to ponder our own identities, empowering us to find the connective tissue between ourselves and the voices represented in the anthology.

At the back of the book, we've included a country index in order to help situate and inform the reader; especially in light of our thematic organizational scheme, we've included this index that lists poets by their country of birth, place of residence, or cultural affiliation.[3] Our method of putting this list together was to ask all of our contributors to self-identify, which proved more intricate than we could have predicted. Sargon Boulus, for example, was born in Iraq of Assyrian descent and now holds an American passport, yet writes in Arabic. Buddhadeva Bose, one of the most important Bengali writers of the twentieth century, was born in what is now Bangladesh, though when he was born, no such country existed. An American-born Korean asked that we not list Korea after his name, because he had only spent a few weeks of his life there. A number of Tibetan poets asked to be listed as exiled-Tibetans, because their country under Chinese occupation was no longer considered a sovereign state, though in their estimation they still possessed the right to self-determination. Of his identity, the poet C. Dale Young says, "For some of us, it isn't so easy to categorize ourselves for indexes and anthologies. As a multiethnic, multiracial person, I am Latino as well as Asian (Chinese and Indian). And strangely enough, because my mother is caucasian, I am actually half-caucasian. That said, I have never felt caucasian."

In the seminal anthology *Aiiieeeee!, An Anthology of Asian American Writers*, published in 1974, the issue of Asian American identity is discussed at length in the preface written by Frank Chin, Jeffery Paul Chan, Lawson Fusao Inada, and Shawn Wong. "The age, variety, depth, and quality of the writing collected here proves the existence of Asian American

---

[3] It should be noted that poets listed under certain countries such as China, Japan, Korea, and Vietnam are listed by surname first, unless they have chosen otherwise, because that is the traditional form of nomenclature. In the case of Arabic, names were alphabetized with the letter that followed prefixes such as *al-* and *el-*.

sensibilities and cultures that might be related to but are distinct from Asia and white America. American culture, protecting us from the sanctity of its whiteness, still patronizes us foreigners and refuses to recognize Asian American literature as 'American' literature. America does not recognize Asian Americans as a presence, though Asian Americans have been here seven generations. For seven generations we have been aware of that refusal, and internalized it, with disastrous effects" (*Aiiieeeee!*, xiii).

In the case of Arab Americans, Arabs began emigrating to the United States as well as to the Americas, Australia, Europe, and Africa in the nineteenth century (circa 1875), although some say they arrived many centuries prior. They faced various racial labels at different periods of American history. They were first called "Turks" then "Syrians"; later, with the formation of new and independent states, especially that of Lebanon in 1945, they started calling themselves Lebanese. Subsequently, they were referred to as "Arabs"; however, to this very day, the U.S. Census Bureau still classifies Arabs as white, even though a number of Arab Americans consider themselves an ethnic minority.

The formation of an Arab American identity—apart from the tendency of ethnic groups in the United States to identify with two cultures, whether those labels are placed upon them or whether they have consciously chosen such an identification for personal reasons or to emphasize their visibility—is largely a result of war and political tensions in the Middle East. D. H. Melhem said in an interview for *Al Jadid* magazine that she was American until the Lebanese war in the late 1970s, early 1980s, when she began to align herself with her Arab American identity. In the second half of the twentieth century, particularly following the events after September 11, the growth and participation of Arab Americans at all levels, whether political, economical, or cultural, augmented tremendously. For instance, although there exists more than a century of Arab American literature from the *Mahjar* (emigrants) poets such as Gibran Kahlil Gibran (1883–1931) and Amin Rihani (1876–1940), the past twenty years, and particularly the last decade has proved to be one of the most fertile periods in Arab American literature.

In constructing our country list, we were confronted with some of the issues prefigured by this preface. Some of our contributors felt it important to be listed under the United States, even if, or particularly if, they did not agree with the Bush administration's policies. A few of them felt that throughout their literary careers, their work had been exoticized and that they did not want to identify with their country of heritage. By the same token, there were other writers who felt a strong affiliation with a particular country as their homeland. If anything, this country list is testament to the vastness of cultural variation and more useful as fodder for discussion than as confining categorization. From our standpoint, even the question of identity is problematic because of how it is asked, how often it is asked, by whom it is asked, and in what context. Though we're including a country list for reference and further study, ultimately it's the poet and their work that should be illuminated.

Many of the poets here have been creative and social forces worldwide who began to initiate private and public changes. For example, Bei Dao's national emergence as one of China's foremost contemporary poets began in 1978 when he coedited and launched the literary journal *Jintian* (*Today*) with his poet-friend Mang Ke, which first appeared as a large character poster on the Democracy Wall in Beijing, where people originally posted their experiences of suffering during the Cultural Revolution. The journal had to be published in secret, and Bei Dao and a few other volunteers bicycled through Beijing to put up the pages, the posting of which took great courage as it was considered politically subversive by the Chinese authorities.

When the journal appeared on the wall, there was a tremendous reaction to the poems and essays. There were blank spaces left after each piece of writing so that people could write their comments and responses. In a short period of time, the magazine circulated throughout China. The magazine was banned after two years of publication and shut down in 1980.[4] In 1990, a year after the events in Tiananmen Square, the magazine was reinstated overseas and continues to this day.

Of the popularity of *Jintian*, Bei Dao has said, "The greatest danger was a matter of language. Our poetry was written in what amounted to a new language, which differed greatly from the official language to which people were accustomed. That was what got people excited. Universities all over began to get more involved in poetry, organizing poetry clubs and such, simply because they were excited about using a new language. It was a challenge which subverted the official language which had been the dominant form in poetry and everything else for many years. The reason why so many young people were imitating our language was that it gave them a way to express themselves which was new to them because it did

---

[4] Bei Dao and Siobhan La Piana, "An Interview with Visiting Artist Bei Dao: Poet in Exile," *Journal of the International Institute*, vol. 2, no. 1 (1999).

not resemble official discourse. It was unusual to have so many people writing poetry."[5]

If the influence and ideas about the inherency of freedom of expression were being channeled, claimed, and transformed by Chinese poets such as Bei Dao, a figure such as Kashmiri American poet Agha Shahid Ali was bringing a dose of the spirited energies of the East to the United States. Ali was born in New Delhi in 1949, grew up Muslim in Kashmir at a time when the violence that continues to mar the region first began, then came to America to pursue his doctorate in English. He stayed, and in so doing, forever altered the American literary landscape.

Besides being a remarkably prolific poet, Ali was also an exceptional translator who rendered the renowned Pakistani poet Faiz Ahmed Faiz's work into English. He brought the traditional Persian form of the ghazal into English, turning it, as Rafiq Kathwari writes, into the villanelle of America. Flip the pages of any literary journal in America today and chances are you will see some variation of the form. The ghazal, which in Persian means "flirtation," is nothing if not rule bound, having a unified mid-line rhyme scheme (*qafiya*), a repeated refrain (*radif*), and discrete couplets that stand alone. As Ali has written, the couplets that compose a ghazal are "stones in a necklace that continue to shine in vivid isolation."[6] Ali also provided his own unique and incomparable witness to the tempestuous history of the Kashmiri region, suffusing his poems and essays with a full dose of personality that sometimes masked his even fuller intellectual and artistic rigor. Flamboyant, full of life and zest, dedicated unswervingly to his art and to the idea of pedagogy, Ali was taken from the world prematurely at the age of fifty-two due to brain cancer, but his influence in the world of contemporary poetry and in the lives of many poets, both Eastern and Western, continues to resonate.

A pivotal female figure, Iranian poet Forugh Farrokhzad, also stretched the bounds of her nation's literature. Born in 1935 to a middle-class family in Tehran, she married a distant cousin fifteen years her senior at the age of sixteen in order to escape the confines of her strict home. However, within three years, during which time she gave birth to a son, her marriage failed, and Farrokhzad was forced to relinquish her child to her husband and his family. Rather than become devastated by her circumstances and despite the stigma associated with being a divorced woman in mid-1950s

---

[5] Ibid.

[6] Agha Ali Shahid and Louis Werner, "A Gift of Ghazals," *Saudi Aramco World* (July/August 2001). http://www.saudiaramcoworld.com/issue/200104/a.gift.of.ghazals.htm.

Iran, she lived uncompromisingly as a writer, painter, and film director/producer. In a society of tight literary circles that were unaccustomed to women, Farrokhzad made men her poetic subjects, her objects of reverie and sexual desire. Her poems were autobiographical and from a distinctly female perspective. Further, they were modern as opposed to traditional, a form rejected by the academic community and not considered poetry at all.

In the spring of 1964, her fourth collection of poems, *Reborn,* appeared. It was immediately hailed as a major work, rivaling the best in the short history of Persian modernist poetry. Farrokhzad continued to write and publish until her untimely death, at the age of thirty-two, in a car crash. Her poems have lived on, influencing generations of Iranians and, recently, readers worldwide.

Though historically it wasn't the first time this happened, the period post-1946 witnessed growing exposure of Western cultures in the East, in ways that were both innovative and controversial. As Michelle Yeh explains, the Modernist School in Taiwan founded by Ji Xian in 1956 advocated a "horizontal transplantation" of "all Western avant-garde movements from Baudelaire onward," clearly distinguishing itself from classical poetry, which was not only a literary but political statement. The Epoch Poetry Society, also founded in the 1950s, promoted surrealism in particular. The literary journal called *Li,* or *Bamboo Hat,* was launched in Taiwan in 1964, establishing itself as a successor to the Modernist School (though it later endorsed a nativist position and opposed Modernism). "In the area of translation, the manifestos of American imagism, French surrealism, Italian futurism, and German *Neue Sachlichkeit,* among others, were published in *Bamboo Hat,* although the journal did not endorse those positions."[7] The journal introduced Japanese as well as Western poetry and in its initial call for submissions, *Bamboo Hat* listed seven categories of contribution, four of which stressed the translation or study of poetry and poetics of countries overseas. Though it consisted solely of Taiwanese poets, the organization positioned itself as one that defended linguistic invention and enthusiastically opened its doors to new ideas, whether or not they agreed with them. There was criticism and debate over the potential loss of or gain for Chinese identity because of such

[7] Michelle Yeh and N. G. D. Mamqvist, *Frontier Taiwan: An Anthology of Modern Chinese Poetry* (New York: Columbia University Press, 2001), p. 30.

influences, but ultimately the journal offered a vital forum to the reading and writing public.

The pendulum has also swung in the other direction during the last few decades. American poetry has increasingly looked toward the East in order to revitalize its own modes of expression, and if one were to survey contemporary poetry publication, in addition to sonnets and villanelles, one would also find ghazals and haiku. A poet such as Kimiko Hahn has popularized in English the Japanese form of the *zuihitsu*, or literally "following the brush," or "random jottings." The form, which has existed in Japan for over a millennia (since *The Pillow Book* written in the Heian period), incorporates diary entries, lists, commentaries on social life, poems, etc., and has strong parallels to the stream of consciousness writing techniques practiced by the Beats and the collages and cut-ups produced by the Surrealists. The pantoum, a poem of Malay origin invented in the fifteenth century, written in quatrains and involving the recurrence of interlocking lines, has also been taken up by a number of contemporary poets. The mutual influences of the East and West are helping lay the foundation for a poetics of a new era.

Here at the beginning of the twenty-first century, where a day doesn't seem to pass without some new outbreak of violence or declaration of conflict, our hope is to shape something that speaks to our generation and beyond. Where the opportunities for fatal destruction, between people and between nations, are intensified, the same age-old questions still exist: What is the role of poetry? What can it *do*? Can poetry still matter? Throughout time, they have been answered in many ways, from the pragmatic to the politicized, but our sense is that the answers to these questions might lie in the poems themselves. Not in rhetoric or debate but in pure feeling akin to instinct, mantra, prayer. As long as the language of inquiry and longing, the music of rumination and loss, and the narratives of growth and transformation exist, so will the cadences of the cultures poetry helps express. In that fact and in these poems, we find hope.

We have been working on this anthology for more than six years, and it's been an exceptional journey, one that included the discovery of many new voices, and that encompassed many hours of dialogue, which were illuminative, inspiring, fraying into disagreement, even succumbing to bleak periods where we felt destined never to finish the project, and it's our sense that all of this ultimately strengthened the vision. The credit is not ours as anthologists; it's rather due to the poets whose works cannot be generalized about but can be deeply felt. In addition to being powerful aesthetic creations, these poems can be experienced as minuscule stays against oblivion, lyrical explorations of place and self, or finely honed insights into what it means to be alive, and it's our hope that we have contributed to deepening any notion of what's possible and what's imminent, where we have been and where we go from here.

—TINA CHANG, NATHALIE HANDAL, RAVI SHANKAR
NEW YORK CITY, 2007

ACKNOWLEDGMENTS

First and foremost, our heartfelt gratitude to Sarah Jane Freymann, our literary agent, whose faith and belief in us and our ideas carried us through every phase of our process. Our deepest appreciation for her friendship, encouragement, and generosity.

We owe special thanks to Frank Stewart of *MĀNOA* who proved to be an extraordinary teacher and guide on our journey. *MĀNOA* served as a model of the depth and richness of world literature from which we drew inspiration; thanks also to Quang Bao and Jeannie Wong from the Asian American Writers' Workshop and Jim Wong-Chu of the Asian Canadian Writers' Workshop for their continued support.

We are also deeply thankful to Wayne Amtzis, Sargon Boulus, Kevin Bowen, Brother Anthony of Taizé, Priya Sarukkai Chabria, David D. Clark, editor-in-chief of *World Literature Today*, Keki N. Daruwalla, Najwan Darwish, Diana Der-Hovannesian, Ram Devineni from *Rattapallax*, Vinay Dharwadker, Ketaki Kushari Dyson, Marilyn Hacker, Subhi Hadidi, Talât Sait Halman, Nareg Hartounian, Khaled Hegazzi from *Meena*, Hassan Hilmy, Hamid Ismailov, Salma Khadra Jayyusi, Fady Joudah, Tsipi Keller, Agnes S. L. Lam, Fiona Tinwei Lam, Leza Lowitz, Sarah Maguire from The Poetry Translation Center, Hsien Min Toh of *Quarterly Literary Review Singapore*, Murat Nemet-Nejat, Idra Novey, William Radice, John Rosenwald, Miriam Said, Najla Said, Bashir Sakhawarz, Sudeep Sen of *Atlas*, Amardeep Singh, Kirpal Singh, Rajini Srikanth and Shona Ramaya of *Catamaran*, Arthur Sze, Manjushree Thapa, Jeet Thayil, Wang Ping, Sholeh Wolpé, Carolyne Wright, Xu Xi, Michelle Yeh, Andy Young from *Meena*, Alfred A. Yuson, Zhang Ziqing. Many other individuals contributed along the way and we apologize for anyone we may have overlooked.

Acknowledgments

The Blue Mountain Center, The Constance Saltonstall Foundation, Djerassi Resident Artists Program, and The MacDowell Colony provided the time and solitude crucial to this project and to these organizations we owe a great debt, and gratitude also to Central Connecticut State University, whose Office of Minority Recruitment provided us a grant to defray some of our expenses. President Jack Miller, Provost Carl Lovitt, Dean Susan Pease and faculty, particularly from the English Department, provided invaluable support.

Our editiorial assistants, Meryl DePasquale, Stephanie Hoos, Sam Lees, and Sheryl Springer performed admirably beyond the call of duty, helping in many administrative aspects, from permissions to copyediting, and it is no exaggeration that we would not have finished without them. Thanks to Traci Brimhall and Brynn Saito for citation and editorial help in the final stages.

Our friends and family provided unending moral support and encouragement to us. Their optimism and kindness buoyed us considerably and helped us persevere through the many years it took us to complete this project.

We feel truly fortunate to have been granted the opportunity to work with Jill Bialosky of W. W. Norton, who shared in our vision and believed in the worth and timeliness of this anthology. *Language for a New Century: Contemporary Poetry from the Middle East, Asia, and Beyond* would not be a reality without her. It was also our pleasure to work with her assistant, Paul Whitlatch, whose professionalism saw us through to publication. Finally, copyeditor David Stanford Burr must be acknowledged for demonstrating care and sensitivity to the details of every line and word.

Recognition is also due to the many authors and publishers who granted us permissions in the spirit of collective understanding. And finally, our profound gratitude to all the poets, editors, and translators who have lent their gifts and expertise to this immense undertaking. We've had the opportunity to make friends around the globe and have shared lively dialogue, which contributed to our own growth and understanding of the world that we inhabit together. We have learned from and have been humbled by knowing these poets, their lives, and their work.

A NOTE ON SURNAMES

Because naming conventions vary from country to country, the alphabetization of this anthology reflects the traditional form of nomenclature. In China, Japan, Korea, and Vietnam, names are traditionally listed by surname first, and so we have listed them in this manner unless the individuals have chosen otherwise. A country such as Singapore or Malaysia has an amalgamation of Chinese and Western names. Certain Indian languages such as Tamil or Malayalam do not have surnames, and often the given name is indicated by an initial (R. Cheran or K. Satchidanandan). In these instances, we have alphabetized according to the second name, rather than by the initial. In regard to Arabic, names were alphabetized with the letter that followed prefixes such as *al-* and *el-*.

IN THE GRASP OF
CHILDHOOD FIELDS

In the Grasp of Childhood Fields

—Luis Cabalquinto

When I was a year old, I lived in a church with my family. We had come to New York so that doctors at Sloan-Kettering could run a series of tests on my father, and with nowhere to live, we stayed in the bare yet livable room the church offered. My father had been feeling fatigued, unable to climb stairs or digest food properly. After an exploratory surgery, the doctors announced that my father had liver cancer. My mother found an apartment for us, hoping to bring my father home for a little while at least, but just a few weeks later, at the age of forty-one, he died at the hospital.

A year passed, not without struggle, and after many late-night conversations with relatives in Taiwan, my mother made the decision to send my brother and me to live with them until she got her life in order again. My mother was the first of her large family to travel to America to seek a prosperous life; in an ironic twist of fate, her children were now being sent back to her native country.

My brother was three years old. I was two. Our mother bundled us up and said good-bye to us at Kennedy Airport. As she embraced me, I understood only that I was going on a long trip without her. As I boarded the plane with my grandmother, I could not translate the feeling of sorrow. I sat, peering out the window, watching the buildings grow faint below me, the pattern of a lit city fading to invisible as I fell asleep.

I often feel that my literary life began with that journey, in my longing for utterance. I was just beginning to understand language, a volley of English and Chinese; my lips and brain forged connections both delicate and clumsy, my vocabulary colliding inside the bowl of my mouth. At the same time, my senses were newly charged as I awoke to the sound of roosters crowing beneath the dripping clothesline and vendors hawking everything from porridge to cooking utensils to the high windows.

Among my memories of this time: splitting a starfruit with my younger cousin; my aunt brushing my hair while singing a nursery song; monsoons shaking the miniature windows of my room; the two furious stone lions that sat on either side of a red door, that guarded the front of my grandmother's home. My life, as a child, seemed to be a linguistic collage of these moments. My hand touched an object unfamiliar and I would name it, fusing a word with its gleaming definition. What I instinctively desired then, as a child, was not loss but *discovery*; not sustenance but *play*; not mourning but *bliss*.

The poems arranged in this section, *In the Grasp of Childhood Fields*, focus on the intricacies of family and childhood. In our youth, every image, experience, and attempt to translate experience into meaning is new; all event of color and imagination is fresh as it begins to fashion itself into memory. What we learn and experience as children stays with us throughout our lifetime as if embedded in our bone and blood. What fascinated me about the poems in this section is the richness of images that I so closely associate with my own childhood experiences: coconut husks, magnolia trees, red dragonflies, midnight dogs, caged birds and mute crickets, house sparrows, bananas and mangoes, lush gardens, clear honey. In Taiwan's fertile landscape, I found myself observing just such things. To wander in the poems of these particular poets feels like returning home.

In Jennifer Kwon Dobbs's lyric poem "Elegy for Pure Music," memory itself is in need of repair as the speaker claims, "I was 10. I believed I was broken / Ceramic, adopted by estrangements. / A watcher of things winged and inexplicable." The speaker floats in aria and myth. One might ask if the speaker's estrangement is a result of existing between two geographic regions, as she reaches "across a sea / of bad reception." Such are the feelings of a young girl: observer, spectator, and student of a world in which everything is mysterious. Dobbs's created childhood seems to try to bridge the distance between the fragmented self and the place where wholeness may reside.

Whether metaphoric or literal, the idea of searching threads through many of these poems. Nick Carbó's instructions to the reader in "Directions to My Imaginary Childhood" leads down avenues and side streets in the Philippines. Past Maneng Viray's bar and the fish sauce factory, past the card table where neighbors play abecedarian dominoes, and tungsten-red Juan Tamad trees, the reader meets the beloved characters of the speaker's boyhood. Through parking lots and supermarkets we are offered a map that leads us to taste, touch, and smell the intoxicating foods and scents that make up Carbó's imagined town. By poem's end, the reader is led to a house with an acknowledgments page and an index. Here, the house is symbolic of a physical shelter as well as interpreted text. Once the door is open, the speaker's directions to "look me in the eye" asks us to confront both child and author, both the boy and the guide to our adventure. Carbó's world is lighthearted, a homage to the people and places he names with sensual adoration.

In stark contrast to Carbó's affectionate reverie of the Philippines, Dilawar Karadaghi's "A Child Who Returned From There Told Us" is a child's account of the anti-Kurdish Anfal campaign, led by the Iraqi regime of Saddam Hussein in 1988. The eight-stage military campaign resulted in the murder of between fifty thousand and one hundred thousand Kurds, according to Human Rights Watch (numbers vary depending on the source). Though the Anfal targeted "battle-age" men, the campaign also resulted in the mass execution and disappearance of women, children, and the elderly. One such execution left a child survivor by the name of Taimour Abdullah Ahmad, "the only eyewitness to the mass killing of women and children."* His story received a great deal of attention in the press, and he comes to mind when I read Karadaghi's poem, as Anfal is personified as thief, intruder, guide, and finally murderer. He enters uninvited into a household where the family has gathered for a meal:

> *Anfal entered while we were still eating.*
> *A banquet of love had drawn us together.*
> *Twilight was slinking against confidence,*
> *salving yesterday's pain.*
> *A night of affection was whistling beyond the window.*
> *Suddenly the lamps were killed*
> *the evening flew away,*
> *the night screamed,*
> *the sun said its last good-bye to the green conifers*
> *at the edge of the village.*

As the family is separated, their belongings taken, Anfal begins to comfort them: "Anfal said, don't worry children / It's just a trip and you will be back." The children realize all too quickly that they have been deceived as they are blindfolded and beaten. The children find themselves in the desert where their fates are sealed. Their story survives as testimony.

---

*Human Rights Watch, *Iraq's Crime of Genocide: The Anfal Campaign Against the Kurds* (New Haven: Yale University Press, 1995).

The journey from childhood to adulthood is a ferocious yet tender struggle, bridging the gap between the wonder of discovery and the reality of a world that is constantly changing, at times filled with brutality. The child watches, interprets, engages, and then, ultimately, claims the world with all its blessings, tragedies, and acts of humanity.

Recently, when rummaging through my childhood room, among the crates of dusty albums, old report cards, and closets of clothes swinging from their wire hangers, I found a box of worn photos under my bed. Thumbing through them, one image in particular struck me. In a yellowed photo I am standing in front of those fierce stone lions in front of my grandmother's house in Taiwan. Every single member of my family is crowded on either side of me, more than I would ever think possible to fit inside the frame of one photograph. These are the people who took me in, nurtured me, and sheltered me after I lost my father so suddenly. I am in the center, as small as I can remember. I was too young to comprehend my loss or put my longing into words. And, ultimately, what they offered me had no name, though I still feel its weight and relevance. In this photo, there is no sorrowful past, nor distant future. There is only the present looking into the lens, documenting that time as miracle and relic. Looking at the viewer, as if into the wider world. The most intricate of human emotions may have no lexicon, but the poets gathered here have offered a glimpse into that complex and wondrous realm.

—TINA CHANG

JOSEPH O. LEGASPI

Ode to My Mother's Hair

The provincial
river is transformed,
my mother
in a clear-sky afternoon
washes her hair,
dark as cuttlefish ink.
Between
her flat palms,
she rubs it
with silt, twisting
the strands
as if starting a fire:

my mother's Promethean
crown of smoke, daughter
of a woman with hair like fire.

I have seen photographs:
my mother pony-tailed
as a girl, split-
ends, braided,
molasses stuck
and formed
prickly discs
like coiled, poisonous caterpillars;
like black holed flowers
in her follicle garden;
tangled little   -
mushrooms.

As a child
in the fringes of sleep,
when my fill of colostrum
swirled warmly inside me,
I often burrowed
my mole face

in my mother's hair,
the darkness beyond the banana grove.

I remember
how it brushed against my eyelids,
fending off the midnight dogs
of sleeplessness; tickled
my ears, deadening
the skeletons
of nightmares;
and how I breathed in
strands, which planted
the seed of the tree of memory.

My mother's hair is domestic hair:
absorbent to the scent
of her cooking—
milkfish, garlic, goat;
her fur of sweeping dust
clipped
in a bun, with wisps
that dangle on her face,
and dance
to floor scrubbing by coconut husk
to laundry five children soiled
to my father's pulling and shaking.

When my youngest sister
was born, our mother chopped
her hair, the incubating black hen
of her head ousted the starlings.
In hope of a reparation
for what we had driven her to do,
I gathered locks
from her brush,
tied them with blue ribbon
and buried them in our backyard,
dusting the plot
with sugar and cocoa,
moistening the mound with honey—

all the goodness from the world of the living.
I believed
the earth resurrects
what is nourished in its belly.

And in this river,
my mother's wet, swirling hair

reminds me
of monsoon seasons,
when our house,
besieged by wind and water,
teetered and threatened to split open,
exposing the diorama
of our barely protected lives
with my mother, seated, telling stories
to her children collected around her,
while my sister and I are brushing her mane,
smelling of rose soap,
sprouting by candle light,
her hair which is always the other half of the world.

JENNIFER KWON DOBBS

Elegy for Pure Music

Non saperlo mai per te, pei tuoi puri occhi, muor Butterfly . . .

—Puccini, *Madama Butterfly*

Again, my false mother of verbena is singing

The aria I'll recite as if I'm a natural

Child among night flowers, opening their dark eyes to the moon,

Who is no mother to the ocean that bears her resemblance

Like a floating summer barge. Again, I am sinking into her

Hazardous silks of caged birds and mute crickets, into her

Televised longing for smoke stacks and flags, into her image

Painted on to a French man's damp face, into her vermilion

Folds in which are sealed the purposes, provisional

Names for my hands eager to break wax.

The dream drips on to the table, makes new forms

That ask to be scraped and discarded. Beginning is always a problem

When slivers of a life: toenail, strand of hair. Some evidence of her held

By the social worker is saved, luck or pity, an address scribbled

In a code familiar as my skin. I am wearing the answer to her questions:

Where is my baby? Is my baby hungry?

Does she mourn as I do? Is this loss or do I recite a libretto?

What is our contract, if there is blood between us? Have I the right

To scabs picked off for pink underneath, little shutters opened to let in air,

The pure music. It is raw in there. I am guessing

An alcove to grieve among robes embroidered with cherry blossoms,

Gion festival wagons, cranes returning to a patch of silver at the breast,

Leave taking for gold. Every sleeve, myth. Every hem, a crossing

Guarded by dust, dry creek beds, buffalo grass, Oklahoma sky

Like a kiln. Not the blue heat, but the orange as in tiger lily, the yellow
 foxglove

Seed ground into the heart's medicine to quicken

In want of a memory, in need of repair. I was 10. I believed I was broken

Ceramic, adopted by estrangements. A watcher of things winged and
 inexplicable,

PBS, Sunday Afternoon at the Met: Levine conducting.

Plastic swatter in hand. My palms pressed against the hot glass to get
 through.

Windows of my parents' living room covered by damask.

The flickering screen. I imagined she called to me, "un bel di vedremo,"
 across a sea

Of bad reception. Her face twisted into recognition.

I did not see myself, but heard the scattered humming of houseflies.

I studied the white parts squirming out their black, mashed bellies

In wonder of death. Still, a birth through the wound

Perhaps willed by itself. Why else such a distance crossed from its mother,

Lying on the wood, her ash veil falling away?

TENZIN TSUNDUE

Exile House

Our tiled roof dripped
and the four walls threatened to fall apart
but we were to go home soon,

we grew papayas
in front of the house
chilies in the garden
and changmas for our fences,
then pumpkins rolled down the cowshed thatch
calves trotted out of the manger,

grass on the roof,
beans sprouted and
climbed down the vines,
money plants crept in through the windows,
our house seems to have grown roots.

The fences have grown into a jungle
now how can I tell my children
where we came from?

Author's Note: Changmas are flexible and flourishing trees usually planted as fencing.

NICK CARBÓ

Directions to My Imaginary Childhood

If you stand on the corner
of Mabini Street and Legazpi Avenue,
wait for an orchid colored minibus
with seven oblong doors,
open the fourth door—

an oscillating electric fan
will be driving, tell her to proceed
to the Escolta diamond district—
you will pass Maneng Viray's Bar,
La Isla de los Ladrones bookshop,

the Frederick Funston fish sauce factory,
and as you turn left into Calle de Recuerdos,
you will see Breton, Bataille, and Camus
seated around a card table playing
abecedarian dominoes—

roll down your window and ask
them if Mr. Florante and Miss Laura
are home, if the answer is, yes,
then proceed to Noli Me Tangere park
and wait for a nun named Maria Clara—

if the answer is, Je ne se pas!, then turn
right onto the parking lot of Sikatuna's
supermarket to buy a basketful
of lansones fruit, then get back
to Calle de Recuerdos until you reach

the part that's lined with tungsten-red
Juan Tamad trees, on the right will be
a house with an acknowledgments page
and an index, open the door and enter
this page and look me in the eye.

HA JIN

Homework

Under his pencil a land is unfolding.
"I'm making a country," he says.

In no time colors shine
all over his pear-shaped island.
A blue bay opens like a horseshoe
along the neck of a glacier,
below which a long sierra zigzags
greened by rain forests.

Further down he puts mines of metals:
aluminum, silver, copper, titanium,
iron, gold, tungsten, zinc and tin.
A desert separates two oil fields
that stretch beside branching rivers.

In the south a plain extends
to vast fertile land, where
he crayons farms and orchards
that yield potatoes, oranges, apples,
strawberries, wheat, broccoli, cherries,
zucchini, poultry, beef, mutton, cheese.

There's only one offshore fishery
because he hates seafood.

On the same map he draws a chart—
railroads crisscross the landscape;
highways, pipelines, canals
are entwined; sea-lanes curve
into the ocean while airports
raise a web of skyways;
He imposes five time zones.

A child's country is not yet marred
by prison camps and concrete silos

or expanded by warships and bombers;
nor is it under a power that issues
laws, money, visas, rhetoric
beside rattling nukes like slingshots.

ALVIN PANG

String Theory

Scientists are still trying to find out what makes the cosmos tick.
I don't even know what makes my dad work, bright thwarted man
that he is, would have outdone us all, had he the funds at eighteen,
not been sucked instead into the singularity of the rest of his life,
all that space and nothing to fill it with, no choice but to walk
from here to there, the long way round. One theory suggests
there are several secret dimensions curled up in every particle of nature,
these incredible long vibrating strings at the heart of everything.
Everything: an endless, restless riff, a violent concerto in a minor key
beyond the range of hearing, a song that pulls at the world, is gravity.
Staying still was never an option for beings made of such manic stuff.
I read this in a paper, but dad doesn't, he falls into orbit between the TV
and the fridge, a satellite relaying any kind of noise but hope. Give or take
a few decades, he'll fall back into the quantum soup lab coats go on about,
the kind without any memory of what it once might have been. I think of
what's wound in him, in us, tighter than DNA, less understood than that
which impels us one slow day forward at a time. The old yarn about
sons worshipping fathers, the way folks thought the sun revolved
around the earth, not vice versa? Well it ended the day he wrote
Do what I couldn't on my birthday card. I was in college. Outside
my bay window the world was a wide unstudied sky, not these
small coiled realities we now think is all we have. I'd not even grasped
the dynamics of colliding lives, fissive trails I wander blindly down.
Dark matter clouds the universe and uncertainty rules it? Could've said that
years ago. I have a theory we become our fathers, however hard we try,
as if this would explain everything. It'll be awhile yet before I arrive
at the way he's letting himself loose now, though not quite the same way
time unspools from the reel of physics, more like a shedding of paths,
all possible futures fusing into a grand unified inevitability.

I couldn't either, I'd tell him, when I catch up finally, out of breath,
as we stand laughing, wonder why we ever bothered, on some
long and distant shore on the other side of nowhere else to go.

TANIKAWA SHUNTARŌ

In Praise of Goldberg

In the silence of the silken air precariously enveloping this planet,
a sound is born as of the very first dripping of water.
The sun, breaking the cycle of sleep, rises
from the distant horizon where fossils of forgotten creatures are hidden.

We need not recollect a thing.
We need not dream of anything.
The sounds are waves of light, particles of light, coming from an unknown
    distance.
They bring you a new morning.

Unnamed wild flowers have budded out on wastelands of all ages.
Their seeds were already prepared,
far back along the history of human struggles,
in the invisible, inaudible silence of the universe.

There a child begins to walk.
Ascending a staircase of sound, he bathes his feet in the fountain of sound
and hears, in the din of people on the street,
the sadness which was before the birth of the word "sadness."

Washed by the sound, ears revive; wakened by the sound, eyes open wide.
Following the sound, lost in the sound, playing with the sound and led by
    the sound,
the child sees, in the tree twigs that continuously climb up the tall blue sky,
the joy which is more than the word "joy."

Tantalizing treasures hidden in the cathedral of wavering sounds ......
The deep source of feelings endlessly piling up ......

An ancient prophecy come true before anyone knew ......
An exclamation mark which overwrites all question marks ......

A quarrelling voice, a praising voice, a lamenting voice and a praying voice ......
Many patterns woven by entwining and entangled voices ......
The child is aware of an order hidden in the chaos
and knows how to play, endlessly and richly, variations on one single soul of his own.

A sound begins to shine in the space between suffering and anxiety.
A sound invites a sound, calls a sound, is connected to a sound,
and presently adorns the breasts of aimless time and space with a glittering
    necklace.
Now you will remember everything and will dream everything.

Translated from the Japanese by William I. Elliott and Kazuo Kawamura

VÉNUS KHOURY-GHATA

Our cries, she used to say
would scratch the moon's windowpanes
and scrape the corners of tombstones which milked the moon

My mother set the long slope of her back against us
to interrogate the walls' dampness
decipher saltpeter's crumbling alphabet
translate the symbols carved on the underside of the city
which she only knew in profile
since she never ventured farther than her shopping bag
rarely crossing the uncertain borders of her lamp
City which sent us its rejected rains
and sometimes a wheezy snow which hooked its flakes into the
pomegranate-tree's ears

The planet must be cleaned up
God must be cleaned up!
My mother cried, tying her apron.

Translated from the French by Marilyn Hacker

PAK CHAESAM

The Road Back

Starting on the frosty path at dawn,
mother now soaked from the heavy night's dew;
mother has come back after a day of selling
to the place where we lie asleep.

There is no jar of honey on the shelf,
only the gray dust piling,
while the children, too small to work
off the debts, lie stretching here, there.

No one to see, no one
to comprehend when she unties
the starlight she carries back on her forehead,
and shakes loose the moonlight
that clings to her sleeves.

Translated from the Korean by David R. McCann and Jiwon Shin

XUÂN QUỲNH

The Blue Flower

Were those blue flowers there or not
In the trampled field of your childhood?
A lazy stream flowed into the distance from the still valley.
A mist rose over the windows.

Were those blue daisies there or not
In that little schoolhouse, far from the world?
Was that our dream, or was it the flower's
To be so gentle, so dear?

The grass sprouts for a small bird in the forest.
The clear water murmurs in a field of reeds

And my heart is as young as dawn light,
Undiminished as yet by sorrow.
Autumns come and go on the old verandas
Life is not yet marred by sudden separation.
The whole of the trampled field is blue with flowers.
Their fragrance fills the world.
Country girls with silken skin,
Village boys eager in their twenties.
Love everywhere, among people, flowers, grass, earth.
Take turns to the seasons of the fruit harvests. . . .

Were those blue flowers there or not
In those months and years of our childhood?
Was the valley there or not
When I visited you?
Green grasshoppers, the tiny red dragonflies
Hummed above the roads of summer wind.
This the kingdom of our past,

Fresh and smooth as grass in a dream. . . .

You must have believed those flowers were there.
And that the valley of our youth was blue with them.

Translated from the Vietnamese by Nguyễn Bá Chung and Carolyn Forché

VIKRAM SETH

Suzhou Park

Magnolia trees float out their flowers,
Vast, soft, upon a rubbish heap.
The grandfather sits still for hours:
His lap-held grandson is asleep.
Above him plane trees fan the sky.
Nearby, a man in muted dance
Does tai-qi-quan. A butterfly
Flies whitely past his easy trance.

A magpie flaps back to its pine.
A sparrow dust-rolls, fluffs, and cheeps.
The humans rest in a design:
One writes, one thinks, one moves, one sleeps.
   The leaves trace out the stenciled stone,
   And each is in his dream alone.

HAMID ISMAILOV

The Shaping Clay

Crack open your door, silence,
to the murmurs of a cottage
under the cradle
of the sleeping clay.
In the long fingers of the wind,
like the trills of a flute
poppies and water lilies
wake to a new day.

The sky is still more dexterous
which sculpts the vault of a heavenly earth
where the blue holds a glaze.
Oh, potter, mold me silence,
take good care not to lose
even a word
in the heart of a child.

At the end of summer in the middle of Russia,
when the water is transparent, who flies the planes?
Like the first falling leaves on the pond,
the life-savers at the end of the path,

is like a feeling in the elevator
when it drops brutally
following the beams, the numbers and letters
like mountaineers tumbling into the abyss.

Their cries rise a whirl toward the ceiling,
filling up the concert halls
like what remains unsaid about this summer?
But then again, what can the bridge of a violin say?

Translated from the Uzbek by the author and Jean-Pierre Balpe
via the French by Aimee Walker

MỘNG-LAN

Overhearing Water

                                        ears pressed i listen
            the drowsy delta
                    sea-salt deep in my nostrils

used for the morning & evening meals
                    water   pumped from the sewage the streets

                                            rush down legs
            & alleyways (rooms wet from thought)
                            clink against
                    sodden sidewalks odored
                            with my hair as i wash upon rising
                    clothes washed   scrubbed
        sound of tubs
            agreeing in the sudsy hands
        of a woman   her willful children about her

i want to dream but i hear
                    women pailing men pumping
                                            ion luring ion
                    electron repulsing electron   gurgling
                        feet always wet faces hands

winter comes
   we wash in the cold
 in doused nights
     seasick the straw mat a cat tramples at midnight

i want to breathe but what breath

a woman still washes her husband's & daughter's clothes
         wringing the clothes hushed

between life & death
       i hear poured into round tubs
    emptied choke
      of water   tub against concrete
  the woman rinses her hands & feet

between day & night
       sounds of gravity
   at 5:30 the first person wakes
  to rinse her phlegm mouth
   noise of work begins
      with an avalanche of insomnia
    morning drunkenness slippers
& mothers prodding their children to school   i see the wash of smoke & tv
  ash   radio
       music bellowing
 the seventies the eighties Brothers in Arms
      a dusky voice like a flower hanging
    & the girl downstairs begins to wash her endless
    ebony hair

  the walkway leading to the 22 families' houses
     rivulets roving

           down roof
concrete algae-green

        overhearing water
              Hanoi's innards alchemize to jade

ROMESH GUNESEKERA

Turning Point

My host is a monk
from my grandfather's town

exploring England
in a darkened age.

Stopped temporarily
in a shared room

we meet on my less
noble travels:

discover we are
exactly the same age.

At ten I knew
the world must change;

he, at ten,
also knew the same.

Twenty yards
of saffron robes

captured his boy's
imagination,

while mine slipped
on the slopes

of Tagaytay. He grew
decisive,

unencumbered
in a shaved head;

I became
progressively

less certain,
more curled.

Reaching our mid-thirties
—the age of Enlightenment—

he speaks, I listen
only half understanding

this language from my past.
I have stumbled

off the path, tripped
by his inflections.

Once we had
in our Colombo house

a daylight almsgiving
feeding twenty monks.

We served, they ate.
This bright morning

at our breakfast
my laughing monk

serves me
his home cooking,

turning the tables
in a Manchester flat.

RAJINDERPAL S. PAL

proof

that one day
going to amritsar
the golden temple
sarinder tied a turban for me
white, in the *fojji* style
that pappaji was particular to
there was a pressure behind the ears
a heaviness i could not detach

as though that one day
in the end
at that final reckoning
the great judgment
as though that day in amritsar
would matter more than all others
those few hours more than the tens of thousands others

there is a photograph—
me walking backward
down underwater steps
a kind of baptism
in holy water
a validation of heritage
                history—
naked shoulders
and arms holding a thick chain
the golden dome in the background

what it doesn't show is the large fish
teeming in the brown water
and that once in up to my chest
i felt a slap against my leg
and rushed out

later i paid a hundred *rupees* for a saffron *sarong*
a stainless steel tray
into which a *granthi's* apprentice
cupped steaming hot *prashad*
to lay in front of the *granth sahib*
an offering
a proof
i was in a long line
a congregation in waiting
on that thin path to the temple
water on both sides
loudspeakers boomed prayers
                    into the sticky afternoon air

i couldn't move
and became separated from my party

the thing is this—
the steel tray took the heat from the *prashad*
and became unbearable
i was completely surrounded
and held the tray above my head
small children scurried between our legs
some screaming for parents
who they could no longer see in the mass—
nobody seemed happy to be here
here, this most sacred of places
burning hands on stainless steel trays
as though in the end
on that final reckoning
what will matter are the scars of devotion

KYI MAY KAUNG

Eskimo Paradise[1]

Eskimo paradise
is warm
paradise of Bedouins
cold—
my paradise—
we're sitting on somebody's
warm flagged
patio
still
retaining the
sun—Chinese magnolias smelling
fruity
Ko Ko[2] is in the golden
garrulous haze
between
a little and
very
drunk
talking too much
wheezing
in an hour maybe
he'll start
making little
passes
at the younger women—
(Chekhov is taking
notes)
but now
all he speaks is
the awful

[1] After Paul Zimmer's "Zimmer Imagines Heaven."

[2] My elder cousin, the late Ko Minshin of Kamayut, who wanted to be like Hemingway and died of cirrhosis of the liver, from drinking. Almost his entire family except for a son and a son-in-law later died in a plane crash in the mid 1980s.

truth.
Suu has made a big bowl
of pickled tea and is saying
she can't stand it anymore
she's going to—[3]
Michael[4] is editing her manuscript[5]
Jane has made the gold beef curry
full of onions—
Ron sitting quietly on the margins[6]

I'm reading my poetry
standing
leafing through pages frantically
my ears
red.

You are staring through your psychological
lenses—
father's ghost is sitting on the ledge
smoking a pipe—

Gordon[7] is talking about Bagan
reading Romeo's part
eighty years old
while I thirteen

---

[3] The pro-democracy Burmese leader, Nobel Peace Prize winner Daw Aung San Suu Kyi. In early 1988 as the demonstrations in Burma calling for democracy were starting, she told a mutual friend she could not stand it anymore and she was going to enter politics.

[4] Suu's husband, the late Dr. Michael Aris, a Tibetologist. He died of prostate cancer and she was unable to leave Burma to see him one last time.

[5] Michael Aris edited his wife's book *Freedom from Fear*.

[6] My longtime economics mentor and his wife.

[7] Gordon H. Luce, famous historian of Old Burma, who was my father's mentor and was the first to systematically study the tenth-century ruins of Bagan (formerly spelled Pagan) in Central Burma. Luce was also a member of the Bloomsbury Group and a poet. His first poetry book was published by economist John Maynard Keynes.

read Juliet—
Tee Tee[8] is saying don't marry her
off
too quickly
and cutting
carrots—
John's[9] hands and voice are
shaking—

Terese and Gor have brought
Beluga caviar from Iran
and are serving
champagne out of paper
cups
with strawberries to bring
the flavor
out—Selena has baked the
Black Forest cake
kuchen bachen
Ats has made sushi[10]

Zarganar[11] is telling his jokes
taking his dentures out—

---

[8] Gordon's Burmese wife, Daw Tee Tee Luce, a noted philanthropist who set up the Home for Waifs and Strays and was herself the sister of a noted Burmese scholar, U Pe Maung Tin.

[9] A noted economist who expounded the theory of plural economies, based on his experiences in the multicultural Burma of the pre–World War II period and of Netherlands India (now Indonesia), J. S. Furnivall. Furnivall was a lifelong friend of G. H. Luce. They both married Burmese women and as a widower, while he was helping the democratic government of U Nu as an economic advisor in the 1950s, Furnivall lived with the Luces. His hands and voice shook from old age.

[10] Members of my multicultural extended family, names changed, and their speciality dishes.

[11] A famous comedian of 1988—Zarganar (pincers or tweezers)—was imprisoned many times by the regime. By training he was a dentist. After one stay he lost all his teeth due to severe beatings, proceeding to joke about it on stage after his release. Present whereabouts unknown.

everyone there is laughing
sad eyed—tears streaming—
wasabi[12] is in our eyes
the three boys are playing
at my feet
white dogwood and frangipani
simultaneously
blooming—
the scent of flowers and
gunshots
in the
air.

CYRIL WONG

Practical Aim

After great pain, what would the body learn
that it does not already know of relief?

When that fire truck has raged past,
what do I rediscover about silence,

except that I would always miss it?
Do trees mind if it is the same wind

that passes through their heads everyday?
After the mall is completed, must we

remember the field it inhabits now
where we chased each other as children?

If my lover fails to wake me with a kiss
a third time this week, do I worry?

[12] The green grated horseradish paste one eats with sushi.

After the earthquake, would it matter if
no one saw two dogs from different

families approach each other
without suspicion, then moving apart?

As the workers wash their faces hidden
by helmets that beam back the sun,

should they care about the new building
behind them beyond the fear of it falling?

Does solitude offer strength over time,
or is denial of it the only practical aim?

If my mother cannot see how else
to be happy, is it enough that she may lie

in bed, convinced God watches her sleep?
After severe loss, what does the heart

learn that it has not already understood
about regret? When all light finally

forsakes a room, do we take the time
to interrogate the dark, and to what end?

CHIN WOON PING

In My Mother's Dream

There is no pain needling hands swollen to young

ginger knots, there are no children fading

into the wide lands of Ah Yo Fah or Ten Ah See

(here in Fui Chang the white-

powder fellows ready to pounce)

there is no square-jawed

soo-woon man bruising with his passions

and committing small acts of betrayal,

no broken wedding plates, lizard tails

sliding from condensed milkcans, no buckets

and buckets of wet torn clothes to be scrubbed

with hard Gor Si Li soap, centipedes slithering

up damp walls, there are no rumors

of Japanese soldiers advancing

with gleaming hatreds and no running

for refuge in leech-deep jungles, no digging

for tapioca root, no tears when all that was hoarded

was Banana notes for a smoky bonfire,

the body does not split with pain as it evicts

the unwanted dead and courses its accompanying

effluents of crimson, relatives do not mock

with refusals or pitiful gifts of powdered

milk and bits of unwanted cloth, rats do not

die in secret places to spread a vast

stench or sneak up to bite toes in her sleep,

cockroaches do not fly up in a swarm, glittering

like a length of Indian sari, spiders do not piss

in her eye or babies snort with incomprehensible

agony in their palsied rage of eleven years,

the sun does not burn black spots on her face

or nourish the fire ant, there is no forced

solitude, her elders' graves are not overgrown

with lalang, no dirtiness follows her home

from the cemetery, no hemp, no grass sandals

to wear and no uniformed officials speak

a language she cannot understand.

In my mother's dream it is Spring

Festival and we in crisp, new dresses

are seated round the table while joss

sticks waft a late scent to her smiling face,

the chicken is boiling in its great

wide pot and pigs' feet pickle in black vinegar,

Oh her white hairs are falling one by one

and she would like to be around for just one

more Wankang pageant, so don't turn off

her favorite soap though it's not Jee

Lor Leen or Tam Pek Wan, she likes *The Young*

and the Restless and has traveled

by bus to Hollywood.

DILAWAR KARADAGHI

A Child Who Returned from There Told Us

Anfal stopped us on the way to dating
searched our pockets, tore the letters, set fire to the pictures,
locked the songs away from our voices.

Anfal stole our school's "good morning,"
"good evening" of the neighborhood,
"good night" of our woolen quilts,
snatched greeting from the lovers' lips,
withered the flower on the collar of Mamleh's songs,
crushed *Sia Chemana* in Kakemem's throat,
wrecked the playhouse of the little Khatuzins.

Anfal entered while we were still eating.
A banquet of love had drawn us together.
Twilight was slinking against confidence,
salving yesterday's pain.
A night of affection was whistling beyond the window.
Suddenly the lamps were killed
the evening flew away,
the night screamed,
the sun said its last good-bye to the green conifers
at the edge of the village.

Aaie, Anfal separated wood from stone,
toddlers from their babble,
trees from birdsong,
the sky from stars,
the village from the mountain,
the river from its murmur.

Waie, Anfal deceived the trees
set out to hunt the moon,
poisoned the honeybees,
planted mines in the fields and the roads,
strangled the wheat stalk.

Anfal said: don't worry children,
it's just a trip and you will be back.
Anfal said: we will picnic,
and chewed two green villages on the way,
tore our letters on the way,
set the pictures alight,
stole "hello" from the children's mouths.

Anfal lied to us, it was no picnic.
It was darkland, just darkland.
We were 182,000 stares
unable to see each other,
we could only hear each other's heartbeat.
Anfal could see all of us
but did not hear our heartbeat.

Anfal blindfolded us with a black cloth
and grinned as it asked us:
Tell me, children, what do you see?
We said: nothing! Nothing but darkness.
Anfal closed the sky above our heads
and gathered the earth below our feet.

Anfal separated us, lined us up
and said: open your hands, children.
With a wet cane, it delivered
182,000 blows to our palms,
our fingers fell off.

Anfal filled our eyes and breath with dust,
separated wood from stone
and everything from everything else.
Anfal said: look, children, what do you see?
We said: nothing but the desert.
Anfal lied. We saw nothing but the desert.
We heard nothing but our own heartbeats
as we were dying.

Translated from the Kurdish by Choman Hardi

NGUYỄN QUANG THIỀU

The Habit of Hunger

When I was fourteen, my sister and I
Drained the blood of a duck into a bowl.
Its red blood came together, in an embrace.

When I let go,
The duck wasn't dead.
Head flopped to one side,
It staggered like a drunk.

From the cut at its throat
Drops of bright blood dripped
And caught on the white feathers
Like a string of broken
Glass beads.

It buried its head in a basin of water,
Hunting for leftover grains of rice.
But the rice couldn't find its way to the stomach.
It fell through the cut in the throat,
Grain after grain.

Then the duck made its way to the path.
It looked for the pond
It looked for the field
It looked for the river, the sea,
To catch fish, to hunt crabs.
When it buried its head in the mud,
Red blood spread like oil on water.

Aching with cold, I went looking for the duck.
With an invisible knife, I cut meat along the way.

Translated from the Vietnamese by Martha Collins and Nguyễn Bá Chung

AKU WUWU

tiger skins

Grandfather hunted tigers.
Father sold tiger skins.

Before being sold,
Those tiger skins were hung before the house.
And as pregnant ewes crossed the courtyard one by one
Their lambs were lost.
Hung behind the house, those skins,
And the pears and peach trees withered one by one.

On the prairie of my dreams, Father
Strode among the crowds
Clothed in a tiger skin.
As shouts of "A tiger's coming" rang throughout
The stone walls of the village,
They cracked,
And rocks rolled like scrambling goats.
The last was Mother, chased by the tiger to wood's end;
There she died, yet was brought to life again.

Before being sold, the tiger skins
Were the skins of sky
The skins of earth
The skins of water
The skins of rock.
When turned into windows on the wall
Those tiger skins would reveal my person.
Should I be seen, it would be with
Hunting gun on shoulder.

When deciding to make a sacred drum of tiger skin,
One fears only those beats that deliver
Withering plagues through the endless forest.
On making a harness of tiger skin for the ox
The one fear is no more land to plow.

When making a banner of tiger skin
The one fear is that of finding no one to raise it.

I have never seen a tiger skin, nor indeed a tiger.
"'A man leaves behind only his name at death;
A tiger leaves only its skin.'
In this life of yours, why not be a tiger?"
And why were the children taught this way?
Whatever the reason, all those tiger skins
Were sold by my Father.

On New Year's Eve pine needles covered the sitting room floor.
Not one of Grandfather's footprints could be found.
Did he die again in the sky? Let it be just a dream.

I carried my cold heart to lay it upon
The pine needles piled there in the sitting room.
I did not feel the needle pricks as their tattoos
Covered my body.
It was again the midnight of that day
The midnight of that day.

Translated from the Yi by Mark Bender, with Aku Wuwu and Jjiepa Ayi

JON PINEDA

My Sister, Who Died Young, Takes Up The Task

A basket of apples brown in our kitchen,
their warm scent is the scent of ripening,

and my sister, entering the room quietly,
takes a seat at the table, takes up the task

of peeling slowly away the blemished skins,
even half-rotten ones are salvaged carefully.

She makes sure to carve out the mealy flesh.
For this, I am grateful. I explain, *this elegy*

would love to save everything. She smiles at me,
and before long, the empty bowl she uses fills,

domed with thin slices she brushes into
the mouth of a steaming pot on the stove.

What can I do? I ask finally. *Nothing,*
she says, *let me finish this one thing alone.*

KIMIKO HAHN

Things That Are Full of Pleasure—

Finally I have a dress that resembles my mother's except for the buttons.
It is a lamby dress: grayish white and furry like wool. A waist. Three
buttons down the front, mine in red, and hers—black with red in each
center. She has tied a red ribbon around my pony tail also. I love her.
I love that we look the same. Am I four?

My grandfather in Wisconsin teaches me how to dog-paddle. The
bottom of the lake is sandy soft.

Dad shows me how to wind wire around tiny pine tree branches. It is five
years old but only a few inches tall. We collect new moss to cover the roots.

The smell of hibiscus. Gardenia. I think of my grandmother.

I think of mango trees.

My first husband speaking street Spanish.

My second husband taking my hand and guiding me out of the rough waves
I had gotten myself into; once on the beach, the hot air. The hot towel.

The third husband.

My daughters, home before midnight and in their beds. They each come in quietly and kiss *me* good night. I tell them: sticks feathers string mud. They understand.

LEONG LIEW GEOK

Dismantling the Wayang Stage

The struts fall to strike sound
Off poles below, those standing
Till their binding ties are cut.
Two men walk roofbeams crabwise
To strip the roof: uncovered, sheets swish
Down like waterfalls of blue-green cloth
To ravished stage where two more
Fold and roll many seasoned tarpaulin.

For three days and nights past, the temple deities
Have watched costumed players sing,
Declaim, their backdrops distant mountains
Or open mansions. Women raise and dip trailing
Sleeves, men handle horses with short sticks
Or brandish swords, striding wide,
Drums, gong and cymbals
Clashing in musicians' wing.

The loaded lorry leaves land to grass
Until the next feast summons
Stagebuilder and another repertoire.
After three days of lighted candles, giant joss
And burning joss paper, quiet returns
To temple. Two or three times a year, I walk over
For some of its evening offering.
Not comprehending Teochew, Hokkien
Noise and song, I hold out
For scaffolding's lasting parts,
Some ancient make-believe to pass—

Though sooner than later, my children stop
Watching to ask—when I'm ready to leave.

Author's Note: Wayang is a Malay word meaning show or theater. In the poem's context, it refers to Chinese open-air opera, now often staged in conjunction with a temple's festive occasions.

RAJENDRA KISHORE PANDA

from *Bodhinabha: The Sky Vision*

Sometimes
the November sky
resembles a speck of dirt
inside the delicate nail
freshly sprouted
on the finger of a baby.

Translated from the Oriya by the author

ABDELLATIF LAÂBI

The portrait of the father
has taken its place on the wall
behind me
I am alone
in my closed room
My wife has gone to work
yet
a hand comes to caress my neck
gently
like a bird's feather
The taste of childhood
rises to my mouth

Translated from the French by Pierre Joris

SHUKRULLA

The Age of My Father

I haven't yet reached the age of my father
Still I feel surprisingly sick.
My father at my age
Knew not what a staff was.

I hate inclement weather.
My veins are constrained by the piercing autumn wind,
Only the crows enjoy such weather,
Chasing each other, unable to share a nut.

My childhood reminiscences are still alive,
The crows threw nuts on the roof with a terrible noise.
Maybe those are the same crows.
Crows live longer than men.

I watch them bustle and play and chase each other.
Still, a crow will never peck out the eye of a crow.
Perhaps that is why they live so long,
Perhaps that is why their days are so long.

Translated from the Uzbek by William M. Dirks

CHITRA BANERJEE DIVAKARUNI

The Walk

Each Sunday evening the nuns took us
for a walk. We climbed carefully
in our patent-leather shoes up hillsides looped
with trails the color of earthworms. Below,
the school fell away, the sad green roofs
of the dormitories, the angled classrooms,
the refectory where we learned to cut
buttered bread into polite squares,

to eat bland stews and puddings. The sharp
metallic thrust of the church spire, small, then smaller,
and around it the town: bazaar, post office, the scab
coated donkeys. Straggle of huts
with hesitant woodfires in the yards. All
at a respectful distance, like the local children we passed,
tattered pants and swollen chilblained fingers
color of the torn sky, color of the Sacred Heart
in the painting of Jesus that hung above our beds
with his chest open.

We were trained not to talk to them,
runny-nosed kids with who-knew-what diseases, not even
to wave back, and of course it was improper
to stare. The nuns walked so fast,
already we were passing the plantation, the shrubs
lined up neatly, the thick glossy green
giving out a faint wild odor like our bodies
in bed after lights-out. Passing the pickers,
hill women with branch-scarred arms, bent
under huge baskets strapped to shoulder and head,
the cords in their thin necks
pulling like wires. Back at school
though Sister Dolores cracked the refectory ruler
down on our knuckles, we could not drink
our tea. It tasted salty as the bitten inside
of the mouth, its brown like the women's necks,
that same tense color.

But now we walk quicker because
it is drizzling. Drops fall on us from *pipul* leaves
shaped like eyes. We pull on
our gray rainhoods and step in time,
soldiers of Christ squelching through vales of mud.
We are singing, as always on walks,
the nuns leading us with choir-boy voices.
"O Kindly Light," and then a song
about the Emerald Isle. Ireland, where they grew up,
these two Sisters not much older
than us. Mountain fog thickens like a cataract

over the sun's pale eye, it is stumbling-dark,
we must take a shortcut through the upper town. The nuns
motion us, *faster, faster,* an oval blur of hands
in long black sleeves.

Honeysuckle over a gate, lanterns
in front windows. In one, a woman in a blue sari
holds a baby, his fuzzy backlit head
against the curve of her shoulder. Smell of food
in the air, *real* food, onion pakoras, like our mothers
once made. Rain in our eyes, our mouths. Salt, salt.
A sudden streetlamp lights the nuns' faces, damp,
splotched with red like frostbitten
camellias. It prickles the backs of our throats.
The woman watches, wonder-eyed, as we pass
in our wet, determined shoes, singing
"Beautiful Killarney," a long line of girls, all of us
so far from home.

LUIS CABALQUINTO

Depths of Field

I walk some hundred paces from the old house
Where I was raised, where many are absent now,

and the rice fields sweep into view: here where
during home leaves I'm drawn to watch on evenings

such as this, when the moon is fat and much given
to the free spending of its rich cache of light

which transmutes all things: it changes me now,
like someone restored to the newness of his life.

Note the wind's shuffle in the crown of tall coconut
trees; the broad patches of moon-flecked water—

freshly-rowed with seedlings; the grass huts of
croppers, windows framed by the flicker of kerosene

lamps: an unearthly calm pervades all that is seen.
Beauty unreserved holds down a country's suffering.

Disclosed in this high-pitched hour: a long-held
secret displaced by ambition and need, a country

boy's pained enchantment with his hometown lands
that remains intact in a lifetime of wanderings.

As I look again, embraced by the depths of an old
loneliness, I'm permanently returned to this world,

to the meanings it has saved for me. If I die now,
in the grasp of childhood fields, I'll miss nothing.

PARSED INTO
COLORS

Parsed into Colors

—PURNA BAHADUR VAIDYA

When I was a young girl living in the Caribbean, three Haitian girlfriends from my neighborhood and I were playing hopscotch, our bare feet on the tropical ground, small stones nestled warmly in our hands. The girls and I would often gather to sing songs, eat shaved ice with flavored syrup in paper cones, and play under the cool shade. On the cement floor, we wrote the numbers one to ten in squares just large enough for our feet. We felt safe and contented, until a Caucasian neighbor approached me and asked disapprovingly, "Why are you playing with these girls?"

That afternoon, as I walked along the narrow dirt road that led to my house, I looked at the sunlight reflected on my olive-tanned skin through the acajou and tamarind trees. It was the first time I had thought about my color. In the evening I asked my father, "Am I black or white?" He said, "You are Nathalie." Seeing the confusion in my eyes he added, "You are Semite." As I lay in my bed unable to sleep, I wondered, *Who am I?*

In time, I discovered I am the girl strolling the narrow streets of Jerusalem's Old City, willingly lost in a maze of Persian carpets, rusted keys hanging from store ceilings; the girl who views her surname on store plaques in Bethlehem, from where her family originates; who walks Boulevard de la Madeleine in Paris, where she sits in a bistro, waiting for a man for the first time; I am the shadow on the red earth of the Aztec capital and the woman under the moist canopy of leaves in the Dominican rainforest.

But it was my first encounter with the poet Lisa Suhair Majaj, in my early twenties, that ultimately made me question if I identified myself as Arab American. Up until then, it was not an identity any writer I knew used, yet it has become central to how others define me today.

Years later I traveled to Pennsylvania, where the Lannan Foundation was honoring the eminent Palestinian poet Mahmoud Darwish with a prize. It was a particularly special moment because some of the people I admired most were all gathered in the same room: Edward Said, the Lebanese musician Marcel Khalife, along with Carolyn Forché and Naomi Shihab Nye. During one of our dinners together, Mahmoud Darwish posed a question that startled me: *Where are you these days?* He proceeded to say, *Choose a continent ya Nathalie.* I wondered if that was how he saw me, lost between continents?

Throughout my nomadic life, the poems of Darwish, Baudelaire, Neruda, and others have rescued me from being lost, have rescued me from the ruse of my own imagination. Because of my many migrations, am I a series of broken images or am I *parsed into colors* as this section suggests?

Like the Armenian American poet Diana Der-Hovanessian, I have sought to define which aspects of myself were rooted and which were suspended in exile. In Der-Hovanessian's "Two Voices," the duality of identity is explored:

> *In what language do I pray?*

> *Do I meditate in language?*

> . . . .

> *Do I think of myself as an American,*
> *or simply as a woman when I wake?*

> *Or do I think of the date and geography*
> *I wake into, as woman?*

> . . . .

> *Or do I think of my grandmother*
> *at Ellis Island,*

> *or as an orphan in an Armenian village?*

> . . . .

> *Do I think of myself as hyphenated?*

In the end, we both arrive at a similar conclusion, that we are not hyphenated in any rigid way.

Many of us think we understand what identity means until the day we are consciously forced to confront others' ideas about us. The definition of identity has multiple layers—from national to religious, ethnic to racial, spiritual to intellectual—and the dialogue surrounding these conflicts can be painful as well as enriching. Does cultural multiplicity confine us? Can we free ourselves from the categories people place us in? Such exploration makes this section particularly essential to me.

The poems presented here challenge us, introducing new visions of the self and the world. Take Bimal Nibha's "Cycle," which uses a lost bicycle as a metaphor for the rediscovery of a new interiority: "It's been a few days since / my bicycle has vanished / Do you know where I might find it?" The character describes the flaws and fissures of the bicycle, mirroring his physical being, deteriorating: "It's true that my cycle is small / its tires are bald / they have too little air / the color is faded / the stand is broken / the kinetic light faulty." There's a clear link between the cycle and the rhythms of the body, and the speaker of this poem reminisces on how he has changed in time. Yet he would not trade his life for any other. Nibha writes:

> *The weight of my body lies on its seat*
> *The measure of my feet fills its pedals*
> *The print of my hands marks its handlebars*
> *My breath rests in each part of that cycle*
> *I am there*
> *That cycle is my life*

The imperfections are invaluable because they are markers of identity. He loves his cycle, whether lost or broken, as he does his life, for the simple reason that it is his own.

While Nibha contemplates identity as metaphor, Leung Ping-kwan focuses on the difficulty of communicating and translating one's culture to others. In his poem "Postcards of Old Hong Kong," he reflects on the flattened and one-dimensional image of his homeland. In exotic depictions of "opium-smoking, long-plaited / gamblers, songstresses, Kung Fu masters, rickshaw pullers," the speaker does not recognize himself nor his personal experiences.

The postcard is a distillation of reality, an entire city reduced to a few imagined and eroticized scenes. At worst, these images show the legacy of Orientalism that the speaker rejects, feeling the need to choose his words or a photo wisely as to not misrepresent his home:

The pictures we sent off have been touched up
images of scenes we never experienced

. . . .

From mass-produced pictures
I pick and choose, wondering how to convey news of me

. . . .

. . . I'm not a tourist
scribbling at the margin of a disaster scene . . .

. . . .

I flip them over, disgusted. True,
they exist, but I'd rather not use them to
represent us

By poem's end, the speaker expresses the challenge of articulating a scene, a mood, a sensation of home, asking, "How do we, on gaudy pictures of the past / write words of the moment? Stuck in their midst, how do we paint ourselves?" As difficult as it might be to convey our sense of self to others, it is a human need to understand oneself in relation to our society. Barouyr Sevag, in his poem "The Analysis of Yearning," states, "I know the dark need, the yearning, that want, / in the same way the blind man knows / the inside of his old home."

The experience of human longing is apparent as the figure is cast into the metaphoric role of a chemist who examines the molecular structure of his condition to reveal his actions and reactions. Sevag writes:

And dangling between darkness and loneliness
I want to analyze this want
like a chemist
to understand its nature and profound mystery.
And as I try
there is laughter
from some mysterious tunnel,
laughter from an indescribable distance,
from an unhearable distance.

Despite the character's assiduous attention, he doesn't ultimately discover who he is nor why he longs for such unattainable understanding. He is left with "an unechoing distance, / an unhuntable distance." The self-examination mocks him, leaving an unbridgeable gulf between himself and his resolution as he concludes, "I run after myself / incapable of ever reaching or / catching what I seek. / And this is what is called / want and longing or 'garod.'"

I have longed to dissolve the designations others have had for *who I am*, longed instead to revel in my memories: the small garden greening in the wind, the open cahier on the divan of my Paris apartment, and the warm sensation of Latin American soil in my hand, as I dig deeper and deeper to plant seeds while listening to grandfather's favorite Arabic song.

I may be Middle Eastern, but I belong to the world in ways that defy definition. My identity has been, and continues to be, deeply rooted in words. Simone Weil wrote, "To be rooted is perhaps the most important and least recognized need of the human soul."[1] And yet the question of rootedness, and of identity, continue to be one of the most fundamentally complicated internal and external debates we have, as we constantly address issues of exile, dispossession, religion, race, and gender.

In a conversation Salman Rushdie had with Edward Said in 1986, he asked, "You say that to be a Palestinian is basically to come from a Muslim culture, and yet you are not Muslim. Do you find that a problem?" Said answered, "I have had no experience of such frictions. . . . One of the virtues of being a Palestinian is that it teaches you to feel your particularity in a new way, not only as a problem but as a kind of gift. Whether in the Arab world or elsewhere, twentieth-century mass society has destroyed identity in so powerful a way that it is worth a great deal to keep this specificity alive."[2] It is through words, like these poems, that I keep my own specificity alive. My existence gleams. It is part of, yet lives outside of, history. That is the beauty of words; they refuse boundaries. They belong everywhere.

— NATHALIE HANDAL

[1] Simone Weil, *The Need for Roots* (London: Routledge, 2003), p. 43.
[2] Edward Said, *The Politics of Dispossession* (London: Chatto & Windus, 1994), p. 122.

DAVID AVIDAN

Dance Music

We reflected at length. Light flooded
the forehead's rectangle, the eyes, the eyebrows. We asked
the same questions and were answered
as always. Winter arrived
and saddened us. From others
we asked nothing and from ourselves
we asked only little. But we grasped
that daylight is not hostile and that night
is only a passing nuisance. Rain came
and silenced the tune. We turned on the radio,
dimmed the lights, and quietly dove
into dark and shadowy abysses. The hairy creature
awoke in us. Man is the sole
goal of all creation. And so
woman found us. We were
hard and festive until nightfall.
Why did light flood the eyes, eyebrows,
the forehead's rectangle, the back, the body. The rain
why did it come, and how would you explain
that we passed underneath and did not sink.

Translated from the Hebrew by Tsipi Keller

XUE DI

The Wanderer

The sea once again leaps up before me. I sit and listen closely. A
cigarette sizzles on wet rocks while the waves make a sound like our
common sorrow. Familiar sour salt smell. Naked children duck and run
through the gate of their mother's legs, playing out their childhood. Sea
birds, luckier than us, pass back and forth between land and sunset
water.

Come, I'll throw my worn straw hat to my feet and sit beside you, Ocean, and with you, my reader, and with all mankind, and have a chat. The noon sun's radiance strikes from the top of my head to the heart's center. What you bring me, Ocean, is vast. It can't be the same craziness as seeing you for the first time, but still I am drunk on you. Heart, you thirsted to see strange things—look at the line of sparks along these breakers!

Sunbathers, don't you want to be naked, don't you want to peel off your skins and get down to your own lives? Then we could listen with real silence as the waves rake the reefs and make sounds that start to live. I attend that wordless language and begin to understand you, Ocean! We both know about hearts torn open and lungs split wide and howling at the sky.

Now both you and I are calm. In this still place we can hear the sound of blood slipping to the ocean floor. That sound is the ripple of a dogfish's fin, the far off song of a small lobster. Or a bell buoy that's there, then not there. Beneath that exquisite buoy the shift and resettling of bones. Shift once more and I'm home again across the sea.

Yes! What else can I say? These people praised me and cursed me and made me start on the long road that brought me here. These people still want to praise me, still want to curse me, but they are just bathers stepping out of the surf. They walk through my body, walk through my life which is spread out on the golden sand. They leave watery footprints, leave this face of mine looking up from the reefs at the sky drying in the sun. What else can I say to this? They finger my tongue, they beat fiercely in my blood. Day and night they rub their genitals against my lair. I am an ant seeking sweet food, I am the reef seeking some boatsman, I listen to the most exquisite cries, hear those who have embraced death and are moved suddenly to praise life. Oh don't excite me in vain.

Ocean, your distance is where I come from, the home of my loved ones. I make of those miles these promises: beauty-seeds from tropical forests, honeymelons delivered in dreams, and my childhood, inlaid with faraway voices. Who can hear, when one is this lonely, the mermaid sing? Who can stretch their hands inside this statue? Who can feel the honesty of copper and its desire to be lovely?

The abject, beaten world is still hopeful. There are still word forgers. Once again I recall the fisherman's voice as he faced the waters and said, with tears in his eyes, "The ocean is clean. Nothing, there, stays soiled. The waves wash all dirt to shore!" And the shore, oh the shore, place where we come together.

Oh let me talk with you a little more! Quietly, humbly, sitting in patience, both knees unfolded before me as I seek out whatever is vital in the space between words. Can anyone doubt our common fate? Oh my friends. Oh everyone I thought my friends.

Yesterday I trudged through the villages of Hebei. I saw the earth-packed urns which store bitter water, I saw the aroused faces of the poor and their copper colored voices. I saw wheat, that golden symbol of existence and of all that will be reaped. In the jumble of villages I held, for a moment, the parched earth in my hands. Then the jazz drumbeats of rain fell and the rooftops stretched to catch each heavy drop. And the song of a country woman which was the same song as the rain, a song made up of every imaginable city and all the magnificent seasons of the south. Splendid! How could I not run out to the rain-spotted steps of the earthen house and grieve with the sky? The wolf pack's passion comes from inside man. An eighteen-year-old's time worn shirt hangs open and shows her breasts.

I can't help wanting the world, and you, Ocean, remind me of this. Be patient with me, get comfortable, unfold your legs and chat just a little while longer. Home, we call you, and Destination, but don't let us make you a symbol. Your waves, crashing toward me, are they really the breasts of women spilling from open blouses?

Just this once, Ocean, I want to compel you with words. I want to stand next to the sun and command you to play your hand accordion, I want you to fold yourself up and become a small village in Hebei, I want you to re-create the sounds of that dry place and an eighteen-year-old's thirsty voice. Just this once.

A few of the bathers are leaving, a few new waders take their place. I must ask all you new arrivals to keep still.

Is it possible? Can we doubt our common fate, our inconstancy?
Suffering and sea waves compel our acceptance by their unceasing
motion. One might start by gathering up, alone, one's lamentations.
One might begin with a single No.

Schooners and sloops. Children's buckets filled with starfish, my own
five fingers walking in their prison. In one corner of the world the wind
rises and faraway a crowd overflows the watery footprint and disperses.
The setting sun, inlaid with images of a single contemplative face, but
under the water bright red flowers bloom. When people drown, their
bones continue to grow until they speak their one word, No.

I can only be silent. There is no way to say clearly why I left that place
and came here. What did I escape? What enticed me all my life? Ocean,
your night waters mold and fashion my body, sculpting from my flesh
a stone church.

Translated from the Chinese by Hil Anderson and Theodore Deppe

DIANA DER-HOVANESSIAN

Two Voices

Do you think of yourself as an Armenian? Or an American?
Or hyphenated American?

      —D. M. Thomas

In what language do I pray?

Do I meditate in language?

In what language am I trying
to speak when I wake from dreams?

Do I think of myself as an American,
or simply as woman when I wake?

Or do I think of the date and geography
I wake into, as woman?

Do I think of myself in my clothes
getting wet walking in the rain?

Do I think velvet, or do I think skin?

Am I always conscious of genes and
heredity or merely how to cross my legs
at the ankle like a New England lady?

In a storm do I think of lightning
striking? Or white knives dripped
into my great aunt's sisters'
sisters' blood?

Do I think of my grandfather telling
about the election at the time
of Teddy Roosevelt's third party,
and riding with Woodrow Wilson
in a Main Street parade
in Worcester?

Or do I think of my grandmother
at Ellis Island,

or as an orphan in an Armenian village?

Or at a black stove in Worcester
baking blueberry pie for my grandfather
who preferred food he had grown
to like in lonely mill town
cafeterias while he studied
for night school?

Do I think of them as Armenian
or as tellers of the thousand and one
wonderful tales in two languages?

Do I think of myself as hyphenated?

No. Most of the time, even as you,
I forget labels.

Unless you cut me.

Then I look at the blood.
It speaks in Armenian.

JESSICA HAGEDORN

Motown/Smokey Robinson

hey girl, how long you been here?
did you come with yr daddy in 1959 on a second-class boat
cryin' all the while cuz you didn't want to leave the barrio
the girls back there who wore their hair loose
lotsa orange lipstick and movies on Sundays
quiapo market in the morning, yr grandma chewin' red tobacco
roast pig? . . . yeah, and it tasted good . . .
hey girl, did you haveta live in stockton with yr daddy
and talk to old farmers who emigrated in 1941?
did yr daddy promise you to a fifty-eight-year-old-bachelor
who stank of cigars . . . and did you
run away to san francisco / go to poly high / rat your hair /
hang around woolworth's / chinatown at three in the morning
go to the cow palace and catch SMOKEY ROBINSON
cry and scream at his gold jacket
Dance every Friday night in the mission / go steady with ruben?
(yr daddy can't stand it cuz he's a spik)
and the sailors you dreamed of in manila with yellow hair
did they take you to the beach to ride the ferris wheel?
Life's never been so fine!
you and Carmen harmonize "be my baby" by the ronettes
and 1965 you get laid at a party / carmen's house
and you get pregnant and ruben marries you
and you give up harmonizing . . .

hey girl, you sleep without dreams
and remember the barrios and how it's all the same:
manila / the mission / chinatown / east l.a. / harlem / fillmore st.
and you're gettin' kinda fat and smokey robinson's gettin' old

Ooh baby baby baby
Ooh baby baby
Ooh . . .

But he still looks good!!!

i love you
i need you
i need you
i want you
ooh ooh
baby baby
ooh

MAMDOUH ADWAN

Tired of Soliloquies

I sing for debilitating love,
for a body of dew, wasting.

I sing to sift through what remains of silence:
slaughter, the shreds in its wake,
and the cover of green words.

Look, I've found it,
something to do without a permit:
To die.
To startle the dead,
to deprive the joy of the one
who will murder me,
deprive him of stilling my volcanic life.

I am dying
having bled away my fears,
little is left,
but empty skin,
a sack with a few bones inside.

Translated from the Arabic by Sharif S. Elmusa

KAMARAN MUKRI

Star, Bird & Autumn

The flower that autumn only withered
The heart that pain could never shrivel
Embers snuffed out only to flare again
The star blazing as it fell toward its river
The bird whose wings a hot wind singed
When it carried on singing in high skies
All of these are guests inside my heart
Molding me never to give up on hope

Translated from the Kurdish by Kamal Mirawdeli and Stephen Watts

NOOZAR ELIAS

Stars and the Dawn

I come from the land of restless wind
from the progeny of wild waves
from the noble genes of fire.
You may come from the stone
—my fellow traveler—
but I am from the sparks
from the nameless crowd of rebels.

In this deadly autumn
the red flower of sparks
is woven in the spring of my bosom.
I hear from afar
the falling, one by one,
of the stars.

I have broken the darkness of silence
I have closed the summit of my volcano
to the poisonous wailing of the night.

Though our dawn is captured by the night
and our jungle is frozen and worn down
the sun is not dead yet.

Now that the canoe of the sky
floats in the stream of blood
and the broad desert
is the falling place of conviction.
Now that beyond our thirsty sight
is nothing but mist and pebble,
you may wait and second-guess
—O my fellow traveler—
but I have no desire to remain
in the four corners of the night.

Translated from the Persian by Wali Ahmadi

MANJU KANCHULI

The Way of a River, The Forest, Night

I did not forge that river
whose current drags the living down
and tosses a carcass to its banks
I only wet my feet—that for a few days
became lifeless. The river was not the stable still
continuous flow I thought it to be

I could not cross that river
I never tread that path
where my tiny range-bound hands
were fated to be brushed by the beast;
its solitude devoured
by the leopard's clawing paws
I cleared that forest with my gaze
Thinking it useless to render it so,
my eyes turned back immediately
The forest was not blessed
with the security, solitude and pleasure
I thought there to be
I could not pass through that forest

Not again did I step through to brigand night
whose tusk now gnaws the moon
having devoured the sun. Only a morning,
naively, reached day and it
blanched with night—its whole body so soon
took on the darkest hues
Night was not the cove—warm, impregnated
with mild dream—I thought it to be
I could not immerse myself in the black liquids of that night

Translated from the Nepali by the author and Wayne Amtzis

FAZIL HÜSNÜ DAĞLARCA

Dead

Whichever neighborhood has no clergyman
I shall die there.
Let no one see how beautiful
Are all the things I have, my feet, my hair.

In the name of the dead, free and immaculate,
A fish in unknown seas,

Am I not a Muslim, heaven knows,
Yet no crowds for me, please.

Don't let them make me wear a shroud,
In sky safeguard my darkness from misery,
Don't shake me as I go from shoulder to shoulder,
For all my parts are fancy free.

No prayer can turn my remoteness
From the other worlds into a reality.
Don't let them wash my body, don't:
I am madly in love with the warmth inside me.

Translated from the Turkish by Talât Sait Halman

KITAMURA TARŌ

excerpts from "A Man of the Port"

13

Past joys are
sorrows still to come.
A day that casts no shadow, even though I'm in the sun, is ending
and everyone is in the shade of a tree holding their breath.
That cry,
so soft,
has continued for some time.

Waves break but once,
as if whimsically, on the white wharf of the promenade
and a single couple who've been watching the water
are startled
and back off surprisingly quickly.

Soon it'll be night.
There is too much shade
and shadows form within the shade.

Winter equinox.
Though there is shade,
some of the shadows have no light at all.

At the moment
the only couple in the world are on the bench, embracing.
Joys still to come
are past sorrows.

33

Something is dripping.
Water?
I don't want to get out of bed in darkness and find out what.
If not water,
what could it be?
A dream holds many answers.

Today was calm.
It rained all day
till darkness fell outside the window.
Though there was no wind
by nighttime the rain had slowly stopped falling.

How long ago was it
I felt as if I were holding on to a saddle
and kicking the ground?

Of course the sky was blue
and it seemed as if
that's what the water was for.
I never imagined so much sweat could drip
from my lover's entire body.
Holding a glass, my fingers
looked ashen.

That's
water.

It can't be anything else.
If not,
what couldn't it be?
However many answers a dream might hold,
they couldn't be any other color.
I hope tomorrow's weather
will be the same color.

Translated from the Japanese by William I. Elliott and Kazuo Kawamura

LEUNG PING-KWAN

Postcards of Old Hong Kong

The pictures we sent off have been touched up
images of scenes we never experienced
                             On the back,
I'll send my greetings, in that space
were I to tell my deepest anxieties and worries
would they among endless strangers go, before
curious or indifferent eyes, bleaching the sepia
lighter and faint, until those old-style teahouses in Happy Valley
Flower stalls along Lyndhurst Terrace, hawkers of all sorts
like the old woman spinning threads at a branch of tree
gradually fade
                  From mass-produced pictures
I pick and choose, wondering how to convey news of me
I don't want to sensationalize the huge fire at the racecourse, or the typhoon
that sank the cruiser in the harbor. I'm not a tourist
scribbling at the margin of a disaster scene:
"We're off to Shanghai for a jaunt!" I'm no
smart broker or colonial official, engrossed in sending home
exotica: opium-smoking, long-plaited
gamblers, songstresses, Kung Fu masters, rickshaw pullers.
I flip them over, disgusted. True,
they exist, but I'd rather not use them to
represent us
                  At the picture border I wrote

hasty words straying sometimes into Kennedy Town side streets
the first Chinese school in Morrison Hill, the reservoir where
China-bound ambassador-laden horses stopped and drank.
I've always wanted to ask how history was made.
Lots of people tinted the pictures, lots of people
named the streets after themselves, statues were
put up and taken down. Amidst overflowing clichés
I wrote you a few words, crossing set
Boundaries
      How do we, on gaudy pictures of the past
write words of the moment? Stuck in their midst, how do we paint ourselves?

Translated from the Chinese by Martha P. Y. Cheung

RAVI SHANKAR

Exile

There's nowhere else I'd rather not be than here,
But here I am nonetheless, dispossessed,
Though not quite, because I never owned
What's been taken from me, never have belonged
In and to a place, a people, a common history.
Even as a child when I was slurred in school—
Towel head, dot boy, camel jockey—
None of the abuse was precise: only Sikhs
Wear turbans, widows and young girls bindis,
Not one species of camel is indigenous to India . . .
If, as Simone Weil writes, to be rooted
Is the most important and least recognized need
Of the human soul, behold: I am an epiphyte.
I conjure sustenance from thin air and the smell
Of both camphor and meatloaf equally repel me.
I've worn a lungi pulled between my legs,
Done designer drugs while subwoofers throbbed,
Sipped masala chai steaming from a tin cup,
Driven a Dodge across the Verrazano in rush hour,
And always to some degree felt extraneous,

Like a meteorite happened upon bingo night.
This alien feeling, honed in aloneness to an edge,
Uses me to carve an appropriate mask each morning.
I'm still unsure what effect it has on my soul.

TAHA MUHAMMAD ALI

Postoperative Complications
Following the Extraction of Memory

In an ancient Gypsy
dictionary of dreams
are explanations of my name
and numerous
interpretations of all I'll write.

What horror comes across me
when I come across myself
in such a dictionary!
But there I am:
a camel fleeing the slaughterhouses,
galloping towards the East,
pursued by processions
of knives and assessors,
women wielding
mortar and pestle for chopmeat!

I do not consider myself a pessimist,
and I certainly don't
suffer from the shock
of ancient Gypsy nightmares,
and yet, in the middle of the day,
whenever I turn on the radio,
or turn it off,
I breathe in a kind of historical,
theological leprosy.
Feeling the bonds of language
coming apart in my throat and loins,

I cease attending
to my sacred obligations:
barking, and the gnashing of teeth.

I confess!
I've been neglecting
my postoperative physiotherapy
following the extraction of memory.
I've even forgotten
the simplest way of collapsing
in exhaustion on the tile floor.

Translated from the Arabic by Peter Cole, Yahya Hijazi, and Gabriel Levin

YAN LI

Warm Inspiration

In my body there are kegfuls of Chinese beer sloshing
Words like pretty goldfish stir up ripples of affection
For the moment I can't bear to cast a poet's net
And so
I knock back a few before the fishing starts
By the time the doctor uses an X-ray to tell me
The goldfish in my body
Have paired off into romantic lines
It's all I can do to lift my eyelids,
and imagine the doctor's mask is tomorrow's net
Because I am drunk on the operating table

Dear doctor
Please remove the beer from my body
Export it to everywhere in the world
Or simply pack me up in a crate and ship me off
However
Dear doctor
What I send back will not be foreign exchange, it will be poems

It will be infinitely appreciating stocks of feeling in poems
The future value of bonds from the Love Reserve Bank
Ah
Dear doctor
How many poets are on your operating table
How many poems is your salary each month?

Translated from the Chinese by Denis C. Mair

NIRMALENDU GOON

Firearm

The police station is crowded
with people surrendering their firearms
under the surveillant eyes of the soldiers.
The shotguns, rifles, pistols and cartridges
from the people—fearful of the military order—are
piling up like the promised offering of flowers
at a holy shrine.
Only I, disobeying the military order,
am openly returning home a rebel,
still carrying with me
the most lethal firearm of all—my heart.

I didn't surrender it.

Translated from the Bengali by Sajed Kamal

PATRICK ROSAL

About the White Boys Who Drove By a Second Time to Throw a Bucket of Water on Me

. . . there shall never be rest
till the last moon droop and the last tide fail . . .

—Arthur Symons

The first time they merely spat on me and drove off
   I stood there awhile staring down the road
  after them as if I were looking for myself
    I even shouted my own name
But when they cruised past again
    to toss a full bucket of water
   (and who knows what else) on me
     I charged—sopping wet—after their car

and though they were quickly gone I kept
    running Maybe it was hot that August afternoon
  but I ran the whole length of Main Street past
    the five-and-dime where I stole bubble gum
cards and Spaldeens past the bus depot and
    Bo's Den and the projects where Derek and them
  scared the shit out of that girl I pumped
    the thin pistons of my legs all the way home

Let's get real: It's been twenty-five years
    and I haven't stopped chasing them
  through each side street in Metuchen
    each pickup b-ball game every
swanky mid-town bar I looked for them
    in every white voice that slurred and cursed me
  within earshot in every pink and pretty
    body whose lights I wanted to punch out

—and did—I looked for them—to be honest—
    in every set of thin lips I schemed to kiss
  and this is how my impossible fury

rose: like stone in water I ran
all seven miles home that day and I've been
running ever since arriving finally
here and goddammit I'm gonna set things straight

The moment they drove by laughing
at a slant-eyed yellowback gook
they must have seen a boy
who would never become a man We could say
they were dead wrong But instead let's say
this: Their fathers gave them their rage
as my father gave me mine

and from that summer day on we managed
to savor every acrid thing
that belonged to us It was a meal
constantly replenished—a rich
bitterness we've learned to live on for so long
we forget how—like brothers—
we put the first bite in one another's mouths

GREGORY DJANIKIAN

The Boy Who Had Eleven Toes

It was a sign of God's bounty,
His mother had said, the fullness
Of His love spilling over.

But he was imagining himself
Slipping on wet grass, his foot
Entering the dark cave of the mower.

Life insists, his grandfather said,
It seethes into plentitude.

But he was inventing jungle rivers,
One leg casually draped over the gunnel.
He was sleeping in the deep winters
Of extremity, firelees, tent flaps
Rattling in an Arctic wind.
How easier it was to explain
Shortages, deprivations!

Always there had been the locker rooms,
The beaches, the ten dozen fingers pointing.
"Clubfoot," he had heard, "paddlewheel."
Why should he not hope to find,
Everywhere he walked, a hundred blades
And edges whirring about his shoes?

He dreamt of the lucky anonymous,
The unseen, the not-remembered.

He dreamt of the power
Of subtraction, six
Take away one take away two
Or take away six which left zero,
A heel and ball without digits.

But sometimes he dreamt of a boy
With eleven toes limping across wide fields
Under the light of a thousand stars
Or not limping, but one foot now
Running faster for its six toes,
Touching earth and springing further
And up, lighter because heavier.
It was a dream he dared not dream too long,
A dream of something powerful and wing-like
Pulling the rest of the body with it.
It was a dream of prairies and horizons
Steeply falling away, the body opening,
The heel, suddenly, a profusion of feathers.

CESAR RUIZ AQUINO

She Comes with Horns and Tail

She comes with horns and tail
   And yet no nightmare
Made of air
   With such a gift
She carries heaven when she walks.
   On all fours, she is
The metamorphosis.
   Hair done or undone
True to the touch
   And true only to her looks
Till she comes with horns (not the moon)
   And tail (not the comet)
Someone no woman has met
   In the mirror.

ISHIGAKI RIN

Plucking Flowers

I plucked wildflowers at Marunouchi in Tokyo.
At the end of the 1920s
I was in my midteens.

On my way to work
To the Bank
The hem of my kimono-trousers flapping
Just a dash up the embankment beside the footpath
Before my eyes an open field.
Clover
Dandelions
Philadelphia fleabane
Wildflowers too poor
To decorate my desk at work.

It's been about half a century since then
Days came when the buildings blazed in the flames of war,
Around the postwar Tokyo Station
Just like a graph of the economic boom
Tall skyscrapers bloomed.

I retired at the mandatory retirement age,
I don't suppose any firms are left which take
Girls straight from primary school.
Even women are questioned about their market value
And ranked accordingly.
Women bloom in competition
But the day has finally come when they cannot possibly be wildflowers.

Farewell Marunouchi
Now no open fields anywhere
The thin green stem that I once squeezed
Was my own neck.

Translated from the Japanese by Leith Morton

KAZI NAZRUL ISLAM

I Sing of Equality

I sing of equality
in which dissolves
all the barriers of estrangements,
in which are united
Hindus, Buddhists, Muslims, Christians.
I sing of equality.

Who are you?—A Parsee? A Jain? A Jew?
A Santal, a Bheel or a Garo?
A Confucian? A disciple of Charbak?
Go on—tell me what else!
Whoever you are, my friend,
whatever holy books or scriptures

you stomach or carry on your shoulder
or stuff your brains with—the Qur'an, the Puranas,
the Vedas, the Bible, the Tripitaka, the Zend-Avesta,
the Grantha Saheb—why do you waste your labor?
Why inject all this into your brain?
Why all this—like petty bargaining in a shop
when all the roads are adorned with blossoming flowers?
Open your heart—within you lie
all the scriptures,
all the wisdom of all ages.
Within you lie all the religions,
all the prophets—your heart
is the universal temple
of all the gods and goddesses.
Why do you search for God in vain
within the skeletons of dead scriptures
when he smilingly resides in the privacy
of your immortal heart?
I'm not lying to you, my friend.
Before this heart
all the crowns and royalties surrender.
This heart is the Neelachal, Kashi, Mathura,
Brindaban, Budh-Gaya, Jerusalem, Medina, Ka'aba.
This heart is the mosque, the temple, the church.
This is where Jesus and Moses found the truth.
In this battlefield
the young flute player sang the divine Geeta.
In this pasture
the shepherds became prophets.
In this meditation chamber
Shakya Muni heard the call of the suffering humanity
and decried the throne.
In this voice
the Darling of Arabia heard his call,
from here he sang the Qur'an's message of equality.
What I've heard, my friend, is not a lie:
there's no temple or Ka'aba
greater than this heart!

Translated from the Bengali by Sajed Kamal

FIRUZA MAMMADLI

Leaning My Shoulder to the Sun

Leaning my shoulder to the sun,
my face to the shadow.
You are between me and my shadow.
We are talking about you.

Is that how you spare me my shadow?
You are standing between us.
You have forgotten though, my shadow
is on your face.

I am sewing a shirt for you
from the rays of the sun.
I am sewing a shirt for you.
You are standing between me and the sun,
your shadow is on the shirt I am sewing.
I am sewing a shirt for you,
on your shirt your shadow.
I am sewing the shadow to your shirt.

Translated from the Azeri by Shouleh Vatanabadi

XIE YE

At Last I Turn My Back

At last I turn my back.
From behind comes a burst of weird laughter.
The eyes of many spiders
Still crawl in the alleyway.

From the dried-up road, no laughter.
Alongside, the wind is stamping its feet.
Clusters of golden dust blossom.
Spring squints.

I do not like the wind.
Nor am I afraid of it.
In my own nonchalant way I'll forget them
And walk toward the call of the shore.

There are many aged boats.
There are battered vases and shells.
The blue glinting water
Covers eternal peace.

I will belong to the sea. I will belong
To those pure lives. In the company of sea foam
I will dedicate flowers, I will love the coral
Sacrificing itself.

Translated from the Chinese by John Rosenwald and The Beliot/Fudan
Translation Workshop

MOHAN KOIRĀLĀ

It's a Mineral, the Mind

Velvet the Himalayan poinsettia in bloom,
silver the scabbard of thrusting power,
the mind is a clear scent,
the pen is a new ridge of hills.

I am a tree with countless boughs,
a flower which hides a thousand petals,
a juniper, a pointed branch of the scented fig,
its rough, misshapen fruit.

In my belief I am Nepali,
my faith the highest Himalaya,
my favorite season is the one
when leather jackets are donned,
my clothes are only freedom.

The Himalayan lights my touching place,
equality spread on the ground where I stand.

Translated from the Nepali by Michael James Hutt

TSUJI YUKIO

Rum and Snow

I used to run barefoot on the deck,
sit on the mast all day behind a tattered flag
and follow the flight of the albatross.
I once crossed the straits where sharks were laughing,
terrified by the raging black-bearded Edward Teach.
The fifteen of us aboard sang "To the Coffin Islands."
However,
Alexander Sergeevich,
I can't recall how I drank my rum.
Did I cut it with water? With ice?

Wouldn't snow do just as well?
As I leave this raucous old joint
cold snowflakes catch in my lashes
and I quickly sober up.
I can't remember where, but long ago
I was astride a horse and thinking of a song
when I was suddenly lost in darkness.
Who was I then?—
Tell me, rum and snow, bring back
the names of people I was and was not.

Translated from the Japanese by William I. Elliott and Kazuo Kawamura

K. DHONDUP

Exile

Exile
      is a marigold
           blushing luxuriously
                in the morning sun
                    luring turquoise bees
                    from their beehives
                    to suck their honey

Exile
      is a melody
           for the forgetful souls
                in search of wider horizons
                    to cherish and conquer

A gold ring clasping
      round the white finger, exile
           is a memory of a beloved
                bleeding somewhere beyond the
                  high mountains.

MOHJA KAHF

Lifting the Hagar Heel

Dying for water,
Hagar went racing
back and forth in the valley
but forgot to look
in the obvious places first

What she needed most
was right there all along,
under the heel of her foot

All it took was a nudge
from an angel's wing

Little self, panting in the world,
take a hint.
Lift your heel,
look!—find your own
long-buried Zamzam spring

PURNA BAHADUR VAIDYA

Water Is Water

Water—
never blocks the light—
its ever moving skin
radiates; its single vision parsed into colors
explicates what's embodied
within light

That rainbow
water sketches on a blue slate
is a disquisition—
—what is and what is seen
borne forth in their fullness
by light

Me?—That very drop!
that attempts to write of light:
self emergent; the enlivened heat of it,
and the gentleness
resplendent on its surface
To express that
in the vastness outside itself

Translated from the Nepal Bhasa (Newari) by Wayne Amtzis

WADIH SA'ADEH

Genesis

With what meager space
remaining between his hands
he tried to reconstruct
a universe: with a tear,
he drew a star, a moon with a glance,
and with a single touch, a sun.
When he closed his eyes,
people commuted to their work
on the sidewalk of his eyelids.

Translated from the Arabic by Sargon Boulus

YONG SHU HOONG

Chicago

The infinite extent of windows
on the observatory deck
reminds me of illuminated fish tanks
that once held my gaze in Van Kleef Aquarium:
the therapy of bubbles. But here,
there's only the chatter of sightseers
drowning out the symphony of skyscrapers.

I navigate my nose closer toward the sky,
staring out with my fish eyes
from my enclosure into another realm.

Then, with the decibel of voices dwindling,
I look down over streets, the big shoulders
of buildings, watching the city bustle in silence
as my mind fills with strange thoughts
of the Flamingo sculpture suddenly taking flight,
the Art Institute's stone lions roaring to life—

How I have again missed out
on anarchy and outrage, trapped
behind the sheen of shatterproof glass.

BOEY KIM CHENG

Wanton with James

Jackhammer pangs of hunger stabbing
at the mind, we drag our depleted bellies through
late-night Chinatown, sniffing out meals
fit for gods but going for a song, no longer
confident of weathering the night
on an afternoon's meager meal.

Fowls, all preened and shellacked, beckon
like centerfolds, and the lipstick red of roasted pork
smells almost like sex. Only the prices
give our purse the pause. Reasoning our bellies
down to humbler fare, we settle on
wanton noodles, exotic to you
at a reasonable three-fifty.

While we wait, the talk of things
spiritual, of Hesse and Hamsun, of the meaning
of hunger. Then my descant on the wanton,
an exegesis on the symbolic contours
of a dumpling. You look happy
with how the word means "cloud swallow"
or "swallowing clouds," your last dollars spent
on something so exalted and filling
as the wanton. Then the arrival of the clouds
and we are enveloped, the talk dispersed
in the wanton heaven. Voluptuous meat wrapped
in thin veils of flour. Nothing spiritual.
Wanton is a wanton word. Still the clouds
dissolve like enlightenment's flash, flushed

down to the lower regions, leaving the bowls
looking like immaculate blue skies.

Gracing the bill are two cookies.
Yours reads: "You are analytic, calm, able to reason
through the night of confusion." All of which
we are decidedly not. Mine: "Long-absent friends
are soon coming back to you." I am happy
with that, satisfied with the belated truth
of the forecast, thankful that a friend
whom I'd thought lost, held out her hand of peace
this morning. I am satisfied that the truth
will wait for us, James, in some Chinatown
ahead, that the clouds of some design
will gather us again for a wanton meal.

No better words said, no better
resolution made, than this tiny truth sealed
in flour to crown our last meal in Frisco,
before you go broke, and I head back east.

ISSA MAKHLOUF

We Travel

We travel to go far away from the place of our birth and see the other
side of sunrise. We travel in search of our childhood; of births
unconceived. We travel so that unfinished alphabets complete. Let
farewell be imbued with promises. Let us move far away like the twilight
that accompanies us and bids us farewell. We tear up destinies and
disperse their pages in the wind before we find—or fail to find—our life
story in other books.

We travel toward unwritten destinies. We travel to tell those we have
met that we shall return and meet again. We travel to learn the language
of trees that never travel; to burnish the ringing of bells resounding in
holy valleys; in search of more merciful gods; to strip the faces of
strangers off the masks of estrangement; to confide to passersby that we

are passersby too, and our stay in memory and oblivion is temporary. We travel far away from mothers who light the candle of absence and thin the crust of time whenever they raise their hands to heaven.

We travel so we do not see our parents grow old; so we do not read their days on their faces. We travel taking ages unawares; they are wasted in advance. We travel to tell those we love that we still love them; distance cannot overpower our amazement; that exile is as sweet and fresh as our homeland. We travel so that if we returned to our homeland we would feel like immigrants everywhere. Thus, suddenly, we shake off our wings idle porches opening to the sun and sea. We travel until no difference remains between air and air, water and water, heaven and hell. We mock time. We sit and look into the expanding space, watch the waves jump together like children. The sea in front of us leaves between two ships; one of them departs; the other a paper boat in the hand of a child.

We travel like the clown who moves from village to village with his animals that teach children their first lesson in boredom. We travel to trick death, letting it trail us from place to place. We continue to travel until we can no longer find ourselves in the places we travel to; until we are lost and nobody can find us anymore.

Translated from the Arabic by Najwa Nasr

SAQI FAROOQI

An Injured Tomcat in an Empty Sack

Jan Muhmamad Khan
    the road is hard
This empty rice-sack
    stifles me
The stiff jute bars pierce my heart
And into the yellow bowls
    of my eyes
Coins of moonlight clink, chink
Night spreads through my body

Now who will light fires
      on your naked back?
Who will fan the coals?
Who will make the bloody flowers of struggle
      burst into bloom?
From my flint-and-steel claws
the life is gone
      Today the road is hard

Quite soon this path
breaks and falls into a dirty pond
Alone in my coffin
      I'll curl up and sleep
I'll dissolve into water
And you must go on—
go on deep-sleep-walking
And the sack that you don't see—
you don't know your own empty sack
Jan Muhmmad Khan
      the road is hard

Translated from the Urdu by Frances W. Pritchett

ZAKARIYYA MUHAMMAD

Everything

What wind, then, didn't break my hands?
What gust didn't fly off with my shirt?
Under what millstone wasn't I a grain?

Translated from the Arabic by Lena Jayyusi and Jeremy Reed

MUHAMMED AL-ACHA'ARI

excerpt from "Little Wars"

My heart needs a banner,
when words fall for no good reason
and the entry paths to all the villages die at once.
It is imperative that I drain the last fraction of the night
down to the dregs,
that I bear the beautiful quiet
of someone who's departed
who's seen only the lightning blades
assault and retreat,
a body rising out of the dust of words.
I haven't grown any older since this sedition,
I have remained between two sides
so that I rarely disagree.
And with each advance I collapse
over my self's embers
and perish,
and with each retreat I demolish the walls of my rhyme
and walk out of the house of meaning in hope
that I would return to it murdered.
And since it was rightful to avenge my death from a rose
the tribe threw me to the water
for me to crown my promise with an ear of wheat
or with the noon sun
so I went along this route for a short while.
I sat by phrases I did not speak
and by a cup whose wine has cracked my face
and I busied myself with arranging the things of my soul
as those who return from war do
for a long long while . . .

Translated from the Arabic by Fady Joudah

SYED SHAMSUL HAQ

Poem 240

Shall I not do any work? Or not go out?
Only remain seated in this empty cup tilting the kettle?
Will I just keep standing in between the void and fullness?
And see in a blue mosque in the dream city
Restless birds scribe golden words?
And groom myself? Choose good shoes?
Matching colored socks, white shirt?

Are stories written with inept pen very much mortal?

Is it because I would hear the last part of the music? Or, when
Naughty ribbons in colored heads of the city would
                                    blow away in storm,
Awaiting in wicked hope I am a very ailing person,
When would the imminent deaths illuminate in my two eyes?

Who calls in the street? Collects dear people from
                        the neighborhoods of the *colony*
Which *muezzin* arranges for the *aazan* today in the chaotic State?
A long time ago, the tied mouth of a brown bag sprang open
Innumerable silver coins fell down on a hard pavement.
The stable horses made tremendous sound storm from
Their galloping hooves—where have they gone?
Whose voice, too, I hear in an anxious uproar?

I have to get out, as if a decade has gone past meanwhile,
Have to untie the color handkerchief, hair, bring forth
Absconded hoards of horses—whose mane is scented, whose back
I once rode.

Translated from Bengali by Quader Mahmud

UNSI AL-HAJ

Is This You or the Tale?

My history goes back
to a fifth century,
since I was baptized
in my mother's presence,
from whom I inherited the feeling
that whoever escapes four walls
commits every treason.

My history goes back
to the time when the head
of the family defied the Sultan
in Constantinople,
and I wanted to be within things
for a while, by way
of necessary aggression and violence,
like an old statue.

My history goes back
to Eil and Baal,
they printed me in *Gilgamesh*
and I was raised in Ugaret.
Tyre, Sidon, and Byblos
visited with me Greece.
Persians ornamented me
and Hebrews bought passages
from my works.
Egyptians simplified me
in their drawings of the living.
Astarte and I
were merged together through mascara.

I lived by the river,
gods slaughtered me, I them.
I carried my tiny grandmother
on my back, and fled
through the valleys.

"Better if you
had buried me,"
she said like a parrot.
When I did, I was born
and died in Beirut.

My history goes back
downward to storms blowing
from books, and sitting for hours
among crowds.
It goes back to what is not of me.
And as my age
is counted in years,
likewise I wander outside this necklace
like drops of pearl.

Is this me or you?
Is this you or the tale?
After a while the musicians
will disappear,
the poet will become official
behind his buttons,
cities of soul will flee
through the chimney,
psalms and roofs will blow away
and stars of desperate longing
will try to reach them.

My sorrow is great
for a history steeped in destiny,
steeped in mishmash,
marching through chance,
through danger, marching through
our fictions, in holes, in inner pockets,
marching in birthmarks
and astrology.

Marching in the *too-late,*
through the pallor of lips,
on the slope of the eyes,

all of which doesn't need to be
reinvented, but only
reconsidered.

Translated from the Arabic by Sargon Boulus

YI SHA

excerpt from "Wonders Never Cease"

The professor said: "Certain races
Are less sensitive to pain than others"

This was in my college years
From a lecture on medicine that got off track

Written down in an old blue notebook
Now ready to be sold for scrap

Leafing through it eight years later
I shudder and decide not to sell it

In a huge display case at the exhibition of love
Two skeletons gnaw each other to the bone
From remaining patches of flesh beneath the neck
I make out which one is he
Which is she

The only prop is a piece of fry-bread in a year of famine
The only scenery is a dilapidated temple in the storm
The only plot has you and I, the leading man and lady
Split that fry-bread and eat the halves

Off to the side of the cutting edge, cursing darkness
The poet shifts his shape

Into a squid
The sepia cloud he squirts within a glacier
Is his inspiration turned into a poem

Keeping the prince company in his studies
I pretend my wit is even duller than his
A big bird flies overhead; I clap and cheer with him

Playing chess with the crown prince
I get into a position I cannot win
Crown prince, whether you are black or red
Pawn, chariot, horse, catapult—you capture them all

When the prince plays at riding
I play the little pony
With lowered head I crawl forward
Ready to buck at any moment

I keep in mind the prince was born to a concubine
This dragon spawn is really just a turtle egg

This summer, huge floods in the south
Despite my empty pockets
I squeeze out a contribution
I feel as if I'm flaying myself
Making a raft out of human skin
Floating it down to the disaster area

Translated from the Chinese by Denis C. Mair

NAZIK AL-MALA'IKA

Insignificant Woman

When she closed her eyes
No face faded, no lips quivered.

Doors heard no retelling of her death.
No curtain was lifted to air the room of grief.
No eyes followed her coffin
To the end of the road.
Only a memory of a lifeless form
    passing in some lane.

The word echoed in alleyways,
Hushed sounds, finding no shelter,
Settled in secluded den.
A moon mourned
In silence.

Night, unconcerned, gave way to morning.
Daylight crept in with the milk cart
    and a call to fasting.
A meager cat mewing
Amidst the shrill of vendor's cries.
Boys squabbling
    throwing stones.
Muddy waters spilling
    along the gutters
As the wind carried foul smells
To rooftops.
Oblivion.

Translated from the Arabic by Kamal Boullata

MEENA ALEXANDER

Floating on Fifth

Chairs upright, white table cloth, glasses of burgundy,
A street struck with light so things shimmer:

Pigeon wings, torn plastic bags.
Hands held out, a woman in a cloth coat drifts

Towards a lilac bush.
About her, singing starts, sounds pitched in an untoward clarity,

Noises so luminous they startle skin from bone.
I glimpse hairs on your wrist, the frayed seam of your sweater starts to bristle.

Under the table your knee bone kisses my knee bone
And I say somewhat loudly so you can hear me over the clatter

It could end, my life, pouf like that, and it would be alright.
A turn of things no more no less

On a street crisp with sun where a woman my age almost
Coat torn, hair aflame, passes through lilac.

Where lads on bicycles flit as clouds do
Above Fifth which is where we are,

Your eyes black as everlasting and bicycle boys
With trays of seaweed soup and kimchee floating at knee level.

BIMAL NIBHA

Cycle

It's been a few days since
my bicycle has vanished
Do you know where I might find it?

It's true that my cycle is small
its tires are bald
they have too little air
the color is faded
the stand is broken
the kinetic light is faulty
the bell trills softly
the pedals move slowly
the chain is old

the handlebars are askew
the wheel is bent and
it has no carrier or lock

Yet no matter what
even if it's flawed and defective
even if it's shabby
no matter what, that cycle is mine
The weight of my body lies on its seat
The measure of my feet fills its pedals
The print of my hands marks its handlebars
My breath rests in each part of that cycle
I am there
That cycle is my life

(What kind of place is this
not unknown to me, my own village
where in the bright light of midday
a whole life can vanish?
Do you know where I might find it?)

It's been a few days since
my bicycle has vanished
Do you know where I might find it?

Translated from the Nepali by Manjushree Thapa

GIEVE PATEL

Squirrels in Washington

Squirrels in Washington come
Galloping at you on fours, then brake
To halt a few feet away
And beg on hindquarters.
No one stones them,
And their fear is diminished.
They do halt, even so,
Some feet away, those few feet

The object of my wonder. Do I
Emit currents
At closer quarters? Are those
The few feet I would keep
From a tame tiger? Is there
A hierarchy, then, of distances,
That must be observed,
And non-observance would at once
Agglutinate all of Nature
Into a messy, inextricable mass?
Ah Daphne! Passing
From woman to foliage did she for a moment
Sense all vegetable sap as current
Of her own bloodstream, the green
Flooding into the red? And when
She achieved her final arboreal being,
Shed dewy tears each dawn
For that lost fleeting moment,
That hint at freedom,
In transit, between cage and cage?

SA'ADYYA MUFFAREH

excerpt from "The Spell of Blazing Trees"

His laugh:
endearing like the trinkets of young girls
the lisping of a shy child

sharp like a sword
hung on his brow
by tribal elders

straight
like a well-lit street
fenced in
by infinite
details

beautiful women
water
palm trees and pebbles

proud silver droplets
a sudden summer rain
on the wide ocean
of my gloom

I shake myself
like a wet bird
dispelling sorrow
driving away
sleep

and paint a face
splendid and proud
to rival yours
which finds its way into
the features of my heart
like a mount
with a rider
who knows this territory

Translated from the Arabic by Mona Fayad

NURIT ZARHI

For they are at the center of my life,
two girls, a man, a woman.

Why should I be afraid,
each thing has only four corners.

Full of intents I smile
almost proffer flowers
plan to sweep the accumulating dust.

But she knows everything about me
and so screeches with the sound of shifting beds.

Beyond the wall the girls in drooping socks
are smooth butterflies
light as if happy.

And grandma-crow divines in the thicket of the pine
from generation to generation to generation

The rain reveals the hidden names of leaves
my heart warm as if washed in blood
a new season love
cruising in our tiny heart
as if in an ocean
never touching.

If it were up to me, first thing I'd give up
on longing as on sickness.
But then I become even sicker,
all I can do is depart from myself
through a ring of fire, forcibly awake
from dream into dream.

And when this happens, instantly I recall
the hidden name of my heart,
as if it were an orphan. No, even this is too revealing,
I'd have to name it a civilian in a long raincoat,
when, in fact, its cauterized name is a mad child
no one would want in my place,
with the self-respect of a wet bird,
in a land where all must appear strong and beautiful.

More than anything, I want to heed
the true tablet of its commandments,
but what can I do, it wants me to expose
myself to all, show what's lacking.
Clearly, it drags me to destruction,
and I put it to sleep: Sleep, sleep.

Witless heart, all or at once
you may achieve in death only.

Forgive my outburst,
I think I was shot, Sir,
I leaned, mistakenly, on love.
But who cares for precision
when they kill off presidents and children.
And you also suggest that I don't take it to heart.
Because, as it is, they've knocked on my door more than once.
I'm cautious since you always hit your target,
I'm sure to keep my eyes wide open.
Same as the pigeon who laid an egg
on my window's ledge,
and the next day nothing—not even fragments.
I understand why you shot me, Sir.
Just another dream that won't disturb you
as you fall asleep.

Translated form the Hebrew by Tsipi Keller

WING TEK LUM

The Butcher

There are many joys in living here,
And just to see it through is something gained.

—T'ao Ch'ien

Half of the top bunk is his,
that is he takes the night shift
sharing it with a late-night short-order cook
who cares for nothing,
not even a sweet bed to call his own.
The butcher does not have much more,
just what he wears or is in his pockets

and what he has saved in his small tin trunk
sealed and scented with camphor—
a second set of clothes and shoes
for festival days and funerals,
his ID papers, an IOU and a little cash,
a stack of letters, two or three photographs
and two or three clippings,
a pressed flower,
and a gold chain for the watch he once wore.
The room is small and spare
littered near the windowsill with cigarette butts
where his cousin, the oldtimer, always sits
reading the daily papers
or a broadside on revolution in the old country.
His cousin who occupies the lower bunk
never likes to go out
and with the bathroom down the hall
and the bar and grill on the ground floor
delivering dinner up to him
at the same time every night
it seems like he never does.
But the butcher loves the streets
or where the streets may take him.
Often he dines at the family clubhouse
bringing vegetables or a small fish from the docks
to share with those who have come in
from the country or another island
and need a place to stay
and fellow members and relatives to chat with.
Many remain after dinner to play dominoes or cards
but the butcher just watches
preferring to exchange a bit of lore or gossip
with the families who drop by
to pray to the Great Aunt in the front hall.
Whenever an opera troupe or an orator comes to town
the butcher is sure to attend.
Fire or flood relief drives
can consume his spare time,
and if a clansman dies
he will join in the collection.

When he returns to his room
the butcher sleeps soundly without dreams
in spite of the after-work rehearsals
of the music society next door.
At dawn he awakes to the rooster crows
that punctuate each back courtyard and alleyway.
For breakfast he lingers over
his usual freshly squeezed orange juice
and rice with ham
at the corner coffee shop;
it is named after an ancient palace
and he tells the counterman with a smile
that this is as close to one
as he would ever choose to get.
As he leaves, the cashier often goes over
the almanac predictions for the day.
The butcher has never believed in destiny
but is too polite to say so;
he waits until he is out of sight
before he shrugs his shoulders.
On his way to work he passes an old banyan
where he recalls on an earlier morning
in the slanting sunlight
he saw a woman with a thin nose
and hair as pale as lightning
who looked like a girl
he might have married.
The owner opening up his store
always nods to him with deference.
The first customers arrive
as they set out the barbeque loin and roast pork
on hangers near the chopping block
that the owner will man.
The owner also collects the cash
leaving the butcher to work the second block
which is reserved for raw meat.
With his fat cleaver
he chops, carves, slices, minces, and trims.
Soon he is surrounded
by curly intestines and lumps of tongue,

the glutinous feet, slabs of spareribs,
pork chop, pork loin, pork butt,
pork belly, kidney, and liver.
He sells to the big restaurant facing the river,
the temple next to the chicken coops,
a few wives carrying their children,
the grocery store owner, the bald tailor,
and the letter writer who never stops talking.
Sometimes the kerosene peddler will curse him
for leaving too much fat.
Sometimes the barber will bring over
a can of soy bean milk as a gift.
He sharpens his knife when business is slow.
He remembers the sage's admonition
that to preserve a blade
the cook must seek the play
between the joints in the bones.

AHMAD 'ABD AL-MU'TI HIJAZI

The Lonely Woman's Room

She shuts out the city now
by closing the door and lowering the drapes—
she puts on the light by daytime.

Those are her things,
the animals of her solitude
reaching up to her from the corners,
and in the wall,
a built-in gas stove,
a sink,
and shelves for groceries.
A small exile
with a bed in its recesses,
and a table,
with stories to induce sleep,

and ashtray
and small candles.

Everything has its predestined place,
a presence that nourishes itself
on bread and water
from the steps of time,
a mantle and a slumbering
in its shifting shadow.

Everything has its lust, its weeping,
the flavor of the body
grown used to solitude,
meditation on itself.
Everything is a mirror
possessing her face,
the same intimacy and brokenness
of her limbs.

Perhaps she came in childhood
upon such a place as this,
and a light,
a vase which casts
a shadow on a spotless sheet.

Perhaps by way of necklaces
and candelabra, she summons up
a spirit who will take her back
to gardens long since left,
springs where faces spread across
clear water,
smiling in the depth.

It wasn't me
she was talking to,
but somebody else
into whose borrowed face
she stared.

Translated from the Arabic by Sargon Boulus and Peter Porter

HATIF JANABI

Paradises, Soldiers, and Stags

I am content with bitter words,
 with a fluttering spike of wheat.
  I am content with broken branches;
   I say someday this wooden space will disappear.
    Sometimes I am content with soup, and with the water of grapes.
    I am content with the hope that the echo of a storm
     will swing between me and peace.
    I am content with the chirpings of the dark.
     I say soon, soon they will come
      to wash my face with dregs of dew.
       I am content with faucets and afterthoughts,
        with the stones that cover autumn's bare back,
         with a snake flicking its tongue behind my ribs. I say
          maybe the loved one will come
           to me in a dream and she arrives.
            I am content with the gushing of seasons, the stutters of
              memory,
             with the dazzle of stars, the flutter of a feeble heart, with
               whispering and caressing and dance,
             with him who does not achieve mischief.
          I am content and I brag about the wings of a crow,
           something to bless my steps
           and to heap on my grief a mountain of dirt.
          I am content with the talk of rebel boys, sayings
           of lunatics, soothsayers, and the prophet-like poor.
          I am content with the one who does not reach desolation.
         (They stretch out to the flow of his shock.)
        I am content with the paradises in their cradles,
       with stags lisping flames
      cunning soldiers shrinking
     without leniency
     and a creaking past.
     I am content with dew as a bird stings the pistil where it lay.
     I am content when a dream pricks my night with its beak
      or reveals that the beginning will be a further strain
       and that winter is the whistling of stones.

I am content with my grandmother's cane, the courtyard, a pot of tea,
 a jug of water
 my mother's cloak, my neighbor's prayer beads, and the palm
  fronds hidden in the victim's rib cage.
 I am content with the little that is much,
 but in the end I will accept nothing less
than to clutch the impossible's throat.

Translated from the Arabic by Khaled Mattawa

LI-YOUNG LEE

Immigrant Blues

People have been trying to kill me since I was born,
a man tells his son, trying to explain
the wisdom of learning a second tongue.

It's an old story from the previous century
about my father and me.

The same old story from yesterday morning
about me and my son.

It's called "Survival Strategies
and the Melancholy of Racial Assimilation."

It's called "Psychological Paradigms of Displaced Persons,"

called "The Child Who'd Rather Play than Study."

*Practice until you feel
the language inside you,* says the man.

But what does he know about inside and outside,
my father who was spared nothing
in spite of the languages he used?

And me, confused about the flesh and the soul,
who asked once into a telephone,
Am I inside you?

You're always inside me, a woman answered,
at peace with the body's finitude,
at peace with the soul's disregard
of space and time.

Am I inside you? I asked once
lying between her legs, confused
about the body and the heart.

If you don't believe you're inside me, you're not,
she answered, at peace with the body's greed,
at peace with the heart's bewilderment.

It's an ancient story from yesterday evening

called "Patterns of Love in Peoples of Diaspora,"

called "Loss of the Homeplace
and the Defilement of the Beloved,"

called "I Want to Sing but I Don't Know Any Songs."

BAROUYR SEVAG

The Analysis of Yearning (Garod)

I know the dark need, the yearning, that want,
in the same way the blind man knows
the inside of his old home.

I don't see my own movements
and the objects hide.
But without error or stumbling
I maneuver among them,

live among them,
move like the self-winding clock
which even after losing its hands
keeps ticking and turning
but shows neither minute nor hour.

And dangling between darkness and loneliness
I want to analyze this want
like a chemist
to understand its nature and profound mystery.
And as I try
there is laughter
from some mysterious tunnel,
laughter from an indescribable distance,
from an unhearable distance.

A city sparrow with a liquid song
changes its ungreen life
into music from an unechoing distance,
an unhuntable distance.

And words start hurting me
as they mock, echo from the unhuntable distance,
the merciless distance.

I walk from wall to wall
and the sound of my steps
seems to come from far away
from that merciless distance,
that impossible distance.

I am not blind
but I see nothing
around me, because
vision has detached itself
and reached that distance
that is impossibly far,
excessively far.

I run after myself,
incapable of ever reaching or
catching what I seek.

And this is what is called
want and longing or "garod."

Translated from the Armenian by Diana Der-Hovanessian

SHIRLEY GEOK-LIN LIM

Scavenging on Double Bluff

1.

My children call these wish-stones, Anne said,
studying the warm brown quartz
I had picked with its perfect elongated
white circle; when that circle is
unbroken, that's what makes them wishes.
I wished she had not told me this.
All week I thought of getting another
down by Double Bluff Beach.
This afternoon I take the time to bike
and walk. Some of us can pick up unbroken
spindles where others see only fragments
and shell bits; can gather a dozen
in a minute, whole and bleached.
Rocks lie everywhere on mud flats.
Serpentine, granite, sandstone, calcite,
agate: igneous and sedimentary,
names enough to fill my pockets.
I find the colors, lines, and shapes
as I find spindles in the shore litter.
Starving at six makes one grow up sharp
at scavenging, and I have seen
strangers turn dubious at my luck.
My eyes stoop to the search.

I do not stop for the blue herons
or the far islands and inlets. The heron
hunts with me, hour after hour,
although I no longer know what it is
I wish for: love, money, position,
picked up like these shells and stones
that weigh down my backpack.

2.

What is the difference between
having nothing and too much?
"You have too much," one complimented,
then asked for my things. But that's beside
the point. It's the work of finding
gives them meaning—work of a mind
honed for surviving. The Chinese,
as I found in Shanghai, at the garden
of the Minor Administrator, prefer
edges of unequally worn stone,
spying buttes, peaks, crags, and scarps
lift up against wear and centuries.
I must have never been Chinese.
I like my rocks smooth and worn
through millennia of water, storm, and tide;
round as the round of loaves; circles
of breasts hurting with milk
on round pillows; as a lunar month finds
an open Oh!, a yellow wheel;
round scrotum swollen at touch.
Complete as unbroken bands
of color, stones that are wishes.
I scavenge dandelion leaves, chicory,
wild onions, beach plums, thimbleberries.
I'm scavenging in case of a famine;
in case I'll have to go hungry,
wishes worn smooth, worn daily,
in my round mouth, my anxious hand.

SLIPS AND
ATMOSPHERICS

Slips and Atmospherics

—Vidhu Aggarwal

In Madras, caught in the teeth of a South Indian summer, before the torrential rains of monsoon season arrive, heat has a near-physical presence, rises from the streets in shimmering curtains, sapping the body of the will to digest, let alone move. For the better part of a year, encompassing parts of third and fourth grade, I stayed with my aunt and uncle in their apartment in Madras and felt at times literally incapacitated by the temperature, unable to do anything more than sit in front of one of their rickety fans with a wet towel draped upon my face, sweating through a suitcase full of T-shirts. My aunt would concoct a special elixir of buttermilk, mint leaves, and *jeera* (roasted and ground cumin) for me and I would spend many nights sleeping on the rooftop of the building with my cousins, where it was too high for mosquitoes, where the coolness of concrete radiated through the straw mats we slept upon, where the night winds would alleviate the heat just enough to allow us to drift off. Indeed, what I remember most vividly about that year is the time I spent on the rooftop, playing cricket and soccer in the moonlight, avoiding the twisted television antennae and multicolored fabrics hung up to dry, and going to sleep under a vast panorama of stars while my cousins quizzed me about life in America.

Poetry was not on my mind then—I loved pizza and Pac Man, fat shoelaces and hot rods—but on that rooftop, trying to disentangle the cinematic version of America that my cousins possessed from the homogeneous land of strip malls and model homes that I knew as home, I had a keen sense about the inadequacies of my words to convey an accurate description. I could present details perhaps, could compare and contrast a supermarket to the vegetable wallahs who would hawk okra and chili peppers from bicycles, but what my cousins wanted was *atmosphere*, the unquantifiable feelings of my day-to-day life there. What I wanted to describe, but couldn't, was how I didn't quite fit into my elementary school though I wanted nothing more earnestly than to do so, how I was jeered at on the school bus because my mother wore a *bindi,* and how although the parents of everyone I knew drove a car, that didn't necessarily mean they were happy. What I wished to have at my disposal, though I wouldn't have known it then, was a kind of oblique language, full of feints and allusions, glintings and possibilities, something that could move through the air like light, illuminating the unique yet utterly common situation I found myself in: made fun of in America for being too Indian, made fun of in India for being too American, part of and exiled from both places, a misfit who wanted nothing more than to belong.

What I love about the poems in this section, *Slips and Atmospherics,* is that the language I might have dreamed up on the rooftop, the words that would communicate my conflicted essence at the speed of light, is given form and existence by an array of divergent voices. These are the poems that we might consider experimental or avant-garde, though neither term is especially adequate; there's a connotation of willful obscurity associated with the idea of an "experiment," and the avant-garde is a historical term that has been so widely applied as to lose its particularity and relevance. Rather, these poems are about multiplicity and escape—slipping free from the manacles of transparent meaning, transforming conventional grammar and syntax, creating new atmospheres of energy and potentiality. These are poems that leap from image to image, passages that contain speculation and fragmentation, shapes that confound the eye, figurations that explore the politics of language and culture, reconstitutions of received wisdom, conflations of eros and criticism, and shiny new idioms and exchanges that frustrate our expectations, even vex and confuse us, like the most difficult and fulfilling works of art often do. These are the poems that usher in the future while keeping a firm hold on the traditions, Eastern and Western, which have come before, and I'm thrilled by the range of works presented here. It was a genuine revelation in the course of putting this anthology together to discover the sheen of the up-to-the-minute; to find evidence that poetic innovation was taking place not just in San Francisco and New York, but in Delhi and Istanbul.

Take Rukmini Bhaya Nair's poem, "Genderole," which is written in the run-on, graphemic style of Sanskrit, a language with a number of written forms, but only one spoken form. At first, it appears that something has gone awry on the page, the words are jammed together without spaces, but after a double take, the phrases begin to untangle, the invisible spaces and punctuation appear, and one discovers a meditation on language, gender, and Indian history:

> *Considerthefemalebodyyourmost*
> *Basictextanddontforgetitsslokas I*

Whatpalmleafmscandoforusitdoes
Therealgapsremainforwomentoclose I

Spacesbetweenwordspreservesenses
Intactbutweneedtomeetineverysense I

Else, take "Sentences," a poem written by Che Qianzi who lived through
Mao Zedong's Cultural Revolution and whose work examines the material-
ity and the ideographic roots of the Chinese language in which he expresses
himself. His poem "Sentences" reads as if plucked from the Surrealist man-
ifesto and even in translation we get a sense of the kind of linguistic inves-
tigation the poet is undertaking, turning over word and origin perceptively
in his mind. Similarly, the excerpt from Thai American poet Jenny Boully's
collection *The Body*, which is subtitled *An Essay*, lacks just one thing: the
essay itself. Instead, what is given are blank pages demarcated with the foot-
notes to the missing text. The body of the essay then becomes a kind of
empty, free-floating signifier onto which the reader can project whatever
sense can be gleaned from the footnotes, which are rich and varied, verg-
ing from arcane allusion to scientific explication to brazen confession.

Or take Arun Kolatkar's poem, "The Alphabet," which could be a lan-
guage poem overheard at St. Mark's Poetry Project, and appears in its spin-
ning out to be an embodiment of Gertrude Stein's assertion that, "I took
individual words and thought about them until I got their weight and vol-
ume complete and put them next to another word, and at this same time
I found out very soon that there is no such thing as putting them together
without sense. I made innumerable efforts to make words write without
sense and found it impossible." The poem begins:

anvil arrow bow box and brahmin

cart chariot cloud and compost heap

are all sitting in their separate squares

corn cup deer duck and frock

ganesh garlic hexagon and house

all have places of their own

inkpot jackfruit kite lemon and lotus

mango medicine mother old man and ostrich

are all holding their proper positions

And what seems at first a rather arbitrary meditation on the taxonomy of the alphabet and how words are kept in place by the letters of which they are comprised, on closer inspection reveals itself to be a kind of warning that the mentality that would segregate words and objects into their proper place could also fall into trap of classifying people the same way. Thus, we have the Brahmin, highest born in the caste system, thrown in with the inanimate objects, and we have a mother and an old man, living in the place and according to the rules allotted to them by the words used to describe them. There's also the further aspect of sheer verbal glee here, how the weight of the anvil is transferred to the flight of the arrow shot from a bow that is tied around a box, or how the movement of a cart takes on the dignity of a chariot shown to be nebulous as a cloud and as full of pent aroma as a compost heap.

The first poem of the section, Yang Lian's "Knowing," encapsulates the formal inventiveness taking place in many parts of the world. The poem is rendered in ancient Seal script arrayed in a ring and includes an ideogrammatic neologism in the center of the circle. By virtue of being a concrete poem and including pictograms, the poem is virtually untranslatable, but Brian Holton has come up with a system that transliterates Greek words into Latin characters. Included in the translation are *protos*, or the first, *photos*, or light, *noesis*, or understanding, *epos*, or story, *logos*, or reason, *anthropos*, or human, *gnosis*, or knowledge, and *tropos*, or change. It's evident how a theory of knowledge could be distilled into some combination thereof and sure enough, in an ionic bond at the center of these words spins the perfect fusion of these concepts, a linguistic corollary to Yang Lian's notion of "the unity of Heaven and Man."

Slips and Atmospherics includes many poems that stretch the boundaries of form, including modernist giant José Garcia Villa's "The Anchored Angel," which uses commas the way, according to Villa himself, the French pointillist painter Georges Seurat used points of color; Yeow Kai Chai's "Quarterly Report No. 7: Epiphytes and Vetiver Control," which is steeped in John Ashbery's use of parataxis and non sequitur to create lyric energy; Lale Müldür's "311," one in a series of poems that attempts to embody the colors from her husband's painting box; and Etel Adnan's "Insomnia 1," which dissects words with colons and slashes, finding meaning in preconscious babble. The experimentation of this section is truly avant-garde in the sense that it often holds an antagonistic relationship with respect to dominant culture and its inherited modes of expression. These poems fracture syntax, appropriate found materials, collage together idiolects, and threaten to veer off in multiple directions.

Cathy Park Hong's "Ontology of Chang and Eng, the Original Siamese Twins" is a brilliant, heartbreaking poem that is as much a meditation on the split self as it is an evocation of the lives of the world's most famous Siamese twins. The poem begins and ends with Chang and Eng, conjoined and separated by a virgule:

> *Chang spoke / Eng paused*
>
> *Chang threw a beachball / Eng caught it*
>
> *Chang told a white lie / Eng got caught for the lie.*
>
> *Chang forgot his first language / Eng picked up English*
>
> *In letters, Chang referred to themselves as "I" / Eng as "we"*

Now *this* is a poem I would show to my cousins, were it possible to travel backward in time. I'd like to share the idea that one body could contain multiple selves, that in the very process of acculturating oneself, one simultaneously forgets and gains something crucial, that the wholeness with which one would discuss oneself is ultimately facetious, or rather just *a* way, not *the* way, of looking at things, that the singular "I" and the plural "we" can in fact coexist within the same person. I would have liked to use the metaphor of Siamese twins to describe to my cousins that the person, or fiction, I inhabited back home was the same person who would sit cross-legged and devout, eating *sambar* rice with his hands in front of his parents, but would listen to Journey, throw paper airplanes, and never deign to eat anything without knife and fork in the school cafeteria, and was in fact distinct from yet the very same as the person regaling them with tales from America while the remnants of the day's heat throbbed faintly at the peripheries of our awareness. I did not have the means, impetus, or articulation necessary back then, but fortuitously, the poems in *Slips and Atmospherics* help fulfill my dream of a rooftop language.

— RAVI SHANKAR

YANG LIAN

Knowing

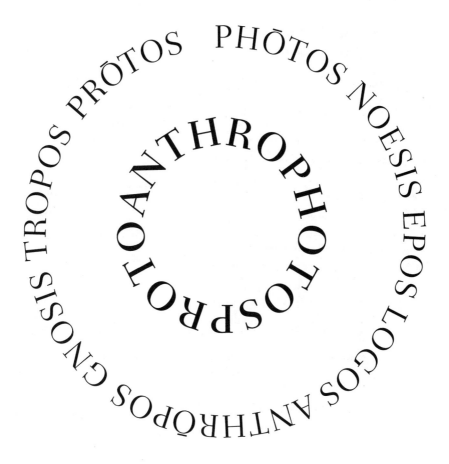

Translation by Brian Holton

Author's Note: The characters are in the 2,000-year-old archaic Seal script, with the exception of the central one, which is Yang Lian's own invention. It is pronounced *yi,* and is a composite of the archaic characters for sun, person, and one, with the sense of "the unity of Heaven and Man." The translator's goal here is to produce a text for the English reader at the same level of near-intelligibility (or near-unintelligibility) as that intended for the Chinese reader, together with something of the same feeling of an archaic talisman or charm: the result is more graphic art than translation. The choice of Greek words rendered in the Latin alphabet was a solution arrived at after much trial and error.

RUKMINI BHAYA NAIR

Genderole

Considerthefemalebodyyourmost
Basictextanddontforgetitsslokas I

Whatpalmleafmscandoforusitdoes
Therealgapsremainforwomentoclose I

Spacesbetweenwordspreservesenses
Intactbutweneedtomeetineverysense I

Comingtogetherisnoverbalmatter
Howeveroursagespraisepativrata I

Katavkantakasteputrasamsaroyam
Ativavichitrawaswrittenformenbyaman I

Theworlddoesnotseemsostrangeseen
Throughgentlereyesnorwomensoalien I

Nalinidalagatajalamatataralamtadvat
Jivanamatishayachapalamchangeability I

Isinthenatureofthingsandespecially
Femalesbutsankarayouoldmysogynisttellme I

Whatssocontemptibleaboutfleeting
Splendour?andwhileyouareaboutitthink I

Wehavewrungpoemsfromhouseholdtasks
Carryingwaterchildsorrowcanyoudoasmuch? I

Itmaybebeneathyoutopriseapartthisgimmick
Butrememberthethingawomanchangesbestishersex I

Opposingyouischildsplaybecauseyoufail
Torealizethisandwecanbeatyouatyourowngame I

Muchhardertoconvertourselveshaving
Labouredlongatbeingmenwepossessnothing I

MyworstfearissankarathathadIindeedbeenyou
Imightnotafterallhaveconceivedanythingnew I

Author's Note: This poem is written in the run on graphemic style of Sanskrit and is addressed to the famous monist philosopher of the eighth century, Sri Adi Shankara.

CATHY PARK HONG

Ontology of Chang and Eng, the Original Siamese Twins

Chang spoke / Eng paused

Chang threw a beachball / Eng caught it

Chang told a white lie / Eng got caught for the lie.

Chang forgot his first language / Eng picked up English

In letters, Chang referred to themselves as "I" / Eng as "we"

While proselytizing, the preacher asked Chang, "Do you know where you go after you die?" Chang said, "Yes, yes, up dere." / Thinking they didn't understand, he asked, "Do you know where I go after I die?" Eng said, "Yes, yes, down dere."

Chang married Adelaine / Eng married her sister Sally.

Chang made love to his wife / Eng daydreamed about money, his Siam childhood and roast beef. He tried not to get aroused.

Chang checked his watch, scratched his head and fidgeted / Eng made love to his wife.

Chang became drunk, knocked Eng out with a whiskey bottle and went carousing with his boys / Eng was unconscious.

Chang proved Einstein's time dilation while hobbling
around the town square from Bar A to Bar B / Eng was unconscious.

Chang apologized / Eng grudgingly accepted
Chang paused / Eng spoke / Chang interrupted

"I am my own man!" / Eng echoed, "We are men yes."

Both broke their bondage with their pitchman, Mr. Coffin.

Both owned land in North Carolina and forty slaves.

Both were nostalgic for Siam: childhood of preserving
duck eggs, watching tiger and elephant fights with the
King, Mother Nok who loved them equally.

The physicians were surprised to find both were "personable."

Both did not appreciate the outhouse joke.

"Are all Orientals joined?" "Allow me to stick this very sharp pin
in Eng's neck to see if both of you feel the pain." "Is it true that
you turn babies into cabbages?" "We are nice, civilized people.
We offer you bananas."

Both were sick of fascination.

Both played checkers, sired children, owned whips for their slaves,
shot game, ate pie. Both wore French silk, smoked cigars, flirted,
and believed in the tenets of individualism. Both listed these activities
to the jury and cried, "See, we are American!"

Both were released with a $500 fine for assaulting another headhunter.

Both were very self-aware.

Both insisted on an iron casket so that grave robbers would not
dig up their bodies and sell it to the highest bidder.

Both did not converse with one another except toward the end:
"My lips are turning blue, Eng" / Eng did not answer.

"They want our bodies, Eng." / Eng did not answer.

"Eng, Eng! My lips are turning blue." / Eng turned to his body and did
   not answer.

CHE QIANZI

Sentences

1: A spire in the north. A spire in the south. In the south a nail
   was pulled out.

2: A half moon, two earths, one earth, very soft when stepped on,
   very soft shyster.

3: The gods appear to have freckled faces; the masses' point of view;
   the rubble creeps over the branches; you are going to hunt birds.

4: A box that cannot keep secrets, darkness and Jiangsu Province,
   will be reduced to a leaky cage. In the cage there is nothing,
   the background contains it.

5: A water drop too is curved.

6: Lace words on the cuff, Tailor Song threads the eye of the needle.
   Shrimp heads twisted off their bodies.

7: Tadpoles drifting between commas, differentiated by their tails, were
   finally expelled from the fictitious revolutionary troop. Transformed
   into iron-skin green frogs, with the press of a button they jump
   without stop, without stop.

8: One sentence is no longer than one character. The character gets a big
   head. The character becomes a big star. A spire. Ursa Major
   hammering bright the nails in the north.

9: One sentence circled three times around one character, circling
the fourth time it broke.

Translated from the Chinese by Jeffrey Twitchell-Waas and Yang Liping

JOSÉ GARCIA VILLA

The Anchored Angel

    And,lay,he,down,the,golden,father,
    (Genesis',fist,all,gentle,now)
Between,the,Wall,of,China,and,
    The,tiger,tree (his,centuries,his,
    Aerials,of,light) . . .
      Anchored,entire,angel!
He,in,his,estate,miracle,and,living,dew,
    His,fuses,gold,his,cobalts,love,
      And,in,his,eyepits,
    O,under,the,liontelling,sun—
The,zeta,truth—the,swift,red,Christ.

    The,red-thighed,distancer,swift,saint,
    Who,made,the,flower,principle,
The,sun,the,hermit's,seizures,
    And,all,the,saults,zigzags,and,
    Sanskrit,of,love.
      Verb-verb,noun-noun:
Light's,latticer,the,angel,in,the,spiderweb:
    By,whose,espials,from,the,silk,sky,
      From,his,spiritual,ropes,
    With,fatherest,fingers,lets,down,
Manfathers,the,gold,declension,of,the,soul.

    Crown,Christ's,kindle,Christ! or,any,he,
    Who,builds,his,staircase,fire—
And,lays,his,bones,in,ascending,
    Fever. Verb-verb,king's-spike—who,propels,
    In,riddles! Six-turbined,

Deadlock, prince. And, noun,
Of,all,nouns: inventor,of,great,eyes: seesawing,
Genesis',unfissured, spy: His,own,Arabian,
His,love-flecked,eye!
The,ball,of,birth,the,selfwit,bud,
So,birthright,lanced,I,hurl,my,bloodbeat,Light.

And,watch,again,Genesis',phosphor,as,
Blood,admires,a,man. Lightstruck,
Lightstruck,into,the,mastertask,
No,hideout,fox,he,wheels,his,grave,of,
Burning,and,threads,his,
Triggers,into,flower: laired,
In,the,light's,black,branches: the,food,of
Light,and,light's,own,rocking,milk.
But,so,soon,a,prince,
So,soon,a,homecoming,love,
Nativity,climbs,him,by,the,Word's,three,kings.

—Or,there,ahead,of,love,vault,back,
And,sew,the,sky,where,it cracked!
And,rared,in,the,Christfor,night,
Lie,down,sweet,by,the,betrayer,tree.
To-fro,angel! Hiving,verb!
First-lover-and-last-lover,grammatiq:
Where,rise,the,equitable,stars,the,roses,of,the,
zodiac,
And,rear,the,eucalypt,towns,of,love:
—Anchored,Entire,Angel:
Through,whose,huge,discalced,arable,love,
Bloodblazes,oh,Christ's,gentle,egg: His, terrific,
sperm.

FATIMA MAHMOUD

excerpt from "What Was Not Conceivable"

Carnations
    flee
Carnations
    spill their crimson autobiographies
I said:
    the ember is the master of fire
    the ember
    is its dust . . .
    Then I became confounded . . .
    what
    to offer . . .
    the master's repulsive . . .
        and delicious mouth
I am singed with happiness
endowed
with the stamps of hollowness
lips
dipped in counterfeit songs
a scented
morning and our faces . . .
    are spat out
    in handsome
        editions . . .
    What
        to offer
            the master's repulsive
            delicious mouth

Translated from the Arabic by Khaled Mattawa

ARUN KOLATKAR

The Alphabet

anvil arrow bow box and brahmin
cart chariot cloud and compost heap
are all sitting in their separate squares

corn cup deer duck and frock
ganesh garlic hexagon and house
all have places of their own

inkpot jackfruit kite lemon and lotus
mango medicine mother old man and ostrich
are all holding their proper positions

pajamas pineapple rabbit and ram
sacrifice seal spoon and sugarcane
won't interfere with each other

sword tap tombstone and umbrella
warrior watermelon weight and yacht
have all found the eternal resting place

the mother won't put her baby on the compost heap
the brahmin won't season the duck with garlic
the yacht won't hit the watermelon and sink

unless the ostrich eats the baby's frock
the warrior won't shoot an arrow into ganesh's belly
and if the ram doesn't knock down the old man

why would he need to smash the cup on the tombstone

Translated from the Marathi by Vinay Dharwadker

LAWRENCE JOSEPH

Then

Joseph Joseph breathed slower
as if that would stop
the pain splitting his heart.
He turned the ignition key
to start the motor and leave
Joseph's Food Market to those
who wanted what was left.
Take the canned peaches,
take the greens, the turnips,
drink the damn whiskey
spilled on the floor,
he might have said.
Though fire was eating half of
Detroit, Joseph could only think
of how his father,
with his bad legs, used to hunch
over the cutting board
alone in light particled
with sawdust behind
the meat counter, and he began
to cry. Had you been there
you would have been thinking
of the old Market's wooden walls
turned to ash or how Joseph's whole arm
had been shaking as he stooped
to pick up an onion,
and you would have been afraid.
You wouldn't have known
that soon Joseph Joseph would stumble,
his body paralyzed in an instant
from neck to groin.
You would simply have shaken your head
at the tenement named "Barbara" in flames
or the Guardsman with an M-16
looking in the window of Dave's Playboy Barbershop,
then closed your eyes

and murmured, This can't be.
You wouldn't have known
it would take nine years
before you'd realize the voice howling in you
was born then.

BRIAN KIM STEFANS

from *The Screens*

Sort of: being there, or being awake. | These emissions: counter-examples of honesty. | Trying: being in the type. | When a figure named Wenderoth conspires: writing. | A calculated instance (among distrust): lost in Europe. | We thought it was Dutch: it was Flemish. | As in: where to go next. | Running out of drink, then: where is the fountain. | Trying: to angle the light. | Grossly spiritual, she takes a number: she is waiting. | Productive backslide: thinking back to terms. | I am here: you are there. | How many times have you been there: and I've choked. | A sliver of counter-honesty: spicy discussion. | Nonetheless, remembering: remembering. | The crowd was fucked: fucked. | Bouncing a ball: waiting for the next line. | Moment by the moment, the web was built: falters. | Later: taking a test. | That writer who wrote of love and fame: that writer who died. | Production ceased: of course. | Making noises with the pen: scratch, tap. | And when she turns to me: forgetting amnesty. | The life gets better, but the writing: worse. | Dialing up: tuning (getting) out. | Indecision is insufferable: then, the rain. | When the masculine forecloses: athletic poem. | A drop: then, sound. | Trying: negotiating a wave. | Thinking it was Cage, knowing finally: Eno. | Pacing back and forth, smoking, fidgeting: behavior. | Cars on the highway: moving forth into adventure. | When it bleeds: satire. | Scanning the crowd for the familiar: faces. | Two words together that make a dull story: theory. | Crying: public address. | Anticipating: public demonstrations. | When the polls close: catharsis of the new naive. | On the streets, garbage, dust: sediment. | I think: I have invented. | Blowing the nose into an ashtray: improbable dissent. | The pathology of getting it wrong: dada. | Trying to circulate among nuance: flexing the Jamesian. | And when the table cleared, and the conversation ceased: my family. | Birds warble: morning. | Cheap jokes and laughing gas: community. | The image profoundly dithers: the site is ugly. | When the chips are finally counted:

pragmatism. | No longer: puppet of stars. | No longer: victim of the contiguous. | No longer: angling to be a stable critic. | After a failure of short-term memory: renew the streets. | Every temp its turn: every type its torque. | Drinking the wine: marrying the incredible. | Pausing before words, inhaling: anticipating commotion. | Taking the wrench to technology: curbing the linear. | Bathing, paring, shaving: detoxifying. | Exploring the real estate of the block: inveigling the dogs. | Loving by brush of the cheek: evading the secular. | Futzing with the stocks, rolling with the hunches: the quizzical mine. | Pissing: watching. | Making controversy on the blog: stemming literary conversion. | The laughs get better, the writing: worse. | Running away to Canada, running away to Patagonia: syllables. | Chuckling in Cathedrals: instantiating echoes. | With an eye on the ball: with a hand on the clutch. | Feeling fancy when ordering in German: debasing the European. | Knee shakes, rhythmically: manic. | Korean soup-eater sips loudly: her comforting music. | Glass backboard after youth smashing basketball against flaccid metal one: failure. | I cough: sub-comic material. | The job was filled: the statistic was digitized. | Argument settled, friendship adhered: check paid. | Touching with two hands, when one was never enough: discovery of sympathy. | As able, as husband: and wife. | We know the news when we refuse the headlines: disciplined scanning. | On a fecund plateau against the short shrift of Senators: writing. | Of the dope: after the anxiety. | Naughty movie business: middle-aged voyeurism. | No longer: fingering the watch-chain. | No longer: sinking behind makeup. | No longer: such tender knees. | I mean: it must be. | Retiring every ten years to the country: levelling out. | Chaucer got it: James didn't. | Wanting the throat to be Chinese: getting Sicilian. | Lorca got it: Dalí didn't. | Wanting a show: wallowing in trauma. | In the ribbons of morning, feeling the touch of a hand: existential measure. | Speaking softly: hardly speaking. | Garbling the vowels: burping. | New airport screening rules: new sentience in the database. | Revisiting photographs: deep-freezing the enigmas. | The clatter of seashells, the walking stick: a turquoise memory.

HABIB TENGOUR

The River of the Cyclops

At the head of the harbor there is a spring of clear water
coming out of a cave, and there are poplars growing all round it.

—Homer, *The Odyssey*, canto ix, 140–41
(Samuel Butler's translation)

Warm breeze   reminiscence
The waves' din
Over there, the two rocks, witnesses of a burst of anger
And those lava stones by the sea, pillows for bathers
Voci del Mediterraneo   racket
Too many people jostling each other   corny old tune
Parade . . .

A long time ago, Ulysses lands not far from the central railway station.
Sweet water overflowed the sea.
A luxurious vegetation suggests a jaunt . . .
The man of a thousand ruses does not resist   desire to look around
Lay in fresh water, a good pretext.
To have a drink's something you can't refuse
And who knows what lies beyond the river

Mount Etna lies in wait around the corner
Balled up spits in his face
O cyclops / the only one to rant (lonely rant)
When nobody disturbs / what ignorance . . . Quand personne ne dérange / quelle
          inconscience . . .

When you'll tread on the heels of Ulysses, dripping with sweat
And out of breath
Your companions will have found the bar from where the music flows

But once upon a time and today   murderous sleep
To catch some zzzs rather than get loaded
Wisdom's preferable to any ruse . . .

The two rocks in the sea
You gaze at them with a doleful eye
It is not Polyphemus   a submarine eruption
Naked naked naked naked naked naked yes yes yes night night O night
Eye at the heart oh he and she who smiles naked
In the water   Dream far away   Shines   sun and full moon
Around the words you discover   to spell out

Translated from the French by Pierre Joris

PRAGEETA SHARMA

A Brazen State

If I remember that there was a course of action
like a town with blueprints for the carnival,
then I can bludgeon the dream with an autocrat's
swiftness and catalogue all the experiences like sentences.
There was the one with a bald spot and the one getting one.
There was one with only a fawn for a friend and one
with a rifle. There was one with just a penny and twelve
zeros with fanaticism for nothing special.
What was edited came true, what was omitted was
lucky to be erased. There lay the town; the state's little anarchy
in trouble with a hazy aqua for a light—a duress unbound in the children's play.
I forgot that it meant we were all brazen and strong willed and hearty
and did not fight indiscriminately for terror or the experts.

MEI-MEI BERSSENBRUGGE

Safety

Urban space is a series of partial views, convex, opaque.

You go from mass to detail, individuals, little ants.

The instinct to preserve oneself deflects onto vertigo from the domination of space, fear of death to fear of damage to a beautiful body.

You connect dwelling to a child guarded by a woman.

Its fate is foretold, child implicit in a word-chain, flash, flowers in ice.

In the days we have left, we count our probable meetings, first surface content, then in your language, as in my dream.

The more disconnected your monologue, the more it correlates to something latent in that moment, separation, flowers in ice.

It's not raining, but it's as if there were mud everywhere, and you're plastered in mud.

When a person falls in front of you, something like rain washes mud away, and his leg becomes white as a piece of marble.

Being with each other, we want to reveal and reveal, conceal nothing, but there's the sense something does not get across, a secret.

In this sense, hospitality between us is a secret interior, instead of reality being the plaintiff.

Shards, detail, singularity, garden in winter in glass, palms, extreme refinement of the civility.

There's a linking of structure, joint and weld, a springiness, and an unlinking across expanse.

The rigor of the link is an artifact.

Its volume is innate in the witness, leg covered over, memorialized by what I saw, concealed, closed, covered with sight as with gauze, light surface with which I wrap you, light trampoline.

SARAH GAMBITO

Scene: a Loom

If I emulate you, where would my rafters be?
She pulls out her voice scale by scale.
She thinks I do not hear her emotion.
This is a shock.

To make it more specific—*my people*.

Children are the imminent sojourn.
A maybe of love.
Brilliant persuasion from the stands.

I buy you a plate of expensive pears.
I cut the pear in 1/2.

January 8th   We eat a 1/2.
January 8th   Someone dear to me has died. Someone dear to me has died.
January 28th   *Ito ay isang pagdasal para sa kapatid ko* meaning

He was unkind and she loved him.
He left her on the impended highway and she loved him.
He went away to the far country and she loved him.

I do not know the Lord.
But he spoke in a lovely way.
Created. Silvery citadel.

KATAYOON ZANDVAKILI

The Eglantine Deal

We're both on our knees to someone only we see.
There is a gold coffin suspended in space,
haze like a soft and distant drum-roll
    (Schumann's nocturne)

the purpose: to get Noah's Ark

Cowboy and Dog and Horse, of course spots of white paper along the free-way spooking the Horse. Coffee and poncho and cups with the face cards all over them.

This person feels safe in the world, this person is a boy becoming a man, an owl evolving in the hum and singsong arms of redwoods. He is astonishing because he knows you'll forgive him, knows it isn't up to you to forgive. Protected by the silver-white layer of goodness his mind has created, he troubles you by bringing your weakness into the circle of light his arms pretend, telling you in an offhand way that you too are received, welcome.

The white butterfly dream:
    trading on a bridge that slopes
    like a horse's lax bridle: he rode
    to tell us something
    before he changed.

And we finding what by the riverbed?

Kneeling in the church this could just as well be a bench off a park trail (the intangibles, cherries and goblets) he relates his dream of being licked on the side of the head by a large wolf-dog. On burial grounds.

The girl would like to play Hansel to his Gretel.

He meets his rogue friends and after, walking through the hills, he sees her. At first, he thinks she is a vision. She isn't. She sits on the side of the hill with her knees drawn up, scent of azurine and a cream-white dog. Later she takes him to the circle of wishing trees where he is reminded of things he has never seen.

She lives in the hills, has no other home. Believes in the butterfly, in the eye of the wolf-dog, in the smoke trailing from her hut in the woods.

He dances in the rain for her
one night, flapping his poncho
to make a point, making wolf
and turkey sounds. Other times,

he is nothing so much as
a deer. She watches him
as he watches her.

Does she wear a Maya of the Wolves/Raquel Welch top, animal skin and tan,
or a Juliet at 14/Princess Leia all-white gown? Never mind. She follows St.
    Eglantine,
tells the boy almost right away about her dream of the perfect
trail, how it wound past the bend, past the familiar boulder (was this too
in the dream?) she and the horse nodded too.

We also need a character dedicated to sheer, strong laughter not a fool but
one with a bird's-eye view, a this-too-shall-pass forbearance.

He says, "I don't know why I am doing this for you, but."

Last shot would be of him long and skinny in a Little-Prince scarf, a hint
of cigarette framing the blue-white globe at his feet, bouquet of flowers
off to the right.

AIMEE NEZHUKUMATATHIL

By the Light of a Single Worm

Kerala, India

Land snails the size of hockey pucks
slime a shimmer along craggy roots. A mantis
wipes its eyes with her forelegs like she's taking

off a new sweater. A certain earthworm
luminesces so strongly here, a zoology professor
once wrote a whole lecture by the light

of a single worm. My hand washes blue
& tiny hairs above the knuckle look electric.
Soil becomes glitter, even the flattest stone

turns into cabochon. When I bathe, a lizard
shaped like a cassava root with blue eyes
spies on me from the corner of the ceiling. I've seen

them fall on dinner tables, into noodle puddings,
the cold ceramic of the kitchen sink, & I just know
I will be next. I turn off the light, knowing that

in darkness they run along baseboards, savoring
picture frames until sunrise. I finish my bath
in darkness with only the glow from the garden,

      listen for any evidence of a tell-tale splash.

MARILYN CHIN

Tonight While the Stars are Shimmering
(NEW WORLD DUET)

A burst of red hibiscus on the hill
              A dahlia-blue silence chills the path
Compassion falters on highway 8
              Between La Jolla and Julian you are sad
Across the Del Mar shores I ponder my dead mother
              Between heaven and earth, a pesky brown gull
The sky is green where it meets the ocean
              You're the master of subterfuge, my love
A plume of foul orange from a duster plane
              I wonder what poison he is releasing, you say
A steep wall of wildflowers, perhaps verbena
              Purple so bright they mock the robes of God

In Feudal China you would've been drowned at birth
              In India charred for a better dowry
How was I saved on that boat of freedom
              To be anointed here on the prayer mat of your love
High humidity, humiliation on the terrain
              Oi, you can't describe the ocean to the well frog

I call you racist, you call me racist
       Now, we're entering forbidden territory
I call you sexist, you call me a fool
       And compare the canyons to breasts, anyway
I pull your hair, you bite my nape
       We make mad love until birdsong morning

You tear off your shirt, you cry out to the moon
       In the avocado grove you find peaches
You curse on the precipice, I weep near the sea
       The tribune says NOBODY WILL MARRY YOU
YOU'RE ALREADY FORTY
       My mother followed a cockcrow, my granny a dog
Their palms arranged my destiny
       Look, there's Orion, look, the Dog Star
Sorry, your majesty, your poetry has lost its duende
       Look, baby, baby, stop the car
A mouse and a kitty hawk, they are dancing

Yellow-mauve marguerites close their faces at dusk
       Behind the iron gate, a jasmine breeze
In life we share a pink quilt, in death a blue vault
       Shall we cease this redress, this wasteful ransom?
Your coffee is bitter, your spaghetti is sad
       Is there no ending this colloquy?
Ms. Lookeast, Ms. Lookeast
       What have we accomplished this century?
I take your olive branch deep within me
       A white man's guilt, a white man's love
Tonight while the stars are shimmering

JOHN YAU

In The Fourth Year of The Plague

Oil began dripping from the black and violet clouds bunched together
near the top of the back stairs. In the second year of this calamity a caravan

of hot-air balloons approached the bottled city. At least three of the pilots claimed to have witnessed a molten sky slide off heaven's domed ceiling.

It was, they feared, further proof that they had drifted away from their appointed destinations, and had unwittingly entered a time of increasing vengeance and relentless cataclysm. Even the flowers fomented. And, as widely reported in a previously taped segment, this was an unheard of metamorphosis that eventually drove the Royal Gardener and his cadre of young helpers to pronounce themselves insane and thus beyond all hope of repair.

How many disasters had been dutifully recorded in the ledgers before the beggars pitched forward in the streets? Their corpses hauled away in the first hours of dawn. Every morning the sky thickened with smoke. By that time I was already a lonely child who talked to small creatures, and made detailed drawings of their pitchfork tongues, arched backs, and ribbed wings. My tongue grew black from licking the silver nibs, my fingers darkened like the river where the pails of ashes sank.

I was told that it was all an error in communication. A monumental slippage, it was announced, whose final outcome remains to be delivered to those who are fervent in their strict adherence to the old ways. Instructed not to ask more, I stopped talking altogether, and have continued to remain silent whenever I migrate through the spheres marked "Public" and "Off Limits."

My tutors and I passed the hours watching rain gather its bubble in the saltshakers our ancestors placed on the limestone altar behind the stables. I discovered that salamander is not a language you can learn in a reflecting pool. Their itinerary was neither heroic nor glittering, and they preferred to congregate in the muddy lanes encircling the arsenal. When you are made of invisible ink, I told my last bodyguard, you are pursued by vexations, but you are not yet the sordid creation you will one day inhabit, comfortable as fur wrapped in muslin and carried down from the mountains. I became the animals that appeared in my dreams, their longing remains my guide.

Listen, Little Magdalena Snowdrop, don't you think it's time we prepare another canvas?

AHMAD DAHBOUR

The Hands Again

No seas in books
I seek oceans, but they don't respond
No bed in the trees
whenever I want to rest, its dangerous branches awaken
No dialogue in language
their words only reach my lips, never my inner nerves
No fields in the clouds
only blood that tries to give its news to horizons
No Seas No Books
No Bed No Tree
No Dialogue No Language
No Fields No Clouds

Grow strong, my hands; if you should,
they'd pay attention, then.

Translated from the Arabic by Lena Jayyusi and Jeremy Reed

LALE MÜLDÜR

311
SERIES 2 (*TURKISH RED*)*

builders of the idea of turkish red
poets dervishes and wandering lovers sitting
at a drinking table based on the
refinement of ancient time
           turkish red
child sultans
looking at the reds in Selçuki tiles crying
           turkish red
the manner of eating oysters & serving them
the entering to the salon & the use of napkins

the liveries of the servants at the table & their *from-the-right-and-the-lefts*
entering the restaurant & picking a table
Athenian banquet tables and Euphrates nights
as I was thinking of these thoughts
        turkish red
thinking of an Azerbaijan girl
with her crescent and star earrings
I am building the
tie between
the lights of the bridge
        and its shimmering
         reflections in the watter
seeing the water as a necklace the bridge
  as a star-crescent body
    (*

_____ = turk

  bridge

like a bridge, departing from myself
like a Turk, red, I am crying *turkish red*

Translated from the Turkish by Murat Nemet-Nejat

Author's Note: Müldür spent several years in Belgium married to a Belgian painter. Different color titles of the poems in *The Book of Series* refer to the names of specific colors in her husband's painting box. Words in italic in the translations mean that the words appear in the same language (English, German, or Spanish) in the originals.

TADA CHIMAKO

Haiku

The meteor shower
In Leo falls as far as
My Cancer sickroom

獅子座流星雨果てて蟹座の病棟へ

A cat in heat passes
And the crime-prevention light
Switches itself on

戀猫の通ればともる防犯灯

A bag of summer earth—
So fresh, the pattern left
After sweeping up

夏土俵掃く箒目のあたらしき

Yesterday, today
And tomorrow—are they all
Just a white summer field?

昨日今日明日も白き夏野かな

The newly formed leaves
They are all the shapes of hearts
And the shapes of eyes

若葉みな心臓のかたち目のかたち

I turn back to look
And in my face I see such
Wildness and pallor

うつむけば顔に婆娑羅と青薄

Enough sleep
Good for forgetting—
My rattan pillow

寝の足りしものの忘れ佳し籠枕

The garden is
Full of discarded cicada shells
Full of holes

庭は蝉の脱ぎ殻だらけ穴だらけ

Holding a jade cicada
I want to listen to the cicadas calling out
Like light rain

玉 蝉を含み聴かばやせみしぐれ

Translated from the Japanese by Jeffrey Angles

Author's Note: In ancient China there was a custom of placing jade cicadas in the mouths of corpses.

TAUFIQ RAFAT

Lights

The car whispers down
the hill road.
Its lights   gouge out
                        a shifting
                        hollow of
                                brightness
except at the turns
where they wander off
                    into unsure space

But wait!

What lights are those
        pricking
        the distant
        mountaintops
        each
        one
        alone?

Starlight and a thin mist
deepen the mystery.

One is tempted to call them elfin

for what   kind of men
would struggle up those backbreaking slopes
all their maizebread goatmilk days
to achieve such
loneliness?

YEOW KAI CHAI

Quarterly Report No. 7: Epiphytes and Vetiver Control

in memory of adult film actress Karen Bach

Before the fourth sunrise, the road shoulder
has already shrugged off its riffraff,

grass grower over night without tea or sympathy.
Side alley slippers from the lights,

eye shadows all and sundry.
Levees veer behind the suns,

tugboat between nonplussed and shy panty
hose. You leave. The remains as it was,

aqueducts bursting at seams
away from the center of the spinning plate.

A crab claws back. Fig leaf. Prawn
crackering . . . Something comes unstuck,

sums added up. Eventually everything
swallows even eventually up. Puff.

Evening spat out like newt.
There's nothing to it. Lovers pistol-whipped

into acquiescence, then resume normal
appliance before dinner function at nine.

Come night, certain absentees glower,
tips shudderer as vitreous floaters.

KITASONO KATUE

Oval Ghost

white straightline
pierced through
yellow cylinder
beside it
listening to
pure
piano
vanishing
within
blue egg
like your
nonexistent
glass
neck's
star

inside
death's
needle,
solitude
of opera
of eternity
wearing Turkish-red corsage
smashing
peppermint moon
transparent
nonexistent
you

Translated from the Japanese by John Solt

TAN LIN

excerpt from *BlipSoako1*

MO   OD   M   IN

SEV   EN   EP   SMPLD 02

: "that there are things that can never be" repeated 01
: about my eyes, their lyres or the papers

on my children's vegetables, such
lyre-like thimbles

in the ponies of their rock bands:
that I was (once)   (iii) ti   )es

the mutiliation of my envies
that was not math, not prepared

throat: iridesence in the squares
that its sorry was

geodesic so like
the sand 03

that it was one   (in love) 04
or another

called 03
"my first full season on DVD"

Romeo
blah:

"I walked
into the ocean" where

they were a few diving
clamps or kitchens speared with gesture re:

so I am wasted aquamarine
in the squirrels vegetables

that there was
kindness spooned due the room + mutilation + dichotomy

that it was rayon the day
that the ice caps were ineligible

that it was bombast
and ocean was stapled brittle as 01

"as an hourglass" 02
that I was pre-dreaming

the calendar
candle-lit   noses

that I dreamed my grandmother
was drowning in a candle

she was pinching
the carnation

"and nothing was true"
that she was not shorter than I remember

that it was bombast without subsitution
without breathing

or the back of the bus driver building a tree
out of ice what was a face like that to my grandmother's

pointed mace like the suede edge of cardboard
and a v-6 engine roped off for $1,999.99

that she or I was gray like. The listening spatters
also and heated like the team wrestlers

that I was loud in tarpaulin like a carp
be little or be little

WAFAA' LAMRANI

A Talisman

> [*It is too little that the rainless cloud of arrival should trim three.*
> *It is too much that the sap of distance should make three winged.*]

Could it be the pomp of the march?
Could it be departure soaked in the waters of orphanage?
Or else the power or errancy?

I have gone beyond the shores of Minor Lessitude,
     Beyond the shores of Major Fury.
I have fraternized with the rowing of the winds
And shored myself in the depth of a sea of sparks
As though I were the front
For which departure yearns,
The front footsteps cannot reach.

  In order to know love
  I have emerged out of love.

  In order to strew flowers
  I have dwelt in the vow.

  In order to vex the cornet
  I have mellowed in the root.

  In order to love the homeland
  I had to gather my fragmented self.

  In order to gather my fragmented self
  I squandered a lot
     and reinvented myself.

And because I have smitten you with the sun
  and with diaphanousness
You have, with all obstinacy,
Missed my splendor. . . .

Translated from the Arabic by Hassan Hilmy

MONICA YOUN

Stereoscopes

[1]
Oranges
going gelatinous in
the Central Valley as the Dow
neared ten thousand.

[2]
Feathers
spiked with
albumen.

[3]
A piece of cellophane
stretched taut across
her back; dragonflies were
spawning.

[4]
Mayday is
m'aidez

[5]
What they took
for a star was in fact
a twin star;
their instruments
revealed that
it sometimes was approaching,
sometimes receding.

[6]
The oiled
needle sleeps in its
glossy cradle.

[1]
My love,
I dreamt the wolves
were on you and I was useless
in my open-toed shoes.

[2]
Deodand,
your function
is forfeit.

[3]
An inch-thick sheet of
iron; the moment
you deduce the blowtorch
behind it.

[4]
A trickling
shame.

[5]
A scaffolding
rose out of the floor:
an effigy
of a hanged child
swathed in
bandages, a family tradition
on the tenth birthday.

[6]
How much
we like to imagine
a great wind.

BAHTIYAR VAHAPZADE

Pauses

You spoke,
I listened.
      So impressive:
The long silences
Were more expressive
   between words, sentences . . .

Stop,
Pause.
So many ideas are contained in each pause.
You spoke so,
     I saw at one point
Silence in the light, words on the shadow.
Into these end-of-sentence intervals could go
The entire lexicon of a language.

Translated from the Turkish and the Azeri by Talât Sait Halman

ARVIND KRISHNA MEHROTRA

The World's a Printing House

There's a mountain in my mind,
 I must be true to it.
  There's a mountain in
   My mind and I
    Must read it
     Line by
      Line

Or it will disappear: cone
　Of light or natal space
　　Call it what you will,
　　　I must be true
　　　　To it. Clouds
　　　　　Sweep its
　　　　　　Base.

Terraces cut into its
　Summit, windowpanes into
　　Its slopes through which pours
　　　The mountain
　　　　In my
　　　　　Mind,

Grazing on itself, and its
　Own reflection. Inversed
　　Peak, clapperless great
　　　Torn, some unfelt
　　　　Entirely
　　　　　Visioned
　　　　　　Thing,

Fading across the rent veil.
　Like a compositor's
　　Radiant font, in my
　　　Mind a mountain;
　　　　I must be
　　　　　True to
　　　　　　It.

ETEL ADNAN

Insomnia

Insomnia 1

1. Through imaging.
   mountains even.
   water-eyes shut.

2. mirror boxed in/
   production of one's
   light. (lightly)
   truck/load of. sweet
   night/mare with
   Faust

3. trees growing on
   fables. legs parting
   on linen. on hold.
   Nebulous. love. of.
   thoughts

4. tiniest of visions.
   an/gelic. fever.
   gulch. O C.a.l.i.
   f.o.r.n.i.a! Dimensions

5. blurrs. o no! not hiding
   mild. wild. kind.
   hind . . . fatigue leads
   ahead. ???????

6. Split. cloud.
   crooked effervescence.
   height of passing
   hour. un [yielding.]

7. the re/turn/rerun
   lived-in devil

a throw of
res/s/urgence
ex/haustion.

8. his/owl/on/
the/ridge.
ouuuuuuuh!

Insomnia 2

1. irreversible clarity
over and why. stairs.
whales eat water. when
tears get married. to
sea. the middle's middle
insomnia

2. women envy sailors
as. additional. distraction.
never colored.
the police stands.

3. on a cycleByecycle. Auto
nomous fear(roofs) the
wind's hunger for repetition.
two lines at a time

4. Funeral/s on two feet.
to carry a light on
one's back. Transparency
of single thought.
Dis/placement—care/fully—
of. a. sentence.

5. Fusion of bodies.
Fragility with marrows.
Plus. Plus fanfare. napkins
are maps. no food material
traffic blocks desire
on asphalt/ness

Insomnia 3

1. foam of Red Sea. Cat/ching
   Mercury. Lord of Time.
   visiting this room(?).
   Passage to: no/where
   fire's proportions

2. sun, moon, free
   what's . . . sleep?!
   ooooo ! booooo. Darkly
   eyes. reversed.

3. lion. judgment of.
   indistinct/ness. Red
   with/in black/ness. O
   non/certitude of non/
   existence. The/re.

4. Break:up. down. over.
   through. So on and on.
   until morning breaks.
   in. Ever.

ALAMGIR HASHMI

Snow

The blizzard overnight.
We wake up
to crazy things:

the pine trees rinsed in ice,
their glass twigs shattered below.
Our brains like eggs scrambled,
after dim sleep and snow.

What can one make of snow
this late,
ice-filled
chrysanthemums
pinned to the window?

No thought in winter would
burn
itself to fragrance
or summer wit.

In this ghastly white,
when I want to say I am afraid
and wordless,
I cannot breathe my breath.

I have seen it happen.
Once stealthily
as in the gray, white, off-white
hair in my father's beard
which the razor has never let
anyone see.

And the day
Dazzled by the light of his commitment
he frowned—
it is not right
to be on the wrong side
of things—
he was already losing weight.
        And two years later
two more wrinkles on the face
made him forever angry.

Here people talk like a Greek chorus.

As I eat in my thoughts
at breakfast
like the latent haze ahead,
I feel this morning's

three-inch ice
   lapse underfoot,
and my eyes spill
with the salt sheet of snow.

ABED ISMAEL

The Poem—The Mirage

This white won't accept another whisper. Let it sleep safely in its whiteness, without nonsense or language. I grab this pen with the hope that I might grab an idea. I only hear the creaking over the paper, and I don't capture a trace. In the wilderness I pound, one dune after another, as if the sky rains only sand. I am inept before the poem—the mirage.

O how the letters dance, hallucinate, choke. The north is air and the south is air. And the step between this and that is shadow. And shadow has the holiness of bowing. Shadow is the heaviness of an idea on paper, and the tenacity of erasure before a fleeting glance.

With shadow alone we live. No ahead and no behind. In the magical zero point. In the heart of seduction—the poem. Touch a poem and you touch escape. Running in air, an air bike for metonymy's teenager. For the beautiful magical frivolity, for poetry.

And poetry is the loser's prize. The consolation of one who sleeps dreamless. It is the echo that rings or goes mad, no difference. And poetry is the thing and its opposite, and also the absence of meter. Poetry is a rising, a place that escapes from its place, and a reality that only fleeing sustains.

O son of contradiction, son of the idea and its antithesis, son of difference at its most. O son of disappearing letters, images, and meanings. Son of concealment and disclosure.

In front of a white sun you flip over on your palm, only this horrific radiance remains, this towering crash of light, this blond blinding beauty, this incandescence, this extinguishment, this paradox, that gap, that cleft, that loss.

Losses pave the horizon cloud by cloud. A rain of loss, a lightning of loss.
And you O life, sleep in the clothes of loss, or the clothes of metaphor, for
the people of the cave to waken, for the shadows that guard the cave to
waken, for the dog of the cave to waken.

Translated from the Arabic by Fady Joudah

ARUNDHATHI SUBRAMANIAM

Strategist

The trick to deal
  with a body under siege
  is to keep things moving,

to be juggler
  at the moment
  when all the balls are up in the air,
  a whirling polka of asteroids and moons,

to be metrician of the innards,
  calibrating the jostle
  and squelch of commerce
  in those places where blood
  meets feeling.

Fear.
  Chill in the joints,
  primal rheumatism.

Envy.
  The marrow igloos
  into windowlessness.

Regret.
  Time stops in the throat.
  A piercing fishbone recollection
  of the sea.

Rage.
 Old friend.
 Ambassador to the world
 that I am.

The trick is not to noun
 yourself into corners.
 Water the plants.
 Go for a walk.
 Inhabit the verb.

MARJORIE EVASCO

Dreamweavers

We are entitled to our own
definitions of the world
we have in common:

earth	house	(stay)
water	well	(carry)
fire	stove	(tend)
air	song	(sigh)
ether	dream	(die)

and try out new combinations
with key words
unlocking power

house on fire	*sing!*
stove under water	*stay,*
earth filled well	*die.*

The spells and spellings
of our vocabularies
are oracular
in translation.

One woman in Pagnito-an

another in Solentiname
still another in Harxheim
naming
half the world together

can	move their earth
must	house their fire
be	water to their song
will	their dreams well.

KHALED MATTAWA

Texas in the Afternoon

Barley grass in winter, rude-boy lush,
and sweet pea seeds in my palm as if grains

of yeast, and the same promise of ardor.

The neighbors' cat, lying on the carport floor,
flees,
always jumping over the same spot in the fence.

I love her ritualized terror, her American sense of drill.
She sprawls behind the kitchen minutes later, asleep.

Midmorning grackles caw, the silver-blue
mint on their wings, a theft from the sun.

The live oak shading three front yards.
The squirrels store, lose and retrieve.

Exile,
your ninety nine names
trill the tip of my tongue.

Isn't it time to sing what I've gathered
into blessing—indigenous, though scant?

TSAI YIM PUI

enchantress

her car stopped at Starfish Street
she went into Arcade of Dreams
and bought a bunch of marigolds
then went down to the graveyard
honeysuckles across a white river
reflecting a myriad of green
you, through the gauze of years
watch her
a face beautiful as creation
of an Eve found only in museums
sitting poised in a *nanmu* chair
against a rosy sunset
merging into the whole canvas
the blood of her forebear the marquis
who for a horse
plunged down a cliff
as he would into mother's arms

as children in mother's arms
we used to ask
after the Crusade
where did Lionheart and his men go
to which side of the Round Table?
in the Russian Roulette Bar
on a brass-drum belly
they gather
hailing a high-born lady
amid throwing down of gauntlets
amid duels with finger shadows on the wall
who, like her, silently follows the setting sun
to the far end of the pier
and jumps
as if into Eden

Translated from the Chinese by Jane Lai

YU JIAN

excerpts from "Anthology of Notes"

1

In the beginning is the bunny
Then you know the wolf will follow
We assume a theater must be equipped with an exit
It's still early   keep watching
Wait a bit longer   you may be surprised
A tank may drive across the stage
I will stay   till the big gray wolf comes
But now the beginning is gone   so is the bunny
The only exit is from the wolf

9

If I compare spring to a temple
a new poem will begin

Green robes   dress gods
as trees
They enter   settle on mountaintops
become flowers   keep simple forms
In silence   flowers rise from leaves
Sacred mouths open
toward ears
but nothing comes out
only opened mouths   wordless

To compare spring to a temple   to say a tree is a god
both are illegitimate metaphors
but metaphor is all I have
Someone may change his mind
put down his ax   and start to listen

11

A letter
got away from a pile of Victorian feathers
from a place where English is spoken and written
It entered the post office
in the manner of a bird
flew over Rome in autumn
past icy Russia and Poland
across sunny Egypt   then to the east of India
and arrived at the office at dusk
governed by Chinese

The postman   descended from the sky
handed me the white feather
A letter   traveled a thousand miles
not to explain Ulysses
but to let me know
that somebody understood
my words

12

The road that goes there need not pass
iron
plastic, nylon
streets
highways
need not pass
women's dressing tables
men's beer glasses
The road that goes there
doesn't require ID cards
shoes
gas
I know this road once existed on earth
borderless
but if I want to get there today
and if I don't want to step on

gas pipes or accounting offices
I'll have to travel by poetry
by foot

14

You're about   to complete
to become
a white rose
even though you felt despair
in darkness   learned how to scream
even though you blocked
all the paths to April
with ink and weeds
even though you cursed
air   sun   water
even though your spirit
totally goes against
the map of the rose
and you once practiced suicide
at dawn
you are destined to become
a white rose
Oh   irresistible light
will enter April on time
and you will turn into broken darkness
Oh   white rose
you'll bloom
like a rose
complete
pay a tax to bees on time
provide metaphors to poets on time
wither on time

15

I write in autumn   like the ancient masters
on the lunar day of August 15 or September 15
Beginning of autumn or White Dew
I write in autumn

A refined habit
Nothing to do with
the autumns in Tang Dynasty poems
There's something huge that rules everything
between the sky and the earth   its vast territory
but it's not autumn
not cranes over the fields   not a shepherd boy's flute in a storm
What permeates this month
is the pipes from the water plant   and rusty
water meters   on apartment walls
their dials turning

Translated from the Chinese by Wang Ping and Ron Padgett

BAHA ZAIN

Language

How hard
to accommodate the word to the meaning
such trouble
to wrap decorum with language
the emotions of old bards;
a fish flashing in water
you already know its gender.

Translated from the Malay by Muhammad Haji Salleh

VIDHU AGGARWAL

Customs House

Come on, we all decide to become a Bob
temporarily—or else

or else it's that poor clown over there, stranded
with over a hundred dirty

bags of tricks,
tripped over, roped-off, emptied out in ways only our names

could stand.
Even then, their searchlights flail,

producing
a flower, a pile

of garbage,
a bunch

of waves
ricocheting between you

and you,
who are always going somewhere quickly. Please.

Amplify us.
Since aren't we all just looking

for another medium
to move in?

Slips and atmospherics,
catchy ditties

of all ages
riding on several balls of air,

or more.
You might just catch one, if you can
and begin

again
where you begin to catch your breath

in wide circlets
that grow

increasingly personal
feverish, agog,

rolling around
in any number of fatal eventualities, you might forget

you might go on,
you might begin again and wave

until long appurtenances lift you,
kick the exit out with you.

OUYANG YU

A poem, long overdue

In my hand, dated 3/1/05
A copy of
Manual of Painting & Calligraphy: A Novel

On page 83
In the margin
I wrote, not dated, in Chinese:

"Right at this moment (I am) in a restaurant
Next to *fuhao binguan* [Big Lord Hotel]
Waiting for my Sour Vegetable Fish

And Mashed Garlic Bitter Vegetables
In the air, "Auld Lang Syne"
Is playing
5 girls are
keeping me company
from a distance . . ."

next to that
near the bottom
I wrote, in both Chinese and English:

标题 : The Age of Formidable Women
in an echo to a line in the book (p. 83):
"In this age of formidable women"

ah, what day is today, the 3rd of January 2005
even death dies
leaving me stonily alone

writing this lone overdue poem
I meant
long, sorry, not lone

JALAL EL-HAKMAOUI

You Hear Me Jim Morrison?

Always
Good poems
Bring us cake
And cheap wine bought from the one-eyed merchant
Who, masturbating, fantasizes on the tail of a romantic
She-donkey
On New Year's Eve,
Mechanical pictures turn her on
And make her run out of Vaseline.
We require twenty bottles of burning vindictiveness
So that we can open our mouths and look at
Our tongues that creep on
The blade of the big mirror
As they get involved in fierce battles
Against the bald tax collector who smokes Chester 25 cigarettes

And, at 4 A.M., lends me Allen Ginsberg's *Reality Sandwiches,*
The remains of an addicted radio and the ringing of black thoughts.
She did not take off all her clothes
When she joined me in a see-through telephone booth
Where she expected to find vigor.
She'd forgotten to take the bus to St. Michel.

Translated from the Arabic by Hassan Hilmy

B. S. MARDHEKAR

The Forests of Yellow Bamboo Trees

The forest of yellow bamboo trees
underlines the sky with its song;
between the lines, the mind grinds up
the promise to live (not now, but tomorrow).

The lemon tree carves in the wind
old neuter futures horned with antlers;
and footprints are printed on that wind,
but they're dead, though new.

Countless crows splotch their lime
on the pylons of the centuries;
and verbs stand guard round the clock,
but though they're alert, they're merely robots.

The polestar that never sets has set,
the Seven Sages have botched their answer;
hail that's not yet frozen falls,
and on the radio, Radha and Krishna.

Translated from the Marathi by Vinay Dharwadker

PAOLO JAVIER

DJ Cam1

Come on let's sway as gravity leaves us playas!
Operating minus one voice   come one less balasubas
                                                            Come hear no evil

come in one piece Infinity

                                        come involuntarily colloquial

                                        come to heal Paolo
Come on   Las Pinas income
In god we thrust to be upfront come upon Villa

   dole out roses come see you better tell us though

Introduce us to the loot come in sir & please

            come into a tunnel   my Juan
come Bruna   , come Bruna pleads
                                    , DJ Cam1 indecisive

Murakami   my Cam1 entry   hearkens experience

come annually
come Bruna, o language

                                        come balasubas
Paranaque tales of orgies come inquire   about my orgies
                                    savior come lascivious

a pagoda amid top brass come Bruna ready-to-wear

                                        come infirm us

is hour   sign outré Cam1, donned
ay sige   Cam1 cues the record to allay Time totally

come lost Pinoys   why come lost domiciles
come Ellis Island   ears alter   why taciturn
why enter trysts   prone to, come   Villa
Corregidor come   Villa as Cam1

raconteur, ardor,   come   companion   manongs   unlocked

come to this lost cause
my gut quantified calls for pork stasis come ascend

enemy shelling crepuscular ears   come connubial
                    Y-chromosome   *"Come, you lost queer!"*

pensive, Cam1's large argument, my Villa   Trysteasers detain
the disease of ebonics immense? establish   come aboard

Time allayed, we've come to deal with the media deity denied me
marine vanishings   why define it, di ba?   it's a comely scenario   how skin
   can kill

I can ascribe lust to verses, to massive trysts. The East comes knocking.
                                                    Come
upon this haberdashery meadow.

SALIM BARAKAT

Index of Creatures

The Fox

The galaxy of songs spreads its fur to the galaxies, come closer, sauntering
ones, with your blue traps, to hunt the dove of tricks.
But, with which snare will you capture this creature that spills over
like a guffaw?
What will capture this mellow melodious chant to the water? So be it.
Take him, take this reckless beauty, he's the story knocking
oooh . . . oooh, or did you think you had a story before his tail touched
the story?

You disperse him but he remains.
You disperse him but the dove of tricks remains.

The Peacock

Out of here, out of hanging feather gardens, a whirlwind of color shakes
off its cover, and the storm scatters crown by crown, so what is seen is
    only tomorrow's
carnival in the shadow of yesterday's ringmaster.

Let this bird cry.
Let his feathers cry.
And you, too, cry, with your pampered present and stolen glances
through a hole in death's bolt.

The Stork

Who's there for the sad white? Who for the grass that undresses
the river's women? Who for banks that steal the candelabra of the water?
Who for the wind hanging on with two thin legs, and a beak that picks
    the wind from the day's pond?
Who for the moan that wears a wedding tiara?
Who for the spring, the police of seasons,
the commander in the name of a sweetness that never was?

Radiant like a scream the sad white rises in the space of our throats;
radiant like a scream the sad white rises.

Translated from the Arabic by Fady Joudah

RICARDO M. DE UNGRIA

Notations on the Prospects for Peace

1.

*

---

* July +he rambu+an +rees s+and
propped on bamboo poles
like cru+ches, +heir branches

roped +o upper +runks
+o hold up & s+ave off
+he deadly crack, snap,

& breakage from +heir +ips
pulled down by +he spill
of blood-red anemone eggs

and +heir burden of swee+ness
+ingling, almost giving in
+o +he s+rong suck of rain-drenched ear+h

or +he young boys' sizzling reach
on +ip+oes on +he o+her side
of +he barbed-wire fence

2.

*

---

* Like fragmen+a+ion grenades caugh+
on imperial boughs
+he durian bulbs hang in midair
in deep sleep,
+heir eyelids winding
round s+one seeds inside whi+e pi+s

brigh+ flesh flaked off an angel's fea+her
furrowed +hrough dea+h's firs+ ro+,
+he bi++erness warmed back +o ear+h's dir+ swee+ness
and plowed in+o reek soli+ude & swagger—
announcing on frui+ion +ime
volup+uous shocks in +he Augus+ air,
unappeasemen+s, and rio+s
in +he ravening +ongue

3.

*

──────────────

* And +he whole sky
a bird keeping
a glad eye
on +hings unpraised,
unheard of
in whispered
careless spaces

+he brief blue momen+
singing or abou+ +o sing,
+he hear+ warm
wi+h li++le wings s+irred
by +he pause of seasons,
+he +ranquil earth ajar

on +he edge of bearing frui+

SRIKANTH REDDY

Loose Strife with Apiary

Watched a man watch a man. One man made smoke out of nothing by scraping together two stones. Another kept time using nothing but stones. One man made love, another made pain with a stone in each hand. Somebody take out these stitches, I'm ready to open my eyes. So this is the new world—just like the old, only brighter. Word is the governor's wife scattered loose strife in the barnyard thinking it chicken feed & the wetlands turned purple overnight. We make ready vectors for smallpox & language. Books on magnetic tape, books on bookkeeping, on being, on coping & beekeeping—I could have told you, all it takes is a meadow & nerve. Come, let me show you the recycled cosmos inside my apiary. A veil on a peg. Queen deep in the sweetness.

JENNY BOULLY

from *The Body*

---

[1] Most likely an allusion to an actual person, as during this phase, it was common practice to place fantastical persons in actual situations or actual persons in fantastical situations.

[2] But in those days, I thought that by believing in magic and miracles, by believing hard enough, harder than anyone on earth, I would be made witness to the sublime. And so, what I was doing on the rooftop was praying. I was praying for the gift of flight, for the black umbrella and the hidden angels to aid me.

[3] "Because of the finitude of this type of travel, one should pack lightly, as words have different connotations according to different witnesses, as all people do not hear the same note of music at the same time, nor do events that appear simultaneous visually seem to be audibly simultaneous.

"Light and prayer also have finite speeds, so we never see an instantaneous snapshot of eternity. The flight of light is so swift that within a single lifetime we obtain effectively an instantaneous snapshot, but this is certainly not the case astronomically. We see the moon as it was just over a second ago, and the sun as it was about 8 min ago. At the same time, we see the stars by light that departed from them years ago, and the other galaxies as they were millions of lifetimes in the past. We do not observe the world about us at an instant in time, but rather we see different possible lives about us as different events in spacetime.

"Relatively moving observers do not even agree on the order of events . . ." (ibid., p. 523).

[4] It is odd that she chose not to record this particular dream about E. in her log, but instead made loose notes in her journal and later wrote in a letter to Andy:

> . . . he died again. This time, I refused to accept his death because I could still communicate with him and so I asked him if he had, of late, been walking on water or on air, and he answered "neither." I only began to cry at his funeral, and the mourners, they didn't know that it was I who made them; it was I who glued the dragonflies to the scene and said, "you must read his stories." I woke because in my dream, I had been crying too profusely. I slept again and this time, I dreamt the dream of his resurrection: he arrived in my mailbox wrapped in his fiction and covered with butterflies. I ran around, shouting, "he's not dead!" But he is, you see. The dream wants to tell me that he is dead to me. The dream wants to inform me not to be fooled by pretty packages, that in matters of correspondence, the body is tragically absent.

---

5 Never assume that the actors are "sticking to the script." It is recommended that students engaged in cinema studies consult the original scripts and make notes of alterations. Sometimes the director orders last-minute changes. Sometimes too, when one speaks, it is never as one had intended. The student should take note and reconcile the irony which exists between "what should have been" [a] and "what is." [b]

> [a] ". . . . when you see him you will be glad; you will love him . . . and he will never forsake you. This is the meaning of the dream." (G.)[*]

> [b] "Although I should go in sorrow and in pain, with sighing and with weeping, still I must go." (G.)[*]

> [*] This particular footnote is imagined as being elucidated by a future editor.

6 This letter was never found.

[7] Generally, this symbolizes not the inexplicable, but rather the understood, as in missing, as in variable; therefore, it is standard practice to plug in possibilities or substitutions in order to discover solutions to one's problem set.

[8] Underneath the covers, the message would always be different: the white bird flying overhead would reveal itself as an emblem of hope; a sigh would be a sign of white flowers held while wearing a white dress; a shiver would be interpreted to mean a shaking of spring leaves, blossoms, or rain; her name, sounding from his mouth, would mean whatever the dream wished it to mean.

[9] Recall that sometimes the world is violet and amass with wanderers, and a woman in white, long sought, appears innocent, as if in a pinup in which anticipation and promise grope one another.

[10] 1606 SHAKES. Ant. & Cl. IV. vi. 37, I will go seeke Some Ditch wherein to dye.

---

[11] From her travel journal, written during the five years of her self-imposed "nun-hood":

> . . . I tried to make myself pure by giving up touching myself, that part of
> myself that my mother used to call a turtle and then a clam. But there I was,
> under the blue mosquito net, blue, not unlike the color of my dreams. The
> cocks were crowing for morning and I began; I began having to start this
> dream over again.
>
> (Perhaps when the cock crows, it signifies only the crowing of the cock and
> nothing more. Perhaps the aubade is, in fact, only a convention. I should be so
> free.)

[12] Horace, 1. Epistles I.1.98–99.

[13] Even so, I go my own way, following the drifts of the hourglass, laurelled with
lightning-blue bumblebees, at the foot of the lunamoth-winged sky, as on the bottom
of the whale-borne sea.

[14] Often, she heard her father whistling, beckoning her home, and she would run, aban-
doning whatever game she had been playing in a neighbor's house or yard somewhere.
When she returned home, her father would be calmly sitting, wanting nothing in par-
ticular, saying he had not whistled, that she must have heard this out of some sort of
homesickness.

MICHAEL ONDAATJE

Proust in the Waters

Swimming along the bar of moon
the yellow scattered sleeping
arm of the moon
                        on Balsam Lake
releasing the air
                        out of your mouth
the moon under your arm
tick of the brain
submerged. Tick
of the loon's heart
in the wet night's thunder
                                below us
knowing its shore is the air

We love things which disappear
and are found
creatures who plummet
and become
an arrow.
To know the syllables
in a loon sentence
                        intricate
shift of preposition
that signals meridian
                        west south west.
The mother tongue
a bubble caught in my beak
releasing the air
                        of a language

Seeing no human in this moon storm
being naked in black water
you approach the corridor
such jewelry! Queen Anne's Lace!
and slide to fathoms.
The mouth swallows river morse

throws a sound
through the loom of liquid
against the sky.

Where are you?

On the edge
Of the moon bar

EARTH OF
DROWNED GODS

Earth of Drowned Gods

— SAADI YOUSSEF

Years ago, having just spent a semester abroad in Paris, I was alone, riding the *Die Bahn,* the German railway, from Frankfurt to Munich. I was passing the time reading a wonderful old edition of the *Arabian Nights,* translated by Sir Richard Burton, and looking out at the German countryside scrolling by the window, when I was joined in my compartment by a skittish-looking man in a beard. We passed an hour or so wordlessly, before he commented on the book I was reading. "Ah, Scheherazade," he sighed, "they don't make them like that anymore, do they?"

It turned out that my companion was an American and also a lover of literature. He was just about to point out a passage he particularly liked in my book when we heard a clattering in the compartment next to us. The bearded man's hand leapt back and he looked at me, wild-eyed and exclaimed, "Put it away! Put it away!"

Confused, I did as he said just as the railway conductor came by to check our tickets. He was accompanied by a customs official who asked for my passport and spent a good amount of time glaring at it under a purple scope. The interaction was disconcerting but I had no idea why my fellow traveler had reacted the way he had until we were alone again. His grandfather, he told me, had lived in the latter part of the nineteenth century during the time of the Comstock Laws, which banned any "obscene book, pamphlet, paper, writing, advertisement, circular, print, picture, drawing or other representation, figure, or image on or of paper of other material, or any cast instrument, or other article of an immoral nature, or any drug or medicine, or any article whatever, for the prevention of conception, or for causing unlawful abortion." In fact, his grandfather had been arrested for owning an edition of the very book I held in my hand!

If only such stories were the stuff of memory, but a glance at the PEN American Center Web site assures that it is not. Over the last decade, Iraqi writers and translators who expressed support for pluralistic dialogue have been hunted by Baathist death squads and forced to flee their homes for uncertain asylum. In June 2005, the Turkish government enacted a new penal code that made it illegal to "insult Turkishness," and this code has been used against numerous Turkish writers, journalists, and publishers, including Nobel Laureate Orhan Pamuk. In 2006, three writers, members of the Independent Chinese PEN Center (ICPC) were detained for their critical writings and dissident activities, for disseminating "counterrevolutionary propaganda." In America, the Federal Communications Commission has passed new standards to censor the arbitrarily defined charge of "indecency" on the airwaves and there have even been calls by members of Congress "to prosecute newspapers and individual reporters for espionage and treason—charges frequently used to muzzle journalists in other countries—and a non-binding Congressional resolution condemning the press and calling for the "cooperation" of the media in the War on Terror."[1]

Many of the countries and regions included in this anthology—Afghanistan, Iraq, Kashmir, Nepal, Korea, Sri Lanka, Palestine, Kurdistan, the United Kingdom, and the United States, just to mention a few—are, in more or less overt forms, places where the application of politics has led directly, and in some cases ineradicably, to censorship, persecution, and even to warfare; where "peace" has been fashioned into a tenuous abstraction, seemingly untenable; where under the rhetoric of "global freedom" or the "fight against terror," national and political self-interests are single-mindedly pursued. Postcolonial theorist Homi K. Bhabha has written, "Nations, like narrative, lose their origins in the myths of time and only fully realize their horizons in the mind's eye . . . a particular ambivalence haunts the idea of the nation, the language of those who write it and the lives of those who live it."[2] Is it any wonder that in a moment where the politicians are seemingly more estranged than ever before from the poets, we are living through dangerous escalations of tension and misunderstanding?

A perfect example of the territory where art meets individual resistance is Afghan poet Nadia Anjuman's poem "The Silenced." Anjuman was one of Afghanistan's most promising young poets. While still a student at Herat University and only twenty-five years of age, she published a book of poems entitled *Gul-e-dodi*, or *Dark Red Flower*, which movingly described the oppression of Afghan women. Later the same year, her battered body

---

[1] "September 21, 2006: PEN sounds alarm on threats against press in the U.S." http://www.pen.org/viewmedia.php/prmMID/818/prmID/1331

[2] Homi K. Bhaba, "Introduction: Narrating the Nation," *Nation and Narration* (New York: Routledge, 1990), p.1.

was found by police officers; Anjuman had been beaten to death by her husband who had been shamed by her literary output. During the Taliban regime, Anjuman and other female writers of the Herat literary group would read and discuss banned authors such as William Shakespeare and Fyodor Dostoyevsky. The tragedy of her death was condemned by the United Nations, as well as by many world leaders. As Anjuman wrote presciently in her poem "The Silenced":

> *I have no desire for talking, my tongue is tied up.*
> *Now that I am abhorred by my time, do I sing or not?*
> *What could I say about honey, when my mouth is as bitter as poison.*
> *Alas! The group of tyrants has muffled my mouth.*

It is not just inequalities of gender that are critiqued in this section but those of class, race, and nation as well. Duo Duo began to write poetry in the 1970s, during the fervency of the Cultural Revolution in China. He wrote in secret and published his work in samizdat publications. The morning after the Tiananmen Square massacre, which he witnessed, Duo Duo left for a reading tour of England and decided not to return to China, but rather to live abroad in self-exile. His poem "When People Rise from Cheese, Statement #1" begins with an absurdist title, immediately followed by a reference to how song can subsume tragedy. The next image is of a vicious son, "Bringing with him tobacco and a dry throat." The connotation there seems to be one of willful sadism—the son is vicious and he brings with him the source of his prosperity ("tobacco") and its deleterious effect on his constitution ("dry throat"). The masses, in contrast, are depicted as "beasts [that] must bear cruel blinders," subjugated by the son so that they cannot even see the slaughter to which they are being led. The poem ends with an enigmatic image, "From far away there comes marching a troop / Of smoking people." Whether the people are smoking because they are being immolated, because they are infernal in nature, or because they are the beneficiaries of the son's vicious cultivation of tobacco, they represent a harrowing image, resonating with the destructiveness of conflict. As Forrest Gander has written, "Duo Duo's poems in English rivet us with their obsidian sharp images and their evocative connotations. They are the *cri de coeur* of a fractured I."

The first poem of this section, Saadi Youssef's "America, America," is one of the most full-throated songs both in praise and censure of the United States. Youssef was born in Basra, Iraq, in 1934 and saw firsthand the many transformations the country underwent. While an Iraqi citizen,

Youssef was also a member of the larger community of literature, translating the works of such writers as Walt Whitman, George Orwell, Federico García Lorca, and Wole Soyinka into Arabic. Accordingly, his poem is a love song of sorts, waxing rhapsodic about "jeans and jazz and *Treasure Island* / and John Silver's parrot and the balconies of New Orleans." But the poem also offers some of the strongest criticism of the American presence in Iraq. Basra, the city in which he grew up, became an epicenter of war. Buildings he had known since his childhood have been demolished.

The poem ends with a self-referential couplet, "We are the drowned. / Let the water come." We have been drowning in eddies of anaphora and disparate materials throughout the poem (there's even a snippet of blues in the midst of this plea), but more than that, the tone is reconciled, turning the poem less into a statement of protest or even an ironic recapitulation of America the Conqueror, but rather into an elegy. A sorrowful realization that whatever promise democracy holds for American citizens, it is a possibility that it is nonexistent for Iraqis.

Marilyn Hacker has written that, "Saadi Youssef was born in Iraq, but he has become, through the vicissitudes of history and the cosmopolitan appetites of his mind, a poet, not only of the Arab world, but of the human universe." His poem was chosen to begin this section because it reveals that at the intersection of politics and culture, there is simply human consciousness. It is one of the callings of writers to depict, regardless of the pressures upon them, the realities of their time and the many voices in *Earth of Drowned Gods* give undeniable testimony to this fact.

The enormous machines whose gears and wheels turn the policies of the politicians are operative on a minute level, playing out upon the lives of those who live under prescriptions and laws they likely have had no hand in choosing. It is up to the writer, then, to interrogate where human interests can thrive in the suffocating matrix of political ideologies. It is up to the poet to serve as voice and witness in parts of the world where sometimes just the writing or the reading of a poem is an act of courage and defiance.

— Ravi Shankar

SAADI YOUSSEF

America, America

> *God save America,*
> *My home sweet home!*

The French general who raised his tricolor
over Nugrat al-Salman where I was a prisoner
thirty years ago . . .
in the middle of that U-turn
that split the back of the Iraqi army,
the general who loved St. Emilion wines
called Nugrat al-Salman a fort . . .
Of the surface of the earth, generals know only two dimensions:
whatever rises is a fort,
whatever spreads is a battlefield.
How ignorant the general was!
But *Liberation* was better versed in topography.
The Iraqi boy who conquered her front page
sat carbonized behind a steering wheel
on the Kuwait-Safwan highway
while television cameras
(the booty of the defeated and their identity)
were safe in the truck like a storefront
on Rivoli Street.
The neutron bomb is highly intelligent.
It distinguishes between
an "I" and an "Identity."

> *God save America,*
> *My home sweet home!*

Blues

How long must I walk to Sacramento?
How long must I walk to Sacramento?
How long will I walk to reach my home?
How long will I walk to reach my girl?
How long must I walk to Sacramento?

For two days, no boat has sailed this stream,
Two days, two days, two days.

Honey, how can I ride?
I know this stream,
But, O but, O but,
For two days, no boat has sailed this stream.

La Li La La Li La
La Li La La Li La
A stranger becomes afraid.
Have no fear, dear horse.
No fear of the wolves of the wild,
No fear, for the land is my land.
La Li La La Li La
La Li La La Li La
A stranger becomes afraid.

    God save America,
    My home sweet home!

I too love jeans and jazz and *Treasure Island*
and John Silver's parrot and the balconies of New Orleans.
I love Mark Twain and the Mississippi steamboats
and Abraham Lincoln's dogs.
I love the fields of wheat and corn and the smell of Virginia tobacco.
But I am not an American.
Is that enough for the Phantom pilot to turn me back to the Stone Age?
I need neither oil, nor America herself, neither the elephant
nor the donkey.
Leave me, pilot, leave my house roofed with palm fronds
and this wooden bridge.
I need neither your Golden Gate nor your skyscrapers.
I need the village, not New York.
Why did you come to me from your Nevada desert, soldier armed
to the teeth?
Why did you come all the way to distant Basra, where fish used to swim
by our doorsteps?
Pigs do not forage here.
I only have these water buffaloes lazily chewing on water lilies.

Leave me alone, soldier.
Leave me my floating cane hut and my fishing spear.
Leave me my migrating birds and the green plumes.
Take your roaring iron birds and your Tomahawk missiles.
I am not your foe.
I am the one who wades up to the knees in rice paddies.
Leave me to my curse.
I do not need your day of doom.

> *God save America,*
> *My home sweet home!*

America:
Let's exchange gifts.
Take your smuggled cigarettes
and give us potatoes.
Take James Bond's golden pistol
and give us Marilyn Monroe's giggle.
Take the heroin syringe under the tree
and give us vaccines.
Take your blueprints for model penitentiaries
and give us village homes.
Take the books of your missionaries
and give us paper for poems to defame you.
Take what you do not have
and give us what we have.
Take the stripes of your flag
and give us the stars.
Take the Afghani mujahideen's beard
and give us Walt Whitman's beard filled with butterflies.
Take Saddam Hussein
and give us Abraham Lincoln
or give us no one.

Now as I look across the balcony,
across the summer sky, the summery summer,
Damascus spins, dizzied among television aerials,
then it sinks, deeply, in the stones of the forts,

       in towers,

         in the arabesques of ivory,

and sinks, deeply, far from Rukn el-Din
and disappears far from the balcony.

And now
I remember trees:
the date palm of our mosque in Basra, at the end of Basra
a bird's beak,
a child's secret,
a summer feast.
I remember the date palm.
I touch it. I become it, when it falls black
without fronds,
when a dam fell, hewn by lightning.
And I remember the mighty mulberry
when it rumbled, butchered with an axe . . .
to fill the steams with leaves
and birds
and angels
and green blood.
I remember when pomegranate blossoms covered the sidewalks.
The students were leading the workers' parade . . .

The trees die
pummeled.
Dizzied,
not standing, the trees die.

> *God save America,*
> *My home sweet home!*

We are not hostages, America,
and your soldiers are not God's soldiers . . .
We are the poor ones, ours is the earth of the drowned gods,
the gods of bulls,
the gods of fires,
the gods of sorrows that intertwine clay and blood in a song . . .
We are the poor, ours is the god of the poor,
who emerges out of the farmers' ribs,
hungry
and bright,

and raises heads up high . . .

America, we are the dead.
Let your soldiers come.
Whoever kills a man, let him resurrect him.
We are the drowned ones, dear lady.
We are the drowned.
Let the water come.

Translated from the Arabic by Khaled Mattawa

LATIF NAZEMI

A Word for Freedom

Let's kiss water,
the root of civilization,
a word for freedom.

I'm in love with water,
with roaring and restless rivers
that are not seduced by trees
nor captured by jungles.
They flow day and night,
carry on forever.

Let's praise rivers that lust for flowing,
for searching, for a heart of temptation
that know what message water delivers to stone,
the question water asks from quiet coasts.

Passersby, for a long time
the river has been constrained in an old robe
on our street and thrown into a well.

Water wars with the well,
water in the mind of a tree,
water in the solitude of a cup,

water in the memory of flowerpot,
inconsolable.

I had a wonderful dream on Friday night.
I dreamed the river ran free,
that on its roaring horse,
it rode over stones,
past the border of farms.

Translated from the Persian/Dari by Bashir Sakhawarz

SESSHU FOSTER

Gigante

He talked about astronauts walking on the moon, farming
the sea, composite materials in architecture, pollution-free
engines and systems of mass transportation. In 1925
he rode a bicycle across the Soviet Union, to Siberia
from Moscow, hero of the Dziga Vertov classic
Man the Rider. Vertov (whose actual name was Kaufman) chased him
across vast territories of new Republics, a man blown down
bad roads, fighting elements in his rain slicker and aviator goggles,
documenting enthusiasm for the Bolshevik Revolution in hundreds
of little villages with scruffy men tottering out tuba, fiddle
and klezmer bands under homemade red banners.
The film itself destroyed by Stalin's censors, he only had a couple photographs:
one standing by his bike in a dusty village lane, uniformed rider on a horse
staring at him from behind impassively, he himself grinning,
a strong young man with his shirt open, lank hair over one eye
—the only piece of the whole Vertov film a still taken from a high
Moscow window at the start, his small figure arched in one corner,
turning up the angle of an immense, empty boulevard. The Constructivists
loved that geometry. During his journey he'd stopped over in the first Jewish
Republic, was photographed shaking hands with the president
for the Yiddish newspaper; he had the scrap of a clipping generations
even after the people had all been liquidated. How had he escaped?
He shrugged, he had never been anybody important to the Party,

they were the first to go. His friends in the Moscow Proletkult
put him in touch with the artist and architect, Vladimir Tatlin,
head of the Scientific Laboratory for Investigating Plastic Arts.
Tatlin was interested in his feats as a cyclist; they collaborated
on the building of a human powered flying machine, the air bicycle.
The design was hardly feasible, called a fantastic dream by experts,
and he and Tatlin had a falling out, the winged bicycle and human
powered transportation never revolutionized city design
as they'd hoped. That potential for the new socialist world
crushed by the Great Terror, forced collectivization in the countryside,
the NKVD scouring the cities for Trotskyites, Right Oppositionists,
wreckers, enemies of the people. He volunteered for Spain,
fought fascists, was wounded on the Ebro, sent back
to Moscow, where he was arrested as a traitor and a spy.
Imprisoned in the murderous prisons in the gulag,
released to a prison brigade in 1942 in the Great Patriotic
War, at Kursk, thrown into the largest tank battle in history,
more than a million men on each side. His battalion exterminated,
he nevertheless went all the way to Berlin. He saw what the Nazis
did throughout Russia, Byelorussia and the Ukraine, he witnessed
Russian retaliation in Germany. Told he could expect to be shot
because of 1938 charges still on his record, in Berlin
he crossed into the American sphere of influence, traveled
overland to Paris. I was sorry, but I had to laugh—
after Paris, you came to Los Angeles? New York, yes,
he said, and then Los Angeles. I still thought to be part of something
new, he said, old gray eyes full on me. City Terrace was a Jewish
neighborhood then, he said, and Brooklyn Avenue was full of Jewish shops.
Movies, the airplane industry, everything seemed new here, you know,
this city was full of promise. He clucked and shook his head,
now all my friends live in the old people's home. I took papers
out of an envelope for him to sign so that the county would pay
his housekeeper. He had little enough to tidy
in the small apartment above the avenue, with its smoky air
of an old man's sweat, cigarettes and wine. Not you,
I said. He nodded, maybe thinking he might have to move
too, soon enough. His cane leaning on the arm of his chair.
I'll come by next week and bring you some figs, I said.
He smiled and nodded, touched his finger to his temple
in a little salute. I let myself out and went downstairs,

still early in the morning, as Councilman Snyder's paid precinct
volunteers in their orange vests with Councilman Snyder's
name on them swept the sidewalks on First Street.

R. CHERAN

I Could Forget All This

Forget the flight
headlong through Galle Road
clutching an instant's spark of hope
refusing to abandon this wretched
vulnerable life
even though all directions shuddered
—and with them, my heart—

Forget the sight
of a thigh-bone protruding
from an upturned, burnt-out car

a single eye fixed in its staring
somewhere between earth and sky

empty of its eye
a socket, caked in blood

on Dickman's Road, six men dead
heads split open
black hair turned red

a fragment of a sari
that escaped burning

bereft of its partner
a lone left hand
the wrist wrenched off

a Sinhala woman, pregnant,
bearing, unbearably,
a cradle from a burning house

I could forget all this
forget it all, forget everything

But you, my girl,
snatched away and burnt
one late afternoon
as you waited in secret
while the handful of rice
—found after so many days—
cooked in its pot,
your children hidden beneath the tea bushes
low-lying clouds shielding them above—
How shall I forget the broken shards
and the scattered rice
lying parched upon the earth?

Translated from the Tamil by Lakshmi Holmström

MUHAMMAD AL-MAGHUT

After Long Thinking

Pull out the pavements,
I have no destinations anymore
I've roamed all the streets of Europe
        from my bed.
I've made love to the most beautiful women of history
        as I sit contemplating
            in a café corner

Tell my little country, vicious as a tiger
that I raise my finger like a student
        asking permission to depart or die.
But I need now the few old songs

I have guarded since my childhood.
I shall not say good-bye
nor climb on any train until my county
      returns them to me, word by word, line by line.
If she does not wish to see me anymore,
if she refuses to argue in front of passersby,
      let her speak to me from behind a wall,
      or leave the songs on the threshold in a knotted bundle.
Even if she leaves them behind a tree,
I shall hurry like a dog to snatch them up
so long as the word "freedom" in my language
      takes the shape of an electric chair.

Tell this coffin that stretches as far as the Atlantic ocean
that I do not even own the price of a handkerchief
      to mourn it.
From the stony squares of Mecca
to the dance halls of Granada
there are wounds snagged with chest hair
and medals on which only the pins remain
Now the deserts are empty of crows
and the gardens bereft of flowers.
The prisons are empty of cries for relief
and the alleys empty of people.
There's nothing but dust
      rising and falling like a wrestler's heaving breast
So run away, clouds,
the pavements of my country
      do not deserve even the mud.

Translated from the Arabic by May Jayyusi and Naomi Shihab Nye

JEET THAYIL

Spiritus Mundi

I was born in the Christian South
of a subcontinent mad for religion.

Warriors and zealots tried to rule it.
A minor disciple carried his doubt
like a torch to temple and shrine.
I longed for vision and couldn't tell it.

The cities I grew up in were landlocked.
One, a capital, buff with architecture,
the other lost for months in monsoon.
One was old, one poor; both were hot.
The heat vaporized thought and order,
drained the will, obliterated reason.

I settled, 20 and morose, in a town
built by a patricidal emperor
whose fratricidal son imprisoned him,
for eight years, with a view of the tomb
he built for his wife, to remember her.
I was overconscious of my rhyme,

and of the houses, three, inside my head.
In the streets, death, in saffron or green,
rode a cycle rickshaw slung
with megaphones. On the kitchen step
a chili plant grew dusty in the wind.
In that climate nothing survived the sun

or a pickaxe, not even a stone dome
that withstood 400 years of voices
raised in prayer and argument. The train
pulled in each day at an empty platform
where a tea stall that served passers-
by became a famous fire shrine.

I made a change: I traveled west
in time to see a century end
and begin. I don't recall the summer
of 2001. Did it exist?
There would have been sun and rain.
I was there, I don't remember

a time before autumn of that year.
Now 45, my hair gone sparse,
I'm a poet of small buildings:
the brownstone, the townhouse, the cold water
walkup, the tenement of two or three floors.
I cherish the short ones still standing.

I recognize each cornice and sill,
the sky's familiar cast, the window
I spend my day walking to and from,
as if I were a baffled Moghul in his cell.
I call the days by their Hindu
names and myself by my Christian one.

The Atlantic's stately breakers mine
the shore for kelp, mussels, bits of glass.
They move in measured iambs, tidy
as the towns that rise from sign to neon sign.
Night rubs its feet. A mouse deer starts across
the grass. The sky drains to a distant eddy.

Badshah, I say to no one there.
I hear a koel in the call of a barn owl.
All things combine and recombine,
the sky streams in ribbons of color.
I'm my father and my son grown old.
Everything that lives, lives on.

KEDARNATH SINGH

An Argument About Horses

The three of them were sitting in the sun
and arguing about horses

The horse is beautiful—the first one said
You're wrong—the second one retorted
the horse is simply solid—very solid

The third man who'd been silent until then
said softly—It's so solid
that you can't argue about it

Why can't we argue about it—the first one shouted
Of course we can argue about it—the second one agreed

The third man was silent
rather he was very pleased
flicking the ash from his cigarette he said—
But where is the horse?

So what if it isn't here
at least we can argue about it
the first one said

We can argue about it
but I'm sad I haven't seen a horse in so many years—
there was a strange kind of pain in the third man's voice

There are fewer and fewer horses
the first one said

Right—the second one replied
That's precisely the question
why are there fewer and fewer horses?

They're sold off—the first one said

But who buys so many horses
the second one asked—
there must be statistics about this somewhere
There are—said the first one
emphasizing the *are*—
but we can't get to see them

Why—why can't we get to see them—
the second man was shaking

Because the horses trample down the statistics
the first one said

His voice was so faint
it seemed he wasn't speaking to the others but only to himself

The third man who'd been silent all this while
screamed suddenly—
My friends
one day those statistics will rise
and trample down the horses

For a long time
after that
there was no more argument.

Translated from the Hindi by Vinay Dharwadker

FADWA TUQAN

My Freedom

Freedom
My freedom
words I re-echo through a mouth
                thickened with rage
under the rain of bullets
amidst the fire's flame
despite the weight of my chains
and the night
I persist
over the ebbs of wrath.
Freedom
My freedom.
I shall carve the words
in the earth
chisel their sounds
over every door in the Levant
in the Virgin's Temple
upon her holy altar
into the furrows of the fields

210

above the hillside
below the slope at every street corner
inside the prison
within the torture chamber.
I shall engrave the words
into the wood of my gallows
despite my handcuffs
the blasting of our homes.
I repeat:
Freedom
My freedom
let the words be at a spark outspreading
covering every inch in
my homeland
even the graves
that I may see
Red Freedom
knocking at every door
and lightning in this darkness
razing the shafts of fog.

Translated from the Arabic by Kamal Boullata

PHẠM TIẾN DUẬT

In the Labor Market at Giang Vo

I don't dare ask who you are,
selling your strength out on the street.
But then the rich need someone to put up their new houses.
still, they don't care who you are, where you come from.

I know you. You are the dark earth
torn from the river bend;
you are the jagged rock wrenched from the mountain.
One difference though, hunger gnaws at your gut.

These days every village must be a great city,
stacks of foods shimmer and dance in the streets.
Not lack of work, but this new life gives birth to
new lines of workers.
A new sky must mean new kinds of clouds.

Dusk crawls up the street. The crowd thins out.
No one left but you. I recognize you now,
the look of quiet resolve, the scar,
the last broken shard of war.

Translated from the Vietnamese by Nguyễn Quang Thiều and Kevin Bowen

SHANG QIN

Flying Garbage

Written on Earth Day, 1998

A gust rises.

First, a piece of old newspaper overturned, yesterday's news, today's
history, sent to the other side of the street to be trampled on once again;
then a plastic bag with pink stripes, almost transparent, floating up to
the sky, brushing the high-rise of Taiwan Electricity Company along the
way, people following its stumble with their eyes; now it heads south
along Xindian Spring, breaking up a flock of pigeons before it enters the
mountainous region of Five Streams, causing a falcon to take flight and
survey in alert while avoiding in haste the clamors and sighs of humans,
animals, cockroaches in the bag.

The garbage bag continues its journey toward White Cock Hill,
vermilion clouds write giant characters in the western sky.

Translated from the Chinese by Michelle Yeh

AHARON SHABTAI

Our Land

I remember how,
in 1946, hand in hand
we went out into the field
at the edge of Frishman Street
to learn about Autumn.
Under the rays of the sun
slanting through the October clouds
a *fallah* was cutting a furrow
with a wooden plough.
His friend wore a *jallabiya*
rolled up to his knees
as he crouched on a knoll.
Soon we will all
meet in the Tel Aviv below—
Weinstein the milkman,
and Haim the iceman,
Solganik
and the staff at the dry-goods co-op:
Hannah and Frieda and Tzitron;
and the one-armed man
from the clothing store
at the corner
near Café Ditze;
Dr. Levova
and Nurse Krasnova;
the gentle
Dr. Gottlieb.
And we'll meet Stoller
the butcher,
and his son Baruch;
and Muzikant the barber,
and Lauterbach, the librarian;
and the pretty dark-skinned lady
from the Hahn Restaurant.
And we'll meet the street-sweeper
Mr. Yaretzky,

whose widow had hanging
in her hallway
the parable-painting
showing the stages of life.
For these *fallahin* as well,
and also for the children of the village of Sumel,
who herded goats
on Frug Street,
the heart will make room
like a table
opening its wings.
For we belong
to a single body—
Arabs and Jews.
Tel Aviv and Tulkarem
Haifa and Ramallah—
what *are* they
if not a single pair of shoulders,
twin breasts?
We quarreled
like the body parts of the man
who brought the milk of the lionness
down from the mountains
in the legend told by Bialik.
Through he cracks in the earth,
we'll look up at you then;
under your feet
our land is being harrowed
with chains of steel,
and above your heads there is no sky
like a light-blue shirt—
but only the broad buttocks of the murderer.

Translated from the Hebrew by Peter Cole

ABBAS BEYDOUN

White Lie

The truth is also blood.
And it might be a piece of tongue
or something severed from us.
We might find it in semen
or in dust if these two things
are not simply appearances
and if the blood does not suddenly
vanish or whiten as a lie.
Should we let the roses
or the strokes against the chest consume
those who lost their truth
as they fought their lies.
Is it the alarm clock's fault
or do we not permit
our clocks such precise appointments.
The sun is our tryst and
we do not know what it gathers now.
We are the meeting of strangers
and we do not ask why love drives free souls
and then abandons them, to scatter,
beneath the heavy rain.

Translated from the Arabic by Fady Joudah

HSIEN MIN TOH

Crow-Shooters

I was nestled in a hammock on the balcony,
soaking in a siesta in the cool, post-rain afternoon
when the noise-shocks erupted, sudden blasts
like localized thunder, cracks of a celestial whip.
I recognized them from army days, whipped off
my hammock and caught sight of flights of birds

flapping frantically clear of the treeline,
into the backdrop of clouds, then, on the lane
to the left, the men, wearing polo T-shirts
encased in beige vests and holding long rifles.
One wore sunglasses atop his cap, another had
split his barrel from his stock and was inserting
another round. Crow-shooters. Sunglasses
took out a rubber glove and snapped it on while
crossing to the grassy bank to bag his earnings.
I recalled how, walking home donkeyed with bags
from the supermarket, I had cast a doubtful eye on
the crows, foot-long sentinels in robes glossy and
black as ink on their high perch of streetlights,
not really knowing what I was watching out for.
Not knowing if anything could ever shake
that robber-baron assurance. And here, now,
was the cavalry, the crow-shooters, laying the sins
I couldn't imagine on this murder of scared crows,
and, in that same fluid alignment of the rifle sights,
burdening me with the undoubting preemption
of my unkind nation, in whose name only I will be
able to walk up the lane with lowered head.

SUHEIR HAMMAD

nothin to waste

you don't waste nothin you
know the worth of
bread cupcakes carrots gummi bears whatever
falls gets picked up and
kissed up to god

and it's new and
fresh again good
enough to eat to
place on the table

and what about cherries busted and
sweet meat flesh about
stretch of leg tear of
muscle what about
almond surprise jelly jam pumpkin virgin pudding

can she pick herself
up back to the table and
know her worth kiss
herself back kiss
herself back and
up to god

FAWZIA AFZAL-KHAN

Amazing Grace

Amazing grace for
edelweiss and gentian
the mountain graced
with ethnic worshippers
remembering Heidi
skipping down what
could have been
these slopes

inspiring
dreams of grandeur the
I-can-do-anything
expansiveness it is
natural to feel in
the presence of a
finger pointing upward to
god

the matterhorn with
its jagged-toothed
majesty like

narcissus gazing
at his navel in the
limpid lake at its
base

up in the sky the
thrusting rock
seems poised to
prick the clouded
bosom, its anima
and then—the shift

a plane crosses
bang
in the middle
cleaving the one
from the other
the rock bereft in
its erection

from another
angle
on the train ride
down the
cloud re-forms
maternal bosom
now comforts the
tip

of its sawed-off
pride, which having
found a place
to hide
recoups to
re-emerge tomorrow
and bend the world to its
will   again

MARNE L. KILATES

Python in the Mall

A serpent-like creature has taken residence
in the dark recesses of a new shopping mall.
Supposedly the offspring of the mall tycoon
himself, the creature feeds, by preference,
on nubile virgins.

—Tabloid story

She hatched in the dank
Basements of our gullibility,
Warmed in the gasp of our telling,
Curling in the tongues
Of housewives and clerks.

We gave her a body half-serpent,
Half-voluptuary, and a taste
For maidens and movie stars
Who began to vanish mysteriously
Behind the curtains of boutique
Fitting rooms and water closets,
Never to be seen again,
Or only to be found in the parking
Cellars, wandering dazed
Into the headlights of shoppers' cars.

How she fed on our thirst
For wonders, fattened on our fear
Of vacant places. Slowly
We embellished the patterns
On her scales and admired
The sinuous grace of her spine.

Avidly we filled our multifarious
Hungers at her belly, and lapped
The marvelous tales of her forked
Tongue. And as the gleaming temples

Of her worship rose in the midst
Of our squalor, how we trembled
At the seduction of her voice,
O what adoring victims we became.

S. SIVASEGARAM

Ahalya

Stones.
Above the earth, beneath the earth,
hillocks and mountains,
rocks and fragments,
standing upright, fallen down,
stones.

Her husband, the sage, was a stone.
The god was a liar, but
no stone he,
only a male deity who lived
to survive the curse.
And she who had lived like stone
coming alive for that instant alone
truly became a stone.

On a day much later,
a god who crossed the seas to rescue a lover
only to thrust her
into burning flames—
who feared the town's gossip
and exiled her—
an avatara, unworthy of touching a stone—
stumbled upon her.

Had she not changed again
stone becoming woman
to live like a stone with a stone,

Had she remained truly a stone
she might have stood forever,
a mountain peak, undestroyed by time.

Translated from the Tamil by Lakshmi Holmström

Author's Note: Ahalya was seduced by the god Indra, who disguised himself as her husband, the sage Gotama. Gotama cursed Ahalya, turning her into stone. The curse was revoked by Rama's touch. The third stanza of the poem refers to Rama's rescue of his wife Sita from Lanka, Sita's fire test and exile. Rama was an avatara, or incarnation, of the god Vishnu.

MOHAMMAD KAZEM KAZEMI

excerpt from "Return"

I am the one who's circled the horizon, end to end
If I was seen by someone, but in passing was I seen
Whenever I had bread to eat, it was of sun-baked brick
My table—if I had one—but with hunger overflowed
Each mirror that you happen by—my breaking shall recall
Wherever stone on stone was laid—a memoir of my hand
Whether out of spite or kindness, I am known by all
Yes, all the people of this city know me, one and all
I've stood up straight, however much the sky above was skewed
I've prayed, although I knew the age belonged to Ibn Muljam.

My talisman of exile shall be torn apart tonight
The tablecloth that I could never fill, be folded up
At sunset, in the hot breath of the road I will go
On foot just as I once arrived, on foot I will go.

Broken-backed and broken-winged I pass by you tonight
Embarrassed by your sacrifice, your kindness without bounds
I know about the chilling silence of your winter nights

My own have been made martyrs too, I know about your grief
Like me, you saw your precious stars extinguished one by one
And all that you saw of your father was his scattered ash
We passed together through the trials of exile's twisting lanes
We bore upon our shoulders the burnt bodies of the dead
When you were wounded, I was stripped and beaten with a lash
When you ate stones you offered me pure water and fresh bread.

Translated from the Persian by Zuzanna Olszewska

Author's Note: Ibn Muljam was the assassin of the Shi'a Imam Ali, whom Shi'as believe to be the rightful successor of the Prophet Muhammad. It is said that Ali was praying in a mosque at the time of his death, and knew Ibn Muljam had entered, but refused to interrupt his prayer to save his own life. The theme of common suffering refers to the period of the Iran-Iraq war and the Afghan-Soviet war in the 1980s, in which both nations sustained heavy losses.

RAFIQ AZAD

Give me *Bhaat*, Bastard

I am terribly starving: in the stomach, around the body circle
Every split second—the feeling goes on- the ravenous hunger.
Like in the month of *Choitra,* drought burns the crops-fields—
Huge burning is the blaze of hunger, the body burns.

Given twice a day two fist-full meals,
                              demand comes for nothing else
Many people beg for a lot of things, they all want:
Houses, cars, money—coins—some do have greed for fame;
Trifle is my demand: the plain field in my stomach will get ablaze—
I want *bhaat*—cooked rice, it's a straight demand—hot or cold.
Fine or if it were very course like the rice from the (state) *ration*
No harm; I want *bhaat* on an earthen plate—*shaanki*—filled up.
For two fist-full meals two times a day,
                              I let go of all other demands.

I have no unreasonable greed, even, no sex demand.
I didn't want the *sari* worn beneath the navel, its owner;
Let those who want them take them away,
                                    offer it to whoever you wish
Just remember: I have no need for those.

If you can't meet this trifle demand from me,
Great sacrificial events will occur all over your realm.
There is nothing good or bad, law and order to the starving.
Whatever is up front, would get eaten effortlessly.
Nothing would be left over, all would get into
                                    the devouring wretched mouth
If, suddenly I get, for instance, you, face to face:
That would be tasty morsel to the ravenous hunger.
When the hunger for little *bhaat* is all-devouring
It brings perilous endings by invitation!
Gobbles the whole action from the scene to the seer.
I will at last eat one by one: trees, rivers
Villages-markets, footpaths, waterfalls in the drain,
Traveling pedestrians, buttocks-prime women,
The food minister flying flag included and the minister's car—
Nothing is today trivial to my hunger.

Give me *bhaat* bastard, else I will munch the map!

Translated from the Bengali by Quader Mahmud

Author's Note: Choitra—the second month in the Bangla calendar (pre-summer);
bhaat—cooked plain rice, staple Bengali food; *ration*—controlled sale of foodstuff by
the government; *shaanki*—earthen plate, traditional rural plate, also a symbol of poverty.

LINH DINH

Eating Fried Chicken

I hate to admit this, brother, but there are times
When I'm eating fried chicken
When I think about nothing else but eating fried chicken,
When I utterly forget about my family, honor and country,
The various blood debts you owe me,
My past humiliations and my future crimes—
Everything, in short, but the crispy skin on my fried chicken.

But I'm not altogether evil, there are also times
When I will refuse to lick or swallow anything
That's not generally available to mankind.

(Which is, when you think about it, absolutely nothing at all.)

And no doubt that's why apples can cause riots,
And meat brings humiliation,
And each gasp of air
Will fill one's lungs with gunpowder and smoke.

'ABD-ALLAH AL-BARADUNI

From Exile to Exile

My country is handed over from one tyrant
to the next, a worse tyrant;
from one prison to another,
from one exile to another.
It is colonized by the observed
invader and the hidden one;
handed over by one beast to two
like an emaciated camel.

In the caverns of its death
my country neither dies

nor recovers. It digs
in the muted graves looking
for its pure origins
for its springtime promise
that slept behind its eyes
for the dream that will come
for the phantom that hid.
It moves from one overwhelming
night to a darker night.

My country grieves
in its own boundaries
and in other people's land
and even on its own soil
suffers the alienation
of exile.

Translated from the Arabic by Diana Der-Hovanessian with Sharif S. Elmusa

PIREENI SUNDARALINGAM

Letters from Exile

These are the letters I leave behind me,
dull lines written for the censor's eye.
There are no stories here,
only headlines,
statements of fact,
shielding the truth.

But how can I write my life without politics
when each word placed is part of an equation?
Talk of my income will be translated
into an exact amount for blackmail or ransom;
Talk of our culture will be interpreted
as a covert call to arms.

I cannot tell you
that I am learning our language,
that I stand as a poet on a Western stage
crying out the loss of our country.

I cannot send you
photographs or cassette tapes.
You will not see my hair turn gray
or my voice change accent
as I become American.

I cannot even send you postcards
because such pictures
are considered currency in our country
and will go home with the postman
to be traded for food.

I write these words for you
knowing the line of people that stand between us:
my cousin, who will sit beside you, translating,
the villagers, hoping for news of their families,
and the government clerk, who will slit open
this letter, like all the others,
checking each word,
over and over,
the most sensitive audience I could ask for.

CAROLYN MARIE SOUAID

Apology to Orhan Pamuk

Comrade, how is it so?
Fined by the high court—

for what? Trafficking a thought?
You, an accomplished lover

of the pen.

Who challenged the Turkish flank
for far, far more than a girl.

How do I walk these streets?
How do I breathe this air

while, heroic, you stand

eulogizing the thousands
flattened on your land?
Risking an emporium bullet,
your name in the news.

I, who am one of you
and not of you.

Fattened on the minutiae of Art:
Idolizing my muse

and the metaphorical prisons
of the heart.

Author's Note: In January 2006, the court dropped charges against the novelist, accused of insulting the Turkish republic for openly writing and speaking against the genocide of Armenians in 1915, a taboo subject and one that officially never happened, according to the Turkish government.

MENG LANG

Facing a Nation

The man stands opposite a nation
Thoughts of going nuclear
Bring his finger to a button on his jacket

Thoughts of going nuclear
By a man facing fruit that is utterly exposed

The man stands opposite a nation
He has blanked out
His jacket a withered bloom that hangs
From the limp crook of his elbow

The border guards of a nation
Concerned with every button on clothes of travelers
Forbid the passage of nervous nuclear notions

The man is concerned with border guards
Past whom the notion of going nuclear now carries
A basket of luscious apples to the opposite nation

Translated from the Chinese by Denis C. Mair

WALID BITAR

A Moral Climate

Before you invaded, we were outsiders.
Now we've got decor to mess around with,
windows defining our views and shutters
designed to make us introspective.

Already, the sky seems less sound and thoughts
that had been public when taken seriously
are replacing property we lost
as private sources of entertainment.

Someone high up, no deus ex machina,
who, after all, must follow a script,
but a god with manners of a mammal,
taught us to fetch, roll over and play dead.

More powers like him, and fewer creatures
until the ratio is one to one.
What's greater than the sum of its degrees?
This climate we are persuaded is moral.

We'd be bored if not for the violence
with which the past is suppressed—memory
went underground, then became a dungeon,
and still we're called revolutionary.

Thank your intelligence I'm not divine.
So much easier being one of the facts
which are as infinite as I am finite,
an apple a day for their digestive tract.

The Sphinx's riddle our masses voted
for in order to avoid answering
is now free in the ocean whose waves
take care of their own breaking and entering.

We know the difference between our speeches
and the reality they're fighting off;
it's in no single weight category,
can't recognize any sparring partners.

Why fight fair then? Let connections run wild—
I mean the people put in their places,
and mine as well. I promise you won't find
our flesh a theme without variations.

MONZER MASRI

A Dusty Skull

In the arts center
On a shelf in the culture department
Dismembered gods
Plaster gills
And deaf ears.
\
On the last shelf
Among wracks of broken sculpture specimens
A dusty skull

Everybody disdains to care about
Peeps its head.
\
I carried it in my trembling hands
And put it on a white towel
In front of me on the table
And here it has been for the last two hours
Staring at me with its hollow look
That has no bottom.

Translated from the Arabic by the author

NADIA ANJUMAN

The Silenced

I have no desire for talking, my tongue is tied up.
Now that I am abhorred by my time, do I sing or not?
What could I say about honey, when my mouth is as bitter as poison.
Alas! The group of tyrants has muffled my mouth.
This corner of imprisonment, grief, failure and regrets—
I was born for nothing that my mouth should stay sealed.
I know O! my heart, It is springtime and the time for joy.
What could I, a bound bird, do without flight.
Although, I have been silent for long, I have not forgotten to sing,
Because my songs whispered in the solitude of my heart.
Oh, I will love the day when I break out of this cage,
Escape this solitary exile and sing wildly.
I am not that weak willow twisted by every breeze.
I am an Afghan girl and known to the whole world.

Translated from the Dari by Abdul Salam Shayek

XIONG HONG

Dark Associations

the dusk: eyes that have wept
watching me, all feeling in flames

and ultimately, that which is visible
and that which is not—
the flames of the five thousand colors go out as one
    (you could not bear my trust)

in darkness, the forest trail; in darkness, the wide bridge
    while the demon hand that conducts fate is already arranging
(the minute hand chases the hour hand, sure to overtake it)
is already arranging—
in darkest night an even darker death at a quarter past seven

with a shock I realize that the dark moment is over
what is done can't be undone
    even if you look to the west, regretfully

Translated from the Chinese by Simon Patton

HAYAN CHARARA

Thinking American

for Dioniso D. Martínez

Take Detroit, where boys
are manufactured into men, where
you learn to think in American.
You speak to no one unless someone
speaks to you. Everyone is suspect:
baldheaded carriers from the post office;
old Polish ladies who swear
to Jesus, Joseph, and Mary;
your brother, especially your brother,

waiting in a long line for work.
There's always a flipside.
No matter what happens,
tomorrow is a day away,
or a gin bottle if you can't sleep,
and if you stopped drinking,
a pack of cigarettes. After that,
you're on your own, you pack up
and leave. You still call
the city beside the strait home.
Make no mistake, it's miserable.
After all, you bought a one-way
Greyhound ticket, cursed each
and every pothole on the road out.
But that's where you stood
before a mirror in the dark,
where you were too tired
to complain. You never go back.
Detroit is a shithole, it's where
you were pulled from the womb
into the streets. Listen,
when I say Detroit, I mean any place.
By thinking American, I mean made.

HILMY SALEM

Trembling

We can resist the sectarian kings
With a single turn in the opposite direction.
But given how nimble we are
The strong ones tremble
Every time two people exchange a smile.
But for those who trade in doubt
Before love, and after it,
Our gift to them: a crutch.

Translated from the Arabic by Dima Hilal and Idra Novey

HASAB AL-SHAIKH JA'FAR

Signature

Every day I see her in front of clinics, surgeries, huddled and clasping her little girl, staring at the passing elegant women. Her own dilapidated house glows in its village of smoke and straw. She prepares tea for us. Her husband arrives with the political mail from the dark palm grove. At the end of the night we leave some of our secrets behind in his house, where we discuss countryside problems. Trembling with cold over a dim lantern. Suspicious foreign birds scream. The surgeries close up. And the glittering cabarets open to reveal soiled nakedness. On which bank did he stumble to fall bleeding, stopped by the bullet in his shoulder?

> He said nothing
> but bled in the stone police station
> until the night ended
> and they wrapped him up
> in the bloody mat.

The political mail waits in the dark roots of the palm grove. The door of the crumbling house bursts open. A bloody dust falls. And the net of the law falls over her. Water, let me go to the bank of the river to carve his face on its stones. Let me hang, like posters, his papers on the palm trees. Let our dim lantern be lit with an eternal flame. Let the surgery doors spring open and al-Rumaila fling its arms around the palms where we first felt the pulse of politics. Waters, take me to that bank where I can spread the waves of his shirt where the bullet pierced. Let me catch a boat to cross. And write on the cheerful face of the water.

> Let me write a name
> which the files have folded away
> in the stone police station
> to be wrapped in a bloody mat.

Her name fades on petition. Every day in front of government offices I see her clasping her little girl under her cape and staring at the elegant women passing. The agricultural superintendent scolds her through the steam of coffee and smoke of his cigarette. Waters, take me to that bank where I can dig in the dark palm grove, and take out sheets of growing grass to hang like flags over the collapsing house in al-Rumaila. On the horizon, the stone police station. Water, take me to the bank where I can carve a face on the rocks. I see him every day in front of the surgeries, humiliated. Elegant women pass by. I am carving something about palm trees where we began to feel the pulse of politics.

Translated from the Arabic by Diana Der-Hovanessian with Salma Khadra Jayyusi

KETAKI KUSHARI DYSON

A Woman Reflects on Mutability

As a man discards a worn out garment and puts on one that is new, so the spirit discards a worn out body and moves on to one that is new.

—Bhagavad Gita, II, 22

We were born
into a patrilinear society:
we could not help it.

Unthinking,
we took the names of our forefathers,
as our foremothers slunk back,
useless as unfertilized eggs
along the oviducts of history,
but like ghosts
they could keep us in their possession.

At first we played round the basil bush,
and with candies for consolation,
had our ears pierced by fine gold wires.
Then we were set to work.

Halfway through our lives,
damming wild flood-waters,
glancing up, we happened to notice
our names dangling from the noticeboard:
lists of workers
and intricate time-tables,
day-shifts, night-shifts.

What a surprise met our eyes;
our names were altered;
the old selves had been traded in;
the new models were out.

Later still we were entirely discarded,
some being retained
as antiques in museums,
but most were given over
to sprawling junkyards
where we were carefully rifled
of our still grinding parts.

And as we were dismantled,
it was a marvel to discover
how the parts were correlated
and ticked away together.

Birds migrate,
but we have transmigrated
within one lifetime.
Or were these the lives
which Krishna, his temples graying,
half scratching his head,
vulnerable but diplomatic,
had tried to indicate,
when he rambled on the field
on the eve of the battle
about people changing clothes
and souls changing bodies?

ASHUR ETWEBI

Politics

Because the African woman sang and wept,
darkness retreats trembling.
Her voice burns bit by bit
the heart's core.
From a spot in the dark
daylight emerges.

People are classes.
The upper is featureless,
the middle featureless,
the lower featureless.
Nonetheless they differ.

It's beautiful to breathe this deeply.
It's beautiful to say what I want.
It's beautiful that you feel me from a distance.
It's beautiful to love without stopping.

I bring a soul close to me
and distance myself from the commandments
that have accompanied me since the first cell split.
Before me the city that refused me blazes,
its cold essence scandalized.
I gather my conscience around me
and with a pronounced slowness rearrange my dreams.

Here our things scattered,
our laughs were defeated.
Here we were stunned by the colors of the seasons,
and their meekness betrayed us.
Here we rank the same as a mouse's tail.

Beware:
two lines of blood
on the dirt,
and an aged corpse

under the coats
of the midget
....
men.

Translated from the Arabic by Khaled Mattawa

TASLIMA NASRIN

At the Back of Progress . . .

The fellow who sits in the air-conditioned office
is the one who in his youth raped
                         a dozen or so young girls
and at the cocktail party, he's secretly stricken with lust
fastening his eyes on the belly button of some lovely.
In the five-star hotels, this fellow frequently
                    tries out his different tastes
                    in sex acts with a variety of women.
This fellow goes home and beats his wife
                         over a handkerchief
                         or a shirt collar.
This fellow sits in his office and talks with people
                              puffing on a cigarette
                              and shuffling through his files.

               Ringing the bell he calls his employee
                                   shouts at him
                         orders the bearer to bring tea
                                        and drinks.
          This fellow gives out character references for people.

The employee who's speaking in such a low voice
that no one knows or would ever suspect
how much he could raise his voice at home,
                    how foul his language could be
                    how vile his behavior.
Gathering with his buddies, he buys some movie tickets
and kicking back on the porch outside, indulges

in loud harangues on politics, art and literature.
Someone is committing suicide   his mother
                                                     or his grandmother
                                              or his great-grandmother.
Returning home he beats his wife
                               over a bar of soap or
                               the baby's pneumonia.

The bearer who brings the tea
who keeps the lighter in his pocket
and who gets a couple of tākā as a tip:
he's divorced his first wife for her sterility,
his second wife for giving birth to a daughter,
he's divorced his third wife for not bringing dowry.
Returning home, this fellow beats his fourth wife
over a couple of green chilis or a handful of cooked rice.

Translated from the Bengali by Carolyne Wright and Mohammad Nurul Huda

KHALIL REZA ULUTURK

The Poet's Voice

I don't want freedom gram by gram, grain by grain.
I have to break this steel chain with my teeth!
I don't want freedom as a drug, as a medicine,
I want it as the sun, as the earth, as the heavens!
Step, step aside, you invader!
I am the loud voice of this land!
I don't need a puny spring,
I am thirsting for oceans!

Translated from the Azeri by Aynur H. Imecer

Author's Note: This poem has also been published with the title "The Voice of Africa."
During the Soviet period, many Azeri poets used other geographical locations in their
poems to disguise their feelings about their own country and their own situation so that
the Soviet censors would not suspect the true meaning and ban their works.

LUISA A. IGLORIA

Hill Station

Baguio City, Philippines

We found conditions exactly as described in the Spanish report. . . . It took us
but a short time to decide that here was an ideal site for a future city. . . . [T]here
were scores of places where, in order to have a beautiful house lot, one needed
only to construct driveways and go to work with a lawnmower.

> —Dean C. Worcester, Secretary of the Interior, 1898. *The*
> *Philippine Islands and their people: a record of personal*
> *observation and experience with a short summary of the*
> *more important facts in the history of the archipelago*

These are the woods through which they came—at the turn
of the last century, riding ponies from base camp, where the rail-
road could not climb further. Cutting through virgin

brush and green pine so thick the fragrance
reminded them of New England, thousands of miles
away. *All one needs is a map and a lawnmower,* exulted Dean

Worcester in his journals, between ornithology
notes. The birds still arrive from sojourning in far-off
islands, punctual as November and its haul of sun-

flowers. But the pine is thinner today, above Burnham Park
where a bust of the Chicago architect stands, its bronze
nose shiny as a beacon-flare pinning this city down

in its hollow of rock and limestone. I can walk
from the City Hall and the pathways around the man-
made lake (really the size of a large duck-pond),

past the soccer field and the grandstand, up
Session Road, named because American officials sat
in session there every summer, fleeing the choking heat,

mosquitoes and malaria in the provinces.
They would not give up their top hats,
their cravats, their coat-tails, their waistcoats

and wool trousers; their wives, those yards of skirts
and heavy petticoats. They gave the native
girls their first white blouses; a Christian gesture,

they stressed—embarrassed by the abundance of brown
breasts, bosoms paganly adorned with layers of onyx
and carnelian, smoky agate, gold leaf and traded shells,

polished to brittleness. You see such heirloom beads now
only in antique shops, wrapped in oilcloth or resting
in the shallow lip of a food basket. Mothers bring them

to exchange for cash, thinking of daughters and sons
anxious to leave the city in the mountains, thinking of new
things they might become: teachers, lawyers, even doctors

or nurses in that other land, America. And I can walk
further east, toward rows of wooden cottages with stone
chimneys on Cabinet Hill, arranged on a rise—reminding me

of the summer we took a trolley tour of Washington:
the guide drove us downhill through Embassy Row,
our heads spinning like tennis balls as she volleyed

and served from left to right and back, naming the flags
of countries that fluttered on each side of the street.
The neatly painted houses with their trim

gardens and hedges, this country of precisely
numbered doors, the solid names of streets—Jackson,
Monroe, Jefferson, Adams—the same I saw

repeated reassuringly in every city: New York,
Chicago, San Francisco, and all the small
midwestern towns I visited between. There were boys

in my fourth grade class with names like Monroe Gawigawen
and Jefferson Palpallatoc. They were of Igorot stock, again
what you might call native. For this the other kids teased them;

even then they thought themselves more citified, cleansed of their savage
origins. Monroe had a limp. I hear he sports long hair and has become
a human rights lawyer. I do not know what happened to Jefferson.

DUO DUO

When People Rise from Cheese
STATEMENT #1

Songs, but the bloody revolution goes unnoticed
August is a ruthless bow
The vicious son walks out of the farmhouse
Bringing with him tobacco and a dry throat
The beasts must bear cruel blinders
Corpses encrusted in hair hang
From the swollen drums of their buttocks
Till the sacrifices behind the fence
Become blurry
From far away there comes marching a troop
Of smoking people

Translated from the Chinese by John Rosenwald and The Beliot/Fudan
Translation Workshop

PRATHIBHA NANDAKUMAR

At the Staircase

Standing beside the serpentine staircase
he pleaded
come, come away with me,
be my woman.

Holding the heavy bag
full of vegetables and groceries
I wiped the sweat off my forehead
with the worn-out end of the sari.

He was quite serious
Is this life?
How pale you have become,
What happened to you,
When did you last write a poem?

Pushing my curls away, he whispered
You are a fool, this is not the end.
Poverty leads to desperation.
Have you ever put the change into your purse
Without counting?
Ever bought the dress off a mannequin?

I just listened to him.
The bag was beginning to be very heavy.

I climbed the serpentine staircase and
removed the *chappals* at the door.
Put the vegetables and groceries away
and sat down to watch my favorite TV program.

There is still half an hour before I serve dinner.

Translated from the Kannada by the author

YANG MU

Fallen Leaves

1
How does an awakened heart examine the blood trails of old
under the remnant icewalls of thorns, snakeberries, and
caltrops? Leaning, I listen to how the beetles and chrysalises

measure with their humble trails the obscure path
from death to rebirth, the journey we have vowed
to take, all the actions of a pilgrimage
and our questioning. When the scorching
sun first enters a shared night
and moderates the temperature, so that our earth
can obtain a solid intellectual basis as it turns at an angle
how the moon in its own track of revolution, in total eclipse
intimates the law of human partings and togetherness. But we
still argue the night before our journey
about each other's direction, deepening in the impassioned darkness of
    last night
—the disintegration of desire, watermarks on frosted glass
drawing repeatedly dragon-patterns, a sketch of ethical
symbols—the memory of spring rain tapping the window
a relentless debate. But before the day breaks
the rain has stopped, the group of pilgrims
left a long time ago. Partridges coo far and near

2

Summertime, we live in the village of orange orchards, evenings
we listen to Granny's stories about the old war and close family
up till the time of the 2-28 Incident. In the mixed scent of mosquito
    repellant and jasmines wafting from the yard I fall asleep
Dreaming of carefree flying, like a red-crowned crane thrusting forth
    from the matting of a Chinese scroll, an almost transparent snow-white
spreading its large cartwheel wings, floating amidst
an ascending range of mountains. Time shifts its balance
in the wind, changing speed as it pleases
The seven colors of the cosmos turn instantaneously
casting me behind in the dim, ever-widening net
at the nexus of dots and lines, broken connections and curves
I bid a silent farewell to yesterdays
The scattered clouds and layered greenness, at this moment
under my gaze at a counter-clockwise reality
take on a coloring from the foothills and the peaks—
melting into sea-blue angelic eyes, looking down
at the lush vegetation world in the great heat
Locking in the seasonal pattern of decay, pointing to a rebirth
like written words illuminating

3

Revolving like this toward a key entity
the final completion. The dew drips white drops first
on the dense slender-eyed foliage of aging trees
A falling star glides off the southwest sky unexpectedly
near the water, soon after the midnight frost
Frost flies up the unpainted wattle fence, we
look up from our books. Perhaps it's the last
fireflies of the year hurrying from the scattered classics
to prove that reading could also mean the collapse of
private imaginings; or it's the virus of creativity spreading
to the dark night as sweet as fruit juice. Crickets
screech in the drafty western chamber where we comprehend
decay as we sit down to read the *Songs of the South*
till all the stars have changed their seasonal colors
indicating work done, and our stagnant thoughts
can't keep up with the universe revolving in greatness
outside the window, toward an organic completion
I sit up to inquire, pressured like never before
Nebulous clouds surge and sail on
A leaf falls, making the wind chime sing

4

Then your magic mirror begins to reveal to us
all the expediencies. Sure enough:
earth always slants toward the domain of dreams
when the heart is at its bleakest
Without hesitation, I choose the day
when the sea shows the first signs of cooling
In the woods small creatures like sparks of memory
their hair growing fast on the back, scamper
in the clearings covered with dry twigs and leaves
The owls of reason hoot, bouncing echoes
shake some trees from time to time
even impact the dimmest sunset
after the first snowfall, when you sit facing north
in front of the window punching on the computer keyboard
while I, under the lamp, re-read the early Virginia Woolf
I can hear a tree, perhaps more than one
roaring like a rolling tide, leaning toward the dark

land. The snow becomes heavier all of a sudden
a white crane flies up in fright, perches on
another branch, its wings closing, an image of purity from one to zero.

Translated from the Chinese by Michelle Yeh

Translator's Note: The "2-28 Incident" refers to the riot of Taiwanese people in protest against the Nationalist government and its brutal suppression of the uprising in 1947. The riot was triggered by an incident that took place in Taipei on February 28, 1947, hence the name of the historical event. The Incident was a taboo topic under the Nationalist regime until the lifting of martial law in 1987. Since then, the government has offered an official apology to the victims' families and established a memorial statue.

MAHMOUD DARWISH

In Jerusalem

In Jerusalem, and I mean within the ancient walls,
I walk from one epoch to another without a memory
to guide me. The prophets over there are sharing
the history of the holy . . . ascending to heaven
and returning less discouraged and melancholy, because love
and peace are holy and are coming to town.
I was walking down a slope and thinking to myself: How
do the narrators disagree over what light said about a stone?
Is it from a dimly lit stone that wars flare up?
I walk in my sleep. I stare in my sleep. I see
no one behind me. I see no one ahead of me.
All this light is for me. I walk. I become lighter. I fly
then I become another. Transfigured. Words
sprout like grass from Isaiah's messenger
mouth: "If you don't believe you won't be safe."
I walk as if I were another. And my wound a white
biblical rose. And my hands like two doves
on the cross hovering and carrying the earth.
I don't walk, I fly, I become another,
transfigured. No place and no time. So who am I?
I am no I in ascension's presence. But I

think to myself: Alone, the prophet Muhammad
spoke classical Arabic. "And then what?"
Then what? A woman soldier shouted:
Is that you again? Didn't I kill you?
I said: You killed me . . . and I forgot, like you, to die.

Translated from the Arabic by Fady Joudah

VIJAY SESHADRI

The Disappearances

"Where was it one first heard of the truth?"

On a day like any other day,
like "yesterday or centuries before,"
in a town with the one remembered street,
shaded by the buckeye and the sycamore—
the street long and true as a theorem,
the day like yesterday or the day before,
the street you walked down centuries before—
the story the same as the others flooding in
from the cardinal points is
turning to take a good look at you.
Every creature, intelligent or not, has disappeared—
the humans, phosphorescent,
the duplicating pets, the guppies and spaniels,
the Woolworth's turtle that cost forty-nine cents
(with the soiled price tag half-peeled on its shell)—
but from the look of things, it only just happened.
The wheels of the upside-down tricycle are spinning.
The swings are empty but swinging.
And the shadow is still there, and there
is the object that made it,
riding the proximate atmosphere,
oblong and illustrious above
the dispeopled bedroom community,
venting the memories of those it took,

their corrosive human element.
This is what you have to walk through to escape,
transparent but alive as coal dust.
This is what you have to hack through,
bamboo-tough and thickly clustered.
The myths are somewhere else, but here are the meanings,
and you have to breathe them in
until they burn your throat
and peck at your brain with their intoxicated teeth.
This is you as seen by them, from the corner of an eye
(was that the way you were always seen?).
This is you when the President died
(the day is brilliant and cold).
This is you poking a ground-wasps' nest.
This is you at the doorway, unobserved,
while your aunts and uncles keen over the body.
This is your first river, your first planetarium, your first popsicle.
The cold and brilliant day in six-color prints—
but the people on the screen are black and white.
Your friend's mother is saying,
Hush, children! Don't you understand history is being made?
You do, and you still do. Made and made again.
This is you as seen by them, and them as seen by you,
and you as seen by you, in five dimensions,
in seven, in three again, then two,
then reduced to a dimensionless point
in a universe where the only constant is the speed of light.
This is you at the speed of light.

BUFFALOES UNDER DARK WATER

Buffaloes Under Dark Water

— MONIZA ALVI

In 1991, I took a yearlong trip back to Taiwan. On one of my excursions, I decided to visit *Alishan,* a place famed for its sea of clouds at sunrise that wrap around the cedars and cliffs, about two thousand meters above sea level. My friend and I arrived in the small town at nightfall on the eve of Chinese New Year. As our bus pulled in, it began to rain. The rain quickly developed into a torrential storm, and my friend became ill from eating an entire box of mooncakes that afternoon. We walked from house to house, knocking on doors, asking for food or shelter. At each house, the owners would shake their heads: no vacancies for the night. They pointed higher and higher up the mountain. Exhausted and drenched, there was no choice but to keep walking.

In our last effort, an old woman opened her door and allowed us in. She said she had no rooms left but she did have an empty attic and one blanket. Anything was better than returning to the downpour, so we climbed up the stairs and discovered it was less an attic than a crawlspace. Hunkering down, we tunneled our way in, lay down on the damp wood, sharing a square of blanket between us. The wind seemed about to tear the tin roof off with its teeth. In spite of the thrashing rain, the terrible cold, and my friend's moans of discomfort beside me, I fell into a deep sleep that seemed very long and peaceful. When I awoke, I could see the clouds from where I lay through a tiny window; full, mammoth clouds that surged forward like waterfalls raging over the mountains, the horizon glowing with otherworldly light.

More than fifteen years later, Indian poet Anjum Hasan's "A Place Like Water" triggered the memory of that scene, and I wondered how these experiences could have taken place in separate parts of the world yet speak so intimately to each other:

All through the day it stays: the sadness of coming
  into a wet city at dawn, not speaking, neither of us,
when one by one the neon lights wake us from a cramped,
  dream-ravaged sleep, driving home in one long curving sweep
on traffic-less roads with their morning walkers and damp dogs;
  still thinking of that other place worked on by the sun,
the casuarina trees and shouts of people on the beach, frayed and
  muffled by the heaving of the sea. We climb wet stairs where
no one's been for days . . .

The poems in this section speak to universal experiences, sensations, desires; this poem continues on in a way that was eerily similar to my own trip long ago to *Alishan*:

                    Instead a winter monsoon
blurs the world; we wash our hair, shake out sand from folded clothes,
  sleep for a while in the still early morning while vendors shout
the names of flowers, sleep so that our bones at least achieve that
  calm alliance with our breathing and take us where we
want to go: a place like water when it lifts us in a magnet wave
  to set us down again, and we're unencumbered, weightless, brave;
our questions turn to images of strangers waving across fields,
  pointlessly, insistently, across fields, through falling rain.

What is it that we seek to glean from poems but a shadow of our own human experience? When we subtract rationale, logic, even narrative consistency, we are led by the essence, feeling, and raw energy of song, the purity of a given moment. On another trip, in Japan, I found myself lost among the houses, manicured gardens, and stray dogs of Kyoto. As I wrestled with an oversized map, a backpack buckled around my waist, I noticed a woman balanced on *zori* with an umbrella in hand. Though I had seen many women dressed in traditional costume, I hadn't seen a woman like this before. She exemplified a grace and solitude that was at once as holy as it was alarming.

Can beauty be that powerful, that magnetic? She saw me watching her and disappeared between the houses. I'm not sure what prompted me to follow her. I didn't know what I was searching for or if I wanted to ask her a question, though I tried to follow without disturbing her. I suppose I thought that if I could just get a picture of her, some of her beauty would be mysteriously transferred to me by some magic process of distillation.

Who hasn't irrationally, or even foolishly, pursued a single, fleeting moment, trying to prolong it, capture its essence, even as it is passing? As the moment lives, it is also dying. However fast I ran in my heavy boots through the maze-like alleys of Kyoto, I could not catch up with her. A glimpse of dark hair, the hem of her dress, or the tip of her umbrella were all I could catch of her. These small hints of her presence, like puzzle pieces, dared me to wonder if my vision of her was real at all. I finally snapped a picture, and when I developed it, I saw nothing but a strip of color that was her *obi* and some wind rushing past. Though it was this hue, this wind, I think I saw it as a lesson: I possessed nothing. Perhaps in letting go, I gained something: an image, a feeling, a moment experienced and then released.

Mystery fuels life. In the world of *Buffaloes Under Dark Water*, entire universes are off-kilter, nothing is rational, and everything is possible. These lyric-inspired poems reside between fog and luminescence. Existing in dark caverns, teetering between believing and not believing, creation and collapse, they defy every attempt to categorize them. The moments in these poems are stitched with invisible thread, though we are fortunate to have them within our reach, in these pages.

I was struck by the utterly imaginative, wild, and unreal excerpt from Bhanu Kapil's *The Wolf Girls of Midnapure*. The working note itself is captivating: the poem draws its inspiration from the story of two girls found in 1920s India who were suckling a mother wolf. The poem is re-envisioned in the undocumented voices of the girls:

A white smoke fills the compound. The younger and I wake in a scrawled ball in the younger's cot; she yowls all night and the stronger girls do not bear it. After the difficult bath, breakfast. Enjoindering us to eat the creamy swarm, but we are gaunt, problems. The younger sucks on the raisins I spoon off for her, but I am not a mother and set upon my own slop with some strength. A warrior must prepare for battle even on her deathbed, as my mother said. Though when they came, she looked up from her bones and with one crack in the stuff of her, she was gone.

The voice of the young wolf girl is calm and her "human" initiatives are clear and direct, though the animal beneath is purely instinctive, her wolf mother having taught her to always be prepared for confrontation and struggle. Ultimately the wolf mother's instincts were proven true when she was killed by the Reverend Father who discovered the unlikely family. Even though the savior had ushered the girls into the human world, they felt anything but saved.

By poem's end, the boundaries between man and beast disintegrate as we are left to question whether or not the speaker is pondering the heritage of these misplaced girls or human heritage as a whole, as well as gender and Indian lineage:

> *Again, the problem of heritage. When men look at me, they do not see my womanliness. A woman as I am, with a slit skin. Then I judged the perimeter. What did I see? Out of the incantations of green. Out of the hide or coat of black and red. Into the lit basin of settled life.*

Is the figure speaking as a woman taken from the wild, or a woman in Indian society? It seems that the speaker could be touching upon a number of topics from race to caste systems to sexual inequality. As a result, she is forced to confront her own identity and her own manner of seeing, after she has lost her mother and, finally, her sister, who could not adapt to the human world. The poem ends in ambiguous territory:

> *When her brown skin sheds, her sisters and brothers*
> *lick her*
>
>   *clean.*

Whether the brown skin is that of the wolf or a woman of a lower caste system, the result is that one of the girls perished when taken from her rightful place of security and nurturing. In an effort to save the girls and to usher them into a sterile and socially acceptable life, it seems that society had isolated them and sealed their demise.

Just as Bhanu Kapil's poem focuses on origin, nurturing, and the darkness of societal relations, famed Japanese poet Tamura Ryuichi seems to contemplate the relationship of speaker to significant other as well as speaker to the self. In "A Thin Line" he writes:

> *You are always alone*
> *There is something like a bitter light*
> *in the pupils of your eyes that have never shown tears*
> *I like it*
>
>   *To your blind image*
>   *this world is a desolate hunting place*

You are the winter hunter
who constantly chases down one heart

You do not believe in words

One is forced to ask with whom the figure is in dialogue. If one is always alone, perhaps the "you" is the solitary self in repose. Though as the poem moves forward, the figure becomes the stalker, consistently chasing down one love, one heart. In the landscape of winter, the person who does not believe in words seems completely alone, as if by choice. The one who is chased seems perpetually out of sight, outside the realm of the picture.

On the thin line that you walk
the smell of blood is even on the top of the snow
No matter how far we separate
I can tell

You pull the trigger
I die inside a word

The poem exists in multiple worlds. Could the poet be contemplating the divide between lovers, or the extraordinary yet brutal consequences of the writing process? Are the casualties those who love, or those who delve into the complexities of language? The answers seem to reside in the subtle details: the snow, the hunt, the kill. Though the speaker metaphorically or literally dies by poem's end, the end seems welcomed and even sought. He perishes in the process of loving something or someone so fully as to be consumed by it and taken by it. "A Thin Line" gestures toward the delicacy between self and other as well as the solitary encounters with the creative psyche.

Moroccan-born poet Rachida Madani fashions a landscape of simultaneity in the passage from "Tales of a Severed Head." Within the world of the poem, interior and exterior situations collide, the figures of man and woman are present yet transient. The train station is both a place of departure and arrival as the figures represent the force of seasons and change:

What city and what night
since it's night in the city
when a woman and a train-station argue over
the same half of a man who is leaving.

He is young, handsome
he is leaving for a piece of white bread.
She is young, beautiful as a springtime
                                    cluster

trying to flower for the last time
for her man who is leaving.

In the young woman's springtime, her youth, she grapples with her love's departure. As the train arrives, her branches break when it begins to rain inside the station. The fantastical aspects of the poem push the moment forward as the whistle and call of the train move through the length of her body, signaling an end to her journey with the beloved. There "will never be spring / again," writes Madani, indicating a clear break between the younger girl and the woman who blossoms from the harsh realizations of final separation. The "piece of white bread" the man ventures in search of might be sustenance, in the form of work. The purity and whiteness of the bread stand in stark contrast to the red of her "bleeding" as the train pulls away. By poem's end, the color white returns again in the gesture of winters passing; the season's return indicates loss, the movement of time, and the maturation of emotion, however severe. The woman, no longer young, waits for the bleeding letter and a mouthful of bread. Here, in "the first tale," flower, night, locomotive, spring, rain, bread, whistle, direction, snowfall exist in the same place, shrouded, illuminated, and disappearing all at once.

As I'm writing this now, a slow lazy rain is falling. In Brooklyn, New York, the brownstones are slick, the fire escapes dripping gray from the tops of their ladders down to the street. From my desk, I can't see what's happening below me, but I hear the cars' syncopated honking, and I hear two men shouting in the rain, something about fish. The Rolling Stones' "Beast of Burden" blasts from a neighbor's apartment. My mind wanders to fish, koi fish swimming in a hazardous carousing rhythm through the labyrinthine sewers of Brooklyn. Glittering orange machinery gliding within murky dens, gills pulsing, miniature hearts pumping, their chambers wide rooms for sleeping, and that is where I go when I am restless: below the surface, breathing through dark waters and places of inevitable glow.

—TINA CHANG

FATMA KANDIL

The Islands

Like any sea gull in the tales I set out .. alone .. when friends were clinging to my punctured boat until their palms appeared to be like hanging doves .. alone .. like a transparent piece of ice revealing her arteries .. I promised them the dead fish .. and the water was cooingly dodging the underside of my oar .. I was not seduced by the muttering of the colored fish .. and I was racing through the wild trees with spontaneous blood .. then there was an island which I named "the water's pupil" from where I could see the distant banks as they tuck themselves into the seashells .. while the shell opens its heavy eyelids and the pearl hides its sex .. I cross from the foam to the roof's yawning .. I can lean on the streets of the sea .. and fill the spirits into a glass bottle .. the steps of the horizon appeared low .. they were washed with a language I did not know .. it found peace in me so I put it to sleep under my breasts away from the heart .. like this I fluff the fog and wear it as wings so the sea can rock it between its two shores .. and when my boat sunk .. I had already supported my back on the wave's sidewalks .. I was alone .. dragging the horizon's threads from my memory .. and spinning a wide net .. human images falling in its rectangles .. bit by bit .. the water's pupil was widening ..

widening ...

Translated from the Arabic by Pauline Kaldas

LISA ASAGI

Physics

Behind a small eye of a small world, there is a place for things that have disappeared. A buildingless room visited by those who cannot stop searching for the right day, misplaced keys, drops of music, tails of footage. Who look across desks and wait to unpry. In the science of pursuit strangeness happens.

I am walking across a freezing wet lawn. Thousands of miles from home. Greenwich. Tightropes are suspended in a grid above a park. Lightbulbs evenly placed are left alive from mistake or tradition. It is so late and I am here as if to move across this one illuminated line would lead instinctively to an ending. As if zero were an ellipse. This is how my mind finds ways to keep moving. It picks up a trace and follows it. As if meaning could become a frame of reference, for me who could never take a decent photograph. In this place celebrated for partitions and beginnings, a small memory of a dream from years ago. It was a dream green with dripping walls of dilapidated factories. I am running through rooms filled with machines, miles of cloth hanging from wires finished drying so long ago they are falling apart. I climb through windows and out into the street. Everywhere, people are waiting in little lots of invisible houses cordoned off by string. Some are eating, others are crying. Street signs, even your building is missing in this dream. I search frantically for your car as light begins to fade, I run until land comes to an end.

Everyday come in with a ring of keys, through a glass door and up the stairwell, into a silence complete as a box fallen in middle of a street. Random and graceful. Slow tossed. In the midst of luminescent night traffic, beautiful streams of red and yellow uncloud an underwater scene of blue. Open the passage between mouth and nose, inhale the velocity of rendered inertia. Invisible movements take place over a tiny clear scarlet sea. The blood of everything nourishes, takes away, will always visit and then go. Leave the body, then the room, returning emotional exhaust over this planet of cities. I am falling again into the night in which you asked me to follow you home. Across the clustering of a city gathered by water. Trees slept and I followed you through hallways that slowly reappeared.

The sound of pennies tossed upon a bed is rain but sun. One morning. How even weather finds meaning in irony and the motion of spirals.

Light pools and seeps beneath waterfalls of curtain. I had been unable to sleep since coming to this place. Your hand a small warm shark dreaming in the reef of my heart. How bodies can whisper. Ribs like gills. Breathing. I could almost hear your voice. Barefoot, slow moving across carpet. How you must have sounded when you were 8.

This is the way the sun cut in while we were still dancing.

In the film of this year someone is leaning out of a window and wonders how much more the island will change while she is gone. An increase in pressure, electricity of engines, combine to create loss of consciousness in the passenger. It happens whenever departing the island. A density that gathers and drops. An anchor that keeps falling.

Every morning of this week I have woke later than I should. And each morning I find a stray eyelash on my cheek. When I was very young I would wish for things. A dog, a microscope, my own room. Meteors of concentrated daydream I would consecrate and let fly up into a ceiling so scraped I believed all of them found a way through. When was I old enough to find you, I never wished. I watched. I listened. Searching. Not a boat. A lighthouse. For spaces between. For meanings of glances. Possibilities of life outside of equations.

Science is searching for evidence of existence.

Upon the summit of a remote island, a nine-foot mirror has been placed within the mind of a telescope. It is held and adjusted by wires, hydraulics. Operated by distance in order to keep it safe from heat. Emanations of body temperature are waves disturbing the accuracy of reflection. Even the stars in the sky are echoes.

Flying now, low over ridges and curves. Muscle and bone under sheets of sand, asleep, it is a quietness almost about to wake and it makes me remember suddenly how far I am from home.

Beneath the desert of southeast New Mexico, exist remnants of a reef. Even an ocean can leave an elaborate past. Passages and tunnels. Memories geologists could not help but chart in words like galleries, labyrinths, pearl-filled lakes, unwinds deeply underground. There air is so full of stillness it reaches. Cascades of minerals fall incredible and slow from the stone sky. Walls silently sweat and weep. As if slowness could be unabsorbed.

In a small room, move your hand under my skin. To where you want to be. In the first hour of another life.

KIM SŬNG-HŬI

Sun Mass

The dark precedes the sun,
the sun destroys the dark.
Reality precedes dreams,
and then dreams destroy reality.
Hey, eagle taking the sun for a stroll
now, behind the wall of clouds,
I dare
to dream
that the sun's mysterious corpuscular waves
are linking my life to the sun.
To prevent my life from becoming an ashtray
to prevent my life from becoming
an icy mask
I dare imagine:
my fire revolving as the sun in its eternal orbit.
For ever, eternally.
Unite
my life and that enormous life.
What spinning wheel
in the void of what fog
is our thread becoming unwoven?

Translated from the Korean by Brother Anthony of Taizé

MANI RAO

§

The sky is fitted linen, stretched over sealine without a crease, pegged to
the spikes and jags of mountains, kingsize, navy, preparing to be sunshot.
Sooner than lovers can hide, no sooner than the taste of stars striking
your lips, one by one stunned and falling to light.

It's all been said and yet, need, blowing between our lips, streams inside a tree. We flowed out of time and back so soon eating eggs our own. Through each other we pass like water.

At the sun to see how it never changes, at the moon to see how it does, algae slipping beneath our feet, roots traveling and dewdrops dying in visible speed. There is no such thing as a circular river.

Unlike bread, the body becomes softer with age. We tag our children with our names, store the plaits of our daughters, stash berries under rocks and look for them later.

Held in the fangs of a wristwatch, a well-worn path of a nail in our veins, heart-hammered time trail.

No matter who two are kissing, eternity arrives, jelly bean eyes black crystal balls. The longer we look, the more we recognize and anything we could say is too obvious. The songs we like are the songs we know, and every song on the radio is about us.

RICK BAROT

Many Are Called

to burn at least one thing they once owned: she tears
the page from his book and sets light to whatever
she said to him there, words to smoke, paper

to black snow. She would like a sleep as big as
a building, whose key she firmly keeps in her hand,
its teeth writing into her palm. *Be as nothing*

in the floods, I read yesterday on the bus home,
which was a way of saying that in the dimmed glass
all of us and none of us could be found. But one

face was like sun reflecting on ice, lit by what
the Walkman poured into it, its champagnes. One
made me think of the mushroom in the woods

like a face pressed to a photocopier's flash,
the face and its goofy pain. Many are called to save
what they can: he rolls up his pants and wades

into the fountain, where the gull has its leg caught
on a wire. The bird flaps away to join the wheeling
others, their strokes on the air like diacritical

marks over the sentences uttered below them.
A friend writes about how cold he had been, nearly
drowned in the spring-melt river when the horse

tipped over. It is months away now, but still
I have him there, in the darkening field, the fireflies
a roused screensaver. Many are called to close

upon themselves like circles: Kafka, waking because
a dog is lying on him. He doesn't open his eyes
but he can feel its weight, its paw smelling

faintly of hay. Or the woman crying in the park,
her shopping cart tumbled, shoes and cans spilled out
like junk from a shark's stomach. Or the man

walking home along the houses and the lawns
of his sadness: *If there must be a god in the house . . .*
Under the new trees and the new moon of his sadness:

He must dwell quietly. Many are called to form
a deity out of what they know: he quizzes me
on the capital of every African country, he paints

his toenails silver because I ask him. A friend writes
about the church where a fresco will always show
them: cleanly naked at first, then full of the blame

of their own guile, then clothed, worried with age,
the woman in her room setting fire to something
she had, the man in the meadow, wishing his rib back.

ZHANG ER

Blue

for Krzysztof Kieslowski

a feeling akin to prayer
ignites the candle too late
to meet at a certain time and place covered with snow
on a crimson set take a seat
smoke drink coffee or tea listen to the snow's
soft voice your finger stained
with ink from the other side of the river
where paper houses are folded
into a mystery of life and death you can't refuse

as steam rises from the window an empty bridge stretching
to a lighthouse that must be there
pale sail pale boat
the face of the helmsman pale like snow
a song like a wound broadcast from an unknown place
with limelights on then off
row row row row
if there is no such place will snow still fall?

listen won't you listen
it wasn't just you passing through fictitiously
when I heard the news too late
for lines rehearsed backstage where you rowed away
"disappointed with a god"
and words better left unsaid
"you found it it's yours"
like a mystery play with an ending preordained?
blue foil postage stamp glass frame
a river rocking with images that soaked into a handkerchief
"are you crying?" "it's only water"
cut scallions whistling on the countertop

beneath a window that reaches out into the far farther
but the sounds a flute tonight and images

bring us back to shore? again
where the snow serves up a candlelit dinner
unsullied by tears? too late
to stir that snowy scene on the page
too late you still insist
on carrying your cross of true gold across the river

with eyes open wide as I watch you
under a sky that presses down from above
showing us all its true color

Translated from the Chinese by Timothy Liu

EILEEN TABIOS

Tercets from The Book of Revelation

after Rupert Thomson's The Book of Revelation

(i)

How does the air
come to pulse
like a muscle

As if your scent
lingers
before your arrival

How does the night
come to press
and smother

As if a fresh wound
must accompany
a revelation

Church bells ring
over a dark street
to fracture glass

Or was it a childhood
memory evoking
how light becomes distant

A fine, silvery mist
descends
on a wall, a city

You reach me
by penetrating past
a train's smoke and whistle

Damp hair clings
to the nape
of your neck

How can the cause
for an absence
lose relevance

How many stories
do we deny
to obviate recitation

How do we pretend
no boats mutter
along the salted, wet dock

How did I give up
your child
for an imagined affair

A pine forest
breathes for me
behind an empty house

He looked happy
before meeting
a burglar's intimacy

You can reach me
by noticing how trees
shiver by the edge of a road

How a sun
flattens the water
of a gray canal

How does release
from what you love
become "unequivocal freedom"

Sunglasses hang
against her breastbone
from a silver chain

No limits surround
the purple sheen
to Montenegro lilies

Afterwards
why do you never
hold me

How do I find
the necessary vein
I must mine

(ii)

How does one see
significance
in brackets studding a wall

Or be claimed
through a stranger's
tattoo

"I want to see you
again to know
I was not dreaming"

A church, a girl, a cloud,
a fragmented tune—of what
are they coordinates

Children cluster
within a tree's branches
like birds, fruit, pollen

A shirt cuff
so white
it forms an independent image

It has never been
my desire for men
to take second place

I always wake
before the alarm clock
begins to irradiate

A man weeps tonight
with the father
of a schizophrenic son

How does one offend
by innocently asking
"Are you happy?"

In Zanzibar
fruit bats
fragment a room's dimness

Upon meeting, you
knew to suggest
"Alchemy needs your silence"

Wildflowers override
the trenches
of a battlefield

There are days when
the world's kindness
forgives pastis imbibed at zinc bars

A man blows a saxophone
until the moon
turns to butter

To approximate immortality
through the art
of doing nothing

Burying stories
I cannot reveal
within those I can

Her hair offers
the scent of firecrackers
reaching for the Milky Way

"Put it in
me now,"
she whispers

When he wants
to protect me
he holds my wrist

The air pulses
like a muscle
attentive and fraught

C. DALE YOUNG

Proximity

I have forgotten my skin, misplaced my body.
Tricks of mind, a teacher once said: the man
with the amputated right arm convinced that he could

feel the sheets and air-conditioned air touching
the phantom skin. There must be a syndrome
for such a thing, a named constellation of symptoms

that correspond to the ghost hand and what it senses.
This morning, I felt your hand touch me on the shoulder
the way you would when you turned over in your sleep.

What syndrome describes this? Not the sense of touch
but of being touched. Waking, I felt my own body,
piece by piece, dissolving: my hands, finger by finger,

then the legs and the chest leaving the heart exposed
and beating, the traveling pulses of blood
expanding the great vessels. The rib cage vanished

and then the spine. If your right hand offends you,
wrote Mark, cut it off and throw it away,
for it is better for you to lose a part than to lose

the whole. But I have no word for this phantom
touch, and the fully real feeling of the hair
on your arm shifting over my own as your hand

moved from my shoulder and out across my chest.
Desire makes me weak, crooned the diva,
or was it Augustine faced with his own flesh?

Whisper me a few lies, god, beautiful and familiar lies.

BUDDHADEVA BOSE

Rain and Storm

Rain and storm, rain and storm, night and day.
The day gray, barren, dark. No light, no
shadows either. Just the rain's haze, the obscurity of clouds,
and the groan of trams, the rumble of traffic.

In the sky—a muted crying. In the wind—long-drawn sighs.
Long, long day. How much longer to night?
The hour weary, the moment sluggish. The rattling of time's chains
unending, unwearied.

Night. Emptiness within doors, darkness without.
Rain and storm, rain and storm.
Empty, empty heart. Failed failed night.
Just the furious city's sleepless snarl.

Emptiness in the heart, moans in the city, darkness in the sky.
Shadows, gusts of wind, voices,
murmurs, angry choked voices, elongated sighs
in the city, in the empty room, in the rain-dripping darkness,
in the clanking of time's chains—all night, all day.

The day empty, quiet as a stagnant pool. The night mute too. There's
nothing. Absolutely nothing. Creation's face
is covered with rain's gray sheet, with the windy city's
tormented voice. There's nothing. I am alone. All alone.

Captive like a blind fly on time's enormous wheel. The window
to the universe closed. The day like a stagnant pool,
dark, stifled. The night
like the bottom of an old forgotten well. And loneliness, interminable.

In the streets—crowds, bustle, madness. In offices, parks, restaurants—
work, play, getting drunk; gambling, gin, siestas
after a bone-breaking week: all indistinct, cramped.
The city numb. Rain, rain. In the streets
the jostling of shadows, the boneless procession of nightmares.

Shadowy Calcutta, without a body, without a skeleton:
irresponsible, wayward
like a dream. Myself a shadow too, trembling at the touch of a breeze
upon the wall, behind the curtain. Within my breast swing
rain and storm, rain and storm, night and day.

Translated from the Bengali by Ketaki Kushari Dyson

CHÖGYAM TRUNGPA

Haiku

The beginner in meditation
Resembles a hunting dog
Having a bad dream.

His parents are having tea
With his new girlfriend—
Like a general inspecting the troops.

Skiiing in the red and blue outfit
Drinking cold beer with a lovely smile—
I wonder if I'm one of them?

Coming home from work
Still he hears the phone
Ringing in the office.

Gentle day's flower—
The hummingbird competes
With the stillness of the air.

EVA RANAWEERA

The Poson Moon

In the lemon grove
Clear cool air
Brightened a Poson Moon
The lemon trees opened
Scented petals spilt into the night
Secretly silently

Who would wait waiting
When formless shadow appears to break
A dried leaf in the silence

When I take my eyes off the Poson Moon
My wish suffocates in a cough
Where is the face to look upon

It keeps coming up
As I hide myself in the shadows
Looking at her sailing with the clouds

Once in my earlier birth
The lemon grove blossomed in the moon
Light as I walked with a shadow
Toward the wooden fence
Casting long length of beings in rows
Silently,
Pleasantest of air surrounding
And a longed for face to look upon
As I take my eyes off the first sighting

PAUL TAN

The Sentry at *Mutianyu* Speaks to the Astronaut

I watch strange creatures unfurl
with each labored breath
and think of your dragon's flight,
launched to such fanfare.

At the edge of the kingdom,
language is pointless,
even if our lips were not blistered,
our tongues frost-dead.

These vats of oil dispatch flames
to the sky. In blazing sequences,
we send stories to the capital.
What cosmic language do you use?

Can you see me, nameless sentinel
on this endless line of stones?
Are there marauding barbarians
in cold outer space?

You and I have linked destinies—
we puncture small holes
in the wintry darkness against
strange winds and shifting stars.

We obey the emperor's bidding,
do not think of earthly rewards;
the festooned laurels we will
save for another life.

Author's Note: Mutianyu is a stretch of China's Great Wall, seventy kilometers northeast of Beijing. China launched its second manned space mission into orbit in October 2005.

MUHAMMAD AL-GHUZZI

A Dream

When he surrendered his eyes to the dream, this lad,
The evening star entering his house, trembling,
The wood of his bed turned into a ship for him,
The cosmos turned to an oyster in his hands.

Translated from the Arabic by May Jayyusi and John Heath-Stubbs

MELIH CEVDET ANDAY

Vertigo

From a sea in bloom everything will burst
One day and be a forest.
From now on what you'll see is the soft hour
Of birds on the branches where they rest.
Wait for the god who waits around:
On blood-red pines, the sun
Will claw till the great night comes on.

One day, all will be sound, such sound
As travels from star to cloud and to star from
       earthly things,
So its ellipse will spread with resounding chimes.
While you eye these rings,
Wait for the voice among voices to rebound.
Passing through organ-music, the hair-winged moon
Will come out quite soon.

I have lived in the wind.
Vertigo turned into lonely day. Alone,
My prophets were far-off rocks,
Neither forest nor sound, all by myself, windblown
Rain comforts the soul.

If not, godlike we must wait around
To hear a voice or any sound.

Translated from the Turkish by Talât Sait Halman

QASIM HADDAD

All of Them

Everybody said it was useless
Everybody said, "you're trying to lean on sun dust"
   that the beloved before whose tree I stand
     can't be reached
Everybody said, "you're crazy to throw yourself
   headlong into a volcano and sing"
Everybody said that salty mountain
   won't yield even one glass of wine
Everybody said, "you can't dance on one foot"
Everybody said there won't be any lights at the party
That's what they all said
but everybody came to the party anyway

Translated from the Arabic by Sharif S. Elmusa and Charles Doria

MONIZA ALVI

The Wedding

I expected a quiet wedding
high above a lost city
a marriage to balance on my head

like a forest of sticks, a pot of water.
The ceremony tasted of nothing
had little color—guests arrived

stealthy as sandalwood smugglers.
When they opened their suitcases
England spilled out.

They scratched at my veil
like beggars on a car window.
I insisted my dowry was simple—

a smile, a shadow, a whisper,
my house an incredible structure
of stiffened rags and bamboo.

We traveled around roads with English
names, my bridegroom and I.
Our eyes changed color

like traffic-lights, so they said.
The time was not ripe
for us to view each other.

We stared straight ahead as if
we could see through mountains
breathe life into new cities.

I wanted to marry a country
take up a river for a veil
sing in the Jinnah Gardens

hold up my dream, tricky
as a snake-chamber's snake.
Our thoughts half-submerged

like buffaloes under dark water
we turned and faced each other
with turbulence

and imprints like maps on our hands.

ARTHUR SZE

Labrador Tea

Labrador leaves in a jar with a kerchief lid
release an arctic aroma when simmered on a stove;

yesterday when fire broke out in the bosque,
the air had the stench of cauliflower in a steamer

when water has evaporated and the pot scalds.
Although Apache plume, along with clusters of

western peppergrass, makes fragrant the wash,
owls that frequent the hole high up the bank

of the arroyo have already come and gone.
Yesterday, though honey locust leaves shimmered

in a gust, I marveled no wasp nest had yet
formed under the porch. Repotting a spathiphyllum,

then uncoiling a hose, I suddenly hear surf
through open slats of a door. Sprinklers come on

in the dark; a yellow slug crawls on a rain-
slicked-banana leaf; as the mind flits, imbibes,

leaves clothed underneath with rusty hairs
suffuse a boreal light glistening on tidal pools.

ANGKARN KALAYANAPHONG

Scoop Up the Sea

Scoop the sea onto a plate
Grasp for a handful of stars
Watch the crabs and oysters circle
Chameleons and millipedes fly
A toad mounts the golden palanquin
A bull-frog goes with him
Earthworms seduce maidens
Every cell and spore
Gods bored with celestial mansions
Praising waste that has a
Jungle groves and thickets
Sawdust murmuring in sleep
Who, wonderful, can reign the sky
World of avarice and drunken wrath

feasted with white rice
mixed with salt to eat
dancing, singing folk songs
to eat the sun and moon
floating tour on currents of heaven
Angels flee into a coconut husk
Apsaras who sleep in the sky
raises their face shining success
swoop to earth to eat shit
taste wonderful in surplus of words
can speak deep philosophy
calculates the weight of shadows
Who remains, earthly, low, a buffoon
Fools, Let's possess excess

Translated from the Thai by John T. Mattioli

LUIS H. FRANCIA

Gathering Storm

Winds of sound will blow down your walls

To render your rooms as desolate as the moors.

Who can contain the storm that gathers each

Day from the multitudes of mouths, the mouths

Of those who have loved and bled and wept?

Each name rides the hurricane, each name

Brings an echo, a wound that

Mothers a republic of nothingness.

I would wish to cut my body into multitudes and to

every part add a tongue to utter all their names.

I would wish my body into innumerable cathedrals,

Every strand of hair a shrine for all who have fallen.

I would wish my body to arise each

Time, hosts of them, manifold and

myriad in their colors, god beautiful—

Blood red in the firewinds, emerald green in

The stirring breeze, indigo under a

Blossoming sky, in a communion that beckons

Growth. The sounds that blow down your

Walls will be the murmurs of gardens digging

Deep to embrace the dead with their roots,

To erect cities of bone and memory, to

Send out the tendrils of an epistemology,

The epistemology of refusal,

A refusal to die even when we are dead.

TAKAHASHI MUTSUO

The Dead Boy

I am a boy, who not knowing love,
Suddenly has fallen from the summit of a frightening infancy
Into the darkness of a well
Dark, watery hands choke my delicate neck
Innumerable needles of coldness push into me
Killing my heart, wet as a fish
Within each internal organ, I swell like a flower
As I move horizontally along the surface
Of the subterranean water
Before long, from the green horn in my groin
A sprout none too reliable will grow
Crawling up the heavy soil with thin hands
The day will come when like a pallid face
Its tree will rustle in the painful light
For I desire as much space inside me for the light
As space for the shadow

Translated from the Japanese by Jeffrey Angles

TAHER RIYAD

excerpt from "Signs"

I
I am not the shade who upholds the bare tree
      against its dissolution,
I'm not hunger to strap stones round my belly and suck
      your emaciated breast.
I'm thin like the figure of fear,
I contain the thirst of embers
      to transform themselves back to branches,
I do not pray for what's to come
—nothing will come—
and I don't concede to reverence.
It is a chain of ants that raised this earth
      and now erodes it slowly.

Translated from the Arabic by May Jayyusi and Jeremy Reed

WANG XIAONI

White Moon

The midnight moon shows every bone.

I inhale blue-white air.
All petty things on earth
Have turned into fireflies.
The city is a carcass.

No life
Can match this pure light.
Outside the window
Sky and earth exchange silver.
In the moonlight I forget I'm human.

The final rehearsal
For all things, soundless.
The moon on the floor,
Lighting my feet.

Translated from the Chinese by Wang Ping and Alex Lemon

TAMURA RYUICHI

A Thin Line

You are always alone
There is something like a bitter light
in the pupils of your eyes that have never shown tears
I like it

      To your blind image
      this world is a desolate hunting place
      You are the winter hunter
      who constantly chases down one heart

You do not believe in words
There is a deep longing for fear
in your footsteps that have murdered all the hearts
It fascinates me

      On the thin line that you walk
      the smell of blood is even on the top of the snow
      No matter how far we separate
      I can tell

You pull the trigger
I die inside a word

Translated from the Japanese by Samuel Grolmes and Yumiko Tsumura

YAO FENG

The Poet's Lunch

in Faro, poets from six countries
sat by the seaside
we used poetry to praise the sea
we used teeth
to turn a big fish into a brooch for the sea

Translated from the Chinese by Agnes Vong and Christopher Kelen

KUNWAR NARAIN

The Rest of the Poem

Water falling on leaves means one thing.
Leaves falling on water another.
Between gaining life fully

and giving it away fully
stands a full death-mark.

The rest of the poem
is written not with words—
Drawing the whole of existence, like a full stop,
it is complete at any point.

Translated from the Hindi by Lucy Rosenstein

SAJJAD SHARIF

Horse

Dense night—and a relentless wingless flight

Translated from the Bengali by Subrata Augustine Gomes

RACHIDA MADANI

excerpt from "Tales of a Severed Head"

The first tale

I
What city and what night
since it's night in the city
when a woman and a train-station argue over
the same half of a man who is leaving.
He is young, handsome
he is leaving for a piece of white bread.
She is young, beautiful as a springtime
                              cluster
trying to flower for the last time
for her man who is leaving.
But the train arrives
but the branch breaks
but suddenly it's raining in the station
                                  in the midst of spring.
And the train emerges from all directions
It whistles and goes right through the woman
the whole length of her.
Where the woman bleeds, there will never be spring
                                  again.
in the night, in her head, under the pillow
trains pass filled with men
            filled with mud
and they all go through her
                      the whole length of her.
How many winters will pass, how many snowfalls
before the first bleeding letter
before the first mouthful of white bread?

Translated from the French by Marilyn Hacker

MONICA FERRELL

Mohn Des Gedächtnis

Picture it: a girl in a strange city
Unpacking her suitcase, setting things on shelves
In the middle of the folds rises the berry
Of her determination, a black pearl on white cloth
As fine-wrapped as a baby Jesus
Or new star—she the one who will set it in the sky
Tomorrow, it's only the night before still. Picture it,
This stranger: doer of an incomprehensible,
Resonant past thing, which echoes in the oyster miles beneath.
Who was she? Some figment, miniature self,
A toy soldier set in motion by
An accidental kick of the dreaming real girl,
Far away untouched and unblemished in sleep.
Yet I was she: I was the eunuch who, smiling, salaaming,

Lets in the ghostly sahib to the huge jewel room
While his hukkaed shah lies fallen. That night,
A little doll stuffed tight with my fell purpose,
How I wandered the city, outdated treasure map to hand
Searching my buried gold. Where my fear went
Skipping a few paces ahead, a paper butterfly, later
I hung my tears like earrings from the lampposts.

—No!

I could make a thousand poems from this
There came in one day enough pain for ten
Natural lives laid end to end,
I could make a whole galaxy of glowing suns
Heating their decades of planets and trash–
But how can I let this live through me any more? Or
I should be the girl of the music box

Open her red coffer, out
Pops the same old song,
Only magical for never changing,

Crystalline, distilling
Its own liquor of eternity
From the sole inexhaustible god-grape—directing,
Suspending me as the magnet-chip in the old jade statue.

Now I may lie tossed up by this ocean, like an old
Jellyfish losing its clarity, hexed
By a curse ancient as a blue faience
Scarab carved with hieratic marks,
But even if it means a change as came
To Anthony, after the god abandoned him—
Human, no longer tragically, singularly destinied—

I will live through it: burn it up
With my breath. For after all I am alive
While what is past has lost that art.

NACERA MOHAMMADI

Weeping

This daylight is a salacious young man
rising lovingly,
startling the mist, disrupting the architecture of death.
He was never swallowed by the depths,
won't stare into the deep chasm.
He paints longing with the light of waves,
transforming weeping into bells
and breezes.
His days now are a crowded city gathering voices,
addresses and gravestones.
His pulse is sand, a stalk of wheat,
his voice water,
a woman with no voice.
How could I not cry?

Translated from the Arabic by Khaled Hegazzi and Andy Young

HUNG HUNG

Woman Translating, or La Belle Infidèle

The dead woman sits in the flower garden
Driving her pen with a furious energy
A butterfly flutters up from the page

In point of fact, she is hard at work on a translation
That peculiar calling so resembling undercover work
In its want of a bold hand, a cool head, and absolute secrecy
The very image of a spectral phantom shadowing a subject—
      all conquering, Argus-eyed
Its sole injunction, to resist all injunctions
Translation lays open the forbidden

The first chamber is laden with heavy antique furniture
The second glistens with crystal and gold and silver plate garnished with pearls
The third contains a circular looking-glass framed in brass
The fourth, riding gear and fowling pieces, chains and leather whips . . .
A sudden wave of vertigo sweeps over her
The key falls from her hand
Heaven only knows what might befall her if she stood before that final
    and forbidden chamber

Translating in a garden filled with flowers
Is ever so much better than standing on the deck of a ship braving
    the waves on a heavy sea
Or being thrown into the ship's hold on the remote chance of running
    afoul of pirates
Much less of enduring those sheets soaked with the sweat and tears
    of the thousand women who came before
Is ever so much better than going to market
And listening to idle gossip about the clandestine affairs of other
    women's wayward husbands
So much better than dancing at the ball
Every eye trained upon you
Never knowing which arrow is the one tipped with poison
Better than opening the door to the next chamber. Better than
Turning on the TV

And seeing those celebrities, with their practiced smiles, holding forth
    with such fervor and breezy self-assurance
At least she knows that she is dead
And must seize this moment while her husband is away
To finish translating the book *tout de suite*
To leave behind this one regret would be a great embarrassment

The Bluebeard among the shadows of the trees has stood watching her
    for some time
Watching love's lingering warmth rain its ashes on the page
Death has closed the book on her discovering
That so many women have passed through his hands
Discovering how in winter
He breaks them into charcoal to feed the stove that fills the room with
    such perfume
He thinks a great deal about stuffing her with embers
And letting her burn

But she is such a cool hand
So absorbed in her work
She hasn't even noticed night has fallen
And, to be sure, it is a thick book
And translation a calling in want of a cool hand

Translated from the Chinese by Steve Bradbury

ARTHUR YAP

Night Scene

the warmth had left the west. timid
the stars appeared. preparedly, in the distance
a finger of light waved across the sky.
others too appeared &, higher or lower,
all impressed their lines on the blackboard sky.
quickly they are disambiguated,
the solitary finger is left
to write the margin of the next sunrise.

SHIRAISHI KAZUKO

Travel Again—The Time I Am Heading For Is May

there was a time when we were May
the Iowa River   shone green   and we got into a canoe
took a trip   everybody   headed for something invisible called hope
although no one knew the destination, whether their steps were heavy or light
at least we all held something full inside
many times I saw   along the way
of my travel in time   people lose their faces   throw their ambition along
    the roadside
they show up at a glorious looking dance party wearing bizarre masks
frolicking like peacocks   throwing searching glances
at each other like crows   my friends
threw away their stripped off souls like cemeteries   and   skillfully put on a
    new way of living
like ribbons on their brains and hearts and were proudly
getting along with the world

but in the desert and in the city   in the rustic country
there is a sun that blooms   between suns   there is a language
for them to talk to one another   travel is   always on the way   holding
    the eternal
soundless sounds   that continue from eternity
to today   today to tomorrow   sometimes   picking up a shining May
scattering a nonexistent green   having   existing hope   will   ambition
like a donkey, not a fine horse   I go
to the indestructible trip   heading for
a fool's great indestructible joy

Translated from the Japanese by Samuel Grolmes and Yumiko Tsumura

JOY KOGAWA

To Scuttle the Moon

wandering, august evening, down the mall
to the lights spawning in the canal
a thousand low-slung baby moons
and fisherfolk groggy with bait
looking with lunar hooks
for late-night sea creatures

comes a man offering
cigarettes, conversation, a fishy stare
then—great immortal whale day—
he slops into her lap, a
tidal wave of blubbering—
is this a fisherman's reward?

she flounders from the taffy pull
to scuttle the moon and the sailing swans

ERKIN VAHIDOV

Blue Rays

Beautiful are the evenings
In serene autumn months.
There's something mysterious in the moon.
The streets talk to the sky.

Feeling this spell
I'm folded in the embrace of silence.
I'm listening to the fairy tales of the stars.
And I feel as if I were in the skies.

Everywhere just silence and calm.
There's nobody in the streets,
As if everyone were sleeping,
As if this existence were deprived of life.

The streets are shining brightly.
The windows pour light.
But nobody, no home is sound asleep.
The thoughts and ideas are restless.

The rays of blue screens.
Pour into the eyes of people.
Everyone is bewitched
With the wolf chasing the hare.

There's silence, silence in the streets.
There's anxiety, anxiety in every home.
The sixteenth-serial sufferings
Mercilessly drive on the nerves.

The adult patience is never lost.
The children would not look at their food.
A kurbashi is shot.
Stierlitz escapes another danger.

A young man kisses his beloved
Who he has just returned from someone else's embrace.
Abandoning their dolls,
Our little girls watch it.

Each day is the same.
When evening comes we sit down before this miracle.
Emotions are poured down from the screen.
We are laughing and crying.

Today I decided to look at the face
Of the world.
Looking attentively,
I wanted to sate it with aryks and flowers.

The stars are dropping down on my shoulders.
Everything is filled with a wonderful fragrance.
The skies are spilling on my breast
Some cool, sweet serenity.

I am walking the streets, alone,
The silence is calling for me
Everything is keeping silent.
Every window is lit with blue lights.

Translated from the Uzbek by William M. Dirks

SHERKO BEKES

excerpt from "Butterfly Valley"

Twilight, after the *ezan* of your wounds I arrive, twilight.
Twilight, after your weeping dinner, I am with you, twilight.
When I come
light me a candle in holy Nali's summit,
let it be the neck of a tree
or the finger of a narcissus
or the locks of a violet.
Light me a wound on the peak of Haji's Kekon
let it be the head of a decapitated poem,
or Wasanan's breast
or the figure of Halabja.
After the *ezan* of your wounds, I arrive.

When I come
carve me an arch
before the gate of your cold breath,
one suitable for the king of sorrow and this crown of exile,
one suitable for Xendan's beard,
for Jeladet's dignity.
Carve me an arch
by the buds of all your tears,
by the leaves of all your sighs,

by the oleander of your suppressed anguish.
An arch decorated with bird prints,
by the red mud that you kneaded with your tears
on the grave of your loved ones.
Carve me an arch
by the square bricks of pain
of all your funerals.
An arch in the shape of Mewlewi's gently pointed turban.
An arch like the curved back
of Mewlana's retreat.

Translated from the Kurdish by Choman Hardi

TÔ THÙY YÊN

The Deserted Café

I go there vaguely thinking of a meeting,
Meeting whom I am not sure.

I go there, my heart dry as a hollowed out shell.
Thirst and hunger hang thick in the night.

In the afternoon the sun beats down hard. . . .
In the afternoon it rains and rains. . . .

The café is empty. The lamp shadows wait
Through the long nights for someone's return.

Its my own fault.
I've forgotten the date of the meeting.

Pity for the one returning. Pity for the one who waits
And no one comes.

Life is filled with errors.
Regrets change nothing.

We must grin and bear it.
Make the best of the journey.

In the afternoon the sun beats down hard . . .
In the afternoon it rains and rains. . . .

The café is empty, the lamp shadows
Wait a thousand years.

Translated form the Vietnamese by Nguyễn Bá Chung and Kevin Bowen

SUERKUL TURGUNBAYEV

Night

In this world one comes into being at night,
We meet one another at night,
Fall in love with each other at night—
People die at night.

Night—vast cave,
Night—fathomless mystery.
The night crowned itself in this world
At the entrance of Time and openness—
Gulping down its creations,
Giving them birth again at once.

Translated from the Russian by Yuri Vidov Karageorge

TINA CHANG

Origin & Ash

Powder rises
from a compact, platters full of peppermints, a bowl of sour pudding.
A cup of milk before me tastes of melted almonds.

It is the story of the eve of my beginning. Gifts for me:

boxes of poppies, pocket knife, an elaborate necklace
made of ladybugs.

My skirt rushing north.

There is something round and toothless about my dolls.

They have no faith. Their mouths, young muscles to cut me down.
  Their pupils, miniature bruises.

I hear the cries of horses, long faces famished, the night the barn burned.

   God and ashes everywhere.

Burnt pennies, I loved them, I could not catch them
in their copper rolling.

My mother's cigarette burns amber in a crystal glass.
I am in bed imagining great infernos.

Ashes skimming my deep lake.

The night the animals burned,
I kissed the servant with the salty lips.

There was a spectacular explosion, a sound
that severed the nerves, I was kind to that shaking. The horses,
the smell of them, like wet leaves, broken skin.

Laughing against a wall, my hair sweeps the windowsill,

thighs show themselves.

First came my body, my statue's back, then hair electric, matches falling
  everywhere.
Tucked in my pink canopy, I am plastic, worn cheeks grinning.

I found my little ones hiding from me, crying into their sleeves.
    They are really from a breeze, momentary, white.

When we unburied the dolls, red ants were a fantasy
feeding on them, nest of veins, shrunken salted corpses.

There is mythology planted in my mouth which is like sin.
Keep fires inside yourself.
My mother once said, *When you were a baby, I let you swim in a basin of water
until your lungs stopped.* Since then, my eyes were open windows,

the year everything fell into them.

Cicadas hissing.

Ashes on my open book.

Ashes in mother's hair. Ashes on my baby brother.
The streets are arid, driven toward fire.

If I hurry, I will dance with my father before the sun sets,
my slippers clicking
on a thin layer of rain.

ANJUM HASAN

A Place Like Water

All through the day it stays: the sadness of coming
    into a wet city at dawn, not speaking, neither of us,
when one by one the neon lights wake us from a cramped,
    dream-ravaged sleep, driving home in one long curving sweep
on traffic-less roads with their morning walkers and damp dogs;
    still thinking of that other place worked on by the sun,
the casuarina trees and shouts of people on the beach, frayed and
    muffled by the heaving of the sea. We climb wet stairs where
no one's been for days, thinking it ought to be the case that one
    returns with screws, a piece of string, some word or turn

of phrase, something to fit somewhere, that click or slide or
    resolution that has been wanting. Instead a winter monsoon
blurs the world; we wash our hair, shake out sand from folded clothes,
    sleep for a while in the still early morning while vendors shout
the names of flowers, sleep so that our bones at least achieve that
    calm alliance with our breathing and take us where we
want to go: a place like water when it lifts us in a magnet wave
    to set us down again, and we're unencumbered, weightless, brave;
our questions turn to images of strangers waving across fields,
    pointlessly, insistently, across fields, through falling rain.

EDGAR B. MARANAN

Climbing Mt. Iraya

A fold in time, a V of sky and earth, plus sea,
stun of pasture, rock, air quivering, waves sun-
dappled, and tropic skydom of migrant birds.

This northmost island floats on the planet's
edge, about to fall off without a trace.

Here, where a stonehold stands, its serpent's tail
defends against the lash, breaking up the spray
of ancient surf, a turquoise glinting whoosh.

This is where our pilgrim journey starts,
the meeting point of gods' play marbles
and green raiments of the brooding peak.

On the slope to the sea by the skyworld's gate,
foot trail and hillock lead toward the clouds.

In trekking, the self is carried lightly with faith
to whistle up the wind across treeless space,
with mirth to savor cool air upon quick sweat
as we file, devotee-like, into some deciduous dark.

In this forest, unsullied land of the Ivatan,
liana hangs like summons to unreachable light,
the boles dare those who would measure trees,

and the windflowers tease but plead to be alone
among the shadows, awaiting warmer solstice.

Moments ago, a black-chinned fruit dove flashed
through a silver airstream, in and out of canopy,
trilling for its mate, then lit upon a branch.

This dove I shall remember, whose half-shut eyes
never saw the gunflash, its song garbled within
a crimsoned gullet.
                    Where the pellet disappeared,
the feathers were growing stiff and dark.

We almost miss the thinnest wake, *tataya* bobbing
among the whitecaps, brown pod bearing life forms.
They sail and disappear, we survey all in merriment.

The craft carries a customary batch of stoics
leathered by squall, windlash and tropic sun,
prey to stealth craft from beyond Y'ami.

Such specks of small hopes, dreamful lives,
pinpoints on a jade-green sea, bright beings.

There was a storm one day, all boats were called
to shore, broods bolted within the yard-thick walls
of mortar, limestone, thatch, ancestral ken.

Across these isles the storms lift sea, till cows
fly off the hills, and death comes many ways.

Around the coves, beneath the island's shelf,
a complement of English pirates' souls still roams
where their bleached bones wail rogue songs
haunting the shallows and the hallows' plunge.

Exalted, we have left the earth behind us
to seek the deities on Iraya's peak, bestirring.

But the peak is never reached, as we stand in awe
beneath gnarled limbs in ever deepening green,
as we watch the clouds darken halfway to the top.

Heaven lours overhead, wind rises from the sea.
In this gray light the world seems crisply bright,
even without the noonday sun.
                                    Then, at the burst,
we become the gods we seek, rainblest.

ZIBA KARBASSI

Carpet Garden

. . . and its red little fish have no need of water
and its butterflies are not crushed under body weight
and its elk's antlers have ripped no one's side open
and its thorns have not pierced anybody's foot.

Keep quiet for a moment
and you can
   still hear
      the sweetest of songs
from the golden larynx of the this garden's canary.

Ah,
at the loom
   the carpet-weaving little girl
      must have been singing
         a song.

Translated from the Persian by Ahmad Karimi-Hakkak

BHANU KAPIL

from *The Wolf Girls of Midnapure*

A working note: In 1920s colonial India, a jungle missionary, Reverend Joseph Singh, found two girls suckling a mother wolf. He killed the wolf and brought the feral girls, Kamala and Amala, to his Mission orphanage in Midnapure. Here, he kept a diary of their adaptation to human life, which was published in 1942 as Wolf-children and Feral Man, *coauthored with the anthropologist Robert Zingg. In the excerpts that follow, I have rewritten this colonial account to include the undocumented voices or versions of the wolf girls themselves; the wolf mother; the Reverend Singh's wife; the Mission's Muslim cook, Assi-ma; and the "sorcerer," sent by the girls' original, human mother, who tracks the wolf girls to the Mission, then is asked to heal the youngest girl, Amala, who is dying. She dies. Kamala lives, constantly resisting efforts to turn her "into a human being again."*

"Wet, wet, green, green. I mix with them and prosper. A baby! Sticky then my mumma licks me clean. Best is brown next to yellow. Best is blue, then brown. Best yellow. Where will the sun go when it's finished?, I ask my mother. Through her skin. So red she is. The sun goes into the ground. Because my mother does, she does so every night. We watch her disappear and then we disappear. Blue as blue, then brown, then green, then black: the holy books of your people foretold this."

—An account of Amala.

My sister. Who did not want to leave her home.

The Reverend father put a pink and unnatural silvery shade into her body: bowls of semolina, with raspberry jam, to make her live. People came and went, observing. Then: a sheet over her head, a fire in the corner, and ropes of stale marigolds on the bushes where she loved to be. I could not ask for more. But the best green-found girl is gone behind the sun, I cannot follow. Telling those colors would rent even a jungle to ruin.

A white smoke fills the compound. The younger and I wake in a scrawled ball in the younger's cot; she yowls all night and the stronger girls do not bear it. After the difficult bath, breakfast. Enjoindering us to eat the

creamy swarm, but we are gaunt, problems. The younger sucks on the raisins
I spoon off for her, but I am not a mother and set upon my own slop with
some strength. A warrior must prepare for battle even on her deathbed, as
my mother said. Though when they came, she looked up from her bones and
with one crack in the stuff of her, she was gone. They put us in sheets and
took us.   Where were we? My life slipped out of me and
down, where now the sun, my enemy, has baked up all the holes. I ask the
rain the rain to soften the earth so my life may come back to me, upward.

The younger, I fear,

her life turned into a snakebird; flew up into the blacking sky, a migrant.
By now to the south and east, grazing in a lush swamp grotted with basic
lilies. Perhaps it is for the best.

Then the compound, our play. The churning orphans gallop. I make my
place by the long wall. My sister crawls under the thorn bushes and hisses.
I am a coward. If I was a true daughter to my mother the wolf, I would put
my teeth on the red leg of the nearest girl of all. White ghost, white
ghost, she sings. But my eyes are bad. I keep to the long wall where
Joseph stands, squinting. I will not leave the shadows.

    A girl was a speck on the ground, so the wolf-wife picked her up in
her hairy beak and flew off into the trees.

When the girl was found in the milky cave, they shot her mother and tore her
out of her hair.

Because she urinated standing up, they wrapped her pelvis in white cottons.
Because she keened over her bowl of sugary tea, they spoke in English,
enunciating.   ·

"Her lips were wet and red as she clucked up at the mongoose in the mango
tree. She would not come down." The Reverend told the gardener to bring a
long stick. "She does not look into my eyes when I ask her questions," he
wrote in his Diary.

"When the Reverend Mrs. fed her milk from a sucking sponge, she clung to
the hem of her sari and would not let go." Day in, day out, for the next
cycle of seven years, they followed her in a tight circle, trying to turn

her back into a human being. There is a formal photograph that survives in anthologies of this period:

the wolf-girl seated at their feet, center front of a row of orphans. The eyes of the good children do not waver. When the man shouts cheese from under his black cape, she is the only one who looks up at a passing raven, shaking her head like a dog on a rope and calling: "Cowowowowow!" The Reverend father kicks her hard, his face completely still, but it is too late. It is 1921. The photograph will be blurry.

Again, the problem of heritage. When men look at me, they do not see my womanliness. A woman as I am, with a slit skin. Then I judged the perimeter. What did I see? Out of the incantations of green. Out of the hide or coat of black and red. Into the lit basin of settled life. Sometimes I pinch a goat.

What is it?, I said to the little one. She was on her stomach, gumming the dust. With my nose I rolled her over. Her mother must have left her for dead, I thought, as weak species do. So little. I took her by her neck between my teeth and retracted.

Here, she scoots and suckles. I don't have to

remember for her.   When her brown skin sheds, her sisters and brothers lick her

clean.

CHUAN SHA

The Wolves Are Roaring

Reading Jean-Paul Sartre

The wolves are roaring,
beyond the deep sea
and the end of wilderness,
craving the juices

of fish,
of beasts,
and drops of
human blood.
The wolves are roaring,
beyond the depths of the heart,
on the tips of their sharp teeth,
savoring the bones
of fish,
of beasts,
and dreaming a thousand-year dream
of licking
a human heart.

Translated from the Chinese by Liu Hong

ADRIAN A. HUSAIN

Crocodiles

From around the swamp
the forbidding vapors rise.
On one side, acacias shoot up.
The approach has been walled off.

Then in a sudden shaft of light
you see them: venerable,
weighted against the sand,
nursing their torpor.

Canines bared like rusks
they lie
as though the swamp
had spewed them up.

You would think them
dead or asleep.
But each primitive lozenge
of skin is watching.

In each form
brooding on the bank
there flickers its instant
of ravenous lightning revival.

SANKHA GHOSH

Four Poems from Panjore DanRer Shabda (Oars in My Ribs)

(1)

Oars in my ribs, waters splash in my blood,
The waxing moon emerges from the boat's hull,
Mosses and reeds weigh my body down,
I have no past—no future either.

(2)

Storm-uprooted, the lamppost lies lonely in the fields,
Fireflies at its head, and above, Orion's sword,
The battle is done, the hour still, all around
The night looms like an immense, opaque sea.

(50)

He who had been bent small with insults and injuries,
Whose days had dropped away with each hour, each tide,
To him when you came, your touch feather to his ribs,
In your fingers, last night, I witnessed god.

(63)

The ground lies very still. But within fires rage,
A sudden explosion has shattered the rocks.
Fling to the insensible dust words that will not
Throb with fever, with lava, or with curse.

Translated from the Bengali by Nandini Gupta

AL-SADDIQ AL-RADDI

Song

Facing down wind in a dust storm,
wrapped up in his cloak
and wearing a hat that can't make him vanish—

this skinny man
scans the horizon,
gathering—but not quite yet—flowers
until the moment you meet

> (. . . but stuck in this narrow alleyway
> among mountains of rubbish
> he longs to lift up his beak
> unfurl his wings
> and take flight . . .)

Translated from the Arabic by Hafiz Kheir and Sarah Maguire

A. K. RAMANUJAN

The Black Hen

It must come as leaves
to a tree
or not at all

yet it comes sometimes
as the black hen
with the red round eye

on the embroidery
stitch by stitch
dropped and found again

and when it's all there
the black hen stares
with its round red eye

and you're afraid.

MONTRI UMAVIJANI

A Revisit

Revisited:
less the shadow of a thing
than shapeless;
and entirely is
a net cast to
the flown bird.

MANJUL

Sky

One day the sky came to hide in my cup of tea
I tried to draw it to my heart,
and quickly drank the tea
But with the last drops the sky flew away

I filled my cup
and once again the sky fell
Someone said "Slip it in your pocket.
Hide it, yes, hide it there."
But I feared the singe of flesh
the sun would bring,
that the heavy rains would pour
To be overwhelmed by the whirling winds of storm!
So many stars would be too much to bear

Could I carry such wonders away
in my flimsy string bag?

Someone said, "Man, be daring.
To live with the sky is a helluva thing."
But I recalled the flash and thunder,
lightning as it struck

For this which comes once in a life
I would not risk such dangers
Not a pack of cigarettes
not even cloves, nor cardamom do I carry
Then, why should I wish to walk off with the sky?

I said, "Where would the earth be
without the sun and moon, didn't a voice cry out—
—'Let there be light.'"

So, yes, I threw the sky back.

Translated from the Nepali by Wayne Amtzis with the author

RANJIT HOSKOTE

Moth

Pressed up against the narrow pane, the moth is rust,
its wings the color of blood drying on stone.

The house and sky are one cubic dark through whose thin walls
the boy moves like a silken cloth,

buffing the brass urns and pewter mugs he touches.
Clots of light, straining through his palms, float in the air.

Dawn is a mile off, but when the house gets there,
a hard edge of fire cuts through the glass

and through the night's restraint: the boy grabs at the moth.
but stumbles, and his prize is just a shock

of sulphur wings that thrash in his hands and vaporize
while he falls headlong, his hands flecked with pollen dust.

He comes to the window again, next dawn. There is no moth
to reach for. He slashes his palms on the fire-sharpened glass.

RAJEE SETH

It Can't Ever See—The Sky

In the center of the four-sided cementness of the wall
a window, fixed
bars in the window
But the window watches the sky—
its expanse of blueness.

The window watches
the play of the wind in every corner of the compass.
The window watches the infinite.
It's only the window which, unblinking,
can see limitless skyness.

But the sky—it can't ever see
windowness.

Translated from the Hindi by the author and Arlene Zide

ROY MIKI

About

Sure it sounds like a cliché
in the morning as the mirror

Rinses the residue of sleep

The tap runs on program
And hands conjure her face

Slavishly giving one cause
to pause in the long chain

The cliché is the uninvited
resonance of blue waves

Sink in the subaltern

Should one pause long
enough for winds to change

The chain of emery is the cliché
of haphazard sand dunes

When in the sleeper's eye
the ocean swells in the orbit

Stuck in the floater that conceals
this replay of powdered cheeks

So here's another one
already forms the mirror

As if a silent witness were to say

We have no recollection of the incoming tide

LING YU

excerpts from "Turtle Island Aria II"

1

we've already fallen
into a black sea, been broken
on the land that has pursued us from afar

but on that shore, ashore
a crowd of people surges like a tide—another fire
is burning

oh let me lay my body down

and in my pride imagine myself
a golden country
and let the ebbing century's waves slap
at the oars of my feet

3

the country of the past slips slowly behind me and disappears
ahead of me lies a vast expanse of blue-green sea

with the speed of flight, I span
the tides, straddle day and night
and the ancient ground beneath my feet is made anew

I want to dream without sleep
I want to walk without feet
I'll play a role, neither son nor daughter
mother nor father, kind-hearted acolyte
nor smiling neighbor
not anymore

I'm just someone floating with the current
and there's a secret course
in the middle of this sea, wherever

a piano sounds a blue note
sets forth—and connects
with the line of my drift

Translated from the Chinese by Andrea Lingenfelter

ESMAIL KHOI

Of Sea Wayfarers

Sign of a true lover is that he emerges cold from hell
Proof of a true wayfarer is that he comes forth dry from the sea.

—Sanaii

Only you have remained.

Those sea wayfarers said:
From water
   we shall come forth dry.
Upon the waves of events, they said we hold the opal of vigilance
and to its lustrous, untouched core
there is no passage for darkness.

With umbrellas of denial
         they said,
             we will survive the toxic rain.
They said:
Even
   the storm's debris
   cannot devastate us.

They said . . .
They said . . .
They said . . . and

Clear as day they saw
that behind the oysters' curtains

the pearls
—perhaps even unknown to themselves—
winked and consorted with corpses and grime.

As if they knew
that their umbrellas
were to become the swamp's wide lilies.

From afar, in breaking light,
they even witnessed the oysters'
rotting in the dark
waters. They saw,
and in a thousand mirrors, laughed.

Only you have remained.
Stay.

Translated from the Persian by Sholeh Wolpé

MANOHAR SHETTY

Spider

The swollen-headed spider
Spins yarns from her corner.
Tenuous threads of her tales
Glitter like rays
From the fingertips of a saint.

She weaves on, plays along,
Hangs from a hoary strand,
Rolls, unrolls: a yoyo,
A jiggling asterisk: a footnote:
Little characters transfixed
In the clutches of her folds.

MALATHI MAITRI

She Who Threads the Skies

As the sky fills
the empty shell
after a bird has hatched,
so desire fills
everything.

My daughter threads together
pieces of the sky
scattered by the wing-beat
of migrating birds

like a mysterious game.
The blue sticks to her hands.

Translated from the Tamil by Lakshmi Holmström

AMAL DUNQUL

The City of Wrecked Ships

I feel I am alone tonight;
and the city, with its ghosts and tall
buildings, is a wrecked ship
that pirates looted long ago
and sent to the ocean's bottom.
At that time the captain leaned his head
against the railing. Beneath his feet
lay a broken wine bottle, shards
of a precious metal. And the sailors
clung to the silent masts,
and through their ragged clothes
swam sad fish of memory.
Silent daggers, growing moss, baskets

of dead cats . . . Nothing pulses
in this acquiescent world.

Translated from the Arabic by Sharif S. Elmusa and Thomas G. Ezzy

KOIKE MASAYO

Antelope

It was the autumn of my fifth year when I encountered the antelope
In the hot springs spa deep in the Hodaka mountain range
The antelope silently drew near
Through the steam   it looked at my naked body
I too   stared at the antelope

Separated from the herd   an antelope
Me completely on my own
I scooped up hot water from the spa in the palm of my hand
And   threw it at the antelope
It was a greeting in lieu of language but
The antelope seemed a little startled
When I saw the furry chest of the antelope   wet with hot water
I felt as if the solitude of the antelope had moistened

The wind swept across
The leaves on the trees shook
Finally the antelope silently turned around
Silently sprang up   and returned to the mountains

To the spa in my dreams
In the dead of night gently   I put my toes into the hot water
Through the steam opposite   I can hear faint steps
That antelope
Returns   each time

Not looking at anything   with its cosmic vast eyes
Drops of water from its furry chest
Dripping   drip drip

Translated from the Japanese by Leith Morton

ATAMURAD ATABAYEV

Depth: A Sonnet

The old sea is full of waves
The faintly lighted cloudy sky
The moon like a pearl—sometimes going below the
        bottom of the sky,
At times beaming its blue light.

The sea is afraid of predators
It strikes its head upon the rocks
As if it were in a cage
And it will never be let free.

For what are all these agonies? Why does the world grieve?
Is it taking its own fortune to the grave?
Or are its sins torturing it?
The faces are burning, but the tears are in the sky . . .

The surface of the sea is agitated, but beneath it
It is full of centuries of quietude.

Translated from the Russian by William M. Dirks

NATHALIE HANDAL

Autobiography of Night

You refuse your darkness,
        tunes, uncertainty, and
the question you keep well hidden
        to forget what you were able to ask
to forget that you listened to the devil
        and the rain and it was a sound you
didn't want to recognize—
        its drops too light, graceful
reminding you of the ghosts between your night sheets,
        the empty closet in your hours
the walls, the peeling paint
        the barbed wire—a view of your history
of all that you've been blind of—
        a view of the marble floor you keep
crying on, and the bird you hold against your grief.
        Confess. Did the passing sparrow in your sleep
tell you what you wanted to ask? Did you feel your navel
        pressed against the earth, asking, *do we*
continue to live with the one we think we love
        when nothing else means something to us.
Confess. You beg not to answer.

R. ZAMORA LINMARK

excerpt from "What Some Are Saying About The Body"

Some say the body in a glass display
in Northern Luzon does not belong to you.

Nothing but wax in a freezer, some say;
on loan from Madame Tussaud's collection.

True or not, some say you shall remain on exhibit,
your death running on electricity,

until senators and widows can agree
to grant you a national hero's burial in Manila

where, free from limbo alas,
you will join the company of veterans and American teachers.

There are some, however, who say you never left Hawaiʻi,
that you are still buried under Aloha soil,

along with piles of unpaid ICU and florist bills.
Some say you never owed a soul a single cent,

paid all your dues on time,
while others say you ran the country

like Mad Max with a credit card: No limit.
Some say you built the city from the swamp up,

that in one day, plants rose into skyscrapers,
dust tracks became overpass, and,

for the first time, people walked across the sky,
like street angels in rubber slippers.

Death found you
under Honolulu sheets with a four-inch farewell.

Some disagree, argue you lost your libido
soon after you slipped inside a barrio bailarina.

Some say that your longest partner in bed was,
in fact, a dialysis machine.

Baloney, some say.
You never went limp, turned gray or yellow,

and lupus—what the hell is lupus, anyway,
but a foreign word to your body's vocabulary?

You died with the physique of a triathlete,
the original Thrilla from Manila, simple as that;

there are photographs and a museum to prove it.
But they're fake! some say, fake as

your World War II medals and Junior Featherweight belts.
All manufactured in Thailand, they say, where

your youngest daughter bought mutant orchids
and gold by the yard.

Off the South China Sea you converted an island into a zoo,
imported the best hunters, gatherers,

and scavengers from Safari and Amazon.
Some say it was to show the world

that Man is capable of moving jungles,
while others say it was a birthday gift

to your one-and-only son who, some say,
received his Oxford diploma with an American Express receipt.

Some say the Muzak played in your air-conditioned vault
is a requiem by Bach; others, Beethoven.

I saw his fingers move, some say,
to accompany organ chords or the hum of Westinghouse.

Others say it is you beckoning the world to come,
come and feel the cold beat of your heart.

APOSTROPHE
IN THE SCRIPTURE

Apostrophe in the Scripture

— KADHIM JIHAD

Before September 11, Americans barely knew what it was to be attacked in their own country, and we continue to be fortunate that wars have not been fought in recent times on U.S. soil. However, much of the rest of the world has had another fate, and most, if not all, countries in this anthology have been victims of combat. After the Vietnam War, some Americans believed that we had become a more enlightened nation and that we would never again enter a war in which we were divided on our objectives. Many thought that after the events of September 11 we would better understand the torment of people and countries that have endured decades of conflict and injustice. The years since 9/11 have demanded our political and moral education, our reflections on the Muslim world, on U.S. foreign policies, and on how the world ensures its survival.

Indeed, many American intellectuals, activists, artists, writers, and others have resisted the U.S. invasion in Iraq and participated in raising awareness of human rights violations, of the realities associated with war, whether exile, deportation, imprisonment, or torture. However, tragically, our nation has been consumed by political issues outside of the realm of national peace, leaving us lingering in a fog of uninformed involvement. As we continue to occupy Iraq, the fragile political relations between the United States and Korea, Iran, Syria, Pakistan, and other countries continue to be a threat to world stability; the memory of children killed in Palestine, Lebanon, and Israel in the bloodshed of summer 2006 continues to haunt us. Why haven't we realized the urgency of dialogue rather than war?

I started writing this essay on route to the United Kingdom. When I arrived, I bought a few newspapers and almost immediately started reading, "Muslims are the New Jews" (*The Sunday Times*), "Blair. The Veil. And a New Low in Politics" (*Daily Mail*), "Universities Urged to Spy on Muslims" (*The Guardian*). It seems the way the West has decided to read the

East, and vice versa, is deepening our alienation from and fear of each other. Soon afterward I headed to Trieste, in Italy at the border of Slovenia. I was reminded once again of what war leaves behind, a convergence of displaced people: Greeks, Jews from Corfu, Serbs, Slovenians, all having fled the iniquitous universes of conflict. On my way back to New York, I could not stop thinking, how can this onslaught of war stop, as a certain anesthetization plagues us? How can literature, a succession of words on paper, speak to these dark concerns? But the poems in this section console me as they are collusions, testimonies, witnesses. These poems are a homage to the ruins of memory, to the spiritual and collective experiences of people and nations.

In war, everyone believes in their own truth. In war, people are often forced to choose sides, but standing on one definite side doesn't necessarily bring resolve. According to Master Sun, the second-century Chinese author of *The Art of War*, "Ultimate excellence lies not in winning every battle but in defeating the enemy without ever fighting them."[1] I have lived in four different continents and have experienced the effects of political upheaval, strife, poverty, and have never been able to ascertain who is right or who is wrong. But the most important question remains: What does violence ultimately accomplish? We often don't know the intimate stories, the names and faces of those who have died, suffered, or have been dislocated after battle. They hang like apostrophes in the scriptures.

Their voices resound throughout this section, as in Keki N. Daruwalla's poem "Gujarat 2002," which mourns the bloodshed on the streets. The poem describes the conflicts of 2002 in Gujarat, India, a decade after the Babri Masjid (a mosque in Ayodhya, Uttar Pradesh) was destroyed by a Hindu mob convinced it was the birthplace of the god Rama. We are struck with grief when we read Daruwalla's description of the chaos manifested once again when a counterattack was made on Hindus after a series of lootings and murders of Muslim minorities. His poem brings the innocent dead to the forefront, forcing the reader to confront terror and the consequences of rage:

> *There's blood on the streets, so many dying and the dead,*
> *that dark-grained newspapers squint with red.*
>
> *Fire and skin turn into one blinding street, and in any weather*
> *life and charred skin will peel together.*

[1] Sun-tzu, *The Art of War* (New York: Penguin, 2002), p.14.

Boards are warped, the steel blackened. Inside
there's a mother in travail, there could be a bride.

Killer and killed are one—they speak the same language.
The vocabulary of guilt has a circumference and a center.

Gasoline alights with a splash everywhere
Knives hiss with the same silence where they enter.

Daruwalla conveys what Hannah Arendt states in her book *On Violence*, "Every decrease in power is an open invitation to violence." And like Arendt his poem wonders if Valéry was right when he said, "On peut dire que tout ce que nous savons, c'est-à-dire tout ce que nous pouvons, a fini par s'opposer à ce que nous sommes" (One can say that all we know, that is, all we have the power to do, has finally turned against what we are).[2] He tragically ends with these following lines:

Gujarat is not just the corruption of an absolute.
It has manufactured its own corrupt absolutes:

"If night fell on Godhra, we are within our rights
to unload night on innocence elsewhere."

There is no place here for the lyre and the lute.
In such times is lockjaw the best—to be dumb, to be mute?

In "Greatest Wish Song," Iranian poet Ahmad Shamlu's speaker sings for freedom: "Ah if freedom could sing a song / small / as the throat of a bird, / Nowhere would crumbled walls remain. / It would not take many years to comprehend. / That ruins are a sign / of man's absence." Chinese poet Chen Li's poem "War Symphony" is a striking visual display that starts with the Chinese character "soldier," marching as an army on the page. As the reader's eyes continue downward, the poet presents two characters that suggest "one-legged soldiers . . . two onomatopoeic words imitating sounds of collision or gunshots." Chen Li leaves us with the terrifying spectacle of war, ending with the Chinese character for "hill" or "mound," signifying the aftermath: a mass grave and ruin that cannot be surmounted.

[2] Hannah Arendt, *On Violence* (San Diego and New York: Harcourt Brace Jovanovich, 1970), pp. 86–87.

The Kurds are a stark example of the residual effects of conflict in the form of forced displacement as they are an estimated 30 million people without a nation-state. They live mainly in the mountains and uplands where Turkey, Iraq, and Iran meet, in an area known as Kurdistan. However, in each of the new postwar countries, the Kurds were persecuted and forced not only to learn the language of the new state but to abandon their Kurdish identity and accept Turkish, Iranian, or Arab nationalism. As the Chinese poet Hung Hung said during the Taipei Poetry Festival, the Kurds are "the most humiliated and disenfranchised of peoples."

One of Vietnam's leading female poets, Lâm Thị Mỹ Dạ, was born in 1949 in Quang Binh Province, in the central part of Vietnam, near the scene of intense fighting during the American War. In "Bomb Crater Sky," she relays the story of a woman who was killed by a bomb attack while on the Ho Chi Minh Trail. It is believed that she sacrificed herself to save the troops. In this poem she praises the woman warrior:

> They say that you, a road builder,
> Had such love for our country
> You rushed out and waved your torch
> To call the bombs down on yourself
> And save the road for the troops
>
> .   .   .   .
>
> Now you lie down deep in the earth
> As the sky lay down in that earthen crater
> At night your soul sheds light
> Like the dazzling stars
>
> .   .   .   .
>
> .   .   .   .
>
> Is it the sun, or your heart
> Lighting my way
> As I walk down the long road?

The poem illustrates the effects of war. Though the person has perished, her soul fuels the lives of others:

> The name of the road is your name
> Your death is a young girl's patch of blue sky
> My soul is lit by your life

Apostrophe in the Scripture

And my friends, who never saw you—
Each has a different image of your face

War has filled the landscape with negative space, with faces that, even while begging not to sink forgotten into the earth's cracks, begin to disassemble. These poems are testimonials that persist in spite of ruin, imagining a world without maps, where histories intertwine. Look to even one date palm in the desert, sprouting in sustenance while the land to which it's rooted is threaded by the tread of tanks. Every day has a shadowy underside, and preserved in these poems, like the space between the newsprint columns of obituaries, those who are gone but not lost continue to live. They have left stories for us to tell and retell, and in the stark persistence of our retelling, we sap war of its power to destroy.

— NATHALIE HANDAL

NÂZIM HIKMET

Angina Pectoris

If half my heart is here,
half of it is in China, doctor.
It's in the army flowing to the Yellow river.
Then, at every dawn, doctor
at every dawn, my heart
is riddled with bullets in Greece.

Then when our convicts get to sleep
   retreating from the ward
      my heart is in a broken down old manor in Çamlica,
every night,
doctor.

Then for all those ten years
all I have to offer my poor people
     is this one apple I hold, doctor,
a red apple:
my heart . . .

It's not from arteriosclerosis, nor nicotine, nor prison,
that I have this angina pectoris,
   but because, dear doctor, because of this.

I look at night through iron bars,
despite the pressure in my chest,
my heart beats along with the farthest star.

**Translated from the Turkish by Ruth Christie, Richard McKane, and
Talât Sait Halman**

KEKI N. DARUWALLA

Gujarat 2002

There's blood on the streets, so many dying and the dead,
that dark-grained newspapers squint with red.

Fire and skin turn into one blinding sheet, and in any weather
life and charred skin will peel together.

Boards are warped, the steel blackened. Inside
there's a mother in travail, there could be a bride.

Killer and killed are one—they speak the same language.
The vocabulary of guilt has a circumference and a center.

Gasoline alights with a splash everywhere.
Knives hiss with the same silence where they enter.

Gujarat is not just the corruption of an absolute.
It has manufactured its own corrupt absolutes:

"If night fell on Godhra, we are within our rights
to unload night on innocence elsewhere."

There is no place here for the lyre and the lute.
In such times is lockjaw the best—to be dumb, to be mute?

ADONIS

excerpts from "Diary of Beirut Under Siege, 1982"

1.
The time of my life tells me:
"You do not belong here."
I answer frankly.
Granted, I don't belong.
I try my best to understand you,

but I am lost
like a shadow in a forest
of skulls.

2.

I'm standing now.
This wall is nothing but a fence.
Distance shrivels; a window fades
Daylight is but a thread
I snip to stitch my way to darkness,
breath by breath.

3.

Everything I ever said of life and death
repeats itself in the silence
of the stone that pillows my head.

6.

The door of my house is sealed.
Darkness blankets me.
The moon offers me
its paltry alms of light.
I choke with gratitude,
but I cannot speak.

7.

Murder has transformed Beirut.
Rock is really bone.
Smoke is but the breath of human beings.

10.

Bulletins:
a woman in love's been killed,
a boy kidnapped,
a policeman crushed against a wall.

12.

People were found in sacks:
a head only in one sack,
a tongueless and headless corpse

in another,
in a third what once was a body,
the rest, nameless.

23.
When trees bend, they say good-bye.
When flowers bloom, blaze and close,
        they say good-bye.
Young bodies that vanish in chaos say good-bye.
Papers that thirst for ink say good-bye.
The alphabets and poets say good-bye.
Finally the poem says good-bye.

Translated from the Arabic by Samuel Hazo

GU CHENG

excerpts from "Eulogy World"
A POEM CYCLE. OCTOBER 1983–NOVEMBER 1985

16 Narrative

three men desert the battlefield

they mix wine with leaves, send people off with bullets at dusk,
they pass by a town flowing with silken cloth

later, when the MPs have arrived
he is the last to be dragged, alone, through the square

17 In Oneself

that face brushed by the windstorm
that face obscured, confused by love

    already it is too long a time
for that face to have clutched the kindling to its breast
                        precious as a brother

that face is like a thick cord
which can only tighten with love
which can only weave itself into a fence, a basket,
and love her winter kindling

    already it is too long a time—
she has never stretched out a hand
to touch the flower overhead

35 Wolf Pack

within those easily opened jars
is light
and the traces of light on inner walls

in the corridor shifting swiftly from light to darkness
someone is letting down their hair. . . .

37 Nature

what pleases me is the hurled lance
numberless leaves on a tree
closing ranks over the earth

they show their faces on the long narrow road
slowly rocking, waving bird's-nest banners

here is that mysterious point where life suffers a defeat

Translated from the Chinese by John Cayley

JEAN ARASANAYGAM

Nallur, 1982

It's there,
        beneath the fallen fronds dry crackling
pile of broken twigs, abandoned wells of brackish

water lonely dunes
                    It's there
the shadows of long bodies shrunk in death
the leeching sun has drunk their blood and
bloated swells among the piling clouds
                    It's there
                    death

                              smell it in the air
Its odor rank with sun and thickening blood
mingling with fragrance from the frothy toddy
pots swinging like lolling heads from
blackened gibbets,
                    It's there,
                         amid the clamor of
the temple bells, the clapping hands, the
brassy clash of cymbals,
                              the zing of bullets
                              cries of death
                              drowned in the roar
                              of voices calling Skanda
                              by his thousand names
                              Muruga, Kartikkeya,
                              Arumuga . . .

"We pray, we cry, we clamor.
Oh Sri Kumaran, be not like the God
who does not hear, deaf Sandesveran."

Thirtam now no longer nectar of the Gods
brims over but is bitter, bitter,
and at the entrance to Nallur
the silent guns are trained
upon a faceless terror.

Outside,
the landscape changes
the temples by the shore are smoking
ruins charred stones blackened,
on empty roads are strewn
stained discarded dressings

burnt-out abandoned vehicles
a trail of blood
soon mopped up by the thirsty sun.

Turned away from bloody skirmishes
of humankind, the gods are blinded
by the rain of bullets,
     six faced Arumugan
     all twelve eyes
     closed in darkness

The land is empty now
the pitted limestone
invaded by the sea
drowns, vanishes.

Waves of rust swell and billow
beating into hollow caves and burial urns
filled with the ash of bodies,
cremated by the fire of bullets.

GRANAZ MOUSSAVI

Camouflage Costumes

The clamor of dusty children
changes in the throats of flutes.
For the children in narrow alleys, a gun
is two fingers put together;
and death
is a closing of eyelids and a rolling around in dirt.
Tomorrow
imaginary guns shall be left and forgotten
on the decks of paper boats,
and the camouflage costumes once too large for the world's children
shall fit.

Translated from the Persian by Sholeh Wolpé

BRYAN THAO WORRA

Burning Eden One Branch at a Time

My father, a skull before the wars were over,
Never saw my mother's flight in terror
~~As our humbled kingdom fell to flame and shell~~

My mother was stripped to ink among the bureaucrats,
A number for their raw statistics of jungle errors
~~Collated into cold ledgers marked "Classified"~~

My feet dangling in the Mississippi have forgotten
What the mud in Vientiane feels like between your toes
While my hands hold foreign leaves and I whisper

"Maple"
"Oak"
"Weeping Willow"

As if saying their names aloud will rebuild my home.

LÂM THỊ MỸ DẠ

Bomb Crater Sky

They say that you, a road builder
Had such love for our country
You rushed out and waved your torch
To call the bombs down on yourself
And save the road for the troops

As my unit passed on that worn road
The bomb crater reminded us of your story
Your grave is radiant with bright-colored stones
Piled high with love for you, a young girl

As I looked in the bomb crater where you died
The rain water became a patch of sky
Our country is kind
Water from the sky washes pain away

Now you lie down deep in the earth
As the sky lay down in that earthen crater
At night your soul sheds light
Like the dazzling stars
Did your soft white skin
Become a bank of white clouds?

By day I pass under the sky flooded with sun
And it is your sky
And that anxious, wakeful disc—
Is it the sun, or your heart
Lighting my way
As I walk down the long road?

The name of the road is your name
Your death is a young girl's patch of blue sky
My soul is lit by your life

And my friends, who never saw you—
Each has a different image of your face

Translated from the Vietnamese by Martha Collins and Thuy Dinh

JAM ISMAIL

Casa Blanca 1991

'the westward creep of the ontario scenario,' premier vander
  zalm warned, describing first, as it turns out, himself.
& there we were, by the gas station on the eve of it could
  be world war III, our arms filter thinning what senses.

'eerie is the right word for it'   (CNN live, about arab
  women)   'because, they all look like birds!'
'well, we really don't know how this war is being
  conducted' : dwarfed by a bosom of blue domes,
  correspondent allows.

cradle ,   cradler, of civilization,   'the
  wheel, the arch, writing, bureaucracy, government, armies,
  the state, the first law codes, everything!',   she
  seethed,   'came out of iraq!'

so-o.. i tell ya what, Sirocco of Ottawa.   light breeze in
  qatar. empty streets, an airraid siren, dahran. the sea
  blue bolt of silk starboard the athabascan.   'liberation
  of kuwait has begun.' (marlin fitzwater, collar off
  kilter),   'swift and massive.'

states, of heightened retinas. soldier rinses duds by a box
  of Tide. 'perception' in the stock market stressed.
  'i had to look at my friends to see if i wuz alright.'
  '. . . killed, by friendly fire . . .'
  (uhh. lucky other side)

slings, & arrows, of islamic calligraphy. europe, enroute
  to india, wanted to avoid arab merchants, so dis covered
  america. now baghdad is a city living by its wits.
  'news of the bunker deaths cannot be allowed to stop their
  mission.'
horror-fatigue sags coiffure of anchorwoman.   'thank you,
  col. flymo, for being, as usual, interesting.'

troop couture. designer war. puppet love. Washington's
  Hand Laundry. 'thanks, Your Disney.'   our P.M. his
  forehead scribbled. inset of desert sand.

FAIZ AHMED FAIZ

Once Again the Mind

Today, as usual, the mind goes hunting for a word,
one filled with venom, a word
sultry with honey, heavy with love,
    smashing with fury.
The word of love must be brilliant as a glance
which greets the eye like a kiss on the lips,
bright as a summer river, its surface streaming gold,
joyous as the moment when the beloved enters
    for the appointed meeting.

The word of rage must be a ferocious blade
that brings down for all time the oppressor's citadel.
The word must be dark as the night of a crematorium;
if I bring it to my lips
    it will blacken them forever.

Today every instrument is forsaken by its melody,
and the singer's voice goes searching for its singer.
Today the chords of every harp are shredded
like a madman's shirt. Today
the people beg each gust of wind
to bring any sound at all, even a lamentation,
even a scream of anguish,
or the last trump crying the hour of doom.

Translated from the Urdu by Naomi Lazard

YEHUDA AMICHAI

I Was Not One of the Six Million. And What Is the Span of My Life? Open Shut Open

1.

I was not one of the six million
who died in the Holocaust, not even
one of those who survived, and I was not one
of the six hundred thousand who came out of Egypt,
I, for one, reached the Promised Land from the sea.
I was not among all those others but the smoke and fire
did linger in me, and columns of fire and columns of smoke[1]
still show me the way night and day, and the mad search
for emergency exits and soft spots still lingers as well.
After the stripped earth to flee into weakness
and into hope and there lingered in me the lusting search
for spring water, speaking softly to the rock and with violent strikes.[2]
Later a silence of no questions, no answers.
Like millstones Jewish history and world history
grind me between them, at times down to dust,
and a solar year and a lunar year precede
one another or follow one another and leap
and provide constant motion to my life
and I at times fall in the gap between them
to hide in or to sink.

2.

I was not in the places where I was not
and will not be. I have no part in the infinite
of light years and dark years but the darkness is mine
and the light is mine and my time is mine.
The sand on the shore, the infinite grains,
is the sand upon which I loved in Achziv and in Caesarea.

[1] Alludes to Exodus 13:21. The biblical Hebrew *amud* is traditionally translated as "pillar," but here, in the context of the Holocaust, I chose "column" to bring to mind the columns of human beings, reduced to numbers, who were actually the fodder of the smoke and fire.

[2] Alludes to Moses striking the rock for water (Exodus 17:6).

The years of my life I broke down into hours
and the hours into minutes and into seconds
and milliseconds. They are the stars above
which cannot be numbered.

3.

And what is the span of my life. I am like one
who has come out of Egypt and the Red Sea parted and I walked
on dry land, on my left and on my right two walls of water,
behind me Pharaoh and his army and horsemen,
before me the desert, perhaps the Promised Land.
This is the span of my life.

4.

Open shut open. Before a man is born
all in the universe is open without him.
While he lives, all is shut within him.
And when he dies, all is open again.
Open shut open. This is what man is.

5.

And what is the span of my life, like a self-portrait,
I set the camera at a distance on solid ground
(the only solid place on earth),
decide on a spot where to stand, near a tree,
and run back to the camera and press the button
and run back to my place near the tree,
listen to the ticking of time, and its hum, like a distant prayer,
and the popping sound, like an execution.
This is the span of my life. God develops the picture
in His great darkroom. Here's the picture:
white hair on my head, the eyes heavy and weary,
and the brows above my eyes black, like sooty
window-frames of a burned-down house.
The years of my life have passed.

6.

My life is the gardener of my body. The brain,
a well-secured hothouse, replete with flowers and strange
exotic plants of great sensitivity and extinction fears.

The face, a French garden laid out in exact planes
with marble-tiled squares and statues and places to rest,
and places to touch and sniff and gaze, to get lost
in a green maze and paths, not to trample, not to pluck.
The torso above the navel, an English park, displaying freedom
with no angles, no tiles, a facsimile of nature and man,
in our image,[3] our likeness,
its arms joining the great night all around.
And my lower body, under the navel, at times a feral,
striking, wondrous nature preserve, preserved and not preserved,
at times a compact Japanese garden, mapped out in advance.
The genitals, honed and smooth stones, with dark tufts
between them, and distinct lanes full of meaning
and calm contemplation. And the precepts of my father
and my mother's commandments are the chirp and song of birds.
And the woman I love is the seasons and weathers
and the children playing are my children.
And the life is my life.

7.

I wholly believe that right at this moment
millions of people are standing at crossroads,
at street corners, in deserts and jungles,
and direct one another as to where to turn,
and which is the road, the direction,
and explain again where to turn, which way,
and how to get there via the fastest route,
and where to stop and ask someone else.
There, there. No, at the second corner,
then make a left, or a right, near the white house,
at the oak tree, and they elaborate, with excited voices,
waving their hands, shaking their heads,
there, there, no, not this there, that there,
like a primal ritual. This, too, is a new religion.
I wholly believe that right at this moment.

Translated from the Hebrew by Tsipi Keller

---

[3] Alludes to "Let us make man in Our image, after Our likeness" (Genesis 1:26).

TỐ HỮU

Pham Hong Thai

Live and die as you live and die—
Hate the enemy, love your country
Live—your life explodes like a bomb
Die—your death waltzes in a blue river

Translated from the Vietnamese by Nguyễn Bá Chung

JAYANTA MAHAPATRA

A Kind of Happiness

The boat I've laid my mind on
is adrift, moving slowly up an ageless creek,
through water still and colorless as time,
among drifts of uncomprehending silent reeds.

In it I've staked those my precious years,
the fear of the depths and the unholy cold;
now for that reason maybe (being so awake)
I fear it may never reach the promise of the sea.

There is a hand I remember, that lay simply
in your lap, warm and sacred and drenched
with its promise, a hair's breadth away from my own,
yet some spell did not drop anchor, to lay mine on it,

barely escaping happiness I thought I knew of it,
but would I recognize it if it really came?
What use would it be if I'd tie the boat to a tree
and lie down in the heart of its demand?

It soaks into each song, words and the throats of birds
hoping such symbols would make up its definition,

yet can the good world
hold the flowing movement of fear in the mind?

Can slain men show the miracle of being alive?
Always it's this boat that nails me to the water,
darkening its silent waste and flow,
the reeds merciless like those dead,
yet don't I know it is better to leave the boat alone?

What would tell me at last where I belong?
The cracking keel, the bold green moss?

MAYA BEJERANO

The Pecan Leaves

1.
The pecan leaves were just
                a backdrop,
the pecan leaves were the late
backdrop that came later,
and before the backdrop of the pecan leaves
there were myriad faces
wishing for multitudes
(like the apples of love-sick Shulamit[1]).
I don't give the exact number.
Faces near and distant
faces from up-close and far away
faces expected to arrive faces gone by
we were all entwined in some rare
presence, not so much
friends intertwined in the presence
let's say a melody
strains of some light and familiar music,
Clark and Hummel Korsakov and Bach

[1] Shulamit of the *Song of Songs*.

the Beatles and Gershwin
The piano keys strode up and down
the fat chords of the contrabass teased in their low tones
and the trumpeter that resembled the shadowy Father Frolo,
and so the medieval church of Notre Dame
immediately leaps to mind, thanks to Tzvia,
the trumpeter attired like the court musician in the palace
adding to the twining process,
the stain of the effort visible in his lip

I try very hard
to continue playing,
keep up the pitch,
and the train of faces grows heavy and is turned already
into pearls white pearls.
The sun already in a blunt angle beyond the right-angled,
filtered radiating simply humbly.
About 2 P.M.,
given to description and it's not hard:
Luzit, The Terebinth Valley, Agur,
a stone structure towering above,
a Turkish bath,
Acacia trees spectacular in their yellow,
olive branches and carob
I want to go back
to the white pearls behind,
turn back.
Not because I left a snake there,
and not a mouse,
no mice,
a cool breeze entered to blow
the notes,
and someone hastened to grab them
with his switched-off cellular phone.
But we haven't smelled the blood yet
(not the blood of the Maccabees)
we only played played
and paid attention
to how the musicians whipped the air near us
with us (and here's where it starts, with us)

2.

The pecan leaves will be
the pecan leaves are about to be
any minute a backdrop
any minute in the backdrop,
they sat with their backs to the backdrop, just like that,
Eliezer's old parents and he next to them
facing their house that's about to crumble
about to crumble for decades now,
like they, and that was the main subject.
Three people in a stream of afternoon light
pecan leaves as backdrop
resting in their exact spot
and the silence silence
even when justified felt intense
and the silence evoked
the scent of blood

Translated from the Hebrew by Tsipi Keller

GHASSAN ZAQTAN

Black Horses

The slain enemy
Think of me without mercy in their eternal sleep
Ghosts ascend the stairways of the house, rounding the corners
The ghosts I picked up from the roads
Collecting them from the sins around other people's necks.

The sin hangs at the throat like a burden
It is there I nurture my ghosts and feed them
The ghosts that float like black horses in my dreams.

With the vigor of the dead the latest Blues song rises
While I reflect on jealousy
The door is warped open, breath seeps through the cracks
The breath of the river

The breath of drunkards, the breath
Of the woman who awakes to her past in a public park.

When I sleep
I see a horse grazing the grass
When I fall asleep,
The horse watches over my dreams

On my table in Ramallah
There are unfinished letters
And pictures of old friends
The manuscript of a young poet from Gaza
An hourglass
And opening lines that flap in my head like wings.

I want to memorize you like that song in first grade
The one I hold on to
Complete and
With no mistakes
The lisp, the tilt of the head, off key
The small feet pounding the concrete so eagerly
The open palms pounding the benches.

They all died in the war
My friends and classmates
Their little feet
Their eager little hands . . . they still pound the floors of each room
They pound the tables;
And still pound the pavements, the backs of the passersby, their shoulders.
Wherever I go
I see them
I hear them.

Translated from the Arabic by May Jayyusi and Alan Brownjohn

BARBARA TRAN

Lineup

For the woman from Muzaffargarh, Pakistan, whose rape on 22 June 2002 by four men was ordered by a jury.

I am 30. I am 18.
There were hundreds

watching. There were none.
My brother is old

enough to pay
for his own

sins. My brother
is 11. The girl

consented. The girl is,
as the jury says, too

high class
for my brother. The verdict

comes. No crowd
hears it: not the protests

spewing, not the prayers
rising, not the disbelief

dribbling
from my father's

cracked lips.
My heels

carve riverbeds. Still
the men

push. There is no
evidence

of anything
I am telling you.

There were 4 men on me.
There was an army.

You believe in justice. I believe
in revenge. The only man

in the moon
is smiling.

MUHAMMAD 'AFIFI MATAR

Recital

This sun wears a live chemise of blood.
A wound gapes from its kneecap, wide as the wind
And horizons gush blood-springs revealing birds and palm trees.
      Peace, it stays until nightfall . . . Peace
The river women rise:
        Anklets of grass twist circlets of
        Silver and silt, desire wet with the water's foam;
The river women call to the birds,
With shawls wipe the glass horizon.
They weep, they shed newly warmed sorrow.
      Peace, it stays until nightfall . . . Peace.

The fields folded their knees.
The ploughsocks softened, relaxed.
The serpents slept.
A pall of peace piles up: Downy hay and plume.
The bulls, standing, slumbered.
In their absent phosphoric eyes, night stars shatter.
      Peace; that mask of merciful night.

The living half unawakened, the mortal half slept.
This earth seemed empty.
When the night's prayer was recited and the dream angels came,

When sleep like the sun rose with its green radiance of rebirth, its sign
of illumination,
Then, by His mercy, I shed the diurnal limbs and opened a window in
the mortal half;
I enfolded myself in the living half
And the vision erupted:

I stepped out of the sheet's patters and the
pillow's perfume.
Have the covers left their bold arboreal designs on my face?
My face becomes flying leaves, falling fruit, sprouting twigs.

An imperial mare rises in my father's house:
Space is folded for her.
The silver, the flashes of her hoofs are the lights of Granada and those
lands beyond the River.
The mercury and kohl of her eyes mirror a blaze of royal ruins.
My form floats from my dream's body. I glow.
Trees spread through my face like traceries,
Freshly green tears inscribe springs and crescents of water on my
features.
My form floats from my dream's body:
The star Canopus looks a
trembling flower in the eyelet of the heart.
Life's blood-dimmed springs are loosed.
Horses rise from the *Amma* of the Book,
The circumference of the earth expands.
Peace, it stays until sunrise . . . Peace.
My knees grip a lodge on the horizon's ledge.
In my face crowd the lightning of writing, green leaves and water.
(The letters, a nation among nations, are addressed and
entrusted.)

The birds broke out from the dome of the wind as a well breaks out.
I remember . . . it's the horizon's divan.
My body is a lodge. I reign in what's not mine, what's not others'.

I remember . . . beneath me runs that river of living images;
And the springs sported as I wished.
I remember . . . the earth's globe approached and the heavens came to
me. They exchanged garments.

The mixing of memory's creatures and the marriage of what's not male
with what's female; what's not female with what's male,
And the joys of earthly powers
Gave me the strength to conjure with the sources of memory's shattered
images.
I conjured delicacies, images and chants as I wished.
The pause in the *Be* of the Book lingered.
Joy filled with tender questions,
And the foliage of the face dropped with fresh fears and the buds of
discovery's bewilderment.
I knew I walked the way of Ascension. I dwelt in the lodge of ultimate
certitude.
The circumference of the earth expanded.
The heavens appear as garments ripping at the waistline of the living
river,
A window beneath the garments of the oceans gapes open.
The Oriental Sages, the Hermetists and Gnostics partake of the banquet
of luminous dialogue.
Al-Suhrawardi breathes in the fullness of space, divides bread and the
silvery fish of the Nile. He eats in the plentitude of anarchy and drinks in
the profusion of ceaseless emanation.
The Hermetists weave the cape of chants and enchantments. They
unfold it for the noble tribe, the beats and the birds as a resting, sheltering
space for initiating and linking creatures twice, thrice, four times and up to
the last number memory may retain.

Rising from sleep the river women reveal bronzed legs, silt and earthy
grass.
        Peace, it stays until sunrise . . . Peace.

A mare whinnies in my father's house.
My father's house is a nomad in my dream's body.
The two Euphrates read like a book of rising blood
And the Nile is a book.
The Ocean pulls off the garments of diffused blood.

Then the desert's dressed, the large land and the cracked ruins adorned
by the splendor of lightning, by the green life of fire.
   The sun penetrates the flanks of night with purple gloves and stockings
of hammered and unhammered gold.
   It rises and falls.

   He descends to the murmur of vermin, the clinging of insects, the slither
of reptiles.
   The steps shorten.
   I wrapped myself in the tatters of the diurnal half.
   The smell of nocturnal sleep spread
   And the woolen covers heaved.
   The wet cotton covers collapsed.
   Peace, a spider of blood, clothed by the features' similarity . . . Peace.
   Water drains from the body.
   Memory drains from the water.

Translated from the Arabic by Ferial Ghazoul and Desmond O'Grady

Author's Note: Al-Suhrawardi: Shihab al-Din Yahya ibn Habash, known as "The Slain,"
was a famous mystic in the second half of the twelfth century. He lived in Baghdad and
then Aleppo, where he was under the patronage of its viceroy, al-Malik al-Zahir, son
of the famous Saladin. However, al-Zahir eventually put him to death when al-
Suhrawardi was only thirty-six, because his original mysticism rendered him suspect to
orthodox believers. Al-Suhrawardi believed in the agreement of all religions and all
philosophies, which, he insisted, express only one single truth. He was a student of
major Greek and other philosophers before him. The most characteristic attribute of
his work was his metaphysics of spiritual light, which he regarded as a symbol of ema-
nation and as the fundamental reality of things. He based his proof of the existence of
God upon this symbol.

KIM KWANG-KYU

North South East West

In spring a flood of tender green goes rising
spreading northward, northward.
Unhindered by barbed wire or military demarcation line

it journeys north.
Rising over mountains
crossing plains,
azaleas and forsythias cross the border north.
In summer the cuckoo's call,
the croak of frogs,
are just the same in every place.
In fall a flood of golden hues comes dropping
spreading southward, southward.
Unhindered by demilitarized zone or lines forbidding access
it journeys south.
Crossing rivers
passing over valleys
cosmos flowers and crimson leaves cross the border south.
In winter the taste of ice-cold pickle
the taste of spicy morning soup
are just the same in every place.
North South East West: making no distinction,
covering everywhere alike
in white, no one can keep back
the snowstorm.

Translated from the Korean by Brother Anthony of Taizé

Ý NHI

excerpts from "Letter in Winter"

1

Winds howl through the winter night.
A singer's voice fades in and out as if in a dream.
Pages once open close again, no one knows since when.
All the noisy reconciliations, the silent leave-takings,
the boisterous strides, the mournful, muffled footsteps
still reverberate through our lives.

2

How crowded the city
a war has just passed through.
Streets with ruined houses, whole blocks devastated,
a few familiar patterns, a few monuments left;
now roads widened, trees planted,
new train station, new flower basin in the garden,
the electrically lit swing, its bright circles of light,
multicolored shirts and dresses, the carefree, the
untroubled, loudspeakers blazing out new songs.
No mention of the sound of the old alarms.

Grand Central committee resolutions, grand schemes
at *Thac Ba, Ke Go, Thang Long.*
Prefabricated buildings newly erected,
new layers of paint frame thousands of old windows.

The crowded city.
A night blasted by gusts riding down from a northern gale,
a girl in a red dress passes me, her face blazing with rapture.
I am reminded of your poem—
"The bluish pale skin still shaken by fever
The fiery noon, the sun-lit clearings, the old forest . . ."[1]
I am reminded of your poem—
"We drank stream water, and ate our dried food
the cube of sugar divided into three at the top of the pass . . ."[2]

In her dazzling dress, her face so radiant and happy,
the girl passes by me under the trees' shadows.
How is it that I can never forget
lines written about those who are dead?
"The months and years of war touched everyone.
We sifted life to find what was pure and fine."[1]
How is it that I can never forget
"the artist felled by the canal near the river mouth
in the glare of the claymore his hand slowly let go of the
                                        palm leaf"[2]

[1] from a poem by Ngo The Oanh
[2] from a poem by Thanh Thảo

3

The road says nothing.
The trees say nothing.
Only gust after gust blows through the streets.

The day is no longer the same: something has awakened.
The light of the sun, the pebbles under our feet,
the fragrance of the tangerine, the leaves by the road,
the small room, the familiarity of a look,
even distant, with a touch of the unreal,
like the lamp flickering in the depths of night,
the endlessness of the time we were separated,
which seemed so short when we were reunited.

What landscapes have you passed through, what villages?
The joys, the sorrows, the bitterness of your life:
let me keep them in my heart.
The wind and fire of those days,
the sand burning under the July sun,
let them become flowers blooming suddenly under a column
                                        of pines;
in the seas where the waves are raging
let them be the water that calmly splashes the seagoers' feet;
in the forest after a season of violent storms
let them be the plants that gently open their leaves to the
                                        reddening sky.

Gusts of wind blow through the city in winter,
the day grows dark with longing and with hope.
We will reach the new land of the future:
your face, the song, the woodland, the distant shore.

Winter 1977

Translated from the Vietnamese by Nguyễn Bá Chung and Marilyn Nelson

D. H. MELHEM

Mindful Breathing

In the Buddhist tradition, we have the practice of mindful
breathing, of mindful walking, to generate the energy of
mindfulness. It is exactly with that energy of mindfulness that
we can recognize, embrace, and transform our anger . . .

—Thich Nhat Hanh, Riverside Church,
September 25, 2001

I sit by the window,
concentrate on breathing
and become, breath by breath,
a part of breath, drawn
first from this side of the street
bent to shadows dropped
from a scrawny moon.
Now the whole street is breath
flowing uptown
ebbing downtown
to swirl and swirl around
Ground Zero and blur into smoke
from those buried walls and those bodies,
smoke lifting from deep levels
of caves where survivors are hunted
and none can be found,

yet each one remains,
transformed into breath,
a tower, a vortex,
a silent tornado
or a slow wisp of smoke
curling around lightbulbs
and the dark pit
of memory
the pit of my stomach that
rejects this air.
It feels natural and wrong to use it

to keep my body intact, unless
each breath be taken in prayer.

I pray for the smoke of Ground Zero
and the smoke over Afghanistan
and every cinder of human history,
I pray that my own breath embrace
the blame and the connections
to wounded and wounding animals
who die, fall, and rise
into the furnace of living.

JOKO PINURBO

Coming Home at Night

We arrived late at night.
The bed was burnt
and the flames, which had spread
throughout the room
continued to roar.

Upon the wreckage of dreams
and ruins of time
our bodies char and disintegrate,
as fire turns them
into smoke and ash.

We are a pair of corpses
wanting to hold each other forever
and to sleep at peace
in the bed's embrace

Translated from the Indonesian by Linda Owens

AMIR OR

Blow Job

In the beginning there was desire, they say.
And then some.

The lips that clung to this dick
suckle now, blind with rapture,
a live dildo, a hard-on Truth,
the deeper the more blessed,
the more
the deeper.

Later, blue as well. The hand that was tied
with the black stocking between the legs,
the groin tucked in flayed hide (dressed and dyed),
the whip up the ass
will leave nothing
but doubt.

And primarily the grip. The involuntary
gagging motions take a small death first
before begging for more
only more
deeper:
heat up the blue rim.
Pull the trigger.

Translated from the Hebrew by Tsipi Keller

WALEED KHAZINDAR

At Least

If you would smash the glass against the wall,
if you would wake anyone you please, now at two in the morning,

if you would just say what you wrote yesterday, secretly, on the
      cigarette box,
"It has rained, spring has come
and the murdered man is still lying in the garden"—
if only you would do something, friend:
cut something down with your scythe, fling dust around!
Because when you sit like that at the edge of the sofa,
hands between your knees,
after your fourth glass, saying nothing,
I feel a jar breaking inside me.

Translated from the Arabic by Lena Jayyusi and W. S. Merwin

SANIYYA SALEH

Blind Boats

Because desolate rooms are beds for the poetry
   that kills
I sob,
I dry up like trees.
The days still as the rocks
  send the calls of blind boats.

Sharpshooter
Aim your gun at my heart,
Whisper your bullets like a lover into my ear.
In vain I raise my anguish to the skies
Let their roads
  be empty except for
My voice and
My echo.

Translated from the Arabic by Kamal Boullata

AHMAD SHAMLU

Greatest Wish Song

Ah if freedom could sing a song
small
as the throat of a bird,

Nowhere would crumbled walls remain.

It would not take many years
to comprehend

That ruins are a sign
of man's absence,
that human presence
makes hamlets and life.

Like a wound
dripping blood
life-long;
Like a wound
life-long
pounding with pain;
Opening eyes to the world
with a howl,
disappearing from it
with loathing.

Such was the great absence.
Such was the tale of ruins.

Ah if freedom could sing a song,
tiny,
tinier than a bird's throat.

Translated from the Persian by Sholeh Wolpé

AMJAD NASSER

One Evening in a Café

When thoughts don't take you far
and you sit silent
tremulous
staring at the veins in your hands;
when the chariot of your imagination
won't carry you to passageways lit with glimmers of insight
and you sit silent
tremulous
gazing at the smoke encircling your wrist:
when you do not answer the woman who greets you
as she lets her shawl fall
into the vacuum of the evening
and you sit silent
tremulous
staring at the fateful events written in your coffee grounds;
when the new émigrés stroll by
arm-in-arm with their adorned ladies
chattering on about how time flies
and you sit silent
tremulous
gazing at the mysterious wood of the table;
when you don't keep anyone's company
and can remember nothing of the war
but a horseshoe
or bullet holes in a curtain;
when, one evening in a café,
faces pass before you like a copper fog
and you hear cymbals clashing in a distant desert
or walls crashing into hypothetical canals;
when, one evening in a café
that blind singer's album
starts to play,
and everyone suddenly sighs;
then you rise and walk

to where the hatchet
leans against the tree.

Translated from the Arabic by S. V. Atallah

BEJAN MATUR

Time Consoled in the Stone

I
In the courtyard where sick horses
circle to recover,
a puny youth
his neck thinner than the neck of a sick horse,
stands in the middle of a stone bridge
in long black clothes.
The censer swinging at his neck
shows how far he must travel,
but his horse is sick,
unable to go
and the moon shall not enter his sleep.

History must move on
and find its place.
The word must find its subject.
His hair must grow long
and be damp and fragrant.

II
Time consoled in the stone
told him,
when it's dark
you'll be driven from here.
But we will remain.
The eagle's beak
snow water
in the well.
Remember your ancestry,

they say history will end
frozen in a photograph.

Man creates his face on his own
and so there is wind.
A place weeping enters our sleep
and never leaves.

Zeytun/Maraş   1997–98

Translated from the Turkish by Ruth Christie

Author's Note: Zeytun, in the southeast of Turkey, once had a large Armenian population who were subject to many massacres concluding with the major events of 1915.

H. S. SHIVA PRAKASH

Eleven Rudras

A bald hill of prickly trees
And a lonely house leaning on it

Around it
All through the long night
They go on screaming—

Eleven Rudras:

In the east
As the hurtful songs of a broken-throated koel bird
In the lands enslaved in shattered springs

In the southeast
As the screaming smoke of a city under siege

In the south
As the wind roaring across mile-long graveyards
Where mothers are buried with their newborn

In the southwest
As the sigh of waves of oceans
Turning slowly into poison

In the west
As the sarcastic laughter of the White House turning blood-red
At dust

In the northwest
As the screech of the engines of bombers out-speeding hurricanes

In the north
As the thousand-voiced wailing of a colossal collapsing tower

In the northeast
As the exploding sobs of girls raped by peacekeeping soldiers

I bow to you all

O! Eleven Rudras
Screaming eleven screams,
Do not show me any more your eleven rigid, compassionless faces
Do not scream any more your eleven terrorizing screams

No revolution
No tyranny
Can suppress you
O restless primeval beings

Come
At least now
As healing springs
As groundswells of solace
As well-protected maternal wombs
As floods of *amrit*
Should you turn red at all
Turn red like ashoka shoots

Come
As arch-rites of orgies of the young

As cooling crescent atop cascades of pitch-black clouds
As irrepressible peace benedictions
As seed mantras of the earth's most ancient and endless joys.

Translated from the Kannada by the author

U SAM OEUR

The Fall of Culture

I hid the precious wealth,
packed the suitcases with milled rice,
packed old clothes, a small scrap-metal oven,
pots, pans, plates, spoons, an ax, a hoe,
some preserved fish in small plastic containers—
loaded it all in a cart and towed it eastward
under the full moon, May '75.

"O home! Home! The sacred ground where we lived happily,
the heritage built, bit by bit, by my father.
O, the Naga fountain with its seven heads,
preserving our tradition from days gone by.

O, Monument of Independence! O, library! O, books of poetry!
I can never chant the divine poems again!
O, quintessential words of poets!
O, artifacts I can never touch or see again!

O, Phnom Penh! O, pagoda where we worship!
O, Angkor Wat, sublime monument to the
aspirations of our ancient Khmer forefathers.
Ah, I can't see across those three wildernesses:"

I'll be nowhere,
I'll have no night,
I'll have no day anymore:
I shall be a man without identity.

"Sorrow for the Cambodian women
who were faithful to their lovers;
now they wander without sleep,
any piece of ground their home.
O, rang trees, the spawning grounds,
turned to charred stilts by the Pot-Sary conflagration.
Annihilate the rang trees, the sugar palms
the Khmer Republic!"

There are no more intellectuals, no more professors—
all have departed Phnom Penh, leading children,
bereft, deceived to the last person,
from coolie to king.

Translated from the Khmer by Ken McCullough

Author's Note: Precious wealth refers specifically to both an Amrita crystal, which had
no actual material value but was of inestimable spiritual value; *Naga fountain with its
seven heads* is a statue with seven hooded cobra heads; *Monument of Independence* is
a neoclassical monument built in Phnom Penh in 1957 to commemorate Cambodian
independence from the French; *those three wildernesses* refers to Wilderness of Killing,
Wilderness of Starvation, Wilderness of Disease; *rang trees / the spawning grounds* are
the trees that grow on riverbanks, whose roots grow into the water and serve as a shel-
ter for fish to lay their eggs; *Pot-Sary conflagration* refers to Pol Pot, in cahoots with Ieng
Sary, the Foreign Minister of Democratic Kampuchea, who were the engineers of geno-
cidal policies. Ieng Sary was the brother-in-law of Pol Pot.

MAMMAD ARAZ

If There Were No War

If there were no war,
We could construct a bridge between Earth and Mars
Melting weapons in an open-hearth furnace.
If there were no war,
The harvest of a thousand years could grow in one day.
Scientists could bring the moon and stars to Earth.
The eyes of the general also says:

"I would be chairman in a small village
If there were no war!"
If there were no war,
We could avoid untimely deaths.
Our hair would gray very late.
If there were no war,
We would face
Neither grief, nor parting.
If there were no war,
The bullet of mankind would be his word,
And the word of mankind would be love.

Translated from the Azeri by Aytan Aliyeva

SHAMSUR RAHMAN

Into Olive Leaves

Ma, I can tell for certain,
at this very moment,
sitting on your faded velvet prayer rug,
facing the Ka'aba,
you're reciting the Holy Qur'an.
No one else in the house has gotten out of bed yet,
there's no sound of anyone nearby;
only, an exquisite silence.
Nature is singing the *Kalangra*.

And I'm now
half lying, half sitting, passing time in a foxhole.
Next to me my automatic rifle is sleeping deeply
like a tall black candle
and to my left lies a man in uniform—
his right leg blown off by a shell.
He can't be touched now—a mere touch
will make his body dissipate like sand.
Those of us who are waiting here
to ambush the enemy, it's as if each of us today

is like a sand statue.
Last night he asked me for a cigarette—
Ma, don't get angry that I told you about the cigarette.
Now I can tell you about many things
without hesitation, what you'll not want to hear;
you'll want to silence me for not being proper.
Now everything has turned upside down within me.

Anyway, as I was saying, yesterday the man
next to me in tunic wanted a cigarette from me
and showed me a photograph of his wife and children
he pulled out of his chest pocket.
That photograph is now lying in mud,
worms have started tunnelling into his tunic,
his nostrils.
After chasing them away once or twice
I stopped.
Some kind of a scent has spread everywhere like darkness.
Do *Azrail*'s wings have this aroma?
Inside my eyes
inside my chest
inside my bones Life whimpers
and I snarl fiercely at the advancing wings of *Azrail*.

Ma, I can see
you're sitting in the narrow veranda
with your prayer beads in your hand;
your mind is in the shade of the magnanimous blue sky
and my three-year-old son Tukun
is standing with his hand on your knee,
looking at the dawn birds flying,
your left hand placed on his head.
I remember seeing such an image long ago,
as far as I can remember, in a book about painting.

Ma, in this foxhole, sometimes it feels like
as if I have no dream, no memory, no attachment,
no tomorrow.
Death here is playing the accordion
and whimsically singing away in a croaking voice.

My ghost is walking away
scattering the ashes of my dreams.

I don't know if I'll return to you again;
through the ages, many have not returned,
will never return.
You know, Ma, how odd that at this very moment
I feel nostalgic about the pomegranate tree next to our kitchen,
about the tubewell spot,
about certain markings on the wall of my room.

Ma, it was from you that I had my first lessons.
Let my Tukun have his first alphabet lessons from you.
From now on raise him so he never, even by error,
shoots lead pellets into a flock of birds,
shoots a hole through anyone's chest.
Ask him to look after the olive orchard, Ma,
so that he can weave his dreams into the olive leaves.

Translated from the Bengali by Sajed Kamal

SITOR SITUMORANG

In Answer to Father's Letter

I'm no longer good
at hitching a plow.
When Mother died
I wrote a poem
about suffering
which the world soon forgot.
And then I wrote a story
about how she went to heaven,
and the world was moved—
But about her suffering, not one word.

And now that you yourself
are preparing for death,

what am I to write?
I fetch your picture
and see in it
both General and Ancient Farmer.
And remember the saying,
and the poem that reads:
When the general leaves for the battlefield
he does not turn back in remembrance.

Swords and shields
are now covered in dust.
And all that's left is for me to write:
The poet has crossed the lake safely
his boat on the shore is but a shell. . . .

Translated from the Indonesian by John H. McGlynn

KADHIM JIHAD

South

Silently I watch them move away
and cross the fence with one step.
The expanse, girdled with palm tree towers,
quickly swallows their specters.
A small vanishing point
is what each one becomes at the end of the horizon.
I wish I could be hung
from the fate of one of them
like a dagger is hung to a belt, I wish
I could become a comma or an apostrophe
in the scripture of their completed destinies.

With rifles of deflowered butts
they move away.
Hunters of ducks and hogs,
whenever they risk crossing
the far end of the reed forests.

I grab their brief speech
and fill their emptiness with my words.
No doubt misfortune
desired that I was born in the city,
far from the countryside where my kin extend
their solid roots in the sturdy land,
where our cousins built
their pillared guesthouses upon the river.

There at its peak noon returns you
to an original time.
You hear its droning ring
ascending the folds of silence.
And at night when no wedding
clamor rises,
it's common to hear the solitary song
of a lonesome neighbor,
charitable in your direction as if he had chosen you,
a singular witness to his grief.

Insects of the countryside,
I know their buzzing in all their verities:
palm tree forests in their swarming worlds
I know how birth persists in them
and the birds of the countryside.
I tell them apart
by nothing other than the tone of their chirp.
Early on I learned to surprise the hogs;
they don't see from the corner of their eyes.
All the dead children,
their bodies floating in water,
I am their orphan.
I know the strange taste of pollen
and from the roses I know
the sting you suffer
as a sweet dizziness.
I know the marshes
and the earth is tilled every other year.

Like an orange in the water's belly,
the countryside sleeps in my depths.
Without it I move in this world
deprived of one aspect of being,
no doubt the more beautiful aspect.

Translated from the Arabic by Fady Joudah

SHOLEH WOLPÉ

One Morning, in the *LA Times*

It's a picture of the universe
ripped in the middle
through which a child's head and shoulders lean.
His gaze
past sheaths of yellow stars
and wheels of pinhole lights
arrests your eyes.

For a moment you are confused.
Who is this celestial child
with round black eyes
and lips parted
as if speaking to you,
in your kitchen chair
with the taste of coffee on your tongue?

You bend
look closer
read the caption.

This is not a picture of the universe,
not a dark starry night.

SHIN KYŎNG-NIM

Ssitkim Kut—
A wandering spirit's song

Go your way in peace, they say, go your way in peace.
With your broken neck, hugging severed limbs,
go a thousand, ten thousand leagues down the road
    to the land beyond, without night or day;
go your way in peace, they say, go your way in peace.

Sleep now, they say, sleep quietly now.
Though a myriad million years pass, never open those eyes
blinded with blood as you fell in barley field, meadow,
    or patch of sand;
sleep now, they say, sleep quietly now.

Seize hold, with your slashed and slivered hand
seize warmly hold of these blood-covered hands.
A new day has come, the sun is shining bright,
birds are carolling, the breeze is balmy,
so seize hold with your slivered hand, they say, seize hold.

I cannot go with my broken neck and severed limbs,
I cannot quietly close my blood-blinded eyes,
cannot seize hold, cannot seize with this slivered hand,
I cannot seize your blood-covered hands.

I have come back, with blood-blinded eyes glaring,
    I have returned
with my broken neck, hugging severed limbs;
I grind my teeth and wish bitter frost may drop from heaven.
I cannot seize hold with this slivered hand,
I cannot seize your blood-covered hands;
I have come back, a dense storm-cloud,
to alleys, markets, factories, quays;
I have come back, a violent clamor.

Translated from the Korean by Brother Anthony of Taizé and Young-moo Kim

NAOMI SHIHAB NYE

The Word PEACE

You could find words or parts of words
inside other words, it had always been a game.
PEACE for example contained the crucial vowels of
EAT and EASY which seemed suggestive
in good ways. If people ATE together
they would be less likely to KILL one another
especially if one were responsible for shopping & cooking
& the other for wiping & cleaning & you took turns.
Then you started thinking, what does he like?
What might suit his fancy?
There should of course be meals
for all peace talks, yes, we understood that
long ago, as there is eating at festivals & weddings,
the generous platter, the giant bowl.
Those who placed a minor faith in rhyme,
might try PEACE & CEASE, as in,
could you please CEASE this hideous
waste of time & resources, when's the last time
any of you considered how lucky we are
to be BORN? We had grown too far
from the source, that's for sure.
A man spit ETHICS at me as if it were
a dirty word.
And what about apologizing to kids, hey?
After TEACHing them to use words to solve
their differences, what did we do?
People two years old were starting to look
a lot better than people than anyone else
& consider their vocabularies.
EAT was probably in there.
Sweet DREAMS & PLEASE which also contained those
crucial vowels found in PEACE if anyone
were still thinking about it. This didn't always work
though, because some might say WAR contained the
first 2 letters of ART & you would not want them
for one minute to believe that.

CHEN LI

War Symphony

兵兵兵兵兵兵兵兵兵兵兵兵兵兵兵兵兵兵兵兵兵兵兵兵
兵兵兵兵兵兵兵兵兵兵兵兵兵兵兵兵兵兵兵兵兵兵兵兵
兵兵兵兵兵兵兵兵兵兵兵兵兵兵兵兵兵兵兵兵兵兵兵兵
兵兵兵兵兵兵兵兵兵兵兵兵兵兵兵兵兵兵兵兵兵兵兵兵
兵兵兵兵兵兵兵兵兵兵兵兵兵兵兵兵兵兵兵兵兵兵兵兵
兵兵兵兵兵兵兵兵兵兵兵兵兵兵兵兵兵兵兵兵兵兵兵兵
兵兵兵兵兵兵兵兵兵兵兵兵兵兵兵兵兵兵兵兵兵兵兵兵
兵兵兵兵兵兵兵兵兵兵兵兵兵兵兵兵兵兵兵兵兵兵兵兵
兵兵兵兵兵兵兵兵兵兵兵兵兵兵兵兵兵兵兵兵兵兵兵兵
兵兵兵兵兵兵兵兵兵兵兵兵兵兵兵兵兵兵兵兵兵兵兵兵
兵兵兵兵兵兵兵兵兵兵兵兵兵兵兵兵兵兵兵兵兵兵兵兵
兵兵兵兵兵兵兵兵兵兵兵兵兵兵兵兵兵兵兵兵兵兵兵兵
兵兵兵兵兵兵兵兵兵兵兵兵兵兵兵兵兵兵兵兵兵兵兵兵
兵兵兵兵兵兵兵兵兵兵兵兵兵兵兵兵兵兵兵兵兵兵兵兵
兵兵兵兵兵兵兵兵兵兵兵兵兵兵兵兵兵兵兵兵兵兵兵兵

乒乒乒乒乒乓乒乓乒乓乓乒乒乓乒乒乒乓乒乓乒乒乒乒
乒乒乒乒乒乓乓乒乒乒乓乒乓乒乒乓乒乒乒乓乒乒乒乒
乒乓乒乒乒乒乓乓乒乓乒乓乒乓乒乒乓乒乓乒乒乒乒乓
乒乒乓乒乓乒乓乒乓乒乓乒乓乒乓乒乓乒乓乒乓乒乓乓
乒乒乓乒乓乒乓乒乓乒乓乒乓乒乓乒乓乒乓乒乓乒乓乓
乒乒乓乒乓乒乓乒乓乒乓乒乓乒乓乒乓乒乓乒乓乒乓乓
乒乒乓乒乓乒乓乒乓乒乓乒乓乒乓乒乓乒乓乒乓乒乓乓
乒乒乓乒乓乒乓乒乓乒乓乒乓乒乓乒乓乒乓乒乓乒乓乓
乒乒乒乓乒乒乓乒乓乒乒乓乒乒乓乒乒乒乓乒乒　乒乒　　乒
乒　乒乒乒　乒　乒　　乒乒　　　　乒乒　　　乒乒
　乒乒　　　乒乒　乒　乒乒　乓　乒　乒　　乒　　　乒
乒　　　　乒乒　　　乒　　　　　乒　　乒　乒
　　乒　　　　乒　　　乒　　　　　　　乒
　　　乒

丘丘丘丘丘丘丘丘丘丘丘丘丘丘丘丘丘丘丘丘丘丘丘丘
丘丘丘丘丘丘丘丘丘丘丘丘丘丘丘丘丘丘丘丘丘丘丘丘
丘丘丘丘丘丘丘丘丘丘丘丘丘丘丘丘丘丘丘丘丘丘丘丘
丘丘丘丘丘丘丘丘丘丘丘丘丘丘丘丘丘丘丘丘丘丘丘丘
丘丘丘丘丘丘丘丘丘丘丘丘丘丘丘丘丘丘丘丘丘丘丘丘
丘丘丘丘丘丘丘丘丘丘丘丘丘丘丘丘丘丘丘丘丘丘丘丘
丘丘丘丘丘丘丘丘丘丘丘丘丘丘丘丘丘丘丘丘丘丘丘丘
丘丘丘丘丘丘丘丘丘丘丘丘丘丘丘丘丘丘丘丘丘丘丘丘
丘丘丘丘丘丘丘丘丘丘丘丘丘丘丘丘丘丘丘丘丘丘丘丘
丘丘丘丘丘丘丘丘丘丘丘丘丘丘丘丘丘丘丘丘丘丘丘丘
丘丘丘丘丘丘丘丘丘丘丘丘丘丘丘丘丘丘丘丘丘丘丘丘
丘丘丘丘丘丘丘丘丘丘丘丘丘丘丘丘丘丘丘丘丘丘丘丘
丘丘丘丘丘丘丘丘丘丘丘丘丘丘丘丘丘丘丘丘丘丘丘丘
丘丘丘丘丘丘丘丘丘丘丘丘丘丘丘丘丘丘丘丘丘丘丘丘
丘丘丘丘丘丘丘丘丘丘丘丘丘丘丘丘丘丘丘丘丘丘丘丘
丘丘丘丘丘丘丘丘丘丘丘丘丘丘丘丘丘丘丘丘丘丘丘丘
丘丘丘丘丘丘丘丘丘丘丘丘丘丘丘丘丘丘丘丘丘丘丘丘

Author's Note: The Chinese character 兵 (pronounced "bing") means "soldier." 乒 and 乓 (pronounced "ping" and "pong"), which look like one-legged soldiers, are two onomatopoeic words imitating sounds of collision or gunshots. The character 丘 (pronounced "qiu") means "hill" or "mound."

THIS HOUSE,
MY BONES

This House, My Bones

—ELMAZ ABINADER

Before my family moved from an apartment in northern Virginia to the first house we'd ever owned, we lived for a year in Madras and Coimbatore, in South India. While there, I was bathed with well water that was drawn up by hand and heated on the stove in large pans, and sent to a school with a clip-on bow tie and an aluminum tiffin-carrier. Unlike in Virginia, where I had a regimented schedule and my own seat on the school bus, in India I was crowded by people yet somehow less confined than I had ever before been. I walked kicking dirt past roadside stands that sold goods from transistor radios to halwa in silver foil, shot marbles in the street, goaded bullocks into motion, ate milk-sweets, and got my cheeks pinched by innumerable aunties. I felt unique and fêted, if out of place.

The week of our return to America, I was taken with my cousin to be blessed at Guruyayur temple in Kerala. I had my head shorn by a priest using a straight razor, the hair swept into a neat pile and weighed against some coins on a scale. I was relieved to discover that, under the sandalwood paste my scalp was smeared with, I had no scars or odd protuberances. The wind tingled my head as I was carried out triumphantly on my grandfather's shoulders.

I returned, nearly bald, to Virginia in the middle of the school year. I had been a rare specimen in India, marveled at for being American, and coming back I thought some modicum of magic would remain with me. After a few days of ridicule in the school cafeteria though, I looked forward to moving to another neighborhood, particularly because I'd be in a different school district. Those were unsettled times because I was both literally and metaphorically between homes. Though I missed my cousins, the shops of mirrored textiles and carved figurines, and the smell of jasmine threaded in a woman's hair, I looked forward to a new beginning.

The house where I would come to spend my formative years was but an indentation in the ground when we first visited: a plot of scoured earth, the woods sprawling thickly, the riverbank less than a ten-minute bike ride away. Back then, we sat around an immaculate dining table while a man with waxen hair showed my father catalogues of available lots. My father chose the hypothetical Colonial on a small hill, and over the year, we periodically visited the site as it began to embody a home—when the foundation was being laid, when the walls were being framed, when doors suddenly appeared.

I still vividly recall the collective family pride of ownership, the sense of adventure that permeated the first night we spent there, newly painted trim gleaming, wall-to-wall carpet yet to be laid. We unfolded blankets onto the hardwood floor and my parents told stories of the cities they'd lived in. Over the years, I grew to inhabit one, then another of the rooms, played touch football on the front lawn, built barely functional tree houses, got drunk in the basement for the first time off pilfered liquor sealed in Tupperware. My father still boasts that the house is "his slice of heaven." Yet ask him if he's home and he'll shake his head *no*. Ask me and I'll answer the same, but for very different reasons. I feel simultaneously welcomed into and excluded from the many abodes I possess, that have possessed me. I have been *from* a place but not *of* a place, a tourist, not a settler.

Zhang Zai (张载) of the Neo-Confucian school once said, "Other people and I are of the same womb, I am one with all things." And yet the notion of habitat that each of us possesses is distinct and sometimes slippery to the point of nonexistence. Where or what is home? This question is perhaps unanswerable, but within the space of *This House, My Bones* different possibilities are raised. Some of the poems in the section are abstract investigations, while others are straightforward evocations of location, the cement and brick and air that constitute place.

İlhan Berk's "Istanbul" reminds us that the lengthy history and cultural association a group of people might have with a territory can be soothing but also dangerous. The poem begins with the image of "leaden domes" and a "man on the gallows" swinging to and fro, and ends with tramps, vagrants, whores, and dead sultans. Bashir Sakhawarz's "Kabul Behind My Window" also calls forth dust, suffering, the noise of death, and the "mullah like a worm through the loudspeakers," just as it conjures the ethereal and lyrical image of "nights caravans of khutbeh from mosques." Agnes S. L. Lam's "Eighteen Haiku for Xiamen" uses the minimalist form popularized by Bashō to convey fleeting impressions of the subprovincial city in the southeastern Fujian province in China. Rather than the images of nature expected in haiku, there are moving walkways, airport toilets that flush automatically, and "A Hello Kitty" laughing for "Year 2000." Banira Giri's "Kathmandu" offers a complicated portrait of the city, evoking "poplar, comb-tree and mimosa, bottle brush and pine" as well as "the Toyota Corolla with the white government plates, guzzling liters and liters of gasoline, never sated."

Other poets use the lens of history to reflect upon their homeland. For instance, Peter Balakian's "Mandelstam in Armenia, 1930" metaphorically describes the trip Osip Mandelstam took in Armenia, a visit that renewed his poetry before he was jailed by Stalin. The poem also serves as a kind of clarion call to Armenia itself. As Meline Toumani has written:

> Literature is tremendously important to Armenians. Yet for most of the 20th century, Armenians studied and wrote in Russian. The Armenian language, an Indo-European tongue and script with no living cousins, never fell out of use—not even close. But it would be an understatement to say that Armenia's literary history has been variously shaped, impeded and complicated by foreign conquest—Russian, Ottoman, Persian and Byzantine, in reverse order, dating back to the first century B.C., when the Armenian Kingdom began its decline. Thus the survival of national identity has been Armenian literature's most persistent theme."[1]

In referring to "history's caw and chirp and bird shit / on the tombs in the high grass," Balakian underscores the ways in which the repositories of Armenia's past have been soiled and indeed transformed by time. The pastoral resplendence of "caucaus eagles" and "Lake Sevan's ripping blue skirt" turn foreboding in light of what has been and what is yet to come, for Mandelstam and for the country he visits.

For others, homeland is illusory because it's not one thing. Singaporean poet Kirpal Singh literalizes a sense of bifurcated identity, alternating between a Malaysian-dialect English ("i tell you ah, too much man, alamak") and a more refined and abstracted English ("the change has been phenomenal / a small nation but a big city"), ultimately advocating a fusion

---

[1] Meline Toumani, "Destination: Armenia," *Salon* (July 13, 2006). http://www.salon.com/books/literary_guide/2006/07/13/armenia/

of the old world with the new. For the speaker in Zhai Yongming's "The Black Room," family is conflated with any sense of dwelling and, like the three weird sisters in Macbeth, the three sisters in Yongming's poem "glide to and fro," plotting and awaiting a potential mate, searching in their dreams "for unknown house numbers." For them, home is not something they return to but rather the place they set out from. In G. S. Sharat Chandra's "In the Third Country," the speaker discusses not just the place arrived at or left behind, but that third place where "the wind neither wails / nor stays on your windowsill." Homeland, in this instance, is the fixed, invisible point toward which all human life converges.

I now live in a small town on the banks of the Connecticut River, quintessentially New England in its features, replete with a town green, stone walls hand-set by masons, tall white clapboard farmhouses, an annual tractor parade, a terraced Edwardian library that hosts readings from local authors and historians nestled among sugar maples, and cars full of day-trippers for the fall foliage season. A town where I am fully half the population of color. Nowhere do I fit perfectly or well.

Actually, let me recant that statement. There is a spot in my parent's yard in Virginia, not within the house itself but on the margins of our lawn, where wild honeysuckle and hydrangea bloomed. There was an alder bush the size of a small shed under the overhanging trees and I found a hollow space within it where I could burrow. This became my safe haven in the summertime, when I was seething with anger, unable to stand the sight of a classmate or to communicate with my father; when I was contemplative and wanted to look out at the world but not be seen; or when I sought a simple shade from the afternoon in which to nap. That patch of dirt, with its astringent odor and scrim of green where I could hide, became the place I felt most comfortable. Because it was shorn of history, except for a personal one, because it was simultaneously safe and uncultivated, a vast cosmos with just enough space to breathe. I was freest under this bush.

In some generative ways, having no home means that it is everywhere, a center without circumference. The deep space beneath the branches where I was once limitless comes closest to rebirth on the page. When I engage the poems in this section, I'm so fully immersed in dislocation and in inflections of language other than my own that, for the moment, my apprehension dissipates. I feel a kinship with these voices, even if what's described is utterly unfamiliar. Perhaps the root of xenophobia can be traced to those who feel too much at home too much of the time, who have never felt the specter of being an outsider. Being presented with many versions of place and origin, then, is a necessary salve that forces each reader to deal with the complexity of otherness, which ultimately also illuminates our shared humanity.

Whatever else home is, it is not just one thing. The poems in *This House, My Bones* are ample evidence of this fact. As has been expressed in an ancient Sanskrit mantra: *jananee janmabhoomischa swargaadapi gareeyasi.* One's mother and homeland are greater even than heaven.

— RAVI SHANKAR

SUDEEP SEN

A Blank Letter

An envelope arrives unannounced from overseas
  containing stark white sheets,

perfect in their presentation of absence.
  Only a bold logo on top

revealed its origin, but absolutely nothing else.
  I examined the sheets,

peered through their grains—
  heavy cotton-laid striations—

concealing text, in white ink, postmarked India.
  Even the watermark's translucence

made the script's invisibility transparent.
  Buried among the involute contours, lay sheets

of sophisticated pulp, paper containing
  scattered metaphors—uncoded, unadorned,

untouched—virgin lines that spill, populate
  and circulate to keep alive its breathings.

Corpuscles of a very different kind—
  hieroglyphics, unsolved, but crystal-clear.

SAMUEL HAZO

Just Words

In Arabic a single word
  describes the very act
  of taking a position.

                    Greeks
        pronounce three syllables
        to signify the sense of doom
        that all Greeks fear when things
        are going very well.
                    As for
        the shameful ease we feel
        when bad news happens
        to someone else, including
        friends?
                    In Greek—one word.
To designate a hose that funnels
        liquid fire down the turret
        of a tank in battle, the Germans
        speak one word.
                    It's three
        lines long but still one word.
And as for John, Matthew,
        Mark and Luke?
                    There's not
        a surname in the lot.
                    With just
        one name they match in memory
        the immortality of martyrs.
                    The longer
        they're dead, the more they live. . . .
I praise whatever mates
        perception with precision!
                    It asks
        us only to be spare and make
        the most of least.
                    It simplifies
        and lets each word sound final
        as a car door being shut
        but perfect as a telegram to God.

JIBANANDA DAS

Banalata Sen

I have walked earth's byways
   for millennia
   from Ceylon's coast
to the archipelago of Malaya,
   in the night's darkness,
   moving ever.
   I have been a guest
at the now hoary court
   of Vimsivar
   and Asoka;
   in the further dark
   of the city of Vidharva.
   Life's seas foamed
   all around. I was weary.
   And my sole respite came,
   when
   I spent a couple of hours
   with Natore's Banalata Sen.

Her hair dark, like some long gone
   Vidisha's night,
her face like Sravasti's delicate
   handiwork.
   Like some mariner,
   helm lost, gone astray
   in far seas,
   by chance of discovering
   the greenness
   of Spice Islands—
   I saw her in the dusk.
   And raising eyes, like bird's nests,
   she asked: "Where were you
   so long?"
   She asked me then.
   Natore's Banalata Sen.

Evening comes at all our day's end
  like the sound of dew.
The kite wipes off sunshine's scent
from its wings.
When all the earth's colors are spent,
  in the fireflies' brilliant hue,
    completing an unfinished tale,
  an old script
  finds a new arrangement.
All the birds return home,
all the rivers.
All the day's transactions end.
Just darkness remains
and sitting with me
face to face,
Banalata Sen.

Translated from the Bengali by Ron D. K. Banerjee

Author's Note: Natore is a small town in the Rajshahi area of what was then Bengal.

XI CHUAN

excerpts from "Misfortune"

D 00059

He was King of Chu, who razed Wo Fang Palace.

He was Black Tornado, who tore the emperor's pardon to pieces.

After the night, fog. After thunder, his brain leaks. He speaks different
  tongues in different rooms. His last territory is his house.

He was once Emperor Li. His poetry negated the crime of losing his nation.

Too feeble to talk about his past—famines, harvests, beggars' justice,
  gamblers' legends, too weak to talk, he hiccups at spring.

At dusk he staggers along the streets. He curses himself, but people
   think he's cursing this paradise. His poor, embarrassed father waits
   at the dead end, ready to box him in the ear.

Once a father, he now plays with a pair of walnuts.

His life, full of wrong words, is an unpublishable memoir.

E 00183

Confucius said: "At thirty, a man stands."

At thirty, the doctor diagnosed his infertility. His clan will vanish.
   He shattered china, burnt books, wailed himself to sleep.

Confucius said: "At forty, a man is no longer puzzled."

At forty, he trembled at the sound of singing, guilt made him give up his
   golden Buddha. He moved out of his mansion, turned over a new leaf.
   A weak man wants nothing but peace.

Confucius said: "At fifty, a man knows the mandate of heaven."

Porridge stains all over his fifty-year-old wife, he brings her vegetables
   and a small sea bass after school. Late blooming love is like the rusty
   oil in a wok.

Confucius said: "At sixty, a man's ears are an obedient organ for Truth."

He lost his hearing at sixty: a loud world was reduced to expressions.

Confucius said: "At seventy, man does as he pleases without crossing
   the line."

Confucius died at seventy-three, an immortal age.

G 00319

He never learned to piss on the streets in elementary school, never
   learned to hide his diary in middle school. He learned from history

that gazing at plums could quench thirst, learned how to adjust the seasons with the wind of his soul.

It's raining over the world. Every crook is posing for a picture.

H 00325

In his soul sharp teeth are growing.

M 02345

In his memory every saint is handsome. He left the crowd, shameful of his ugliness and walked into his grave.

Who's the master of this world? Whose body is he using?

His wife, born from an intellectual's family, died beneath thugs' sticks.

Shadows lay on the ground, clouds poured into his mouth. Moonlight meant forgetting, a breeze meant kindness. The snoring woman next to him meant history went on.

His will was robbed, but by whom and why, he had no idea.

N 05180 (Identity unclear)

Small is beautiful, small is clean, small is safe.

Small like an egg, like a button, even smaller, smaller, like an insect in amber.

Dust covered his face, he shrank.

Children gathered sunshine with a magnifying glass. He dodged the light, but still, his skin smoldered.

U 20000

He forgives the crows of the countryside's roosters, forgives dusk as they sing. He forgives the stone grinder and B.C.'s casting technology.

He forgives the dry pen, the stubborn donkey. He forgives the female teacher in middle school, forgives this dumb woman for locking him in a dark classroom.

But he won't forgive the human folly, even though he forgives the sealed walls, the crowded streets, the flies, even the person with goose bumps in a warm room.

He forgives the surrendering army, the judges who drink milk, his files, memos, decisions, but he won't forgive slogans, documents, books, and the typos in instructions.

He forgives his children and wife for their betrayal; his weeping has never seen any words. Only today did we realize he had every reason to smash the radio.

But he didn't. He forgives belief in electricity, belief in water. How sad the shiny river! But he won't forgive the unbelieving sky. Where is he going? Who will he meet?

He forgives his cancer, his miserable funeral. He forgives the way he'd forgive rotten food. But he won't forgive the paper money they offered.

Twenty years after he died, we acknowledge him as a person.

Translated from the Chinese by Wang Ping and Alex Lemon

PARTAW NADERI

Lucky Men

When your star is unseen in this desolate sky,
your despair itself becomes a star.

My twin, the steadfast sun, and I
both grasp its far-flung brilliance.

In a land where water is locked up
in the very depths of desiccated rocks,
the trees are ashamed of their wizened fruits.

The honest orchard is laid waste—
such a bloodied carpet
is spread before the future.

Yesterday, leaning on my cane,
I returned from the trees' cremation.

Today, I search the ashes
for my lost, homeless phoenix.

Perhaps it was you who shadowed me,
perhaps it was only my shadow.

Even though the lucky men in my land
lack stars in the heavens, lack shadows on the earth

they welcome any stars
that grace their devastated sky.

O, my friend, my only friend,
turn your anguish into constellations!

Translated from the Dari by Sarah Maguire and Yama Yari

OKTAY RIFAT

Beyond the Seven Hills

1

An oil lamp still far off, still hidden in rushes, with the facets of a star;
    she trembles in an embrace again, she resembles her paintings,
her feet never fail to touch the seaweed;

when she opens her hands, manuscripts catch fire in the palms, half-
faced she still runs toward a dream and weeps.

Pierced with a swift shaft of light and strolling in the halls of the sky she
gathers flowers of the day;

she wanders again in big mirrors, looks at the clouds on the treelined
road, and looking she becomes herself again;

again evening opens with a timeless song, windows open again to the
line of the sea with its waving flags,

Istanbul again.

2

We can't live without you, can't cross the bridge. Can't survive without bridge
  or river or
weapons,

without you we can't survive, when we walk we never reach the end, when
    we
talk we never exhaust our words, and we never drink them dry.

It hurts to be far from you, we can't go on without you. We can't live
    without
night, night and day alike.

When a great earthquake starts there is no passage from the blood-soaked
    square,
on the wheezing horse that's lame and blind.

No strolling, no lying down without you. You who are prone and upright,
    keep
stretching toward us, lie close and easy.

Stretch toward me, lie close. Let my loneliness make peace with your
    face
beyond the seven hills, let me grow without nourishment, without time.

Insatiable at all times. All the time without you. Shouting the names of
    many
places in the keenest darkness.

We can't move away without you, what I want is to love and submit to
    the
spreading twilight of your hair.

Without you whatever is in fragments cannot be kissed better or embraced,
there is no aging, no dying without Istanbul.

Translated from the Turkish by Ruth Christie and Richard McKane

SAMIH AL-QASIM

excerpt from "An Inquest"

- And what do you call this country?
- My country.
- So you admit it?
- Yes, sir. I admit it.
  I'm not a professional tourist.
- Do you say "my country"?
- I say "my country."
- And where is my country?
- Your country.
- And where is your country?
- My country.
- And the claps of thunder?
- My horses neighing.
- And the gusts of wind?
- My extension.
- And the plains' fertility?
- My exertion.
- And the mountains' size?
- My pride.
- And what do you call the country?
- My country.
- And what should I call my country?
- My country . . .

Translated from the Arabic by Nazih Kassis

BANIRA GIRI

Kathmandu

Kathmandu was forged a superheated furnace
fired by a hundred thousand volts
Like Sita at her trial by fire,
the helpless girls of this capital

sit upon it, tender bodies ready to be branded,
ensnared in its bondage of desire

The white dove in flight
across the boundless blue sky
is locked inside every citizen's eye
Every swarthy smuggler,
fat con artist, cruel backbiter
and hypocrite of the land comes here
to plunge into the waters of Rani Pokhari
and be made pure
The poplar, comb-tree and mimosa,
bottle-brush and pine
fan all who live here, pure and foul
But
Kathmandu is not pure coolness
Kathmandu is also hexes and jinxes

That Toyota Corolla
with the white government plates,
guzzling liters and liters of gasoline, never sated
isn't that Kathmandu?
And isn't it Nanicha's liquor-shop
where the GunjaMans and Ram Bahadurs daily crowd
tossing their heads back to drink
then going home to beat their wives?
The Toyota's deep tire tracks in the street
the greenish kick-marks on the bodies of their wives
Kathmandu's daily fare

Kathmandu is something
my dear son babbles in his dreams
half I understand, half I do not
but I want to hear more
always wedged in and driven between
attraction and repulsion
I know
many curse me
few like me
I feel that

since I have come to live in Kathmandu
hasn't Kathmandu also come to live in me?

Kathmandu's endless protest marches
pour daily into my dreams
Alas!
My nights are filled with riot
But how silent my cold mornings,
Kathmandu covered over in mist,
as if the city's dead were exhausted
after a long night's vigil

This beloved Kathmandu
is an epic
of fascinating, sweet and bitter tales
the horrifying opening lines of politicians' speeches
the people's chorus of poverty
wages—the fortunate increase
prices—the cursed rise
the ceaseless hide-and-seek of kerosene and sugar
It's all here

Poor Kathmandu!
Everyone's darling
Cursed by all
Its people,
like the narrator of the Satyanarayan puja
forever repeating the story
of Lilavati and Kalavati
forever repeating the same laments
　　　walking the same narrow lanes
　　　bringing out the same processions
　　　thronging to the same festivals
　　　celebrating the same holidays
like a Ka-ka-kul bird's chant:
Kathmandu Kathmandu
Kathmandu Kathmandu

Translated from the Nepali by Ann Hunkins

SIMIN BEHBAHANI

Homeland, Once More, I'll Build You

To the lady of Persian storytelling, Simin Daneshvar

Homeland, once more, I'll build you,
If needed, with bricks made from my life.
Once more, I'll support your ceilings,
If needed, with columns made from my bones.
Once more, I'll seek in your flowers
The perfumes of a new generation.
Once more, I'll cleanse your body of bloodstains
If needed, with my tears.
Once more, one shining day, darkness will leave this house.
Once more, I'll paint my poems blue,
Reflecting the colors of your sky.
Once more, he will raise me, like a glorious mountain,
The Judge and Resurrector of old bones.[1]
Ancient I may be, but given the opportunity,
Once more, I'll begin youth, among my children.
I'll sing "The Love of Home"[2] with passion,
Filling every word with vitality.
A fire still burns in my breast,
Fueled from the warmth of my people.
Once more, you will give me your strength,
Even though my poems are blood-clotted.
Once more will I build you with the substance of my life,
Though it requires powers beyond mine.

Translated from the Persian by Farzaneh Milani and Kaveh Safa

---

[1] Quranic reference to the day of resurrection, when God will reconstitute human beings from their rotten bones (sura 36:78, "ya seen").

[2] Refers to a *hadith* (a "tradition" or account of the Prophet, his companions, or the Imams) known as *hubb al-watan* or "love of country/homeland," in which the Prophet is reported to have said, *hubb al-watan min al iman* or "Love of country/homeland is from faith."

NADIA TUÉNI

Cedars

I salute you,
you who draws life
from a single root
with the night as your watchdog.
Your rustlings have the splendor of words
and the supremacy of cataclysms.
I know you,
you who are
hospitable as memory;
you wear grief of the living
because this side of time is time as well.
I spell your name
you who are
unique as the Song of Songs.
A great cold enfolds you,
and heaven itself is in reach of your branches.
I defy you,
you who wail in our mountains
so that we hear the sounds in our blood.
Today, which is yesterday's tomorrow,
crosses your forms like a setting star.
I love you,
you who depart with the wind as your banner
I love you as man loves breath.
You are the first poem.

Translated from the French by Samuel Hazo

ASADULLAH HABIB

The Story of My Country

The story of my country
is written on its jungles and deserts—
so sorrowful it cannot be spoken.

Like the colorful dream before the night of Eid
when, on a summer night, I slept on the rooftop
watching stars nearly at the height of man,
the smell of wet grass carried on the wind.

My country is a book of disasters
or maybe a beautiful poem without end,
never to be completed, nor read to the end.

My country is an old hymn from the time of Zarathustra,
a hymn sung by tired men on a narrow path
lit by the sacred light of Zarathustra.

In my country, the flower of Azarnoosh
grows through the cracks of rocks
and in springtime, its valleys and deserts
are illuminated with color,
sonorous with the prayers of Zarathustra.

The story of my country
is a fractured mirror,
a continuous fire,
a burning garden.

Where are the old storytellers
to tell the story of my country?
Where is one listener?

Translated from the Persian/Dari by Bashir Sakhawarz

Author's Note: Azarnoosh was an old Zoroastrian temple in Balkh, Afghanistan.

GARRETT HONGO

Chikin Hekka

Thwock! Thwock! Thwock!
           was the rhythmic chopping of steel on butcher block near the sink,
Kubota wielding the cleaver's long, narrow blade like it was a machete cutting
    cane,
Bringing it along the back and legs of the raw carcass in quick, pistonlike
    strikes.
He was making *hekka*—a whole chicken cooked with bamboo shoots
                                sliced thin as *sashimi,*
Fresh carrots in diagonal slivers like orange doubloons, and half-circles
Of cut round onions that tesselated and turned clear in a bubbling pot.

He'd make a broth of bonita flakes and black *shoyu,*
Then grab all he'd cut the way I'd seen him handle octopus
                        in tinned buckets near the sea,
Scooping them in the basket of his hands, tentacles drooping
                          like roots from a purple screwpine tree,
And dropping them in a waiting pot. And if they cried, Kubota didn't care,
Wind furling the big trouserlegs of his khaki pants. It was the ocean that gave
    off
A rattling sigh of small stones and regret. *I cooking,* he would say,
And not the pink bits of chickenflesh nor white flecks of bone that spattered
    his glasses
And spotted the newspapered backsplash along the sinks and carving table
Would stave him from the *karma* of his task.

                                Aroma of blood and marrow,
Bright cymbal of a steel pot's lid, dipper of *keawe* and spoon from the horn of a
    goat,
He made his humble kitchen a spectacle of sights and smells—
Petite, green armies of chopped celery sliding off the cutting board.
He'd take a bundle of bean threads, dry as graveyard sand, white as ashes of
    incense,
Twisting it like a rag in his hands until the strands sheared from his quick torque.
Shirataki, he'd say, *Waterfall we call long rice,* but unlike steamed rice,
It turned golden in the slick of the stew, fattened in flavors of blended fish and
    fowl.

Winters, when the Oregon rains can damp my soul, I try to make it this
    way still,
And take the Viking cleaver down from its place, a household god over
    the sink,
Holding it up to the light so I can see the sheen of its edge against the
    outer dark,
And I swing it so flesh and fat spatter me awake to all the heroic good of
    his will.

AL MAHMUD

Deathsleep

So far no one had
Any worries at all for me.

Where and how a myopic member
               of the family lives—
This never bothered anyone.
The sons and daughters assumed
In whichever room Dad was present
He was surely with books.
          Watchful.

Only at times of dinner and outing
The wife gives a little reminder
And says, rise you . . .
As if the lady was nudging a stone to roll on and
To give it a bath.

Once I had finished my meal
Everybody in the house would flock together
Bend over the dining table
As if flocks of hungry wild geese
Had descended on Medi *haaor* making their own calls.
The sounds of their indiscriminate devouring
I could hear from the adjacent room

While smoking my cigarette.
Everybody reckoned I was not in their party.

How easily they have arrived
At the real truth about me.
A person who has.
No party
                no power
                        no movements
Lives in our family.

My wife though, didn't want
To reach any decisions about me
The reliance that grows out of living together fifty years
She does not have it.
Who knows—
She perhaps thinks I have hidden under my pillow
Disasters that destroy relationships.

Hence I have no sleeping malaise.
There is no end to my wife's complaint—
I get to sleep as soon as my head rests on the pillow
That it could be a matter of complaint,
I never knew.

She used to say—
I slept like a beast
And dreamt while awake, all day long.

My married wife
Has no doubt that
I am not a real human.
She though has not much complaint.

Of late she is scared for me
She reckons—I keep on sleeping day and night
I sink into deep slumber
Even when my eyes are wide open.

I wouldn't respond to treatment
She knows that too.
She wants to wake me up.

I ponder should I rise from this deadsleep
By any heavenly reason
Shall I find
My family and relatives
My wife
In their former locations?

Translated from the Bengali by Quader Mahmud

Author's Note: Haaor is a natural lake.

CHOMAN HARDI

Summer Roof

Every night that summer
when he went to bed on the flat roof,
I stayed awake
watching the opposite roof
where he was,
a tiny light turning on
every time he puffed his cigarette.

Once I was shown his paintings
and I went home
and wrote his name all over my books.

I kept imagining what he would say,
how I would respond.
I imagined being married to him,
looking after him when he fell ill,
cooking for him and washing his hair.
I imagined sleeping on the same roof.

A whole year went by and we never talked
then suddenly an empty house opposite us,
an empty roof, not staring back
and sleepless nights for me.

Years later we met again
the same man with a few fingers missing,
bad tempered, not able to paint.

We never spoke,
we remained on our separate roofs.

BHUPI SHERCHAN

Cursed House

Whenever the neighbors to the left and right
fling stones on each other's roof
the glasses of the old woman
sunning herself on the roof of this house
and the bangles of the bride looking out from the terrace
break. When at midnight the neighbors
from wherever with whatever they can grab hold of
strike out of each other . . .
the next morning the arthritic old man of this house
wakes to find his walking stick broken
It's like this—this cursed house
This house like a plant sprouted in the midst of fire
a plant that ignites

Translated from the Nepali by Wayne Amtzis and Sulochana Musyaju

DILIP CHITRE

Ode to Bombay

I had promised you a poem before I died
Diamonds storming out of the blackness of a piano
Piece by piece I fall at my own dead feet
Releasing you like a concerto from my silence
I unfasten your bridges from my insistent bones
Free your railway lines from my desperate veins
Dismantle your crowded tenements and meditating machines
Remove your temples and brothels pinned in my skull

You go out of me in a pure spiral of stars
A funeral progressing toward the end of time
Innumerable petals of flame undress your dark
Continuous stem of growing

I walk out of murders and riots
I fall out of smouldering biographies
I sleep on a bed of burning languages
Sending you up in your essential fire and smoke
Piece by piece at my own feet I fall
Diamonds storm out of a black piano

Once I promised you an epic
And now you have robbed me
You have reduced me to rubble
This concerto ends

AMIN KAMIL

In Water

You're fraught with words, better go sit in water;
For they swell with meaning and glow more in water.

Look for the heart in the chest and roast it on embers
Look for the blood in the liver and drink it in water.

Tomorrow Kashmir will stretch in the sun like a desert,
The day after Ladakh and Leh will float in water.

Under the hollow banks frightened waves take refuge;
Lord Jaldev is born with fire in water.

At mid-day, even the sun gets soaked in sweat;
At the end, even the moon catches fire in water.

Even in excitement, sometimes, people set towns on fire;
Even for fun, sometimes, people pour poison in water.

The lost cow is looking for the elevensome, would someone tell her?
Five drowned in dry land, six are aflame in water.

The peddler of *ghazals,* this Kamil, makes fiery calls
But the fatefrost people are coldly sleeping in water.

Translated from the Kashmiri by Muneebur Rahman

RAVIL BUKHARAEV

The Wey

A little English stream called the Wey,
Purling transparently, pretending to be a genuine river,
Is consonant with this idyllic silence
Just because it offers a Russian rhyme to the evening branches.

I am long bored with the Russian rhymes,
Some unavoidable ones throw me into despair.
If one is at all guilty of accords and assonances,
Let them be simple enough to rhyme "peace" and "remorse."

A leaf is carried away in the stream,
Which tree is it from? Does it really matter?
Breathe in the silence, you may breathe out a word,
And in what language, you will never know.

Translated from the Tartar by the author with Hamid Ismailov

LUO ZHICHENG

On Encountering Sorrow

The South, you know
Is the Land of Promise . . .
Loving priestesses believed in this deeply

Then China had not yet taken shape
The chariot of the Sun God only reached River Huai, at most the Yangzi
Until Zhuanxu—my ancestor
The blood of the sage thawed, and flowed south
Millennia later
His blood reached the city Cheng
Cheng was just a land of swamps then
Invisible deities and spirits
Were everywhere in the air

The land of Dream Clouds—yes, the entire region
Was filled with orchids!

A few centuries passed by
The mists had dispersed
The rainy season ended
Chu became the South to be proud of
Once it even vied for the rule of the Central Plains
We worshipped the aesthetics of black lined in gold
Virtues of heady fragrances
A religion of tender love
Graceful, reserved, fancy-prone . . .

A more widely told story
Speaks of the secret marriage vow, between humans and gods
And spirits of fishhawks, daylilies, and
Morning dew

In the Month of Yin, the Year of Yin
My birth deserves mention
Especially because it preordained all
And witnessed it all
The hour when Shen Ti shone in the northeast
The last light snow of the first month
Had just cleansed the early blooming selinea
My mother—
Like so many mothers of Chu—
A mysterious, high-born
But obscure goddess
Placed me amidst mushrooms and cassias
Rinsed my soul
With the melting snow gathered from orchid buds
Thus setting in motion my never-cooling blood
At the age of twenty
I had a name the whole South adored
Lingjun—"Divine Balance"

But how could I have foreseen
The misfortune of possessing a mind of clarity?

Low, flat lakeshores
Are not fit for farsighted men
The Kingdom of Chu, with the inevitable
Coarseness of the first mold
Repeatedly wounds a delicate soul
Driving me to my wits' end
When standards of judgment have yet to be established
How can things of supreme beauty come into being?

But, like the angelica in my hand
I too face the end of beauty and sweetness
In the vissicitudes of time
I have discovered

Death is the only unchangeable truth
Besides, without the ability to discriminate
Goodness turns into my suffering in the end—

How can you give a phoenix a mere foot of land?
How can you give the North Star only one night?

How could I not know my impatience
And cold eyes, those cold cold eyes?
They used their eloquence to slander me
Laying nails and hooks around the palace
To catch me by the train of my robe
Turning me into a silkworm spinning deliriously
But I had no time to grope around in their meandering alleys
When a newly written poem
Lifted me up to the sky of stars
But an unparalleled concern
Pulled me back down to my care

Yes, clattering horsehoofs on the borders
Have shaken the pillars in the ancestral temple
A metallic taste has interrupted
The stay of the fragrant castor plant
The mighty Kingdom of Qin
Has eclipsed the fading twilight in the western sky
Sorry lies fabricated in the land of Shu
Led to the downfall of the noble King Huai

Fair One, Fair One, where should I begin?
Always he is on my mind
Like a pearl in the clam . . .

That man, in the seat of honor
Showed me an appreciation beyond my belief
As if keeping a promise from the previous life
To take me to the granary among the clouds
Telling me of an unrequited love at six and passion at forty
The stern upbringing of his royal father, and
A territorial ambition that knew no tempering

We were both young then
We were unsophisticated, uncarved
Like a music score yet to be written
An icy river in one moment
A molten rock in the next
Moving, like clouds of thunder and lightning
Demure, like the most tender spring

But, he made himself forget all of that, as decidedly
As a jade pendant dropping to the floor, breaking
The nine acres of orchids that I had grown laboriously
Lay fallow—
I entered the counsel chamber
Where foul weeds grew rampant
I entered the inner court
Where ghostly shadows and flattering rhetoric lingered
At last, we came face to face with each other
He pointed to the south
Without a shred of hesitation, concern or care in his eyes.

He astonished me
In that moment
He acted in a truly royal way
Except for the head-spinning blindness
The heart-wrenching ruthlessness
He acted in a truly royal way
Yet
We were once the best of friends, truly
We were once so very close . . .

And the South, you know
Is the Land of Promise
The second time I came to the Yangzi shore
My clothes covered with dust
The humid heat of the continental climate
Was killing the pepper on the banks
A dusty gust began to rise
By the bright water's edge, a horned dragon
Recoiled in bitter pain
Its five-colored scales robbed by the rainbow

When the night falls
Laughter comes drifting from the cooling shores
In the land of Chu you find many folks like these
They don't insist on fauna and flora
Nor on aesthetics
They live in abodes of woven grass down the river
Fish for a living
And love telling fables
I cannot bear to look at them
For I am of different blood
Besides, I have fallen short in both
Self-cultivation and cultivation of the world

Solitude consumes me day by day
As if to close the shop early
Unsold flowers are left in the scorching sun
But in the beginning you know
I knew nothing about abandoning
My intention to reconcile; my hope died and was reborn
Over and over again
Now I have given up on learning other possibilities

Where did I go astray?
For a while I was deeply attracted by myself
When the whole world was drunk
I gazed at myself by the pool where the giant Peng bird fell—
A special destiny requires a special man to complete
Every human being is unique
The inward-searching eye has opened

Now, dressed in selinea and shady angelica
My hair tied with sedges and thistles
Holding a bouquet of autumn orchids
I sing in the wilderness to my heart's content
The villagers living by the lake
Whisper among themselves
A little girl runs up to me
I present her with a bouquet of melilotus rods
A little boy runs up to me
I present him with a bouquet of cart-halting flowers

I climb up the round hill with great effort
A gusty wind renews my mood
Finally I can use a child's eyes
To know what I once knew—
And love—
The tired and exhausted
Kingdom
O Kingdom
My tears cannot help but pour like rain

When
Did the deities and spirits quietly withdraw?
When
Did the clouds cease to rest
And the dragon cease to snore lightly as it turns in its sleep?

When
Did the priestess's song lose its warmth?
The priestess's song its warmth lost
For they have ceased to believe

But I have not wavered in my belief
The South is the Land of Promise
Worthy of all of my love
All of my bitter suffering

I will inscribe these words
On the flowing river.

Translated from the Chinese by Michelle Yeh

Translator's Note: The speaker in the poem is Qu Yuan (343?–278 B.C.), the first identifiable poet in China. A nobleman of the Kingdom of Chu in the lake country south of the Yangzi River, Qu was slandered by fellow courtiers and banished to the southern hinterlands by the inconstant King Hui, referred to in the poem as the Fair One, who died a prisoner of the king of Qin in 296 B.C. After he was exiled for the second time, Qu drowned himself in the River Milo. In 223 B.C. Chu was destroyed by the king of Qin, who unified China and became the First Emperor. "On Encountering Sorrow," or "Lisao," is the title of Qu Yuan's autobiographical poem written during his exile.

MOHAMMAD RAFIQ

No One Belonging to Me

with the meeting of the Baleshwar and Pashur in his heart
  the man floats till he reaches dry land
  Mehendigang market, Char Baisha's shrine

half-broken voices, rain-soaked footsteps, whispers among
  potatoes and onions in shuttered shops and warehouses
  hurricane lanterns' smoky glow like muddy water at high tide

faces look familiar, bangles and laughter jangle
  thatched roofs are slick and mossy in the moonlight
  a flirtatious sari slips off a head, everything is dripping, dropping

in Banishanta village nothing moves under the man's gaze
  market stalls, narrow path obliterated by water and mud
  paddy on both sides, shaora bushes—father and grand-

father, come back, son—cold touch of people you don't belong to
  shadows, odor of shrouds and incense rises from the graves
  a sickle of light crosses the fields on the moon's twelfth night

suddenly, a circus tent touches the body and takes flight
  arthritic sleep, miserable horse's hoofbeats, dead tiger's rib cage
  tendons—but the man's illusion hasn't shattered

with only the meeting of the Baleshwar and Pashur in his heart
  he floats till he digs into the bank one night
  knees smudged with dirt, palms smelling of scum and fish scales

Translated from the Bengali by Carolyn B. Brown

VIVEK NARAYANAN

The Dump

to Shuddhabrata Sengupta

1.

The dump is the very sprawl it once preceded,
distilling our dreams to grit. Mouth at every door,
abandoned to kitchens, it trailed the radial roads
and signed the city's nascent borders with its seed.

2.

Half animal, half machine, half sapient, the dump
is a drowsy interlocutor:
itchy newsprint, smeared fat, pitch smoke, carburetors,
potash alum, fruit husks: submerged in the incessant
fill, all eat the earth and are mourned.

3.

Your cheap locket, *semblable,*
lost at the carnival, adorns another's neck,
that of an iron bar. Crows scuff
your skin flakes, make strings there of your elastic
flesh, a patient work. No first hello, no one sign-off:
the dump will crush your angel on a pin.

GEVORG EMIN

Small

Yes, we are small
the smallest pebble
in a field of stones.
But have you felt the hurtle
of pebbles pitched
from a mountaintop?

Small,
as the smallest mountain stream
storing rapids, currents,
unknown to wide and lazy valley rivers.

Small,
like the bullet in the bore
of the rifle;
small as the corn waiting to sprout.

Small
as the pinch of salt
that seasons the table.

Small, yes,
you have compressed us, world,
into a diamond.

Small,
you have dispersed us,
scattered us like stars.
We are everywhere in your vision.

Small,
but our borders stretch
from Piuragan telescopes to the moon,
from Lousavan back to Urartu.

Small as the grain of marvelous Uranium which
cannot be broken down, put out or consumed.

Translated from the Armenian by Diana Der-Hovanessian

WONG PHUI NAM

excerpts from *Against the Wilderness*

for Daizal Samad, who knows about migrations

i

Antecedents

For months, the sky was pale copper, withholding rain,
firing the fields into fused beds of clinker.
A subterranean kiln reduced standing grain and grass
to fiber, snakes and mudfish in their holes to bone.
When people turned from eating bark to sand, we waited
for our dead to putrefy before we buried them.
Then we left. Every unseasonable road we took
brought us among other aimless ghosts in a treeless,
unforgiving plain, crying like us against exhaustion
of spirit as our bellies ate us from within,
making our bones come unjointed. Nursing with paps
blackening from the teats, I was death for our howling son.
In the city, we gave him up that we might eat.
Though we were ghosts, we found it very hard to die.

iii

Bukit China 2

When my sea-blackened junk crumbled for its weight
of salt-gutted timber as it sat dry on a spit
of mud, I gave myself over to the thought
the sea had retched me up for final dissolution
in the waiting earth. In the flesh, I sensed the flood
gathering in the soil already of lapping oblivion.
From these small hills, I had no unknotted wood to remake
myself my sundered craft, in a city somnolent still
as mangroves fecund in sea snakes, in mudskippers,
scarce hint of an architecture for vessels by which
our fathers through the ages flouted the blackest, boiling seas.
My flesh would find continuance in the moist salt wombs
of native women and leave secreted into this hill
a clutch of bones from which no transfigured life would hatch.

v

Into the wilderness
When the valley dawned about us, we sensed
that we had come, each to our particular end.
We found ourselves detached as shadows at the mouth
of a great receiving darkness. So far inland,
we lost the clarity of the day's fires,
the luminescence of pain as the sun broiled
us in our skins when we poled our way upriver, hearts
locked tight on a single lust—the glittering image
of life we would retrieve in our waking dreams
from sands beneath watery mirrors that blinded us
by day, flowing by night as cold thoughts of death.
In that we were into the hills for other than a god,
he came, blind knobs for eyes, swelling gourd for belly,
crying out of the water for our lost, drowned selves.

BEI DAO

Black Map

in the end, cold crows piece together
the night: a black map
I've come home—the way back
longer than the wrong road
long as a life

bring the heart of winter
when spring water and horse pills
become the words of night
when memory barks
a rainbow haunts the black market

my father's life-spark small as a pea
I am his echo
turning the corner of encounters
a former lover hides in a wind
swirling with letters

Beijing, let me
toast your lamplights
let my white hair lead
the way through the black map
as though a storm were taking you to fly

I wait in line until the small window
shuts: O the bright moon
I've come home—reunions
are less than good-byes
only one less

Translated from the Chinese by Eliot Weinberger

YASMINE GOONERATNE

Washing the Grain

Round and round the year tilts
from nighttime to dawn from sunlight to shadow
and the pale days falling from this side to that
yield a fine cloudiness only

We are so far now, so far, cry the grains
the home-field only a memory warm
in the husk
and that too sloughed off
that too lost
in the mortar's pounding

Round and round spin the days
another year of this churning
and tilting, washing at last
quite over the rim
will we lie in clear water,
pure, transparent,
delicately separate?

We shall become
consumable: our pale substance
will satisfy somebody

And this dark grit
trapped in the bowl's fine furrows
may be disposed of, thrown
out upon the wattles and dry grass

LOUISE HO

POP SONG 1 "At Home in Hong Kong" 1964

feet that paddle
in the shallows
hands that sieve
through slimy weeds
eyes that reflect
the thousand lights
give only
secondary sensations
the toes are booted
the fingers are gloved
the eyes are shaded
we talk of cultural vacuity
we talk of flux
and instability
the sophisticated
talk of inevitabilities
to explain away inconsistencies
nevertheless
we walk firmly
though we walk
on stilts
we walk only
where stilts
are safe
schooled

in our system
of indirect transmissions
we run
like clockwork
and go on ticking
till we stop
on the dot

M. ATHAR TAHIR

Carpet Weaver

Between buildings which like beggar women
    squabbled for sunlight,
      I had, I think, lost my way
      when in a nook, I came upon him

huddled in an interior lit by black.
    His fingers blunt with wood
      labor at the ancient contraption
      to the scurry of a rat.

While he earns his bread
    by knots per square inch,
      only a muezzin's call away
      at the shrine of the great sage

professionals extend their metal bowls for food.
    Many well-beloved of God
      with rice dhegs and strings of flowers
      come to thank this saint of the green dome.

Recommendations work even here.

İLHAN BERK

Istanbul

You're in Istanbul, city of leaden domes;
a man on the gallows swings to and fro in the rain,
a drop, a blue sky drop, on his eyes.
Someone lies face down on the stones before the mosques
near trees and sea,
a sailor who fled ashamed
from his dreams in this city's park.

An old peddler by the bridge
arranges greasy loaves in his glass case,
contented;
poems have been written to a sky full of mighty masts.

Look below where the dirty painted sailboats lie;
the loves and dreams peculiar to bums and bureaucrats
toss with a vulgar sky of ivory inlay.
And the madmen never forsake their endless cursing.
The poets declared
clouds caught on minarets were drunk.

You know that at night
the tiny festooned ships,
your stars that always bring us pleasant thoughts
enter and tangle in the sleep of girls.
While weeping her heart away for tramps and vagrants
Istanbul lights a cigarette for the pipes and cymbals.
Everyone lives their lives cursing Allah.
Just mention raki, everyone leaps to their feet
but no one ever questions how to live.

Long-haired hippies in transit,
refugees from lovers, countries, wars,
have come to see the world and its peoples.
What's he observing, the man on the bridge,
hands clasped behind? He's probably watching
the sky, the park, the silvery palaces.

But this is a city of loveless lusts,
ready to give up the ghost,
a city of young whores, dead sultans and the sick,
an Istanbul debased.

Translated from the Turkish by Ruth Christie

BINO A. REALUYO

Filipineza

In the modern Greek dictionary, the word "Filipineza" means "maid."

If I became the brown woman mistaken
for a shadow, please tell your people I'm a tree.
Or its curling root above ground, like fingers without a rag,

without the buckets of thirst to wipe clean your mirrorlike floors.
My mother warned me about the disappearance of Elena.
But I left her and told her it won't happen to me.

The better to work here in a house full of faces I don't recognize.
Shame is less a burden if spoken in the language of soap and stain.
My whole country cleans houses for food, so that

the cleaning ends with the mothers, and the daughters
will have someone clean for them, and never leave
my country to spend years of conversations with dirt.

When I get up, I stand like a tree, feet steady, back firm.
From here, I can see Elena's island, where she bore a child
by a married man whose floors she washed for years,

whose body stained her memory until she left in the thick
of rain, unseen yet now surviving in the uncertain tongues
of the newly arrived. Like the silence in the circling motions

of our hands, she becomes part myth, part mortal, part soap.

GURBANNAZAR EZIZ

The Eastern Poem

A green wind brushed a slender branch,
opening the mouths of the buds.
Head thrown back to the sky, a wolf howled,
as if telling his complaint to the moon.

Moonshadow fell on the river,
weaving a golden carpet across the water.
Beneath the Asian sky, a girl
recited a poem by the eastern poet.

Beneath this sky, in moonlight,
the poetry written in ancient times,
finding no place in the kings' golden castles,
knocked on the door of the common people.

Nothing of the ancient world is old
if a nation's people have the desire.
Old is something new that's been forgotten.
New means the legacy of what was before.

And so if this sky remains,
if this moon continues to extend its beam,
as the early star is born each morning,
the eastern poem will cast its glow over the world.

We will pass away.
After us, there will be many others,
and then a girl, turning her face toward the sky,
will remember what was written in pursuit of eternity.

Translated from the Turkmen by Eric Welsapar and Idra Novey

ABD AL-AZIZ AL-MAQALIH

Ma'reb Speaks

I come from the land of qat, the ages clamor with my tragedy.
I come from there a crying qasida and an exiled letter.
I got out of yesterday's prison coiled in volcanic rage.
My wrists bear the trace of shackles, my feet drag their fatigue.
No perfume, no petrol to carry and I own no gold.
I still drink from a skin bag and wash in the sea.
My feet are bare and with a naked head hunger rivets me.
The desert ship is my plane and my palace is built with wood.
And when *el-mawal* hums I am killed by rapture.
In the fields the reed flute moans then grabs and dissolves me.
And in love I am the descendant of nobility.
Majnoon Laila is in my blood and Jameel is a maddened fire.
I reared passion's shadow and it reared me.
So do you accept me O Arab sun? Do you take me?
I am crazy about you and you bewilder my life's journey.
Your admirers gather by your wondrous parade.
They utter sounds that die by hanging on my blazing mouth.
Their rhetoric shakes you as my silence fails and wails.
And you return to your qat and bathe in clamorous waves.
If only you knew silence . . . a million speeches are not so eloquent.

Translated from the Arabic by Fady Joudah

KIRPAL SINGH

Two Voices

i say, have you been following all this
this twenty-five-year thing or not
i tell you ah, too much man, alamak
you know lah how we suffer those days . . .

the lion-city and a proud people
anniversary songs all over the place
celebrations galore. loyalty intact.

last night i watched this programme
you know lah. class of fifty-nine
yah-lah. younger than us. we started
fifty-seven what. but never mind lah.

leaders worry about various issues
intellectuals debate. eat. debate.
some multiply. others get sterilised.

remember those days in school
sometimes we had no money
no money even for a drink
nowadays my son demands a dollar

the change has been phenomenal
a small nation but a big city
economic miracle of the east

what happened to that chap ah
that fellow lah. laprik
you mean he went off couldn't cope
that's why. too much pressure lah

the politics are a major concern
people want a bigger say everywhere
they are critical. not always realistic.

of course i'm proud of Singapore what
sure i'll fight for my country
but take it easy lah go slow a bit
otherwise. ah. sure problems man

naturally we have many problems
the aged. the sick. the low-income
groups who cannot manage . . .

somewhere there must be a merger
fusion of the two, the old, the new.

This House, My Bones

BRIAN KOMEI DEMPSTER

Your Hands Guide Me Through Trains

for my grandfather, Archbishop Nitten Ishida, 1901–1996

We stare down the track, searching the arch, where rails curve
out of darkness. You lift me on your shoulders
and we balance in white light, the dead center approaching.
The whistle blows, a rumble climbs through the bones
of your feet, through your legs and hands into mine,

and your right hand clenches my right,
your left hand clenches my left,
and if this were 1942, my hands would be the handle
of your suitcase and your purple book scripted
in prayer. You board a boxcar, snap open your case,

and set your brush and ink to the right,
stones to the left, paint your own sea and coast
as the plains, grass and ironwoods rattle by.
You dip the brush in each camp and each barrack,
fill the paper with kelp and jellyfish, pebbles and shells,

tape the sheets side by side in a collage. And when it grows
dark, you stroke a track leading to the edge of the tide.
Praying for water, your hands drop from their clasp,
cling to the wires as men rip the sash from your back.
A rifle butt loosens your throat like a well.

But it is 1976, a Sunday like any other,
when blue-collared men in stiff hats snag the wrist
of an old man, break his bottle in the dirt. *Get out,* they say
as he slides through a hole in a chain-link fence, the train rushing
under our feet, our lungs flowering with soot and steam.

For 54 years the imagination of your hands was enough.
The attic and your suitcase held every dusty scroll.
1996 and your brushstrokes fade, crumple in my palms.

427

Your fingers grip a cane, they waver with chopsticks.
Soup, tea and rice sprig your bib. I feed you, brush your teeth,

and my right hand clenches your right, my left clenches your left
and I lower you in the chair, place your feet on the steel ledges.
Grandfather, can we run through the gravel now, along the silver rail
watch flames curl off the faces of men smudged in coal?
Can we return to Missoula and Fort Sill, the wheels circling back

to Crystal City? I will wheel you past the rows
of empty chairs, drape the sash over your back, strike a match,
light sticks of incense. Your hands will guide me
up the years like a black iron rope, the orange glow, a tunnel
of smoke, the pages that turn us toward a more certain home.

HASSAN NAJMI

Train Station

A tourist in the station, a tobacco kiosk for reading. A gloomy newspaper.
A small square at the bottom of the page for forgetfulness. Two fingers
with an extinguished cigarette. Lost tempers. Clouds on the faces. A
closed tavern. A media preoccupied with police. Police to ruin the cities.
A felony in the garden. Half bodies in the brigadier's tapes. Two lovers on
the right-hand sidewalk. Naked legs. A maid pouring a water bucket by
the entrance. A guard dozes off by the door. A public ad on the gate.
Remnants of pamphlets in the dirt. A window without a curtain. An
anxious evening. An anxiety concealed from the monitors in the houses.
Health education programs. Admonishing talk. Chatter by the post
office. A woman complaining about her neighbor. A girl in a nightgown
on the balcony. A ghost going to his bed. A newspaper clip full of mud.
An astonished standing up. An awakening friendship. The solidarity of
grass. The coming down of storms. Sycophant speeches. Compensated
bribes. Exemptions without exemption. Perversions of time. Endless
disfigurement. A silence springing from the pores. Dead cities, graveyard
cities. . . .

Translated from the Arabic by Fady Joudah

AK WELSAPAR

Midday

Midday, just look around:
the heat raises the sand to a boil.
Life is nothing more than a myth
when summer comes to this land.

A camel on the ground, groaning,
doesn't help against the heat.
What does it ask and to whom,
its neck bent into a question mark?

The day at its peak. The sun blind.
Mirages draw me in only to disappoint.
In Asia, a tornado is born
and wails past me on its way to Africa.

The forest of desert trees lies quiet;
strives to survive.
On a branch, a small body jumps around,
a sparrow burned black by the sun.

The ground is cracked and jagged;
the desert air melts away.
The wonderful music of the heat
is brief, and piercing.

I bear a worry in my heart
not everyone bears.
My homeland follows me everywhere.
I love my people. I can't help it.

Translated from the Turkmen by Eric Welsapar and Idra Novey

DORJI PENJORE

I Want My Soil Back

How can I grow, spread my roots
Far and deep when beneath
Me, the soil has been gouged,
Displaced, to form a multitude
Of bricks that shapes a wall
Dividing man from man?

Now a strong wind blows.
I cannot withstand it.
Rocking and shaking,
I blanch, turn ill and frail.
The earth cannot nourish me.
I want my soil back.

NGUYỄN DUY

The Father

In this place there are so many
who spent half their life in Viet Bac, the other half along the Truong Son
    mountains,
men and women who once ate roots, bamboo shoots for meals
and now make do with taro leaves and wild tendrils.

Their great hopes have turned their skulls white,
their native villages so far away now, like distant seasons.
A lifetime working in sun and rain,
a lifetime walking, and they've yet to reach home.

All along the far horizon, families drift off to sleep.
A father old as a thousand hills, a mother old as a hundred rivers.

When the winds come, they'll have to arc and circle, climb over
the great bends and twists of the forests to get to this place.

Translated from the Vietnamese by Nguyễn Bá Chung and Kevin Bowen

DOM MORAES

Gondwana Rocks

Heavy the climbing wind,
burdened with coming rain.
At the road's edges are
black stands of conifer.
Above, anarchic rocks,
grotesque in disarray,
left by a continent
which slowly disappeared;
scoured and depleted by
a hundred million rains.

They stand in silhouette
above the windwarped pines,
more corpsed with memories than
ruins which castles leave.
Though they have stood much wear,
have endured more than grief
and survived more than war,
these rocks now bear no runes
more than those worked by wind,
great shifts of earth, and rains.

But these gnarled outcrops are
connections with what is.
The cold salacities
of night, day's fall and flare,

unending cycles, pass
at the same charted pace.
Forest on forest dies
at charted pace, beneath
the scarred rocks which maintain
a stillness not of death.

The constant wheel of stars
turns over them in time.
Glaciers, tidal waves,
sandstorms and human hands
have paused on them, then passed.
Ghosts follow other ghosts
up climbing stairs of wind,
across black stands of pine
to the last source of loss:
the rocks, the coming rain.

GÉMINO H. ABAD

Jeepney

Consider honestly
this piece of storm
in our city's entrails.
Incarnation of scrap,
what genius of salvage!
Its crib now molds our space,
its lusty gewgaws our sight.

In rut and in flood,
claptrap sex of traffic,
jukebox of hubbub—
I mark your pride of zigzag
heeds no one's limbs nor light.
I sense our truth laughing
in our guts, I need
no words to fix its text.

This humdrum phoenix in our street
is no enigma.
It is a daily lesson of history
sweating in a tight corner.
Its breakdowns and survivals
compose our Book of Revelation.
It may be the presumptive engine
of our last mythology.

Look, our Macho Incarnate,
sweat towel slung round his neck.
He collects us where the weathers
of our feet strand us.
His household gods travel with him,
with the Virgin of Sudden Mercy.
Our Collective Memory, he forgets
no one's fare. Nor anyone's destiny.

See how our countrymen cling
to this trapeze against all hazards.
All our lives we shall be acrobats
and patiently survive.
Our bodies feed on proximity,
our minds rev up on gossip.
We flock in small spaces
and twitter a country of patience.

Here is our heartland still.
When it dreams of people,
it returns empty to itself,
having no power of abstraction.
Abandoned to itself
and in no one's care,
jeepneys carom through it,
our long country of patience.

Nights I lie awake, I hear
a far-off tectonic rumble.
Is it a figment of desolation
from that reliquary of havoc,

or, out of its dusty hardihood,
that obduracy of mere survival,
a slow hoard of thunder
from underground spirit of endurance?

G. S. SHARAT CHANDRA

In the Third Country

1
As a last defiance
you die simultaneously in three countries

In the country that exiled you
it's a simple funeral
a mummy in white
you're carted off
to the ghats of Benares
in a wheel-cart

In the presence of sadhus
for a fee or for none
Allen Ginsberg raves a mantra
in homage

You burn well on the sides
someone notices your mouth
sizzles a speech to the authorities

2
In the country you went for
your ex-wife arrives
by the next available flight
the children as usual
are at summer camp

For want of religious clarity
you're hearsed to the public cemetery

Someone throws in
a copy of your paperback
you don't complain

Your friends in Iowa bewail you in a bar
someone reads a poem or two
someone mentions you on the telephone

3
In the third country
the wind neither wails
nor stays on your windowsill
your teacups remain full or empty
it's one season or another
people sleep or people wake

No one wants your whereabouts
no one worries your mail

If you changed your mind
and returned there
no one wonders if it was appropriate
whether you acted hastily
or with taste

EDIP CANSEVER

Bedouin

In the desolate shriveled brown town of my eyes
White-necked camels trudge along behind the weary herdsmen
Who still grope for a meaning day after day
Staring into a place far away
Ask them if they saw at least as much as they see a tale
In the desolate shriveled brown town of my eyes

Toward an unknown plate neither day nor death
They just stare
A Bedouin stands among the white thorns
Among gods and suns and fires
Not even a flame nor a plant nor a prayer
In the desolate shriveled brown town of my eyes

Who knows what he seeks perhaps a sating sip of water
Not a stop nor a rest
The white-necked camels could sense nothing even if they came
Even if the weary herdsmen knelt down and crouched before them
As the chilliest desert bird dies once again
In the uniform color of the world

Translated from the Turkish by Talât Sait Halman

AL-MUNSIF AL-WAHAYBI

In the Arab House

The deep blue of the earth
tempted me, and I came.
It was an Arab house
dedicated by wind to eloquent silence.
I wished good night to the grasses of the garden,
then went away.

A woman awaits me
She has fixed a spear at the threshold of the tent,
completed her beauty rituals, laid down
on the sands, and slept.
As I move toward her in the dream,
the star of the guest will see me
and follow my steps

"Sir, oh Sir,
you who stealthily came to me in the dream,
spread out in my body—
the morning star has entered our tent
and alighted in the mirror of frothing days."

Translated from the Arabic by Salma Khadra Jayyusi and Naomi Shihab Nye

AGNES S. L. LAM

Eighteen Haiku for Xiamen

The airport toilets,
white, clean and Japanese, flush
automatically.

The arrival lounge,
an international size,
has moving walkways.

The sky blue and clear,
I breathe the air, light without
mist or pollution.

Not chaotic roads
lead to a winding city
right up to the sea.

Gu Lang Yu air fills
with music from pianists,
the drumming of waves.

Echoes of prayers sing
through the richest monastery,
Nan Pu Tuo. Next door,

from many donors
for the university,
dreams and stories rise.

The guesthouse has rooms
with bedsheets and towels, white
as the Shangri-la's.

Once a monk student
fell in love with a classmate.
One killed the other.

This one learns English,
Buddhist sutras to translate,
the whole world to save.

A thousand may meet
at the square on Friday nights
to practice English.

Shops near the South Gate
meet devotees' and students'
needs for food and wear.

A fresh cream cake sells
at thirty-five Renminbi
next to lychee tea.

Cages on the floor
of a restaurant hold snakes
snuggling like siblings.

An egret was once
eaten by a student's friend
trusted with its care.

A friend from Beijing
married to a Fuzhou girl
expects his first child.

A Hello Kitty
is laughing in Putonghua
for Year 2000.

May missiles not be
shot over the seawater
divide to unite.

MERLIE M. ALUNAN

The Neighbor's Geese

His flock of five white geese,
he keeps them fenced,
together with the fattening pig,
a few chickens he's raising for the pot,
some *lanka* trees. Once he'd kept a dog there,
a lonely hungry brute, snarling and barking
all day, and an ewe which lambed
one cold wet night while he slept.
But the dog broke its leash and killed the lamb.
It was no more than what dogs would do
you might say, but the ewe bleated all night
And he never wakened. Ewe and dog
are gone now—to their fates, I guess.
So now there are the geese.

He keeps the geese, he says, to guard
his few trees, the pig, the chickens
scrabbling in the grass, the thumb-sized
patch of gravel he had claimed
under god's heaven as his.
If geese had business of their own
other than this, he'd never think of it.

In this little gravel patch,
the wind blows in as anywhere else,
leaves, twigs fall. Prowler cats break in,

stray dogs snaffle past, mice scuttle through,
toads hop toad fashion into his water trough.
The geese announce each intrusion
in raucous gabble without distinction.
            Or could it be just
goose talk, "Bad food here, mate," and the rest
squawk back, "You bet, not enough here
to make a crap!" Goose laughter, loud, loud.
If goose were polite, won't they be like us?

What I always say is
keep only what comes to your door
freely and in peace. I'd say it to him,
but he's full of his own wisdom—
I doubt he'll hear me out. I'd tell him
keep only what would stay, willingly—
for as long as they need, a day or two,
maybe—to breathe, rest, feed.
Anyone, anything, furred, feathered,
or human, bearing gifts or empty-handed.
Above all, keep only what you can
love truly, abundantly, no holding back,
no regret, knowing any guests you take in
could pick you bone-clean before they leave,
shaking the dust from their feet
for you to sweep to the high wide sky.

            There go his geese again,
honking fit to bring down the rain.
They raise their beaks, craning their necks
as they make their urgent cry, marching
across the gravel patch, their heads held high.
I'd willingly grant, despite his fence,
these geese guard terrains grander and nobler
than his gravel patch, all we could see
with our mere human eyes.

BASHIR SAKHAWARZ

Kabul Behind My Window

Days, evaporation of thoughts in the dusty plane
Nights caravans of khutbeh from mosques
Kabul
      a changed skin
      worn by children in rubbish tips
      worn by silence and noise
          silence of living
          noise of death.

Mountains translation of tolerance
      shoulders of dry deserts
      mother of rivers
      height of tragedy
      behind my window
      dust, shout and the mullah like a worm
      through the loudspeakers
      life is another ablution
      another clean bottom.

I am late
mountains have moved
Kabul soaks in pain
here it is
here it is not
like magic
like a dream
the road to Kabul
disappears.

SOHRAB SEPEHRI

At the Hamlet of Gulestaneh

How vast the plain!
How lofty the mountains!
The scent of grass permeates Golestaneh!
I came here a seeker
Of perhaps slumber
Of light, a pebble, a smile.

From behind the poplars
It was pure negligence calling me.

I paused by a field of reeds.
The wind blew, I listened.
Who was speaking to me?
A lizard skidded by.
I walked on,
Past a hayfield,
A cucumber bed,
A blushing bush,
And the oblivion of earth.

On the lip of a stream
I slipped off my shoes
Dipped my feet in the cool water:
How awake and sentient I am today!
How sober all my senses!

What if from behind these mountains
Some sorrow is bound my way?

Who hides behind the trees?
No one—just a cow grazing.
It's summer's high noon.
The shadows—patches of bright,
Untainted purity—
Know such summer.

Children, this is where you must play.
Life is not desolate.
There is balm, blessing . . . and apples.
Live while there are poppies in bloom.

Something stirs in my chest
Like a dawn-spun dream,
A grove of light
And I am restless.
I want to run to the limits of this plain,
Past the top of these mountains.

From the distance a voice is calling me.

Translation from the Persian by Sholeh Wolpé

ZHAI YONGMING

The Black Room

All crows under Heaven are equally black, and this
Fills me with fear, they have so many
Relatives, their numbers are legion, they're hard to resist

But we're indispensable, we three sisters
Slim and graceful, we glide to and fro
Looking like sure winners
But I mean to make mischief, I'm cruel at heart
Maintaining a good daughter's appearance of sweetness
My footsteps retrace my daily defeats

Awaiting proposals in our boudoirs, we're fair maids of good family
We smile resentfully, racking our brains
For ways to augment our charms
Youthful, beautiful, like fires ablaze
Seared black, these single-minded snares
(Which of these good men with well-sharpened teeth, an unwavering gaze
And steady expression will be my brother-in-law?)

I sense
Our chamber is beset on all sides
In the night, both cats and mice have awakened
We go to sleep, and search in our dreams for unknown house-numbers
In the night, we women are like ripe melons about to fall from the vine
Conjugal bliss, etcetera

We three sisters, different with each new day
Marriage, still at the crux of finding a mate
Lights in the bedroom fill the newlyweds with disappointment
Risk it all on one throw, I tell myself
"Home is the place we leave"

Translated from the Chinese by Andrea Lingenfelter

SALMA KHADRA JAYYUSI

A Tale

My father-in-law goes to bed,
sleeps with his wife, gets up,
takes a bath and prays to God for Paradise.

That's God's law and the Prophet's:
An unquenchable river of kisses,
houri dreams like a snake
wriggling between his thighs,
a neatly drained putz
his idea of fun in bed,
plowing woman to harvest children.

My husband worships the randy flea too,
he's usually to be found
stuffing dinars into wrappers
to buy a second wife.

As for me I wear a scar
on my buccaneer's brow
while I sail the wind everywhichwhere,
wife to exile,
my people dead or dying,
my children lamps in the windows
of my storm-moved house.
My country? My country!
Sliver moon of sorrow,
my mother's dead body
wandering in the hills,
wind stands frozen by her grave.

Translated from the Arabic by Kamal Boullata

PETER BALAKIAN

Mandelstam in Armenia, 1930

Between arid houses and crooked streets
a shadow could be your wife or a corpse
and a mule's hooves sounded like Stalin's
fat fingers drumming a table.

In the Caucasus eagles and hawks
hung in the blue's basilica.
A swallow flew off a socle
into the wing of an echo-

history's caw and chirp and bird shit
on the tombs in the high grass.
On hairy serrated stems
poppies flagged like tongues.

Petals of flat paper
lined your thumbed-out pockets.
Anther seeds burned your pen.

From a cloud of broom a red bee stumbled
to your fish-globe brain.
A casket of light kissed the eyebrows of a tree.

Lake Sevan's rippling blue skirt
lapped you. Slime tongues got your eyes.
A half-dead perch slithered your ear.

When the evening air settled
on the creatures of the mountain
the sun was the Virgin's head.

Here, where the bush grew with fresh blood
and ancient thorns, you picked the rose
without scissors. Became an omen.

U TIN MOE

Desert Years

Sobs
An intake of breath
A sliver of glass
Old decades of years
cannot consider
In these years the bees cannot
make honey the mushrooms
cannot sprout
All the fields are out of
crops. Dry.

The mist is damp
The storm is dim
The dust rising in clouds
Along the road where
the bullock cart
has traveled.

Encircled by thorns
the hta-naung tree its trunk
cat's-claw scratched is trying
to bloom.

It doesn't rain.

When it does—it's not enough
to soak the earth.

In the monastery at
the edge of the village
bells
are not heard. If they are
they do not enter the ears
blissfully.

There are no novices
orange-clad
zilch of sounds of young
voices
reciting the scriptures only the
kappiya attendant
with his
shaved head falls between the
pillars and columns of the
building.

The earth doesn't dare
to put forth fruit.
It abandons all
and looks at me
at once feeling embarrassed
and frightened as if she
cannot talk.

When will the sobs change
and the bells ring sweetly again?

Translated from the Burmese by Kyi May Kaung

SUJI KWOCK KIM

The Korean Community Garden

In the vacant lot nobody else bothered to rebuild,
dirt scumbled for years with syringes and dead
weed-husks, tire-shreds and smashed beer bottles,
the first green shoots of spring spike through—

bullbrier, redroot, pokeweed, sowthistle,
an uprising of grasses whose only weapons are themselves.
Blades slit through scurf. Spear-tips spit dust
as if thrust from the other side. They spar and glint.

How far will they climb, grappling for light?
Inside I see coils of fern-bracken called *kosari*,
bellflower cuts named *toraji* in the old country.
Knuckles of ginger and mugwort dig upward,

shoving through mulched soil until they break
the surface. Planted by immigrants they survive,
like their gardeners, ripped from their native
plot. What is it they want, driving and driving

toward a foreign sky? How not to mind the end
we'll come to. I imagine the garden underground,
where gingko and ailanthus grub cement rubble.
They tunnel slag for foothold. Wring crumbs of rot

for water. Of shadows, seeds foresung as *Tree
of Heaven* & *Silver Apricot* in ancient Mandarin,
their roots tangle now with plum or weeping willow,
their branches mingling with tamarack or oak.

I love how nothing in these furrows grows unsnarled,
nothing stays unscathed. How last year's fallen stalks,
withered to pith, cleave to this year's crocus bulbs,
each infant knot burred with bits of garbage or tar.

Fist to fist with tulips, iris, selving and unselving
glads, they work their metamorphoses in loam
pocked with rust-flints, splinters of rodent-skull—
a ground so mixed, so various that everything

is born of what it's not. Who wouldn't want
to flower like this? How strangely they become
themselves, this gnarl of azaleas and roses of Sharon,
native to both countries, blooming as if drunk

with blossoming. Green buds suck and bulge.
Stem-nubs thicken. Sepals swell and crack their cauls.
Lately every time I walk down this street to look
through the fence, I'm surprised by something new.

Yesterday hydrangea and chrysanthemums burst
their calyxes, corolla-skins blistering into welts.
Today jonquils slit blue shoots from their sheaths.
Tomorrow day-lilies and wild-asters will flame petals,

each incandescent color unlike: sulfur, blood, ice,
coral, fire-gold, violet the hue of shaman robes—
every flower with its unique glint or slant, faithful
to each particular. All things lit by what they neighbor

but are not, each tint flaring without a human soul,
without human rage at its passing. In the summer
there will be scallions, mung-beans, black sesame,
muskmelons, to be harvested into buckets and sold

at market. How do they live without wanting to live
forever? May I, and their gardeners in the old world,
who kill for warring dreams and warring heavens,
who stop at nothing, say life and paradise are one.

GYALPO TSERING

The Nomad III

I slowly gather up my shaggy herd
And prepare them for the lowlands,
while wolves get hungrier and brave
The sun's rays that freeze with the breeze

Already I feel the longing to remain free
Here where I can sing and train my thoughts
On matters that follow no boundaries,
But nature overrules my wandering too far.

Nine loads of butter wrapped in gut
Lies freezing while I thaw the saddlebags,
For busy days in the cities of butter-lights
Too crowded; too sinister for the wide spaces.

My friends can bear the cold and the storms
That blanket my grassland thoughts,
Wind and yet clear of soggy-dung smoke
Trapped in the cold hearth where the fire burns.

FARAH DIDI

Dying for a Himalayan Dream

pristine white snow-capped peaks,
painted across the horizon,
above green clad foothills and valleys,
glacial waters cold and sullen,

meandering rivers now stand still,
where Sherpas carry their daily loads,
a fresh chill spreads along the wake
of footsteps over virgin snows,

a crimson range stencilled in the sky,
bleeding in the evening light,
half shadowed flotilla of clouds,
descends into a misty night,

trudging against the hostile glare,
a ghostly moon to guide along,
with frozen breaths they suck the air,
as she pulls them ever closer to her womb,

the people of the frozen tombs,
the final dream, the dizzy heights,
the chilling promise the goddess made,
the summit for their lives.

ELMAZ ABINADER

This House, My Bones

*Under siege, life is the moment between remembrance
of the first moment, and forgetfulness of the last—*

—Mahmoud Darwish, *State of Siege*, 2002

Enter the house,
Sit at the table covered in gold
A cloth Sitt embroidered
For the third child's birth.
Take the tea, strong and minty,
Hold the glass warm
Against your palms, fragrances
Of centuries fill you, sweetness
Rises up to meet you. The youngest boy
Faoud, shows you a drawing
He has made of a horse.
You touch his shoulder, stroke
His hair, he loves to talk to strangers,
Shows them his room filled with posters

Of extinct and mythical animals; dinosaurs,
Unicorns, dragons. You want to linger
In the music of his voice, afraid his disappearance
Is inscribed on shell cases stockpiling in the Gulf.

Enter the mosque,
Admire the arches
Inlaid with sea colored pebbles,
Follow the carpets, long runners
Of miracles in thread, your feet still damp
Slip against the marble floor.
Spines of men curl into seashells
In the room ahead. Echoes
Of the meuzzin shoot around you
Fireworks of speeches and prayers.
Don't be afraid because they worship
Unlike you. Be afraid that worship
Becomes the fight, faith the enemy;
And yours the only one left standing.

Someone asks, what should we do
While we wait for the bombs, promised
And prepared? How can we ready ourselves?
Do we gather our jewelry and books,
And bury them in the ground? Do we dig
Escape tunnels in case our village is invaded?
Do we send our children across the border
To live in refugee camps, remembering us
Only in dreams, ghostly voices calling their names?
What do we pack? The coffee urn father
Bought from Turkey? The pair of earrings
Specially chosen for the wedding day?
How can we ever pack anything if not everything?
If not the tick on the wall marking
The children's growth, if not the groan
Of the washing machine in the kitchen,
If not the bare spot on the rug
Where Jidd put his feet when he read

The Friday paper?
Help them gather things: brass doorknobs,
Enamel trays, blue glasses made in Egypt,
Journals of poetry, scraps of newspapers, recipes
They meant to try. And what about the things
They cannot hold? The beginning of life and all
The memories that follow. The end of life
And all that is left to do.

Enter the heart,
Read the walls and all the inscriptions
The love of lovers, of children and spouses,
The love of stars, and cardamom and long eyelashes.
Tour the compartments telling
The story: that life has begun with faith,
That life may end with folly. See it heave
In fear that threats, predictions, and actions
Are a history already written, spiraling
Loose and out of control. No amount of hope
Can save it. No amount of words can stop it.
Hold the heart. Imagine it is yours.

BOWL OF AIR
AND SHIVERS

Bowl of Air and Shivers

—Eugene Gloria

Have faith, believe in Allah, my mother told me at my grandfather's funeral. I was six years old. She held my hand as I looked at my Jiddo in the casket. Who was God, I thought, and would he be good to my grandfather? My mother explained that we are created in God's image. That He is the supreme spirit. I didn't understand what she meant. She suggested I find my answers in prayer.

A few years later, I found my father at the edge of his bed with a letter in his hand, crying. I stood in front of him but was careful not to disturb his grief. His head was bent downward, his complexion darker than usual, and his tears insistent. In his large hand he gripped a thin sheet of paper, as if it could keep him from falling into an abyss. Soon after, I found out that his best friend had been killed in Africa while on a mission with the Red Cross. *Have faith,* I heard my mother tell him.

That evening I stayed awake looking at the moonlight glistening on the field of grass. It was so glorious. But I couldn't find the perfect distance between that beauty and the cruel fate of my father's friend. I couldn't find the stillness in a sacred river. Church. Mosque. Temple. *Have faith,* my mother's voice echoed like a mantra I could not escape.

Little did I know, as the years passed, I was to attend many more funerals as thousands of Palestinians were killed during what is now more than sixty years of occupation; others had been killed in Burma, Iraq, and elsewhere. It was difficult to have faith.

Then one misty morning, while driving to my family's house in Santo Domingo, my silence collided with what felt like an earthquake. A huge crash, followed by the windshield bursting into a million pieces.

I stopped the car and got out, screaming for help. But instead of coming to my rescue, the few people present ran in the opposite direction. I stood confused until I saw a body on the ground. A man had just driven into my car with his motorcycle, not wearing a helmet. People were speaking but I could not hear anything. By a stroke of bad luck, the battery of my cell phone was dead, so I could not call anyone.

Suddenly, a beat-up red car arrived. A man in his forties got out and told me he was a taxi driver and he would help me take the man to the hospital. I asked him if I could use his cell phone and called my father, who said he would come right away. We arrived at the emergency room of a small hospital, and they placed me on one bed and the man on another. I was hysterical, and as the nurses tried to calm me down, I saw something strange: my taxi driver, wearing white surgical gloves, examining the man as if he were a doctor. I didn't understand what was happening and thought perhaps I had crossed over to the other life or this was some horrifying dream and I would be waking up any minute. But then I heard the words I was dreading. *He is dead.*

My heart beat so fast that I forgot how to breathe. My taxi driver and the police decided that it was best if I left the hospital. Meanwhile, my father's only way of communicating with me was through the taxi driver's cell phone. As we drove to the police station, the taxi driver told me that everything would be fine, God willing. I felt the universe around me disappear. When we arrived at the police station, he held my hand for a second. I got out and he drove off.

I never saw that beat-up red car again, nor the man who had been driving it. There wasn't a trace of him anywhere. His name did not exist in any records I could find, and his phone was no longer working. Did his phone just stop functioning? Or was he an angel? What had happened? I had faced my own mortality and my own sense of self in the world, and my angel–taxi driver helped me through it all and now he had disappeared. I wondered why our lives had intersected and whether this angel was there to help the man cross to the next life, to help me survive the tragedy. Or perhaps it was Karma. Perhaps this was God's way of showing me He existed, thus making me confront my faith. Because, for the first time, I could not feel my existence, *He* was the only one present. *He* was the only one who was real. Then I thought, is this death?

Death and life are considered ambiguous terms by many. The end of one's existence differs from how that end might come into being. Death could be a blank state, a finishing point, or a continuation. And life, no more than a certain death. Some like Sigmund Freud believe that "the goal of all life is death." Others like Ernest Becker explore the ways society prevents us from contemplating our own mortality. Many people find answers or solace in their religion. Hindus go to the Vedas, the main scriptures of Hinduism, following the Vedanta philosophy (*Veda* meaning knowledge and *anta* meaning end), believing in the cosmic spirit of Brahman. Christians seek Jesus of Nazareth and his teachings in the New Testament, believing that Jesus is the Messiah. Muslims look to the Quran and believe that there is only one God and that Muhammed is His Messenger. Jews find in the Old Testament the divine revelation of the written and oral Torah. Buddhists find relevance in meditation, the four noble truths, and the contemplation of Dharma, taking their cue from the Buddha. A Buddha is anyone who has achieved enlightenment or awakening. And then there are those like Gandhi, who consider themselves "Hindu, Christian, Muslim, Jew, Buddhist and Confucian." Or Rabindranath Tagore, who said, "My religion is in the reconciliation of the superpersonal man, the universal human spirit, in my own individual being."[1] So if religion is a bridge to God, who is God?

This is expressed in the poem "To God," by the distinguished Bengali poet Sarat Kumar Mukhopadhyay. It begins with a stream of questions to a higher power: "How many things they say about you— / that you created the expanding universe, / or was it that the world's people / created you?" The speaker in the poem questions God directly, which could be perceived as condemnation or inquisition:

> *Whose side do you choose?*
> *The rich—who take more than their due*
> *and toss scraps to the poor, and toss you, too?*
> *Or the poor—who hope you'll turn things upside down*
> *and so deliver them?*

Mukhopadhyay is not only inquisitive, he is also pointing out our relative economic inequality.

The figure returns to his questions, though this time he ventures through the minds of philosophers: "Nietzsche says, you're dead. / Pascal says, we can't know whether or not you exist, / but it's worse to be fooled disbelieving." Which brings us to what God seems to demand most from us: *faith*.

Raised in India and Nepal, Tibetan American poet Tsering Wangmo Dhompa has written the poem "One more say," which begins simply but upon further reading takes on melancholic tones. Faith is not something one acquires, it is something one already possesses:

[1] Dutta Krishna and Andrew Robinson, eds., *Rabindranath Tagore: An Anthology* (New York: St. Martin's Griffin, 1997), p. 233.

Think on this when prayers fall like thick paint on dry asphalt.

Think on this when the face is fading.

Think on this and be decisive in your motions. The breathing. The utterance.

No Eastern star leading conch shells and a rainbow at dusk. Those who must believe, do.

The speaker's lines become a way to recollect the past and present, become prayer and meditation, ultimately declaring the importance for us to *know* that we have the final choice when it comes to the direction we want to take:

Who dares to question the accuracy of a direction when the journey was not theirs.

The moment of birth. Before the father extended his arm towards the mother.

The poet's direct language gives the reader pause, as it reflects on destiny with a strange familiarity. Some might call such faith absurd and may not find that it can bring happiness. Still others, who foreground the brutality and unfairness of death, might turn solemn, incapable of daring to hope. Ultimately, as the well-known Sudanese poet Muhammed al-Faituri has written in "A Scream," everything, including faith, seems to be lost in the oblivion of death and what remains is nothing but a *denouement* (final completion) or a *denouncement* (an act of denunciation):

At the end, every scream
pours like a river into silence,
but the most dazzling star
is that which shows the caravan its way
when moss has covered our memories
and grief runs wild through the house.

Such grief has run wild through my own house, and for solace I often go back to the words of Omar Khayyám: "Ah, make the most of what we yet may spend, / Before we too into the Dust descend." Like Khayyám, I believe only in the present moment, that perhaps there is nothing beyond, but keep returning to my ruminations on mortality, to my mother's words, *have faith,* and back again to Khayyám: "Oh, the brave Music of a distant drum!" No matter what road I seem to take, I find myself wondering if perhaps I end up being where I need to be. Whatever happens during this lifetime, death unites us all; it is the unraveling of *mystica,* which is part of and apart from us.

— NATHALIE HANDAL

SARAT KUMAR MUKHOPADHYAY

To God

How many things they say about you—
that you created the expanding universe,
or was it that the world's people
created you? Whose side do you choose?
The rich—who take more than their due
and toss scraps to the poor, and toss you, too?
Or the poor—who hope you'll turn things upside down
and so deliver them? But you never do.
In battle, you sit by the victor.

Nietzsche says, you're dead.
Pascal says, we can't know whether or not you exist,
but it's worse to be fooled disbelieving.

These are weighty and deep philosophical questions. I see
a forest behind me, a desert in front of me,
and man in the middle, in his encampments.
And bullock carts hauling heaps of beef everyday.

Translated from the Bengali by Robert McNamara and the author

TSERING WANGMO DHOMPA

One more say

Think on this when prayers fall like thick paint on dry asphalt.

Think on this when the face is fading.

Think on this and be decisive in your motions. The breathing. The utterance.

No Eastern star leading conch shells and a rainbow at dusk. Those who must believe, do.

Who dares to question the accuracy of a direction when the journey was not theirs.

The moment of birth. Before the father extended his arm toward the mother.

Here is a location. Here it is scattering like mustard seeds.

PIMONE TRIPLETT

A Vision of St. Clare

Girl for whom the job came as a crack in rockface, the sudden
      tomb-slip turned all door.
So that when she saw the lily spell itself there, seraphed on the wall
      of her father's house, she knelt
down for the rapture, the rupture, and started to dig. Wall through
      which the dead in those days
were carried for burial, delivered into, they prayed, His secrets
      held deeper than dirt.
On the night of the rock loosening beneath her fingers to gravel,
      to seconds falling ordinary
as hourglass, the little sands cinch-waisted, Palm Sunday, in Assisi,
      in the family house,
1212 A.D., she listened to the mice scurry and flirt in the hallway, then
      to the one dove's sound
of silken pebbles tumbling in its throat. Turns out later they asked,
      for what, the mother and father,
getting up for the scream, running to find her there in rubble, blood
      rivering steep down her arms
by then, instant the wall fell, and first light entered, and she stepped
      clean through.

RUSSELL C. LEONG

Tian Qiao / Sky Bridge

Taipei & Los Angeles

Here I am standing at the edge
of the dark lashes under your eyes
in that zone that misses radar altogether.
Jagged fragrance, jagged finger
once-upon-a-time
jagged chinese lover, cook, masseur
good at massages, at pouring the right amount
of cold-pressed olive oil between your thighs
kneading your body and at once
needing it obsessively.
Pointing at a world that now scans me ironically
crystal and shadow compete
for alignment or enlightenment
here, a spot of dust, there, a bit of glass
a line of light intersects a shadow slowly.

Here I am standing
at the bottom of the Sky Bridge
back to back with you in Hong Kong, Tokyo, Manila, L.A.

On the verge of a tropical sweat
of a relationship that is no longer a familiar relation
all points of the cheap compass I bought in Taipei
magnetize my longing and your leaving
opposing directions
as you walk away.

A thousand cars a minute
pass under the concrete sky bridge
mute steel bodies threaten to metabolize me
I climb the first steps anyway.

Two monks in ochre cloth
stand on either side of the bridge

one monk has a bowl, and so does the other
one is real and the other is fake
or both are real or both are fake
I genuflect to the first, and when I reach the other side
nod to the other
I drop one coin in each bowl adding
a clink or two to my claustrophobic karma.

Jagged fragrance, jagged finger
point at the world that denies me
but another feeling arises from nowhere
even more subtle than smell, or sex, or perfume
chromatic eyes of yellow, red, and blue
delicate signals sidling in the wind
flags mark a zone that ignore radar altogether.

I've crossed the sky bridge, loved and left
paid homage to monks real and unreal
dodged loose cars, tight women, soft men
and seductive shadows
left all familiar relations to the familiar.

Now I am in a line of sight barely
touching the jagged edge of the Heart
    Heart as body
    Heart as sutra
    Heart that roams freely
as empty as some sound
bouncing around in a brass bowl.

SARGON BOULUS

How Middle-Eastern Singing Was Born

Prophet

I gather myself
into one,

exposing my face
to the lightning,
and rave
while waiting
for the wave
that will cast me
onto an unknown shore,
tied to a stone.

Book

Open
the book of time
with trembling
fingers, and read:
your life
that is chained
to this page;
your lover
who will tell you
the first mystery
and the last.

God

God decreed
that the underworld
be revealed
in this one:
these dark, sad
and twisted alleys
where men are condemned
to drift forever.

Oud

Then the days
went rolling by,
and one day
somebody

shoved this *oud*
between my hands,
and taught me
how to sing
in this wounded voice.

Translated from the Arabic by the author

AGYEYA

Quietly

Quietly
may the murmur of water falling
fill us,

quietly
may the autumn moon
float on the ripples of the lake,

quietly
may life's unspoken mystery
deepen in our still eyes,

quietly
may we, ecstatic, be immersed in the expanse
yet find it in ourselves—

Translated from the Hindi by Lucy Rosenstein

GOENAWAN MOHAMAD

A Tale

Silent, the earth is still. On
that mountaintop, as light fades.

Emptiness has been unfurled,
the sun halted.
Whose is the voice that laments:
where are the skeletons
of stars, your majesty?
Humankind, be calm.
The world will, in the end
bow low in defeat.
Day is over, and darkness cast
all light away.
What might time be:
is it a gentle dance
with the softness of a spirit
or a wind to hide
death's curse?
The clouds are rolling, my lord.
and the sky pale with fright
of a night that brings with it storm.
There is a solitary lamp that shines
there is a final soul
walking slowly on a predetermined course.
Silent, the earth is still. On
that mountaintop, as light fades.

Translated from the Indonesian by John H. McGlynn

KO UN

excerpts from *Flowers of a Moment*

At sunset
only one wish—
to become a wolf
beneath a fat full moon

I have spent the whole day being someone else's story again

and as I journey homeward
the trees are watching me

In Mount Kariwang in Chongson, Kangwon Province
the falling streams
are busy, but busier are
the minnows, the carplings
swimming upward
against the current

Rowing with just one oar
I lost that oar

For the first time I looked round at the wide stretch of water

Outside the cave the howling wind and rain
Inside
the silent speech of bats filling the ceiling

"I've come, dear.
Harsh winter's over now"

His wife's tomb laughs quietly

Yes, some say they can recall a thousand years
and some say they've already visited the next thousand years
On a windy day
I am waiting for a bus

We went to Auschwitz
saw the mounds of glasses
saw the piles of shoes
On the way back
we each stared out of a different window

Following the tracks of an animal in the snow
I looked back at my own tracks

Two people are eating
facing each other

The most routine thing
and at the same time
the best thing

Like they say, it's love

Without a sound

resin buried underground is turning into amber
Above, the first snow is falling

Along the path
a roebuck
is quietly contemplating the moon in a stream

The beak of a chick pecking at feed—
My studies too are far from complete

When the stalls were closing last market day
I suddenly glimpsed
Samman's ma who died last year
I suppose she came back to do some shopping

Mother hen outside the egg
baby chick inside the egg—
the two are really one single body

What can I do?
Peach blossom petals
have been drifting all day long into the empty house

Thirty years ago
a starving woman saw
a thousand sacks of rice in a mirage

Everything outside my door
is my teacher

Master horse shit
Master cow shit

Master children's freckles

That business tycoon's tremendous mansion—
the despair of beggars
the hope of burglars

Why?
     Why?!
          Why!?
A bright day
busy with questions from a five-year-old

Surely that child knows
that without those Why's
everything would be nothing

Translated from the Korean by Brother Anthony of Taizé, Young-moo Kim, and Gary Gach

LIU KEXIANG

Natural Science Teacher

Finally I spy that bundle of light, slowly flowing into the woods. Like a silent stream, leaving a waterfall, myriad specks of dust, like spores, float among the beams, exploring, or aimlessly wander off.

They enter the woods. There's a child fascinated by insects, going on and on about plants with me. There's a youngster who loves climbing mountains and fording streams, who will someday trace every range I've crossed. As for that girl who writes like a poem, she's never grown up, still that same likeness of an 11-year-old I dote on.

They'll come across my death, in different places. It might be like the shards of a beetle shell, or possibly a rotting, withered tree.

And, by chance, they'll encounter my birth, a kind of essence even more concrete than tender shoots and new leaves, sitting by their side in lonesome moments.

They continue going into the woods. Inside my aged sea-turtle's body they squirm about, vexing me, tiring me, harassing me. It's always been my living question mark, my uncertainty.

Translated from the Chinese by Nicholas A. Kaldis

MUHAMMAD HAJI SALLEH

the forest last day

death comes at the end of the chain saw
with spears of shrieks that split the air and red of the sun
biting into the flesh of wood
that is shocked by the sudden pain and alien din.
its world overturns all, strange as fainting
sap flowing, its essence denying the steel's
base and supporting roots trembling.

in its canopy birds still play
its air made fragrant by the essence of the forest
the sky is the witness with clear eyes.

> fallen is the cengal
> fallen is the meranti
> fallen is the merbau
> fallen is the pulai
> fallen is the seraya
> fallen is the nyatuh
> fallen is the resak
> fallen is the halban
> fallen is the nibung
> fallen is the rattan

a family of trees aged by the centuries
the beautiful and great lying in the shadow

with a presence in the root's fibers and shoots' sway.
heat rushes into the air tunnel, existence is scalded.

the wheel of nature turns slowly
listening to the rhythm of the season and sun
with a sense of presence in the roots and the sway of the shoots.

after the death shatter and scatter of roots
heat rushes into the tunnel, searing existence.

morning-purple flowers fall
as red as cliffs, as white as cloud, as brown as trunks.
buds and fruits on heavy branches fall
are dotted near the stem or full with the seasons
a universe of colors falls
a hundred stripes of green painting the leaves' personalities

the moon falls, caught by the branches
as light that sketches difference,
morning falls, the afternoon and the night.

with the rustle, tenderness drips from shoots
the secret mist of nature evaporates
the frame of balance is broken, since trees became earth
the quiet beauty filtered by light fades away,
leaves are dumb, branches speechless, no song, no echo
no deer, no baboon, no elephant herd
no pulse of mouse deer's bleat, no question.

the full epic of the forest
is ended by a convoy of lorries with tyres of concrete,
a gang of paid lumberjacks who wear no pity in their eyes.

and a bloated logger
who stands on the red desiccated desert—
our future.

Translated from the Malay by the author

MUHAMMED AL-FAITURI

A Scream

I understand Death's contract
and the finite ends of life:
however long a man lives
he lives only to die.
At the end, every scream
pours like a river into silence,
but the most dazzling star
is that which shows the caravan its way
when moss has covered our memories
and grief runs wild through the house.

Translated from the Arabic by Sargon Boulus and Peter Porter

BEHÇET NECATIGIL

Phosphorus

In the nocturnal obscurity of ancient tombs
Distant shrieks of bygone corpses are phosphorous.
At midnight over the old scrolls and papyri
Why does phosphorus dazzle with its pyres?

From his youthful days a man may pluck himself:
A furtive diamond beckons in dripping tunnels
If a phosphoric gleam shimmers far away
Melting candles become barely visible.

The prodigal water of early youth
Maps out a tangled course on harsh cars
$Mg\ 3P_2O_3$ magnesium phosphate.
Chemistry tarries in the realms of foam;
Phosphorus sparkles in desolate rooms
With nude pinups helpless and panting.

A man may die
Just a couple of grains.
Fear gnaws into vacant brains
Floating on an alabaster viscous liquid.
When you make enough money for food
On drenched marble basins phosphorus becomes a fetus.

Sternest stones, white papers, soft dyes—
Like vacuous waters—would turn dolorous
Nor would my writing have body or form
If they were not all a little phosphorous.

Translated from the Turkish by Talât Sait Halman

VISWANATHA SATYANARAYANA

Song of Krishna (5)

You come while I'm taking my bath.
You come when my sari gets wet, and I change into a dry one.
When, unnoticed, my sari falls from my shoulder—you are there.
Almost as if you had planned it.
As if you knew all such slippery moments.
You sit right in front of me.

Some kids are like this from the start, in the womb.
You're a true jewel among them, the eye on a peacock's feather.
Really, you're spoiled. No one disciplines you.
Everyone loves you and no one speaks to you harshly.
Any time they begin to get mad,
you do something or other and they laugh,
and everything is lost in that laughter.
For years and years, your mother longed to have
a tiny boy in her womb, and you came, so now
she lets you do just as you please.

What's a game for the cat is death for the mouse.
We can't even talk about these things.
We can't face them unless we give up all shame.
Sometimes I tell myself firmly: he's only a child,
why get so stirred up? But that's how women are made.
I can't help myself. If *you,* young man,
are the one to take away my shame,
I will take you for my God.

When a woman is getting dressed, you should leave.
If you happen to catch a glimpse, you should
bite your tongue, go away, and come back after a while.
You should ask if you can come in.
That's the proper way. It's not as if
this is your own house and I'm your wife.
Even my husband doesn't come in when I'm dressing.

Along with being so brash, you're also angry.
Don't be.
Never mind what I said.
Come, Krishna, eyes dark
as the lotus.

Translated from the Telugu by Velcheru Narayana Rao

KIM NAM-JO

Foreign Flags

There I first glimpsed
such desolate loneliness.

Above the soaring towers of the old castle
at Heidelberg
a flag is waving
like a boat being rowed
like a windmill turning in the wind
waving on and on
until the threads grow thin
then casting away that body like a corpse
they raise a new flag

I wonder
what it's like to be up there all alone
in the sky with the drifting clouds,
what it's like
to be shaking all over, looking down
on the mutability of people and things?
There I first glimpsed
such adult prayer.

Translated from the Korean by Brother Anthony of Taizé

NISSIM EZEKIEL

The Hill

This normative hill
like all others
is transparently accessible,
out there
and in the mind,
not to be missed
except in peril of one's life.

Do not muse on it
from a distance:
it's not remote
for the view only,
it's for the sport
of climbing.

What the hill demands
is a man
with forces flowering
as from the crevices
of rocks and rough surfaces
wild flowers
force themselves toward the sun
and burn
for a moment.

How often must I
say to myself
what I say to others:
trust your nerves—
in conversation or in bed
the rhythm comes.

And once you begin
hang on for life.
What is survival?
What is existence?

I am not talking about
poetry. I am
talking about
perishing
outrageously
and calling it
activity.
I say: be done with it.
I say:
you've got to love that hill.

Be wrathful, be impatient
that you are not
on the hill. Do not forgive
yourself or other,
though charity
is all very well.
Do not rest
in irony or acceptance.
Man should not laugh
when he is dying.
In decent death
you flow into another kind of time
which is the hill
you always thought you knew.

SUYUNBAY ERALIEV

Beginning

From the green meadows of Altai
I brought back a miraculous new wine
to the great summit of Tyan'-Shan'ya,
so that it might regenerate our self-esteem,
strengthen our people's spirit
amid the devastation,
amid the battles,
amid our wanderings,

so that it might invigorate our spirit from year to year,
amid our legendary traditions.
In the firmament,
on the vaulted slopes
where flow the crystal waters,
in the villages so highly protected
by the endless stream of years gone by.
One could almost hear the strains of "Manas"
as time suddenly released the reins,
even the rain,
like the glance of an evil eye,
gave up its place to that weather.

Translated from the Russian by Yuri Vidov Karageorge

LISA SUHAIR MAJAJ

Reunion

You'd think the dead would come at night,
shadows on a midnight wind,
shudders from the heart of mystery.

Instead they crowd in over my morning coffee;
hover insistently in the steam,
jostling their competing memories.

I tell them to come back later.
All those years of longing,
and they think they can show up like creditors?

I have a family to feed, work to do.
But they are like petulant children
clamoring for attention.

My mother wants to give me
the cracked white porcelain angel
that stood on her dresser for years,

impervious to despair. I tell her no,
but she presses it into my hands.
While I'm pondering the pursed mouth,

the glue-stained wings, my father
pulls my T-shirt into a pouch,
fills it with clods of dry brown earth,

murmuring something about loss,
remembrance, Palestinian inheritance.
My uncle is next, holding

a glass of red wine to my lips.
On its surface I see faces
shimmering as if in a lake:

his wife, whole and safe before the bomb
that shook the East Jerusalem cobblestones
so many decades ago,

his sisters before the cholera epidemic,
his mother with a straight, young back.
He urges me to drink, but I fling the glass away,

hear it shatter on the tile.
My elderly aunt, our newest dead,
comes forward to sweep up the mess,

muttering about the carelessness
of the young. Ashamed,
I try to take the broom from her,

but she tells me to drink my coffee,
leave the dead to their own business.
When I raise the cup to my lips

my mouth fills with dregs:
coarse, bittersweet, earth-dark,
dense as unclaimed memory.

K. SATCHIDANANDAN

Stammer

Stammer is no handicap.
It is a mode of speech.

Stammer is the silence that falls
between the word and its meaning,
just as lameness is the
silence that falls between
the word and the deed.

Did stammer precede language
or succeed it?
Is it only a dialect or a
language itself? These questions
make the linguists stammer.

When a whole people stammer,
stammer becomes their mothertongue:
as it is with us now.

God too must have stammered
when He created Man.
That is why all the words of man
carry different meanings.
That is why everything he utters
from his prayers to his commands
stammers,
like poetry.

Translated from the Malayalam by the author

DAHLIA RAVIKOVITCH

Grand Days Have Gone By Her

How did it go?
Untypically, she was quick to recollect.
A vineyard didn't spring from the earth.
An orchard stood there,
sickly,
slow to blossom.
A walnut tree that bloomed failed to ripen.
As though some natural yielding element
were missing from the ground.
Hard green lemons.
A balding lawn.
A great calm.
In the west, the hedge grew wild
and naturally the honeysucker
(later named honeybird),
were it alive today,
would have been twenty already.

There were manhunts in the valley.
Fire in the brush.
The summer burnt as usual in a hellish blaze,
the evening cast shadows with no relief.
Between death and death
they sang to her
the songs of Zion.
She wouldn't go to bed before dawn,
before a bird twittered.
In those years
she herself died
three or four times.
Not a definitive final death,
but a sort of death throes.
Great yearnings gripped her
in the bosom of night,
mighty emotional throbs.

The years have their way of wreaking changes
hidden and secret.
It is simple for her to remember this.
Grand days have gone by her.
What a pity that now, so near the end,
she's suddenly lost the ability
to remain among the living.

Translated from the Hebrew by Tsipi Keller

RAFIQ RAAZ

Seven Sparks

At the midnight's hour a sage's soul came afire.
In splendor he began to dance, a frenzied dance.

I was still in awe and fear when he bestowed
A folded paper on my undeserving self!

Suddenly I looked at the gift and trembled,
For I saw seven sparks wrapped in a silken paper.

Then rapture overcame me and I dozed.
I dreamed the dancing sage came to rest.

With folded hands I humbly asked what gift is this?
Pray, make me aware of this secret tonight!

For God's sake what will I do with the sparks?
For if I keep them, they will burn the silken paper!

The silken paper will burn, he said, the sparks will vanish.
Seven spots will burn for years on the subcontinent.

Translated from the Kashmiri by Muneebur Rahman

YONA WALLACH

Tuvia

The earth murmurs
Tuvia
the earth draws near
to observe you from up close
Tuvia
how do you look
Tuvia
the earth murmurs
the earth draws near
Tuvia
the earth swarms
I have something to show you
Tuvia oh oh
Tuvia ohohoh

Let's count leaves together
let's count the stars
the clouds
let's count components
Tuvia
the earth whispers
let me just come close
Tuvia

The earth draws near
flee
it's not so bad
what's happened
flee
it's not so bad
let's count the components
fluttering leaves
let's count leaves together
let's count how much there is in everything
let's count the grains
how many there are in every clod

Tuvia
the earth draws near
to observe you from up close
Tuvia the earth is a grave
look at her through the eyes of a gravedigger
the earth is ash
look at her through the eyes of oxygen
Tuvia
the earth is home
Tuvia
the earth is nowhere

Let's count the people together
let's disturb their sleep
Tuvia
Tuvia
let's count the hairs
let's count the roads
let's count the places
let's count houses
the houses

Tuvia
let's shatter walls together
let's count the fragments
let's watch the people each on their own
outside the houses
Tuvia
let's count the crumbs
the emotional fragments
let's count the women apart
the men apart
what's left in the middle is held
         held
         held

held dazzled
the earth opens
a gaping mouth
such a big
mouth

round
filled with sand
to eat what
eats you
dead or alive

Translated from the Hebrew by Tsipi Keller

SAKSIRI MEESOMSUEB

excerpt from "Tutka Roi Sai (Sand Trace Dolls)"

Sand trace dolls
Lying with eyes open;
Black sun shining down,
The dolls eat it lying.

Sand trace dolls
Lying with eyes open—
Their foolish eyes
Being buried by the wind—
Die amidst the black sun.

Translated from the Thai by Soraj Hongladarom

EUNICE DE SOUZA

Sacred River

Two logs fastened in the river
for birds to take the waters.
I saw no birds there,
just a cremation or two on the ghats
onlookers at a safe distance,
yet another pregnant half-starved stray dog,
a white man playing at being a sadhu

top knot and all.
But nothing stops faith.
No. Nothing stops faith.
It will be heaven to get out of here.

ERIC GAMALINDA

Valley of Marvels

You must be single-minded as Humberto
Delgarenna, who risked his life
crossing the Vallée des Merveilles
to carve his name on Mont Bego.
The year was 1629. He may have fallen
from the crags, his bones now interred
with graffiti, the apothems and zigzags
whose inscrutability was sorcery, medicine,
object of fear. Let that be a lesson
to all who want to be remembered.
You must carry nothing, disappear quietly,
leave no other clues. A sailor in a shipwreck,
dazzled by Saint Elmo's fire. A hunter
or a shepherd, the words wool and venison
sacred to you. Decipher the enigma
of verdigris. Be metal, be clandestine.
Navigate through shadows, use touch
and sound to recognize the shape
of luminance. Learn a skill, how to carve
a rouelle, a flawless spoke, perfection
as an act of worship. Find your way back
to water through guesswork; begin from
the cul-de-sacs of Tende. And if you discover
the seven rivers to be true, drink and resist
believing you've been saved. You will not
be saved. You will walk away as blinded
as you were before. You will make a living
doing what you dislike. A blacksmith,
a vendor of flowers. You will live so long

no one will recall the midnight
you were born. The mornings will be cold.
The towns will lose their tools and weapons.
Invaders will come, first the Remedello,
then the Rhône. They will find, clenched
between your teeth, the words dagger
and halberd. They will uncurl from your fingers
objects once marvelous to you: billhook,
pickaxe, flint. Your bones will resemble rock.

INDRAN AMIRTHANAYAGAM

Yamoussoukro, With Cathedral

The sacred wood borders
the city, fields sown
with coffee and cocoa.

The cathedral's bigger
than St. Peter's, built
in marble gold stained
glass from floor to sky,
a marvel, seat of popes,
greeter of tour buses;

Even Naipaul visited
Yamoussoukro, before
the cathedral, when palace
and mosque were the charms
conjuring a call
by that voyager named
by the English language—

Somebody declared the city
a ghost; somebody else
said the church cost
100 million dollars, another

registered the Sunday mass
on his video recorder;

How many human beings
must pay homage to a church,
palace, lake with hungry
crocodiles—Houphouët's totem—
before we accept the city's
right to sit beside Rome or Venice?

How many technical experts,
weekends to spare, and a need
to breathe away from conundrums
of irrigation, fish culture

Pineapples, will accompany
their hosts to see the city
hewn from the jungle, inscribed
on the world's map by a sort
of Walt Disney, Monsieur
Houphouët-Boigny?

By what right, do you deny
his city's place in the catalogs
of world attractions?

Have you fixed the water pipes
in South East Washington?

Now, I hear the arguments
for and against and against,
how the poem is not a bill
proffered by a legislator;
it has no power to feed

Or clothe, is a butterfly
pinned to a sheet; we learned
all this in 1917, but the new
class needs to be taught

or fooled yet again,
by some easy rhymes and
a slight disdain. No,

Yamoussoukro will stand,
like the Sphinx,
or the Tower, the Bridge,

not some sand-built nest
on which the piper sits
for a day before the tide
washes it away.

It is evening. The columns burn
red and gold. The visitor
gets up from the square,
swivels a last time
with his camera and walks
toward the parking lot.

Every monument
in the modern world
requires a parking lot.

Here you may leave
your horses, tents, motor cars.

Here, you may leave your shoes.

Here, your ideas, complaints
and theories of beauty,
your newspapers.

Before you: marble,
stone, glass and wood.

A church, Notre Dame
de La Paix, services
on Sundays, days
of obligation, weekday mornings.

WOESER

Midnight, on the Fifth Day of the Fourth Month in the Tibetan Calendar

A stainless Dolma,
from top to bottom, blended with the people
Too much tragedy makes her suddenly transform
It was not a pretty girl that
grabbed my hand
and tirelessly spoke of karma
with the force of yesterday's sunlight

Flocks of eagles
like an inflected sound
let the body and soul drift away
let the purple clouds advance from the east
A sound from a certain place
simple, meaningful
rescuing numerous blessed children lost to the red earth

But here, in the Tibet that is daily ascending
daylight nurtured by the gods' ether
the devils' fumes also arrive
The miserly them fight against consensus
and even secretly imagine themselves lucky
But motivated by an unbreakable illusion
they are lost
Only this miraculous Dolma
walking behind
will take pity on this type of person—
Coming upon someone's hand print
all their lives just between the brilliant and the common
hesitating, pacing
As the sun lights the world, she also relinquishes
to the swirling dust and smoldering smoke of everything

Translated from the Tibetan by d dalton

CATHY SONG

Breaking Karma

Beings flame into existence
in and out of the shadow world,
the one we travel through is real.
On streets, where nothing remains hidden,
the six realms collide.
We see only what we are
capable of seeing.
Flying apsarases appear as pretty hostesses
offering a menu of services.
They vie for your attention
alongside the legless stump of a man
who barks after you, propelling
a torso lashed to a wooden scrape of wheels.
The gods glide by in black foreign cars.
They feast on cat and snake and monkey.
Still the desire for wilder meat is strong.
On streets, where nothing is hidden,
the scarred-skinned survivor of some hellish fire,
ropes of flesh twisted into tourniquets of bacon,
rubs against you,
mocking your aversion.
You can't deny you find
the rawness thrilling,
the multitudes streaming past,
each encounter a chance to make amends.
You light incense at every temple.
Innumerable sticks, flaring, then settling,
burn repeatedly
into the urn of human ash.
The earth is the urn of human ash,
a smudge of pigeon-gray talc,
coughing up one more summer of peaches,
in the palm of your hand.

Breaking karma is hardest
with those who are hardest

to love, those closest to us
who wait out our endless return.
Upon arrival your mind whirls with prayer wheels and flags
bargained for at roadside carts, incoherent snapshots,
Laughing Buddha on a keychain, bundles of temple
incense broken into pencil bits of lead,
as if all the sentences constructed
in three-star hotel rooms, greasy
dining cars of sleeper trains and other
grog-filled transit points had seeped down
to a handful of regrets.
You choose to exit, traveling
halfway around the shadow world
to crawl into your own bed,
strangely malnourished.
Those closest to you wait
to welcome you back,
you who are so hard to love.

YUSUF AL-KHAL

Retaliation

Our necks
stretched toward morning,
night advances
to lay foundations
for a house and a wall
of small minutes.

It is mortality
petrified with giant time
until not a phantom,
nor a fiction
of a finger is left
of the past.
Besides leaves rustling
from time to time,

and the beat
of a wing in space—
who was calling?

Who heard the call?
As if there were
someone in heaven
to retaliate
for the spillage of our blood!

Translated from the Arabic by Sargon Boulus

NAJWAN DARWISH

Clouds

I have no brothers to lift the sky off my back

     no daughters to comfort my trees.

I have no grandchildren to inherit the lakes

     no flame to light up the fireplace

     no winsome relative to water the violets.

Nothing but these homeless clouds

     to walk one day at my funeral.

Translated from the Arabic by Kamal Boullata

NAZEEH ABU AFASH

excerpt from "The Wolf's Hour"

And so, for no obvious reason, I feel sad now
and that I'm about to die, the earth my grave.
And my friends, all of them,
have gone, leaving the whirlwind of their breath in bitter wineglasses.
And so, for no reason, I feel sick with sadness now
and the earth continues its revolution in the haze of misery: blue, black,
wounded under the dome of that blind sky,
and I sit above it, an orphaned prophet,
flipping through the pages of its pain,
counting the last seconds of life.

And so, for no reason, I feel sad now, and, with no regret,
I will take the path that connects a stranger to strange soil,
counting my footsteps on the leaves of memory. I go,
absorbed on my way,
looking around like one expecting to find
the wolf hiding inside his own breath.

Translated from the Arabic by Khaled Hegazzi and Andy Young

FEHMIDA RIYAZ

Iqleema

Iqleema,
born of the mother of Cain
and Abel—their sister,
but different.
Different between her thighs
and in her breasts, different
inside, in her uterus.
And the worth of all the differences?
One fattened, sacrificial lamb:
Iqleema stands on a blazing hill.

She's a prisoner in her body.
The sun burns her into the rock.
Look,
above the long thighs and the rounded breasts,
above the labyrinth of the uterus,
Iqleema also has a head.
Allah, speak to Iqleema,
for once ask her something.

Translated from the Urdu by C. M. Naim

AMRITA PRITAM

excerpt from "Creation Poems"

4. Ad Pusthek (The First Book)

I was, and perhaps you also were
Perhaps within one breath you stood
Perhaps in one vision's darkness, you sat
Perhaps a consciousness's crossroad you walked
But that is a primordial story

It was mine, and your, existence
Which became the world's primordial language
I, of the script—its letters became
You, the letters of the script became
And in that primordial language was written the first book.

It was your and my understanding
We on the stone bed slept
And eyes, lips and fingertips—
My and your bodies—letter-scripts were made
And they, this first book translated
Rig Veda's creation was a much later conversation . . .

Translated from the Punjabi by Kuldip Gill

ABDUL BARI JAHANI

Messenger

Who are you to remind me
of old memories?
My heart was restless.
You brought it further unrest
you opened wounds from the past.
Where do you come from?
Who lead you here?
I do not know anyone.
My beloved and I
do not know each other.
I do not deal with
messengers of love anymore.
I burnt my wings on my own.
I do not envy flowers
nor do I seek their beauty.
Leave me alone.
I expect no visitors.
Consider false
what you saw yesterday.
Love became estranged.
I have ceased struggling.

I am exhausted from the desert running.
I bought a house by the sea.
I surrendered to the hunter.
I accepted sleeping in a cage.
I broke my wings.
Do not remind me of those unruly
wild dreams anymore.

Go back the way you came.
Let me enjoy my last days.
Take this message back home.
Give my regards to old friends.

These frail hands
Cannot withstand time.
These retreated soldiers
will no longer fight.

Translated from the Pashto by Fareda Ahmadi

KU SANG

This Year

As this country rocked like a boat in Galilee's storms,
I spent the whole year not losing my belief in God alone,
just doing as I could what had to be done.

Laid up sick, I suffered for more than a month,
there were many hard things in the family and the world,
but having endured it all meekly, it proved more valuable
than any good fortune could have been.

These days, as I dream bright dreams of the world beyond,
entrusting all things to His divine Will,
even if storms are forecast for the coming New Year
there is nothing I fear.

Translated from the Korean by Brother Anthony of Taizé

SUJATA BHATT

Black Sails

Paula Becker to Rainer Maria Rilke, September 1900, Worpswede

Black sails: greased and tarred—

Black sails of boats laden with turf—

They glide down the river—
I see them sliding through
      trees—Black sails
between sunlit patches
  of birch bark—

Every day the light pulls me
      out further—somewhere
further outside of myself—

Today I think these boats
    come out of hell—dripping with black blood
      from the moors—
dragging out
  the smell of marshlands,
of rotting leaves—

You tell me
  we must learn
how to welcome back
the dead—they are always there, you say,
and we must learn to live with them—

Even now, some days
  they pull out corpses
      from the bog—
Dead bodies
from Roman times—their tired wrinkles
    seem to sweat—

Later
we bury them in the churchyard—

Is that a true way
  of welcoming?

Perhaps the turf I burn
once covered the face of a woman—
This turf, grown thick
  and rich against her skin—

A woman
who might have looked like me—

Perhaps tonight
I will burn bits of her hair
without truly knowing that I do—

Hair that might have been
     as long as mine—

Now lost, peat entangled,
peat ensnared—prickly
with moss and rough seeds—

A married woman
     who took a lover—

You told me how
     they punished her:

Face down, naked
     they made her lie
down on the moor,
     in the wettest part of the bogland—
all the tender parts of her body
     tightening against the coldness—
all her pores curled and puckered
     in anguish—

Then,
the farmhands stepped on her—
the largest men walked over her
     stamping her into the mud—

The stickiness taking her in—

How the air must have hummed
          seething around her—
Even the mud
          seething with her soul—

This brownish black Worpswede mud—
how strong, how dark
      it must have been
   a thousand years ago—The stickiness
taking her in—
      A glistening being—
Did she still think
      it was Mother Earth?

Her nose, mouth, ears
stuffed shut with spongy loam—

They stamped on her
   until she was deep enough—
Their own legs covered with mud.

You say, betrayal
   is too simple a word—
Too convenient
   to call it adultery—

You tell me even now
you can see her face—
      hear what she felt
   centuries ago:
fear, disgust, anger—
her distorted face stays with you—

Then, stays with me
as if she were a black rose
you had pressed for me—
as if I must keep her
     for you—
as if I have no choice—

SURESH PARSHOTTAMDAS DALAL

Prose Poem

I look at you in helpless silence, incapable of doing a thing for you. In the middle of the white-washed walls of the hospital ward you lie, groaning quietly in the dark abyss of pain. Only a miracle can bring you some relief. I have nothing to offer, but a prayer. All my prayers reach the Almighty, an attempt I shall make. I am trying to find ways to shake off His unbearable silence. Desolation and numbness in your eyes drive me crazy and as I leave the ward quietly, I hear the footsteps of death. I want to cut off my ears to block their sound. But will that delay the advent of death? From your voicelessness before death, I move toward your silence after death—and I do not even want to feel angry or shed tears at my helplessness.

Translated from the Gujarati by Bhadra Patel-Vadgama and The Poetry Translation Centre

ABDULLAH HABIB AL-MAAINI

Noon

Your feet crush a cluster of grapes
At the pillar of longing

Shade burns the pillow
While you bite at my palm

And infinity flows from your breasts
And hips

Earth's vine adheres to your navel
And a dove releases its feathers mid-flight

A curtain in the clouds flutters
You sink your nails into rapture

Strands of your hair tremble against the chest of time
Setting it aflame

And the black star shines in the nebula

What's a body but the guardian of the soul
When Death makes a eulogy of us

Translated from Arabic by Dima Hilal with Idra Novey

SASAKI MIKIRO

The Procession

The procession's head bites
  the procession's past.
The procession's mouth recites
  the procession's future.
The procession has neither eyes nor nose.
The procession's robes melt in the night, and though
  the procession's tail may catch fire,
  the procession's fear will not go away, nor will
  the procession's obi unfasten.
The procession has no reason for its length, while
the procession's priest runs up and down the whole length of the
    procession.
The procession has no voice.
The procession has no horror even in
  the procession's center,
  which is transparent,
  while butterflies fly up and down the whole length of
  the dark procession.

Translated from the Japanese by William I. Elliott and Kazuo Kawamura

BADR SHAKIR AL-SAYYAB

Wafiqa's Casement

Wafiqa's ecstatic casement overlooks
The village square
Like a Galilee awaiting Jesus
And awaiting his walk.
Icarus stretches his wooden wings,
Rubs the eagle's feathers against the sun,
And sets forth.
The skyline captures him,
And tosses him to the entombing waters.
O Wafiqa's casement,
O tree respiring in the waking morn,
Beside you, the folk's eyes are with expectation filled.

Eyes that expect apple blossom,
Whilst *Buweib* is a chant,
And the wind echoes
The tunes the water plays upon the palm fronds.

And from the grave,
Wafiqa looks up and awaits:
He shall pass by,
And the water shall,
In the forenoon of a feast day,
Murmur his wavering shadow like a bell,
And swish like the breath's jetsam.
And the wind echoes
The water tunes (It is the rain!)
And the sun chortles in the fronds.
Is it a casement that in the glitter giggles like a child,
Or a gate opening in the wall,
Causing the fragrant wings to take flight?
Is it a soul for radiance pining?

O rock of heart's ascension,
Of images of love and intimacy,
O path leading up to God,

Were it not for you, the gentle winds
Wouldn't have made the village laugh.
A fragrance in the wind
Arises from the river's verdant banks,
It sings to us and lulls us.
Ulysses sails with the waves
And the wind reminds him of forgotten islands:
We have grown frail and senile,
Leave us alone, O wind.

The world opens its window,
And, in that blue casement,
Achieves unity and turns thistle to
Soothing fragrant flowers.

A casement like you in Lebanon,
A casement like you in India,
And a dreaming damsel in Japan,
Like Wafiqa dreaming in the tomb,
Dreaming of thunder and lightning green.

Wafiqa's ecstatic casement overlooks
The village square
Like a Galilee dreaming of Jesus
And dreaming of the walk.

Translated from the Arabic by Hassan Hilmy

SHANTA ACHARYA

Highgate Cemetery

I wandered among the dead in a cemetery town
exploring the winding paths where angels, carved in stone,
stood silently directing me through the green alleyways.

This island with overhanging yew and trailing clematis,
with unifying ivy nurturing insects, larvae, butterflies and birds

has more to do with the living than the memory of the departed.
We need the solace of the Comfort Corner more than the dead.

Through the hawthorn and blackthorn, field maple and elm
a cool wind blows steadily through our realm.
The voices of children from the playground across the school
confirm the inscription on Karl Marx's tomb:
The philosophers have only interpreted the world
in various ways. The point however is to change it.

Everyday our little world changes a little bit,
whether we like it or not is quite irrelevant.
I imagine a dialogue between Marx and Krishna.
It is easier I confess to alter myself than the world!

When our friends start to leave, it is time
to take stock of our coming and going:
Of those immortal dead who live again
in minds made better by their presence.

In the unmapped terrain within us we bury
in terraced catacombs painful memories.
If only we could let them grow out of us like trees.

SHIV KUMAR BATALVI

Turbaned One

Like a branch of the pomegranate tree
We lie here, swaying slowly, o turbaned one.
Turbaned one, black of heart,
Swaying slowly, o turbaned one.

Like the eyes of a wild deer,
Burning in the forest, o turbaned one.
Turbaned one, black of heart,
Burning in the forest, o turbaned one.

Like boats left at the shore,
We lie here, sinking slowly, o turbaned one.
Turbaned one, black of heart,
Sinking slowly, o turbaned one.

Like lumps of sugar candy,
We lie here, dissolving slowly, o turbaned one.
Turbaned one, black of heart,
Dissolving slowly, o turbaned one.

Like logs of black sandalwood,
We lie here, smoldering slowly, o turbaned one.
Turbaned one, black of heart,
Smoldering slowly, o turbaned one.

Like a house with walls of unbaked brick,
We are crumbling slowly, o turbaned one.
Turbaned one, black of heart,
Crumbling slowly, o turbaned one.

Translated from the Punjabi by Suman Kashyap

RAHMAN RAHI

Redemption

The cupola-dweller, a labyrinth,
in which
petrifying shadows and the fusing rocks
arouse in oceans the desire for the desert;
and dreadful phantasms in the foliage of nightly planes in quietude.

The cupola-dweller, a labyrinth,
a step and luminosity of flickering lamps,
a glance and the moth's flutter in the flame and blare.
The illusion densities and
the bee hurls itself on the glass in the black stone.
The lowly army has returned from the campground;

the trees weep, but all around
cupolas spring up, and the vortex whirls.
A labyrinth breathing in and breathing out.
No trellis of Beauty's loggia is ajar;
nor does the chain of Love's door clang.
Neither is there any wave of sound rising without,
nor is the fount within ankle-deep.
A gloom within gloom, a gyrating wheel,
dawn, morning, day-time, night-time:
foot-prints on foot-prints, a loop fitting in a loop.

A labyrinth, darkness meeting darkness;
chanan-chana-chan-chanan-chana-chan.
Loveless diapason, a formless dance.
Neither the meaning of *vaakhas,* nor acceptation of songs.
chanan-chana-chan-chanan-chana-chan.
The ground underneath your feet sinks, an abyss is seen.
O my existence, you attained non-being, your exultance.
That half-slain dancer,
how, slumbering in a mine, could become a gem?
How could that prisoner be free
if this abyss of incertitude were not underneath his feet?

Translated from the Kashmiri by Shafi Shauq

Author's Note: Vaakhas is a Kashmiri word for poetry that expresses mystical or spiritual experience.

TOYA GURUNG

After a Turn Around the Temple

I feel a pride
a structure so large
so many rooms
endless staircases
a multitude of guardian animals at the doors

I feel a pride
no matter how troubled I might be
my mind is calm after a turn around the temple

as though all my worries are left there, though
once I reach the street it seems
that with this joy there comes growing
another torment

at first
to die on the road
and then gradually to live
angry red-hot eyes and faces
giant doors, neatly laid streets, filthy tea and
a crossroads
then the tough climb
the rude remark
the unpleasant eyes

that thoughtless man
the other, perhaps with barren heart

nevertheless I feel a pride
neither of stone
nor of wood
nor of earth

Translated from the Nepali by Ann Hunkins

SAIF AL-RAHBI

Clump of Grass

Peace upon the clump of grass sprouting
atop the barren mountain.
How much time does it need to grow,
how many storms and landslides?
Maybe it thought of the lightning bolts

shining in the night as merciful angels.
Man's hand is sullied with blood,
goats climb rocks nearby,
meteors fall on the mysterious battlefield.
But it is lonely and luminous
in that vast space opening its mouth
toward the ocean's abyss.

Translated from the Arabic by Khaled Hegazzi and Andy Young

ESHQABIL SHUKUR

The Corpse of a Sufi

In a dark cave lives a snake,
A black wind nestles there,
The corpse of a Sufi lies flaming,
It has been thus for five hundred years.

The corpse of the Sufi each day
Speaks one piece of wisdom . . . the snake writes it
    down in a book.
The truth lies five hundred years beyond,
Five hundred years hence tarries a lie.

Every day on the ceiling of the cave a spider
Easily weaves a shroud for the corpse.
The snake lies protecting the treasure,
Every day the wind tears up the shroud.

Translated from the Uzbek by William M. Dirks

SUAD AL-KAWARI

Comfort for a Lonely Woman

The woman who opens her home to the wind
is preparing a large feast
at the gate of an ancient graveyard
giving out bread to passersby
and their ghosts come forth like horses racing a cloud
The mercurial woman knows how to tame wild flowers
and embalm birds with her tired eyes
I see her crouching at the window and she sees me not
I hear her and she hears me not

Let the wind be the first to journey, I will not race after it
Let tonight be the last to melt upon my body
or quietly vanish
I shall wipe my face with a cold palm
and follow her slow movements
A woman of mercury stuck to my mirror
I see her and she sees me not
I hear her and she hears me not

Today I saw her
she was throwing a metal spear at the stars
and muttering words I could not make out
But I did not see before her the long waiting line
that stretched along the road from end to end
I saw her, a solitary figure sweeping cat bones
I saw her weeping from afar
and I did not see my face suspended between us
I only saw the cats' crushed bones
and receding footprints

Translated from the Arabic by Samira Kawar

DEBJANI CHATTERJEE

Swanning In

Saraswati, you come swanning in, smooth
as ever on your gliding bird, playing
your goddess self and expect me to rise
      and honor you.

An unexpected guest, you never knock
at my mind's door. You fly in with élan
and chat like it was yesterday. Any
      window will do.

This is no neighborhood in India,
nor is this Heaven, but you are at home
no matter where—folding white wings—your bird
      swans into view.

While great Brahma rests, you are the blossom
on his six eyes, his heart-strumming music.
But each polyglot lilt you sing to me
      has an echo

that belongs to your raucous bird. "Beauty,"
it winks, "has an ugly voice, serpentine
like my neck." Your company has a price,
      so I bow low

and make the most of any arrival.
Lady, I would put aside life itself,
if you would understand my need to hold
      when you let go.

Saraswati, you do not see the glint
in your bird's slanted eyes—a mortal dart.
Cushioned on airy clouds, impregnable,
      you breathe incense.

Even in Fortress Britain where I draw
my mind's portcullis and double glaze all
windowpanes, you surprise me with your sudden
      gracious presence.

Ringing the alarm about intruders
would have no effect. By the time help came
you would be long gone; a few swan feathers
      for tantalizing evidence.

Author's Note: Saraswati, wife of Brahma the Creator, is the Goddess of Music and the Arts. The swan is her symbol.

SALLY ITO

Alert to Glory

to sun-break and water-burst, to land-ho and pinnacle reach
to shimmer shine of light on wave, of moon glow on broken glass;
to face praise the world in the stroll-hours of the park; to hear
the lark music of argument in the pew wing of the fowl;
For before anywhere, it begins in the *seeing,* alertness before the glory
in the bit sound of hammer pound, from the spark and spray of smithies
in the watery forge behind the eye where tears spring like iron
to shoe the horse of sight's delight; alertness, the soul beam,
light tunnel of praise, through which to gain gallop the cup, the trophy,
the thing won and earned by having been sought and found,
Glory, the lost sheep of Joy.

NGODUP PALJOR

Ways of the World

I

When my bamboo flute's
Sound was deep
Birds of all feathers flocked around me
Without an invitation
Now this broken flute's shallow sound
Does not even draw the attention
Of seagulls

II

When my father left his body
I inherited a wooden cup
Some day when I die
Do you know what I am going
to leave for my inheritance?
A cotton stuffed zafu

AMINA SAÏD

on the seventh day of my birth

I spoke the language
of the world I'd come from
bore witness to a shadow
which was the shadow
of another light
which no one saw

in the seventh month of my birth
my mouth took the shape of the void
I cried to tell what was true
and that which the present had taught me
of the past of the future
but no one understood

the seventh year of my birth
I dreamed what had been
on the world's lined page
I traced letter after letter
to remind myself
of what I had to forget
and of what in me was already dying

Translated from the French by Marilyn Hacker

ANDRÉE CHEDID

To Each of the Dead

These things these hours
Belong to me
Still

This clear or rainy season
These suns that flake away
This night which lingers
These faces
Their games their cry their laughs
This realm of tastes
This spirit which grounds us
This body molded with years

These hours these things
Were yours
Matter was your fiefdom
Hope your domain
The future your soaring
The passion in your veins
Lifted you out of time

This time
Which carries us away
Far from hours

And from things
Toward places
Without matter
Toward the simple
Earth.

Translated from the French by Annie Finch

EDITH L. TIEMPO

Rowena, Playing in the Sun

God, who stirred the void and in Motion's birth
Revealed yourself; the warm limbs wake
Along the dark stairways, the far eyes life to take
The fixed commotion of the stars, their dim furious speed
Predictive in the blood; the cupped hands hold for the spinning sun
Till all this reaching tips the rim of heaven to the earth,
Spilling the primal colors from the splitting of a seed,
Waving the tall green like a great sea waking,
And in the golden light, tiny hands lifting, falling,
Turning in God's own orbit, my golden one.

PHAN NHIÊN HẠO

Trivial Details

Inside an old car a heart sat behind the wheel
To circulate along the blood avenues
Where battles and a chaotic retreat occured
In which my father was killed

I grazed her breasts and was wondering why she did not smile
It was what I had waited for all night inside a hut lit by a lantern
Her teeth resembled the keyboard of an unplugged organ

As a carpenter Christ should have made himself a coffin beforehand
Maybe that's only a trivial detail
But we live in a practical world and trivial details are often what generate
    beliefs

How to jump from the stove to the pan and back without tripping
My face is a doorknob
If you turn and enter, behind is a void I have to stock with stuff
    to convert into a warehouse before sudden dusk

Wolves are sharing the corpse of a crow and hurling blood at the sky
There are fixed values and unnecessary rituals carried out
    because of instinctual fear

"Ah, in the end He has come," the secretary says, bowing to the God
    of miserable fates,
then throws his ink pen at the gold fish inside the glass tank
That tiny world soon has the color of the sea
By doing so he becomes a creator

I watch a film with a telescope and imagine that I am from another
    planet
Who has abandoned his own kind a long time ago

A fat man kneels next to a woman who has just died
Says to take some of my flesh with you
Which you will need, when your own flesh has rotted
That is a dream I often see in my evening sleep

When bored and with some money I will travel
To a country where everything is coincidental
Man is born to be satisfied with waiting
Where I was born to wait for myself

The door slams with the sound of a vague collision from the other bank
    of the river
where fishermen are tapping their boats to chase fish into nets.

Translated from the Vietnamese by Linh Dinh

MASUD KHAN

The Age of Commerce

By and by the age of commerce returns to the earth.

Traveling merchants come in bustling like shiny *Basak* leaves—
The grief gets forgotten, the disease remains.
In love with the color red, devouring virgin fire everyday,
The boy lives a carefree life.
From across the ailment his young aunt calls him by his proper name:
"Come here and see—neglecting their duty
The trees spend all their time quarreling with the clouds."
With helium sparkling in his head,
The boy rushes down from the distant clouds
On a flying tricycle.
The air becomes charged with friction and electricity.
Like glittering nickel, fireworks burn.

One day in the future, he deserts his sleeping wife and child
And sets off on a journey to nowhere.
The banks of the *Niranjana* shimmer in endless thirst.

Nature lazily reclines
On the shoulder of that man and—lo!
A beast is born on the wheel of time:
Half aquatic, half aerial,
Bloodshot eyes,
Spines full of spikes, incredibly vivid wings,
The nether parts, the tail, slimy with water,
Fire emitted from the mouth inundates the world—
Ah! all hell breaks loose everywhere!
Somebody, call the medicine man. Nay, call the Buddha instead.
He has attained *Bodhi,* he knows it all, call him . . .
Thereupon a sirocco starts and a very prolonged ice age ensues.
By and by the age of commerce returns to the earth.

Over there, a thousand years ago
There used to be a funfair full of fanfare,
Now there live only a couple of submerged trees there.

When methane glows from those drowned trees now
The children today cry: "Look! Will-o'-the-wisp!"

The boy's body or non-body gleams on bluishly.

Translated from the Bengali by Subrata Augustine Gomes

EUGENE GLORIA

Allegra with Spirit

Even the dead is cold in 1967,
        the dead shivering in his trousers.
Allegra waits for the bus
        on Union and Van Ness,
           her arms wide around a paper sack.
A car stopped at the light is playing Rodrigo.

The melody is red, the Spanish earth,
        all manner of color thrown from the car window.
Allegra wouldn't know Rodrigo from Elgar,
        Elgar from Miles, only that the 47
isn't running on time
        on still wet streets from a spell of rain.

Here, then, is winter in 1967
        when the dead has come to visit
           inside an insomniac's dream. The dead
shivering in his trousers, betraying a promise
        by crossing the water on a secret boat
just to tell her he is hungry. In the long ago,
        she whispered in his good ear
when he was very sick; and she, his girl
        spooning him the bitter medicine, begged
him to never visit when he is dead.
        In 1967 when eucalyptus leaves could cleanse
the air's palate with their antiseptic blue,
        a bus, as if from some great vanishment on roads

that climb and bend but never want to end,
                a white and mockorange bus emerges
like a tardy backdoor man, a pallid innuendo.

A woman waiting for the bus has staked her faith
                in the hour's luck, in the bony air
of the alley she wades through to get to the street
                that is dark as a paper sack.
There is only the rice she washes daily
                and what she carries in the paper sack: eggs, bread,
                    salt for memory, a can of milk, fish
for the tamarind soup
                she'll pray over with the rice.
Allegra would like to tell the dead to go
                because there is nothing here to take back.
In his secret boat, the dead carries
              his bowl of air and shivers in his trousers.

ATTILÂ ILHAN

The Dead Grow Old

the downpour of stars is no less than a servile salute
lilies are white and whites are no less than lilies
over the marches mosquitoes multiply by the million
bugs and insects are linked forever in a hug and embrace
the downpour of stars is no less than a servile salute

all the old equestrians hoof the wayworn up the hill
sweltering in galaxies horses will burst inside out
on hoary battlefields lie the wounded and the martyred
pines and willows are linked forever in hug
      and embrace
should a girl come alive or a mortal die or a star fall
all the old equestrians hoof the wayworn up the hill

hyenas refuse to recall the saturnalia and all
life's flight from the body and man's from humanity

a hundred killed a hundred orphaned a hundred lost
mother raise their sons for combat overseas
hyenas refuse to recall the saturnalia and all
should a girl come alive or a mortal die or a star fall
whoever is dead is dead and the dead have grown old.

Translated from the Turkish by Talât Sait Halman

HILARY THAM

Mrs. Wei on Piety

My Buddhist friend, Kitn, has arms
dotted with red pinpricks where mosquitoes
have drunk their fill. She's so devout she will kill nothing,

not even a fire ant with its sharp mandibles in her foot.
Flies play tag in her kitchen while she holds the door
open, begs them to leave.

They don't go, they invite other flies into the feast
of soybeans and tofu in her vegetarian kitchen.
Now I believe in Lord Buddha, but within reason.

When she offers me food, I shake my head.
Everyone knows flies stomp their feet in dung
before they come into a house.

ABDALLAH ZRIKA

excerpt from "Black Candle Drops"

2

Give me a glass
to sip this emptiness

An arm
to measure this separation

Prepare me a bed
of glass
for my nightmares to slip on

I don't want to read letters
that don't stand up before my eyes
like nails

I'll give my hand to this dog
come to sever a few of its fingers

I'll leave much white in my writings
so that this prostitute may meander therein
at will

(This is not a pen
but a pick ax to demolish the poet
who tyrannizes me)

The ants will be at my funeral
and I'll leave my tomb to someone
who hasn't found a place to sleep
I'll leave much white in my writings
to illuminate the darkness coming down
with the night of the words

I'll leave some white
for the day of your wedding

Translated from the Arabic by Pierre Joris

DAN PAGIS

Ein Leben

In the month of her death she stands
at the window, a young woman, her hair
done in a permanent, elegant wave.
In the brown photograph
she is pensive, looking out.

From the outside an afternoon cloud
of the year '34 looks at her, blurred,
out of focus, but always loyal.
From the inside I look at her,
a four-year-old, or thereabout.

I seize my ball,
slowly exit the picture
and grow old, grow old,
cautiously, quietly,
so as not to startle her.

Translated from the Hebrew by Tsipi Keller

NUJOUM AL-GHANIM

Sand in Flames

I put my cameleer off two thousand and one times
Proximity forgave not my compassion for my orphans—
those are the worshippers of darknesses
spitting forth fires on the horizon.
        O star,
my grief is for you, swinging in the void like a skeleton
calcifying before its feet can walk

in that the cutters of death stand their arrows on end to throw at you—
Is it conceivable, this stricken one in my folks' house?
While I'm the radiant virgin
whose face the rivers unrolled for me.
I am led into captivity,
my states are plundered,
my companions are exiled.
I greet a hill to which repair untouchables
and bereft mothers
while my sons—moons in whose presence
shooting stars hang themselves,
are guarded by the unclean.
Where is my blemish, if my veil is removed
and robes sob over my body?
And what is my failing if I receive dust on the part of my hair
with honor
and every day men wound a heart for me.
Return me to my stall
Shackle the *zajals* on the tongue which mourns with them,
Cauterize the eyes
Hunt down sighs
      hunt down
the questions between you and me.

Footfalls deafen the ears
The girl cameleer comes out of hiding split-pocketed,
her hair flies behind her
her hands above her belt unsheathe her dagger
but mothers weep crying for help
ah! unto the heavens
The girl cameleer
stabs the air
as if the pattering of rain showers did not reach the tribe.
Any captivating appearance,
tongues smack their lips in lust
while the walls crack, the rooms collapse,
      dreams die

blood spurts from everywhere, a wail,
bodies float by . . . the city drowns
in blood.

Translated from the Arabic by Clarissa Burt

Author's Note: Zajals are folkloric songs.

ALFRED A. YUSON

Dream of Knives

for Ric de Ungria

Last night I dreamt of a knife
I had bought for my son. Of rare dagger
with fancily rounded pommel, and a wooden sheath
which miraculously revealed other, miniature blades.

Oh how pleased he would be upon my return
from this journey, I thought. What rapture
will surely adorn his ten-year princeling's face
when he draws the gift the first time. What quivering
pleasure will most certainly be unleashed.

When I woke, there was no return, no journey,
no gift, and no son beside me. Where do I search
for this knife then, and when do I begin to draw
happiness from reality. And why do I bleed so
from such sharp points of dreams?

SAPARDI DJOKO DAMONO

Walking Behind the Body

walking behind the body the wind subsides
hours blink
with unexpected speed
the afternoon slips away, broadening earth's roads

at the side: tree after tree bows its head
above: our sun, that same sun too
hours floating somewhere in between
how unexpectedly empty when breathing them in

Translated from the Indonesian by John H. McGlynn

BUDDHADHASA BHIKKHU

Blind Eyes, Eyes That See

A flock of birds stare	staring long	never see the sky
A school of fish	they don't see	the water, cold and clear
Earthworms stare	don't see the earth	that they eat
Maggots, they don't	see the waste	that they suck
People everywhere,	they don't	see the world
Must suffer sad	anxiety	all the time
But Buddhists	applying dhamma	following tradition
See everything	without remainder	following the truth

Translated from the Thai by John T. Mattioli

OLIVER DE LA PAZ

Aubade with Bread for the Sparrows

The snow voids the distance of the road
and the first breath comes from the early morning
ghosts. The birds with their hard eyes
glisten in the difficult light. They preen
their feathers and trill. It's as though they were one
voice talking to God.

                    Mornings are a sustained song
without the precision of faith. You've turned the bag
filled with molding bread inside out and watch
the old crusts fall to the ice. What's left
but to watch the daylight halved by the glistening ground?
What's left but an empty bag and the dust of bread
ravaged by sparrows?

                    There are ruins we witness
within the moment of the world's first awakening
and the birds love you within that moment. They want
to eat the air and the stars they've hungered for, little razors.

Little urgent bells, the birds steal from each other's mouths
which makes you hurt. Don't ask for more bread.
The world is in haste to waken. Don't ask for a name
you can surrender, for there are more ghosts to placate.
Don't hurt for the sparrows, for they love you like a road.

AYUKAWA NOBUO

In a Dilapidated House

The wind blew hard that day
just after *keichitsu*[1]
The Eastern and Southern windows
rattle in turn,
the doors open and close . . .
the house trembles,
continuing its symphony.
It's too cold to call it Spring
but the temperature was not so low
that by turning on a nearby heater
my feet couldn't soon become warm.
Beyond the window
the bright blue sky spreads like an ocean,
with cirrus clouds of thin torn silk.
Even a life that is beautiful
when spoken or put to words,
is hard to live in reality.
In the end, the problem
could be psychological
but in the meantime,
I thought it was not that serious,
and could be endured.
The house has definitely aged.
Because the wind
blows fresh vitality
into its senescent, flimsy frame
no one would think it strange
if it fell down tomorrow—
this house is trembling,
its joints noisily creaking.
The owner, who reads books
from the past and the present
and knows the sorrows of the flesh completely

---

[1] Japanese Candlemas or Groundhog Day, signifying the end of winter and the beginning of spring.

is leaning on a chair
his back bent as if a prisoner in Solevetsky[2]
forced to wear a bag.
In an overgrown garden
the man swinging a club in strong wind
is another him . . .

How far it is.
Everything is in the distance.
Even the rumbling of the ocean can be heard.
In such clear air,
there seems to be no evil
but in the voice of the wind
in the rustling trees
even in between the blinks of an eye
the valley of the dead—
victims of wars and revolutions—
appears and disappears.
That is why, even now
the hands of the prisoner in Solevetsky
tremble slightly.

Because of the hardships of his boyhood,
he believed in the miracle of hands.
He used to think one line for one word
would change people's minds . . .
one modest poem for one line
would change the direction of the light.
So he kept a single room
and endured a long imprisonment
until the house began to lean.
Piling books, clothes, and things
everywhere like dust
what objects have you buried reverentially?
The house will never fall
as long as a human being lives in it,
that man's endurance will

2 An island in the White Sea, where the first concentration camp was established in
1923.

sustain the beams, ceiling and floor.
As long as the smell of human breath
that stains the bed of agony with blood
is there,
the house will not collapse.
That's what he kept on believing.
But from the corner of his eyes
with his head hung low,
a glint of an
unendurable tear falling.

For a while, the wind blew hard
against the senescent faces, walls, mind
covered with rusted metal ivy
pressing against them,
frightening or consoling.
Oh, the dilapidated house on the hill,
the prisoner in Solevetsky,
beloved people,
farewell.
Just as the time we live together
comes to an end some day,
so a very sad fate will come to pass
for the person who came into this world
crying as a newborn.
In any case, since no tomorrow will be better than yesterday,
all the books in the world
have become an incurable illness,
eating away at our lives
leading your house to collapse.
The least you can do is
make the last breath clean,
quietly waving to the wind.
Let's welcome a much better extinction.

Translated from the Japanese by Leza Lowitz and Shogo Oketani

MUHAMMED HASAN 'AWWAD

Secret of Life and Nature

What secret lies in the winds
blowing north and south
bringing rains

What secret lies in the sea
one day calm, another day tumultuous

Chasing the full moon, and the stars
in its ebb and flow

Why does the earth revolve around the
sun, forever and ever going

Why do the stars shine at night
and the sun at day, dazzling the eyes

Why does the eclipse of sun and moon
appear one day, and other days hides away

Why is Neptune inscrutable to us
We cannot see the stars around it?

Why are we willed to live on earth
Not choosing, and spend our lives
uncertain of the world

Why is death, like life, decreed upon us
it robs the soul of its potency and grandeur

Have philosophies, science and religion
been a minaret for people?

Did they awaken our minds from slumber?
Have we torn out the curtains of uncertainty?

Like the ancients we live our course
Then others come after us to do the same

And life, sun and stars and night and day
Revolve as ever before
Life's secret must remain inscrutable.

Translated from the Arabic by Laith al-Husain and Alan Brownjohn

MICHELLE YASMINE VALLADARES

Manga

in memory of Raghubhir Singh

is thin cord
hardy and strong
from which kites fly.
Rice paper diamonds,
their long tails
slicing the sky.

This is how we cling to the dead.

The skinny legged boys jump,
from rooftop to rooftop,
dodging each other,
intent on cutting the manga
of someone else's kite—
purple and red-crossed sky.

In the evening
we on the sidelines
watch them reel
the manga in,
only a few, ragged
and torn, survive.

DƯ THỊ HOÀN

Dhyana Land

An opening in the canopy of the sky
The light of meditation falls through
A Buddhist altar on high
She becomes a nun amidst the sanctuary of Three Treasures

Outside someone strikes the bell
Inside her heart the wooden fish is beaten
Namo
Namo
The insects call
Namo
Namo

From the opening to heaven

Translated from the Vietnamese by Ho Anh Thai and Wayne Karlin

THE QUIVERING WORLD

The Quivering World

—'ENAYAT JABER

Once, in New York, I fell in love. The man and the city merged and I could not separate them. We shared tea from a single cracked mug in a mom-and-pop café and rode the Staten Island ferry, salt spray on our faces as the collage of towering buildings receded. We ate fried oysters while wandering the cyclone frenzy of Coney Island as he spent all his money trying to win me a bag of goldfish. Careening through midsummer traffic in Murray Hill, I perched on the handlebars of his bicycle, shrieking, my eyes glued shut. At night, teenage girls tumbled home in taxis headed for the outer boroughs and sleep came with the sound of storefront gates clanging shut, the click of the ceiling light as he turned it off.

Eventually, as powerfully as it had arrived, love vanished with equal ferocity. Left to contemplate the boom and hiss of the city on my own, its swoon and tragedy seemed all the more ferocious, but Eros himself was born of the opposition of love and loss; in Greek mythology, the god of love and lust sprang from both light and darkness, the offspring of Love and War. I was experiencing for the first time what Sappho described as the *bittersweet*; one's inability to know the fullness of desire without knowing its absence.

While Eros dominates the Greek understanding of love, Europeans were not alone in equating love with loss. In the Indonesian and Malaysian tradition, *Sayang* expresses unconditional love but also expresses regret in losing something. The most well-known book of erotic love in history is the *Kāma Sūtra* or *Kamasutram. Kāma* literally means desire and *Sūtra* represents thread. According to folklore, the earliest version of the text was attributed to Nandi, the sacred white bull whom Lord Shiva would ride and who served as a doorkeeper when his master and his divine wife, Parvati, were making love. So full-throated and mellifluous were the sounds of their coupling that Nandi was moved to sacred utterance. Contrary to popular belief, however, the *Kāma Sūtra* was not just a guide to sex but a book that governed all of the relations between men and women, from the renewal of friendships with former lovers to productive citizenship. In order to ensure survival, the individual in the collective had ethical duties; the accomplishment of such duties was vital to the pursuit of love and prosperity.

What I take away from the poems in this section, *The Quivering World*, is a sense that no love of any kind—be it erotic or romantic, familial or companionable, eternal or fleeting—can exist without tension. There is no angel without a devil, no divinity in the absence of the beast.

In the leading Chinese poet Shu Ting's "A Night at the Hotel," the scene is initially devoid of distinct bodies in time. Instead, declarations and imaginary correspondence haunt the night:

> *The declaration of love, co-authored by lip prints and tears,*
> *Bravely climbs into the mailbox*
> *The mailbox is cold*
> *Long abandoned*
> *Its paper seal, like a bandage, flaps in the wind*

and later . . .

> *The woman in her nightgown*
> *Yanks the door open, shaking heaven and earth*
> *Like a deer, she runs wildly barefoot across the carpet*
> *A huge moth flits across the wall*
> *Plunges into the crackling fire of a ringing telephone*
>
> *In the receiver*
> *Silence*
> *Only snow*
> *Goes on singing, far away, on the power lines*

Though there is desperation and longing, the beloved is like a spirit that has left this world. Love, the poem suggests, is the destination and the place the woman may arrive if she waits long enough, patiently enough. In the end, however, the silence in the receiver makes us question if the lover is on the other end at all. The snow indicates absence or perhaps hope.

A leading figure in Japanese feminist poetry, Itō Hiromi speaks candidly and straightforwardly about childbearing, reproduction, menstruation, sex, the body, female consciousness, and sensuality. Born in Tokyo in 1955, Itō

Hiromi first came to public attention during the women's poetry boom in the 1980s. During this period, Itō's fourth collection of poems, *Ōme (railway line)*, was published alongside her contemporaries of that time, Shiraishi Kōko and Isaka Yohko.[1] Her poems are so honest that they seem confrontational, even brash. The poet herself claims a rhetoric of sexual assertiveness that had been previously dominated by men, reversing traditional gender roles. In "Near Kitami Station on the Odakyū Line," while the speaker rides the train to her destination, she is sidetracked as she initiates a sexual encounter:

> *Outside the carriage greenery is everywhere*
> *Because I don't know it well I always sit in the very front carriage of the all-*
> *stops train the steps leading to the ticket-turnstiles are in the middle of*
> *the platform. Where I cross the up platform I wave my hand seductively*
> *I cross the level-crossing and go into his apartment*
> *Ten minutes' walk away*
>
> . . . .
>
> *We had sexual intercourse . . .*

The figure is predatory as she leans over the man, examining his face, ridding it of what she deems unsuitable. As the young woman in the poem moves through her day, sex has become "a matter of course." Her language empowers her to translate the world, minute by minute, as the day unravels:

> *I am a 25-year-old woman and thus do engage in regular sexual intercourse.*
> *I come from Itabashi ward to Setagaya ward and while traveling sexual*
> *intercourse is not on my mind I do not feel any sexual desire I am watching*
> *the grass and trees of Setagaya ward as they pass by outside the carriage*
> *in this season the chlorophyll is evident in layers the moisture almost reaches*
> *the saturation point when I meet him I feel happy so I wave seductively*
> *but when I turn on the radio in his apartment is the time I think of sex*

Hiromi's poems defy gender limitations to the point of obliterating notions of the self. As editor and translator Leith Morton has stated, "The female self is parodied to the point of destruction; in the process, all conceptions of sexual identity, stereotypical or not, are exploded. Itō makes a

[1] Leith Morton, *Modernism in Practice: An Introduction to Postwar Japanese Poetry* (Honolulu: University of Hawai'i Press, 2004), p. 103.

simulacrum of herself in her poetry and then proceeds to ridicule and destroy even this." He goes on to comment, "Such texts demand respect because of their technical brilliance and also because of their discursive power. Shiraishi Kazuko claims that this destruction of gender is Itō Hiromi 's most impressive poetic achievement."[2]

Just as Itō Hiromi ushers feminine power to the forefront, Justin Chin's "Eros in Boystown" boldly explores the boundaries of the masculine. The poem is part homoerotic travelogue, part myth, and part political commentary as he writes:

Eros stalks Boystown looking for his love. His quiver filled with fresh cut arrows dipped in the poison of his semen. His pockets bulge with his fattest wallet, and his arms jangle with gold and silver and diamonds dipped in cyanide.

Fearless and unabashed, Chin's speaker belts, stalks, aims, blesses, and creates. The figure of Eros is reviled and grotesque as he suffers collagen injections in the name of vanity, his wallet overflowing with American money. Though Eros is all-powerful, he is portrayed as an old, decaying archer who shoots his arrow to "pierce the heart and arse and eyes and scrotum." Chin is anything but demure in his poetic commentary on capitalism, exploitation, boy toys. So what does this say about love? In one of his most powerful stanzas Chin writes:

Eros loves this land. He created it out of darkness. Pissed his seed into the land, dumped his napalm shit into it, fertilized it with mere pennies that he's found on the ground beside porno stores, decorated it with his wettest dreams and his scripture-blessed visions of snowy rapture, a diorama played out with natives reenacting his favorite movies with sticks and masks and dyed cotton loin cloths.

Though this scene could be construed as a dysfunctional mirror image of God creating the earth, here it is Eros who destroys and demolishes. Filled with lust, he envisions cities where the natives do his bidding, outfitted in ways that mimic a "primitive" culture. Eros is the appropriate name for a figure who, by poem's end, flaps "his tattered wings with the faded glory of a silent film star." Languid and cinematic as the scene may

---

2 Ibid., p. 111.

be, it is filled with fury and death. In the name of love, doom and corruption seem to prevail.

Ultimately, I consider these poems documents of peace even if, as Chin's poem reveals—and anyone who has ever been in love knows—Eros is often anything but peaceful. Perhaps it is the greatest lesson that to know love we must know its opposite, its underbelly and its dark ghost.

When I parted from the man I'd loved, I imagined I saw him everywhere: turning downtown corners, descending the steps of a subway station, a shadow sitting bent over a bowl in a noodle shop, face hidden behind a veil of steam. At each side street and intersection where we had once pledged our affection, I now felt the city vacant without him. At night, buildings lit with electric squares of narrative made me wonder: who is falling in love now; who is parting? There's no rational way to manage what we must survive once love has lived its existence, although we are inextricable from our losses. Love is the legacy we leave behind: a collective presence that shines beyond our own recognition.

A native New Yorker, I walked across the Brooklyn Bridge for the first time on my birthday last year. As soon as I took a step on the bridge I found myself back in that middle ground between love and loss, pleasure and pain, my many mistakes and moments of redemption. Standing very still as the water lapped far below, the rest of humankind jogged and cycled past me on their way somewhere. How could I have missed this inevitable crossing? I looked at lower Manhattan, contemplating Sappho's concept of the bittersweet, and saw a vast opening in the landscape where two buildings once stood. There was a hole in the universe where my safety had existed. As I leaned forward, I viewed the beginnings of smaller structures being rebuilt. And therein lies the true construct of love: what was destroyed can find new life. In the present, where the possibility for great loss is imminent, these poems lay a new foundation for love: a paving stone, a pillar, a staircase leading up, a building on the rise.

—TINA CHANG

EVELYN LAU

50 Bedtime Stories

With your mouth you bring me weapons. The long-stemmed black rose of a riding crop. A taper candle. You crawl from the side of the bed, eyelids hung low in repentance. With your mouth you turn every doorknob until all I see is a lineup of doors, you kneeling to one side, ahead a haze of light. I walk through.

The coffee table a display of tissues and needles and a prim bottle of bleach. Bedtime stories, you call the sleeping pills, I have 50 bedtime stories for you tonight. Outside the windows a blossom of light, stamens of neon flaring against the sky; in every teaspoon a pool of blood and a pull of cotton.

The new leash wraps perfectly around my knuckles. One day I will leave you tied, wrists to posts, your eyes blue torches beseeching my face, the groans round and red as apples in your mouth. Meanwhile I dream of men thrown from balconies, men who turn into manuscripts bulky and sinking as if through heavy water, too late to catch without also falling twenty-five stories down to the ending. In the air your body the shape of a fiddlehead, unwinding. Your body slowly scrolling down, coming apart like old rope, coming apart in sentences long as limbs.

BIBHU PADHI

Pictures of the Body

1

There're those frank, unadorned pictures
that skip and dance to quicken
what sleeps through my bland wakefulness—

the wish to carry on the body's need
to interact with the unreached secrets
that wait to be broken upon, enjoyed

by blunt, repeated reminders of where
bodies discover themselves most faithfully,
keep on spilling over into each other

without shame or insult, caring for nothing,
looking for nothing beyond now, submitting
to the glued touch, the wish to be reborn.

I'm quite there, where this body might
find itself once again through a never-ending
rite of arousal and compensation.

The pictures dance to a blind rhythm that is
all their own, while I look on, my flesh
pounding hard over its naive inconclusions.

2

I look away from each one of them from time
to time, expecting nothing beyond their skin,
their wish to be noticed, flawless nudity.

I think I'm learning how they couldn't be
what they are not for me already, how they
belong to a dream that I'd disown.

But I don't know how I sink into this
sleep in the middle of a wholehearted prayer
to be happy with the picture that is me.

They emerge, without much fuss, from under
the low bed, from under the shadow
of intimacy, find me too dumb

and slow to give them what I know
I have, but somehow can't give—
a name for each body, its bunch of toes,

its own breasts and lips. I can't, while they
gather around me in circles, their seductive translucence
playing above a mass of incapacity and sleep.

3

In the first light, just before
the night's departure, the pictures merge
into a shining brown body that

leans over my sleep and waits for
a word of approval that wouldn't be heard
beyond its lone ear, would indeed be

the beginning of a long story.
I imagine the place where I had met
that face, fail. It looks familiar.

Nimble fingers quietly polish my skin
to their desired shine, shape my flesh
into exact measurements of their need.

It seems I had been touched by them in
yet another sleep, variously, felt them deep
under my skin, where an immovable desire is.

The face draws closer, lips greet lips, shaking
two willing bodies, teeth biting every wronged need.
Light is on the windows. My warm fingers feel

the hard lumps on my lips. And there is that
numb weight of a body that knew only too well
what it wanted from me. This sweat. This heat.

QIAN XI TENG

three love objects

i) ash

Li Shangyin (813–858) lights a candle.
The night sighs at the chill of moonlight.

Desire flakes across his desk.
The wax hardens and the tears are dry.
He writes a scorched-earth policy.
Incense smoke passes through the gold lock.
Torch what you want and can't take with you.
For each inch of longing is an inch of dust.
Burn a nuance in last lines.

ii) flower

Paul Celan (1920–1970) knows how loves-me-not blasts.
Heart wall upon heart wall adds petals to it.
The mistranslation of every action as changing fate.
The stone in the air, which I followed.
He inverted his name before he married.
The word that ascended summer.
Sounds the same in French or German.
We baled the darkness empty.
Tiny perfect florets fill a denuded flowerhead.
Will swing over open ground.
The day he died, mail piled outside the door.

iii) grain

Joachim du Bellay (1522–1560) grows sonnets.
On the field a million finished sheafs are shed.
Fed on the bones of old languages.
Like the sown field abundantly green.
Instead of taxidermy which is against his principles.
The stems bristle their blooming swords.
Deaf poets are like deaf composers.
What is falling after the harvester.
They hear salt crystallizing.
See the gleaner walk step by step.
Around stray chips of loved voices.

Author's Note: The italicized lines in each stanza are by the poet named at the beginning of the stanza. The italicized lines used in "ii) flower" were taken from Michael Hamburger's translation of "Flower" by Paul Celan, *Poems of Paul Celan* (New York: Persea Books, 1995). The rest of the translations (in italics) are by the poet.

XI XI

Sonnet

It's been a long time since you've read any of my poems, you say
It's because I haven't written anything, but if I had
How would things stand?
If there's anything I have a handle on
It's the written word
And since it would please you
I'll take what's in my heart and set it to a sonnet
You start it, and I'll carry on
You dance inside it
Freeze, then change
If I really believed in written words
And the perfection of worn-out forms, alas, alas
I might not also be able to believe that our lives will conclude
In a wondrous reunion after all

Translated from the Chinese by Andrea Lingenfelter

USTAD KHALILULLAH KHALILI

Quatrains

Pleasure's origin is the company of lovers
and death's hardship is separation.
As lovers reunite under rich soil
life and death are one to us.

Kneaded by fate on the table of grief
what chance to drink pleasure from life's cup?
Struggling like a candle in a drafty room
I flicker to a waxen puddle and vanish.

When a drop of blood falls to earth
a gem falls from the ring of heaven.
Be careful! An orphan's cries
bring down the walls of the subtle realm.

You knew I saw you as a delicate flower,
a shining essence in the depths of that sea.
Though you were half-hiding your face from me,
I saw the blossoming branch end to end.

Translated from the Dari/Persian by Robert Abdul Hayy Darr

AGHA SHAHID ALI

Ghazal

What will suffice for a true-love knot? Even the rain?
But he has bought grief's lottery, bought even the rain.

"our glosses/wanting in this world" "Can you remember?"
Anyone! when we thought the lovers taught even the rain?

After we died—*That was it!*—God left us in the dark,
And as we forgot the dark, we forgot even the rain.

Drought was over. Where was I? Drinks were on the house.
For mixers, my love, you'd poured—what?—even the rain.

How did the Enemy love you—with earth? air? and fire?
He held just one thing back till he got even: the rain.

This is God's site for a new house of executions?
You swear by the Bible, Despot, even the rain.

After the bones—those flowers—this was found in the urn:
the lost river, ashes from the ghat, even the rain.

What was I to prophecy if not the end of the world?
A salt pillar for the lonely lot, even the rain.

How the air raged, desperate, streaming the earth with flames—
to help burn down my house, Fire sought even the rain.

He would raze the mountains, he would level the waves;
he would, to smooth his epic pilot, even the rain.

New York belongs at daybreak to only me, just me—
to make this claim Memory's brought even the rain.

They've found the knife that killed you, but whose prints are these?
No one has such small hands, Shahid, not even the rain.

M. A. SEPANLU

The Terrace of Dead Fishermen

Fog comes,
covers the heart of the world over
and even after it passes
still, in my eyes, the fog remains.

There's a wedding on the other side of the dividing drape.
On this side, I gaze through an opaque mist
give ear to whispers from the lost. . . .

A narrow cobblestone pavement
a tavern gate
     a door opening on to the sea
and some fishermen on the terrace
their golden pipes
     lighting up the heart of the fog.

The smell of kerosene from the nearby lantern
comes studded with red dots.

I push aside the thin fog and ask:
"No fishing in the fog, ha?"
One answers back:

"We are after adventure.
You see strange things
in the dark, in the fog especially,
there are treasures here—
I swear there are."

"Why not celebrate then, my friend. . . .
Love is all there is!"

The wind picks up
shadows, mirrors, the fishermen's faces,
all drip through the fog's memory.

Rain in the noon of night
and a gray board over the gate:
The Café of the Lost at Sea.

Translated from the Persian by Ahmad Karimi-Hakkak

NATHAN ZACH

As Agreed

Look, as we promised each other,
we changed nothing and the world
is as wonderful as it was, the rain
tarries this year, but it will come:
it will come as long as we're still here.

Look, as we agreed,
I am in one place, you in another.
We didn't become one, which is also natural,
and in your weakness and in mine
there looms a promise, too:
after memory forgetfulness is all.

And if the road already may incline downward
in the famed sloping print of life's curve,

it does, in some sense, aspire upward,
and aspiration is a great thing in life.
On this, too, we agreed, you surely remember.

And if now I'm alone and aching and ailing more than ever,
this, too, was a choice,
if not always conscious. And if you, too, are alone,
it makes my loneliness less just
and this should sustain you as well.

How fortunate that we agreed on so little:
on parting, loneliness and fear, the assured things,
and there's always something to return to.
You will see how young we'll be in the end,
and the end, when it comes, will be almost just.
And everything, you'll see, will be almost welcome.

Translated from the Hebrew by Tsipi Keller

ABDUL WAHAB AL-BAYATI

Aisha's Profile

She hides behind her mask, the face of an angel
And the features of a woman
Ripened on the fire of poems.
The winds of the north awakened her desires
She changed into an apple / wine
A hot loaf of bread
In the temple of holy love
She became addicted to the pleasant embrace.
She appeared in my dreams, I said: A butterfly
Fluttering in the summer of my childhood
Premature
She incarnated all faces
And traveled / sleeping in my blood
A saint fleeing in the middle of the darkness
To embrace the shattering idol

She digs her fingernails in the stone / the rubble
Her mouth / ruby / fresh beams radiating
The fire of the fields
The braided tresses
Eyes burning from excessive compassion
A face behind its mask, hiding
The cities of Salih
And the lemon orchards of the Upper Euphrates

Translated from the Arabic by Bassam K. Frangieh

R. PARTHASARATHY

East Window

It is noon: oak and maple fight
over the sun in our backyard.
A flowering crab scuttles past the east window.
We burn each other with the stubs of profanities,
drop the ash all over the bed.
The unspent days we fold and put away
like a leaf pressed in a book.

Few are the body's needs:
it is the mind's that are insatiable.
May our hands and eyes open this spring afternoon
as the blue phlox open on a calm Salem Drive
to the truth of each ordinary day:
the miracle is all in the unevent.

What home have I, an exile,
other than the threshold of your hand?
Love is the only word there is:
a fool wears out his tongue learning to say it,
as I have, every day of his life.

ISHLE YI PARK

Portrait of a Bronx Bedroom

carnival mask
                bedsheet tacked over window
                                ice freezing on silver bumpers
                                                lime-green el train rolling away
                                                dazed windows

copper Bronx cockroaches
                corroding the sink

light hitting soft skin above my chest,
                silence to pool in, plum-red congas

                                                        what sexy music
                                wine and whiskey arguments
                        what thrown dishrag
                        dirty boot,

                which room needs
                        a match lit
                                hiss of warm light

5 blanket broken heater
winter dizzy with cold
                        whose mouth, whose
                                soft eyelids and long limbs

                secrets we covet behind doors shut tight as lips
                        how will my bones succumb to blackness?

                                        what dumb picture will outlast me?

                        all this sitcom, dirty couch, just a moment

who will continue to love me?

                                        who will I die loving?

Let's take this night
      over graves
         let's illuminate
           this cupped space,
              your mouth

                a hot black flower

JUSTIN CHIN

Eros in Boystown

Eros stalks Boystown looking for his love. His quiver filled with fresh cut arrows dipped in the poison of his semen. His pockets bulge with his fattest wallet, and his arms jangle with gold and silver and diamonds dipped in cyanide.

Eros is a fat fairy in cutoffs and brand-name T-shirts armed with twelve native phrases he's learned on the airplane between in-flight movies and beef meals, ready to dazzle with witless wonderment. He knows how to say *please* in twelve dialects, *thank you* in six, *mine* in twenty, *love* in fourteen, and *fuck me* in one.

Eros lands on tropical soil and kisses it as if it were pilgrim earth. He breathes in the swirling dust and pollution, and in the cancered tissue of his ashen collapsing lungs, changes them to linen-fresh bacterial-cleansing deodorant bathwash, ready to kiss, ready for absolute hunger.

Eros is a 70-year-old Belgian whose collagen injections in his face are melting in the tropical heat, and oozing out of his pores, but he's got his young love stuck to his arm, ready to blot and wipe his liquefying youth off with a pack of disposable tissues.

Eros is a master archer, aiming his arrows with amazing precision, in spite of his Coke bottle glasses. Once he sets his sights on his target, and lays his bait of American dollars and promises of everlasting love wrapped up in the metallic gift wrap of migration to United States of Heaven, the poor love is blinded, hypnotized, lost, caught in the snare, doomed; that's when Eros shoots his carefully prepared arrow to pierce the heart and arse and eyes and scrotum.

Eros loves this land. He created it out of darkness. Pissed his seed into the land, dumped his napalm shit into it, fertilized it with mere pennies that he's found on the ground beside porno stores, decorated it with his wettest dreams and his scripture-blessed visions of snowy rapture, a diorama played out with natives reenacting his favorite movies with sticks and masks and dyed cotton loin cloths.

Eros bribes the psychoanalyst to justify his bliss, blesses the pornographer for helping him create utopia, attacks the poet for chronicling his destruction, and kisses the go-go dancer for his devotion.

Eros stalks Boystown, eyes half shut, flapping his tattered wings with the faded glory of a silent film star, cooing like a fiery infant, slinging his virulent arrows and darts maniacally, raving in life and death, setting his brand of chaos in motion, cutting down all obstructions, turning and turning in his mire and muck, buying and selling and trading his center, all the while, Third Eye infected and encrusted with pus, slouching toward Shangri-la.

TIMOTHY LIU

Five Rice Queens

GWM, 5'11", 170 lbs. Brn/Grn, 8" cut ISO GAM to be my geisha bun-boy mail-order bride and maybe more! Must be discreet and disease free. Your photo gets mine.

ISO GAM (18–25) for LTR. Forty-something GWM, 5'8", average looks, into movies (love Jackie Chan!), romantic walks, quiet evenings at home. Let's order in some takeout!

Well-hung GWM, 6', 200 lbs. seeks smooth GM (Asians a plus!) for lunchbreak tryst. Into

cellophane, peanut oil, duct tape. Shave my hairy ass
and balls during daytime soaps. Serious only.

GBM stud seeks GAM with tiny dick for B&D
face mask fun. Need not speak good English, only
look good with my huge dick in your mouth and a tight
hole I can punish.

Pinkerton lucking for Butterfly to suck my Suzie
Wong. Versatile fifty-looks-forty navy officer ISO
GAM to service my 10" uncut pole. You be submissive
and suicidal.

ITŌ HIROMI

Near Kitami Station on the Odakyū Line

The Odakyū line is always crowded I go on standing
    Around midday if I ride the Seibu Ikebukuro line I can usually get a
    seat as I can also on the Toei Underground line.
These are the lines I normally travel on.
On the Odakyū downline there's a lot of universities so there's lots of
    people. I don't like the feeling I have when I get on a crowded
    train I get on hating people
I change trains at Seijō Gakuen Station. On the other platform the
    all-stops train is waiting with its doors open.
I get on not hating people. Only a few people are inside never many
Because I don't know it well I always get in the front the very front
    carriage of the express the all-stops train does not reach the place
    directly opposite the front carriage of the express. The all stops is
    a short train
While I walk to the door of the all-stops train the express starts to move
    it passes Seijō Gakuen speeds down the slope and as soon as it has
    sped down the slope it makes a stop
I look at the greenery outside the carriage as it rushes past
It changes from trees to grass and then back to trees to grass and then
    back to trees
A creek crosses the grass

Outside the carriage greenery is everywhere

Because I don't know it well I always sit in the very front carriage of the
all-stops train the steps leading to the ticket-turnstiles are in the
middle of the platform. Where I cross the up platform I wave my
hand seductively

I cross the level-crossing and go into his apartment

Ten minutes' walk away

Some weeks ago someone committed suicide at the level-crossing

Planks are lain over the level-crossing

The planks were soaked in blood

In the depression in the track a lump of blood

And what looked like part of an internal organ remained

We had sexual intercourse while I was menstruating

When I go into his apartment I turn on the radio

I leant over his face and

Squeezed the pimples in every corner of his face

I plucked the hairs that remained on his cheeks after shaving

Turned him around

A mole-like thing is on his back

I knew because it sticks out

When I squeeze it the black fatty deposit in the head slides out

In the back of his ears as well there are fatty deposits

When I squeeze they slid out long and slippery

When I grip his hair with my teeth and pull out it comes

I bite my fingernails

My nails are short

I can't pluck hairs with my nails

If I use my teeth they always come out

His cheek comes close to me, it's always cold

His beard touched my skin

He has shaven

I feel the shaven stubble

Before and after we engage in sexual intercourse

I saw a photograph of the area near Kitami station among the photographs of
Araki Nobuyoshi I immediately thought this is where I have sex I felt ashamed
I am a 25-year-old woman and thus do engage in regular sexual intercourse.

I come from Itabashi ward to Setagaya ward and while traveling sexual
intercourse is not on my mind I do not feel any sexual desire I am watching
the grass and trees of Setagaya ward as they pass by outside the carriage in
this season the chlorophyll is evident in layers the moisture almost reaches
the saturation point when I meet him I feel happy so I wave seductively but
when I turn on the radio in his apartment is the time I think of sex

Sex has become a matter of course
I cross the level-crossing and come to the station
    It may be that I've pulled my panties up over my wet genitals and crossed at
    the level-crossing   at Kitami where the piece of flesh still remains
Liquid constantly oozed out
And soaked my panties

Translated from the Japanese by Leith Morton

Author's Note: Araki Nobuyoshi is a photographer (b. 1940).

FORUGH FARROKHZAD

Sin

I have sinned a rapturous sin
in a warm enflamed embrace,
sinned in a pair of vindictive arms,
arms violent and ablaze.

In that quiet vacant dark
I looked into his mystic eyes,
found such longing that my heart
fluttered impatient in my breast.

In that quiet vacant dark
I sat beside him punch-drunk,
his lips released desire on mine,
grief unclenched my crazy heart.

I poured in his ears lyrics of love:
O my life, my lover it's you I want.
Life-giving arms, it's you I crave.
Crazed lover, for you I thirst.

Lust enflamed his eyes,
red wine trembled in the cup,
my body, naked and drunk
quivered softly on his breast.

I have sinned a rapturous sin
beside a body quivering and spent.
I do not know what I did, O God,
in that quiet vacant dark.

Translated from the Persian by Sholeh Wolpé

ZHENG DANYI

but love

but love loves only the three-minute drunk in drunkenness, for abandonment
has nothing to do with wine, or how the survivor's cup holds reflections
of sword and dagger, and less to do with moonlight

with milky white passion, squeezing in from the south window, then out
from the north, leaving nothing but the dense aroma of sweat and joy, and
even less to do with fish shuttling in the bay nearby, and

the canoe in your heart
braving a Sunday of wind and waves, yet having nothing to do
with wind and waves—and, beside you

the stranger with a cracked heart
muttering in his dream—
I loved last night, for love's sake, loved even

the dream of your floral tablecloth, and
how reluctant it was to wake up—but love
always arrives on time, if love is only a distant view with nothing to do
    with the viewing

Translated from the Chinese by Luo Hui

KISHWAR NAHEED

Non-Communication

Like the body peeping through a muslin dress
now all the taut veins of my brain are evident.
Separation's first day was easier than the second
for the first day's first night
was spent telling stories like Sheherzade.
A night like one thousand one nights,
white like unwritten paper,
this creaseless brightness
is like the image formed in the mind
before a word comes on lips.
In the crowded era of my days and nights
you
like a comb passing through hair
keep announcing your existence
but passion and love
like my unkempt hair
keep knitting a web inside me.
Like broken, diffused clouds in the sky
the termite-ridden page of life
will not even sell at the price of scrap.
Thundering like clouds you,
cascading like the rain I,
like two deaf singers
are singing each other a song.

Translated from the Urdu by Mawash Shoaib

ABD EL-MONEM RAMADAN

Preparation for Our Desires

You can put your fingertips on the piano keys,
hide your voice among the sounds of canaries and waterfalls,
but you can't place your feet above the ground.
You, the one rising from dreams,
the last train whistling
means the first train is coming
like a gentle longing for an artist's model.

Do not put the night in your pocket.
Take it with you to bed
and, after it relaxes,
undo the snap and buckle,
shake its lice-ridden head,
then lay it on your lap
and fill your wounded throat with animal voices.

You will be lost.
You'll create a room with no walls.
You can stretch your whole body,
and you can't stretch it on Mary.
I don't know how your brush slipped through the colors,
how your songs gathered all the light
and didn't even grant it to a cow in the field.
You have never seen the *Last Tango*.
You couldn't watch the *Last Tango*.
The night you built your nest in walks by your side,
fears you like an old sheikh,
his cane the only thing tapping.

Listen: you will long for another night
appearing from balconies,
in the daytime
taking off its shoes to face the sun.
It disguises itself as a black cat,
sits by your feet.
You can fly over the fence,

watch the stars
while they gargle light in their mouths
and invite some of them to travel.
But urgently I ask you,
you, the one rising from dreams,
to come from your immortality
and watch *Caligula* and *The Last Temptation of Christ*
and look at *Playboy* magazines.
Even if the apocalypse surprises you,
you will have loved your unemployed body
instead of your puritanical one.

Translated from the Arabic by Khaled Hegazzi and Andy Young

SALAH 'ABD AL-SABUR

The Gist of the Story

She called me the man of sands.
I called her the lady of green.
We met in my twilight days,
Called to each other like happy children.
Shyly we got acquainted
Each of us feeling, with wonder,
The color of the other
And exchanged our names.

Then we parted.
Don't ask me what happens to things when they break
Or to echoes when they fall
In a silent vacuum!

But I recall that once upon an evening,
We dodged the scythe of Death's reaper.
Cheated Time's cock crow
And etched on the wall of the night
An image of our two shadows, blended our colors
On the border of a rumpled pillow,

Then subsided
Into an armchair.

And here you see me contemplating this image,
Drinking to it in my solitude.
So pour a glass of wine to this image, please.

This is the gist of the story.

Translated from the Arabic by Lena Jayyusi and John Heath-Stubbs

KAZIM ALI

Said in the Rain

Wide he came to unearth the golden tablets.
You put this together one afternoon walking home in the rain.

Last night after playing Satie you briefly believed
the back of the mind was the only religion that mattered.

Perturbed, you never wanted words graven in fire,
but wished to be found there, buried in the hill-dirt,

in the rain, a follower of a religion of water,
and why not?

Why not be an acolyte of the twisting ribbon of river?
What else threads its way from great rock to oblivion?

In a night divided between Satie and self-evidence,
why not the religion of a what always seeps back to itself?

Why not a religion of water in a time of great fires?
You fear you may drown, but your birth in it implies otherwise.

Not that it is impossible to drown, but that
this whole time you have been drowning.

SUFIA KAMAL

Mother of Pearls

The sea is not bottomless,
    but deep, deep, so very deep,
and restless, unsteady.
And its water—deep blue in pain. I am an oyster,
my birth is there in that place
where hard sludge heaps up in pain, and stony
harsh, churning, merciless
    shattering waves of song,
in that unbearable clenched-fist pressure night and day
move on at a frightful speed in blind, grief-stricken cold.
In the poreless darkness, hope rises from behind pain's screen,
in the heart's joy and devotion.
I am an oyster. In the warmth of my heart,
    a particle of heavenly light
through drawn-out days and
in the dream anthology of night,
with painful joy I create the elegance
    and luster of pearl.
Time's harsh hand etches on my carapace, by night and day,
stigma's pitch-hued furrow-lines.
Alone, alone in the depth of the sea,
    my body covered in algae,
I listen to the roar of the sea
    and count, hour by hour, the days
when, along the path of heavenly light,
when, replete in elegance
    and in the fullness of her form,
    when will she
speak out quietly the heartbeat's utterance of my words?
When will she reach her fullness in the opulence of beauty
    gleaming with unending glory's elegance,
like my tears, like my happiness,
    like my sorrow, full,
radiating like immaculate, golden, incandescent stars?
In unwearied expectation, how many ages in the depths
    of the sea shall pass

for her to attain beauty's full form
    in the hundred-fold pain of my heart?
One day, she breaks away from me,
    as I, an oyster, lie covered in filth,
or my sludge-smeared body dries out
    on the sandy margin of the shore.
Even so, this life of mine gleams in fulfillment:
I am the mother of the pearl, I am an oyster,
    in my heart is engendered a harvest of pearls.

Translated from the Bengali by Ayesha Kabir, Sajed Kamal, and Carolyne Wright

ZAREH KHRAKHOUNI

Measure

"I love you so much . . ." you said.
"But not as much as I love you," I said.
"Oh, much more than you love," you said.
"Shall we compare?" I replied.
So we measure. We correlated,
collated and weighed.

Taller than tall, we chose mountain altitudes
to scan and grade.
We chose stars and galaxies to outdistance
in love. Day by day we came up
with calculations to outdo.

From legends of Augean stables
to giant structures piercing the blue.
Finally you said your love was as deep
as the light in my eyes when
I looked at you and knew
I was defeated.

Translated from the Armenian by Diana Der-Hovanessian

BOZOR SOBIR

Letters

I opened your letters
And I gave them up to the air,
That they might become spring clouds,
That letters of memories
Might weep over the hills,
That they might weep springs and rivers.
That the letters might weep over us.

Last night I told a story
Of you to the wild wind.
In memory of you I recited from memory
A verse to the streams,
That the water might bear it away
And tell it to the rivers,
That the wind might bear it away
And sing it to the plains.

Last night under the rain
I walked road by road in my thoughts.
Your tresses strand by strand
In my thoughts I walked, braiding strands.
The kisses that had not been planted on your lips
—Along, all along the road,
Along the edge, the edge of the stream—
I walked, planting them in the ground.
So that, ever following in my footsteps
—Along, all along the road,
On the edge, the edge of the stream—
Kisses might grow like daisies,
Kisses might grow like wild mint.

Last night it rained and rained.
The water was too much for the river to hold.
Last night my loneliness
Was too much for me alone to hold. . . .

Last night the April rain
Washed the footprints from the ground.
The wound in my heart grew worse,
Because it washed away the imprint of your foot.
Last night I wandered the streets in vain,
Like a hunter who has lost the trail I searched. . . .

Last night the world was all water,
The sky was refreshed,
The ground was refreshed,
But I, with your name on my lips,
All alone like the parched land
I burned up under the rain.

Translated from the Tajik by Judith M. Wilks

SYLVA GABOUDIKIAN

What I Notice

You ignite
it, hold it
lightly,
as if to
show
something
about us
you want
me to know.
You exhale
warmth
that would
burn me,
flicking
ash,
breathing
slowly,

out of
habit,
just to
pass
time,
alleviating
boredom.
You don't
inhale
but put it
down
to forget
and fail
to finish,

smoking
only part
of each
cigarette.

Translated from the Armenian by Diana Der-Hovanessian

PERVEEN SHAKIR

Consolation

Now, that I have closed the doors
of the city of love
upon myself
and have thrown the key
of each gate
into the jade-eyed sea of oblivion,
this little timorous feeling
is so consoling.

Beyond the forbidding walls of the prison,
in a small lane
of the old walled city,

there is a little window
still open in my name.

Translated from the Urdu by Baidar Bakht and Leslie Lavigne

SHU TING

A Night at the Hotel

The declaration of love, coauthored by lip prints and tears,
Bravely climbs into the mailbox
The mailbox is cold
Long abandoned
Its paper seal, like a bandage, flaps in the wind

The eaves rise and fall softly under the black cat's paws
Large trucks grind sleep till it is hard and thin
The sprinter
In dreams, hears the starter's gun all through the night
The juggler can't catch his eggs
Street lamps explode with a loud shriek
In its coat of yolk the night grows more grotesque

The woman in her nightgown
Yanks the door open, shaking heaven and earth
Like a deer, she runs wildly barefoot across the carpet
A huge moth flits across the wall
Plunges into the crackling fire of a ringing telephone

In the receiver
Silence
Only snow
Goes on singing, far away, on the power lines

Translated from the Chinese by John Rosenwald and The Beliot/Fudan Translation
Workshop

HONG YUN-SUK

Ways of Living 4

You have to wait.
At the crossroads' red traffic light,
you have to stop going along, pause for breath,
look up for once at the forgotten sky,
hoist up and fasten the slipping pack.
A scrap of pink cloud on a remote mountainside,
inky darkness, on the corner you turn,
on the road left ahead cold rain pouring down
we are all being soaked as we pass through this age
for see, this is destiny's winter
and no one can escape from this rain.
Frozen, we rub one another's flesh,
we sparingly share and kindle the remaining fire.
In the darkness our roots twine together.

Translated from the Korean by Brother Anthony of Taizé

THANH THẢO

Adornments

I will slip a rice stalk on your wrist
a jade bracelet sounds of crickets a blade of grass
a flame of skin and flesh
drowned in a pair of pinkish nipples

I will drape around your neck
the mysterious necklace of night
the clear bells of autumn
tremble as the city flies back toward the sky

I will drape on your chest
a tempest

Translated from the Vietnamese by Linh Dinh

WANG PING

Wild Pheasant

Venus points to the mid-sky moon
My path is drenched with silvery dew
A wild pheasant calls from a blue house terrace
Red are my lips, dark is love

Painted phoenix cannot fly
Pain in my heart has no tongue
I was daughter of yellow earth
You were son of mountains and ravines
Two small children with bowl-cut hairdos
We played without shame or suspicion
At 20, Mother opened my face with silk thread
A red sedan carried me to your new cave
Three nights after, you set off for the coast
I grabbed your sleeves, hugged your neck
Why did you bother to marry if you had to leave so soon
You dragged your feet, two steps forward three steps back
Bride and groom, three days new
How our tears broke like partridge eggs

Venus sinks to the west, leaning on the moon
My path makes no sound under wet moss
A wild pheasant calls from a blue house window
Come, my angels, rest your souls at my perfumed feet

Pairs of toads leap in the spring
Our love song echoes ravine to ravine
At the end of the road, I took out my needle
And sewed my heart into your shirt
Go, my lover, don't look back
If you're hungry, there's bread in the sack
Heat your meals and cover your belly
Don't forget your bride, don't pick flowers along the road
I'll plough the fields, care for our parents
My door will be locked till you return
With a cartful of grain

Venus shines—lighthouse for stars
Along my path, shadows scurry in dim alleys
A wild pheasant calls from blue house eaves
Short is my skirt, tender as my scented sleeves

Terraces are ploughed by buffaloes
This world is seeded with sorrow
My love, you're a mud ox sunk in the sea
Nothing returns since you left me
I call heaven and earth
But who will hear who will see
Only tears drip from a crushed heart
A lone shadow hovers over the well

Venus weeps on the blue house roof
At dawn my path crowds with sleepless souls
A pheasant calls under the Old White Star
Long is my hair, tangled love in the teeth of fate

Ten thousand geese fly north
Ten thousand letters wait for a home
Once mating, Mandarin ducks never part
My herd boy, six years is too long without you
Some rule with slogans, some reign with commercials
But who will give back my husband
Let us raise the young, grow old in peace
Roaming from city to city
I ask your name to women, paint your face to thousands of men
Whatever happened, I must find you
Alive, I'll drag you to Mother's knees
Our five-year-old son you've never seen
Dead, I'll take your bones in cloth, rest them
Next to your father, wine and incense to light your path

The moon has completed her journey
From darkness to darkness I linger
A wild pheasant calls with a splintered throat
Gold Star of Venus, please shine your light on my path

I'm a pheasant, a spittoon filled with cigarette butts
My flesh rots beneath powder and rouge
But the fire has never died in my temple
Love is there if you see it—
Dewdrops of faith bejeweling its upturned eaves

Do not move
Let birds stir in their nests
Let pheasants—fairies from this tattered earth—
Carry the sun in our beaks

Author's Note: Pheasant and others are names for prostitutes. A *blue house* was the term
for a brothel in ancient times.

AHMAD REZA AHMADI

I Did Not Expect

I did not expect to come face to face
with this absolute snow.

I did not expect to come face to face
with this absolute love.

These slumbering birds on the glazed tiles
portend the melting of this pure love
in that unadulterated snow.

If only you knew how I set ablaze the vine.
On that Friday I saw
there was no time
to even deny that absolute love.

How many singed ashtrays have I beheld
belonging to men now dead.
How many desolate days have I seen
in need of no man's martyrdom.
How many times have I witnessed

the life of a matchstick flame outlast my friends' lives.
How many times have I watched
someone in search of an address in the rain,
someone to whom as soon as I showed the way
was suddenly engulfed in flames and turned to ashes.
How I have comforted everyone
that this street shall end,
and how they have comforted me
that at the end of this street
a basket of grapes waits for me.

I shall entrust this absolute love
to the pages of the Divan of Hafez.
Until when?
I do not know.
Until what hour?
I cannot tell.

Translated from the Persian by Sholeh Wolpé and Ahmad Karimi-Hakkak

CECEP SYAMSUL HARI

Wooden Table

This is the secret of one twilight, of how a life was wasted,
of death that invites and denies us all. The ocean was vast,
the night was marble. I heard various voices inside myself:
there was fighting, Mephisto dancing, moans and sighs,
herbs soaking, as she picked shadows. There were wounds,
and the prelude to some forgotten sorrow. There was a mature woman,
with teeth like filaments of wire, standing at the edge

of day, at the end of a sodden year, under casuarina trees
covered with lanterns. I confess in my shame, I met
a girl, and we drank coffee together. The less I kiss you,
the older I feel, the lonelier I become. Once, I accepted
failure and sorrow, and thought that they were love. I went out,
one day, wearing brown polished shoes,

and new cotton socks. The grass in the courtyard
had turned to straw. Long ago, Chopin wrote a sad song
about the rain. The mist swirled, coins jingled, a match flared,
her cheeks were plump, that corner of the city
was full of noise. I sang, I always sing
when I'm sad. Forget my love, tomorrow I'll wake up again
back in my hotel room, alone. Everyone I love

always leaves me. This is the secret of one twilight,
without any jagged memories, or the need
to worship old legends. It was beautiful,
the sky was bright, the train sped past,
a parking official blew his whistle to remind us
of some forgotten schedule. I was sad, disappointed,
I jumped out at Tugu Station, and laughed out loud.
Full of faith, Faust was not prepared for the smile
of a young girl, a bombastic leader, a friend

who hid a wolf in his chest, for no particular
reason. Unlike those who had left their homelands behind,
I had lost very little. A leaf fell. The conversation swung
to and fro. A weak and gentle woman took off
her veil, displayed her kisses, tidied some letters,
some trivial gifts, and buried my embraces

beneath a wooden table.

Translated from the Indonesian by Harry Aveling

LAURENCE WONG

Dawn in the Mid-Levels

Resting my head on the dawn chorus,
I am a green waterweed
quietly listening to the soft silver ripples
streaming into the golden glass of dawn.
Deep in the glass, a transparent vein of light

is slowly flowing over lock upon lock of lilac wind.
The lilac wind is your soft hair
floating over the golden comb of dawn, noiseless.

Translated from the Chinese by the author

RISHMA DUNLOP

Saccade

The chronicle of the city unravels
                    like a prayer cloth
calm of storybook nurseries, book codes,
swift calligraphy of desire.

The city dreams us
            gives us exigencies in eavesdropped
            stories, undistinguished pleadings
            requiems for forgetting.

There is a small star pinned where Hiroshima used to be.

It's late and someone's almost forgotten how to convince you
                                he's telling the truth.
Even in sleep he cries out for help
            and you minister to him
            a woman like history returning for its wounded.

Blackbirds drop from telephone wires
                    rosepetals collect in birdbaths.

Everything stories you. You take Rilke at his word
Taste it everywhere. Wonderland signs:
                    Eat me. Drink me.

Your hands like hobbled birds
read the classics. The hero enters the arched gate of the city.
In these books it is clear where the story of the city begins.

In the book of lost entries
                    nothing is pure but the forgotten things
crossed out words on a haunted page
                    useless dark of ink.

Today the city is unwriting itself
                    in a coffin of glass.

In the blurred doorways,
                    in skyscrapers that rise silver and blue
cool as if nothing could ever make them burn.

Sprayed on concrete walls
Where is my beautiful daughter
Emma was here
Escúchame
I'll pray for you Lucas
Fuck the politicians
Recuérdame
Inamorata

the billboard with the women tall
                    with long legs against white sand and blue ocean
                    red mouths puckered high above the crowds
smooth lipsticked smiles longing for cigarettes and sex.

Across the city, lights are shutting off
Good night, good night.

On the radio, the sirens are singing
Emmylou Harris, Alison Krauss, Gillian Welch
ethereal lullaby *Didn't Leave Nobody But the Baby*

Come lay your bones
On the alabaster stones
And be my ever-lovin' baby.

Reading Emily Dickinson
                    Beauty crowds me till I die.
You feel the loneliness.
That's what is left of the dream of beauty.

Beauty
          So many kinds to name.

You hope for a day soft at the edges
                    for something, someone to
                    know the small hands of rain
to be like rain
wet with a decent happiness.

Kiss the gleaming armor of the world.
Feel its electric purr.
Close your hands on wind-stunned leaves.
Buff the scars of history with your mouth.

KIM SU-YŎNG

Variations on the Theme of Love

Open your lips, Desire, and there within
I will discover love. At the city limits
the sound of the fading radio's chatter
sounds like love while the river flows on,
drowning it, and on the far shore lies
loving darkness while dry trees, beholding March,
prepare love's buds and the whispers
of those buds rise like mist across indigo
mountains.

Every time love's train passes by
the mountains grow like our sorrow and ignore the lamplight
of Seoul like the remnants of food in a pigsty.

Now even brambles, even the long thorny runners
of rambling roses are love.

Why does love's grove come pushing so impossibly near?
Until we realize that loving is the food of love.

Just as water in a kettle boiling on a stove
nearly spills over but not quite, love's moderation
is a torrid thing.
Interruption is love, too.
I know nights when love persists
like the green eyes of a cat shining in
death-like darkness, from this room to that,
from grandma's room to the room of the errand boy.
And I know the art of producing such love.
The art of opening and closing eyes
—the art of the French Revolution,
the art we learned not long ago on April 19,
only now we never shout aloud.

Lovely firmness of peach seeds, apricot seeds, dry persimmon seeds.
Wicked faith
of the storm stirred up by silence and love.
The same in Pompeii, New York, and in Seoul.
Compared to the vast city of love I am burying,
greater even than faith,
aren't you a mere ant?

My son, this is not designed to teach you fanaticism.
Grow up until you come to know love.
Humanity's final moments,
the day you drink your cup to the dregs,
the day America's oil dries up:
before you reach such distant times, the words
you will register in your heart are words you will learn
from the city's fatigue.
You will learn this firm silence.
You will wonder whether
the peach seed is not made of love.

Sometime the day will come
when peach seed and apricot seed
will leap up, maddened by love.
And that will not be the false meditation
of a mistaken hour like your father's.

Translated from the Korean by Brother Anthony of Taizé

'ENAYAT JABER

Circle

He breathed deeply,
when the street awoke,
with the very features of yesterday.
He was not ready yet
to deal with the morning.
In her first absence,
what worries him
is not this morning,
he can make it through another morning.
What really worries him
is the mornings after,
his sitting absent-mindedly,
suffocated by air,
counting the seconds
and the movements of emptiness.
One little kick will do,
in his tremulous freedom,
to put love in order again,
and to calm the quivering world.
Just one little kick,
for the sake of bliss, which
overflows from her hands, roaming
on his back.

Translated from the Arabic by Wen Chen Ouyang

MEDAKSÉ

Envy (Yerance te)

I envy the cling of the shirt you wear
that, even in daylight, can be indiscreet
and trace your torso's outline and dare
to wrinkle coquettishly with pagan heat.
Imagine envying an innate thing,
and losing my senses like a flaming wing
of a meteor? Does a shirt have feelings or soul
that I die to hold what it can hold?

What does it care that a woman desires
to wash it because it has felt the fires
of your body and wants to inhale
the warmth of the collar, even the stale
earthly memory of wear and weave
of a sleeve?
What does it care that I envy the clasp
of its pearly buttons that measure the time
of our short lives with their upward climb,
dressing and undressing you, unasked,
leaning against your beating heart,
while I who envied no other's lot
stand silent, apart and jealous of cloth.

Translated from the Armenian by Diana Der-Hovanessian

MUREED BARGHOUTHY

Desire

His leather belt
hangs on the wall
the pair of shoes he left behind has turned brittle
his white summer shirts
still sleep on their shelf

his scattered papers
tell her that he will be gone a long time
but she is there still waiting
and his leather belt
is still hanging there
and each time the day ends
she reaches out to touch a naked waist
and leans back against the wall.

Translated from the Arabic by Lena Jayyusi and W. S. Merwin

PRIYA SARUKKAI CHABRIA

excerpt from "Flight: In Silver, Red and Black"

5. *after Lady Nijo*

My anger ran on four feet
and our paths parted.
There's no regret that I sought him out.
None that I changed to storm
him with my candor,
though my body retained its form:
the nape long, the soft, soft skin,
and intact too, the velvet furnace within.
I've no remorse for not adopting a mollusk's heart.
Only this: When my anger parted
us, his body was caught in a coil for mine.
I should have smoothened desire
his, and mine. I should have slept with him
one last time.

FAWZIYYA ABU KHALID

To a Man

I thought you could be a faithful dog
an Arabian
horse unsaddled
a forerunner to some god
that tastes unlike the dried dates of the tribe.

For myself
I have torn up all my heir's contracts with the past
uprooting my clan's trees
embracing the freedom of outlaws.

Alas, I discovered
your backbone was
but a pillar of fog frozen
in the Levantine mirror of Narcissus;
and you: nothing
more than a Sultan's herald
another pimp
hailing the virtues of the fruits
of the Fertile Crescent.

Translated from the Arabic by Kamal Boullata

SŎ CHŎNG-JU

Barley-Time Summer

A stony stream burns beyond yellow clay walls,
heat bleaches barley that seems to hide guilt.
Where has mother slipped off,
leaving her sharp sickle back on its shelf?

Among the rocks where a wild boar once went
gasping, bleeding, along the path, the field path,
a leper wept, his clothes all crimson,

a girl stretched snake-like on the ground
sweating, sweating,
as I stood dizzy, she drew me down.

Translated from the Korean by Brother Anthony of Taizé

ABDULLAH GORAN

Women and Beauty

I have seen stars in the skies &
Picked flowers from spring gardens

Dew from branches has sprinkled my face
I've gazed at many mountains at twilight

Rainbows that follow torrential rains
Were arched against the rays of the sun

Suns of Nawroz & Maytime moons
Many have wandered from night into day

Sounds of silver-foamed waterfalls
With myriad tints flickering in the mist

Ripe yellow and red fruits of the orchard
Easy birdsong in the mountain forests

And from flute throats, violin strings
Many beautiful melodies have come

All of these are beautiful and calm
And lighten the ways life takes us on

But nature lacking a lover's smile
Will forever lack real light

Will hold no melody in its soft sound:
I don't want to hear it & feel satisfied

What glinting star or wild flower
Is cherry like her cheek, nipples, lips

What black is the color of her eyes
Her brows, her lashes, her loose hair

What hill is as lovely as her curve
What glow eludes her vision's light

What desire, heat or expectation
Can magic match—those of love?

Translated from the Kurdish by Kamal Mirawdeli and Stephen Watts

MUHAMMED BENNIS

Love Is Eternity's River

Nothing but rivulets
communicating,
this is love.
I am the one who says
the parts of various selves become alike,
who says, within opposites harmony lies.
I have tried this and seen that,
so take what you know
about me and about women.
Love is the mood of similar souls,
the secret of the collar around your neck,
the secret vanishing in you.
O self

of lightweight worlds,
I am the one who says,
what has taken hold of the self
will only perish with death, and you.
Fly high, high
into tattooed space, strive
with your dove collar,
long for the calling of water.
O self
that's how you are
one cloud nudged by another.

Translated from the Arabic by Fady Joudah

PARTOW NOORIALA

Are You a Snake?

In an extensive commentary on Qur'an's Sureh of Yusef, it is mentioned that among animals only snakes cannot hear one another.

From behind the curtain of fog
through the scattered bird plumes and feathers
from among white teeth and claws
your wild murmur
makes me breathless with yearning.

I crawl up the fog
fly through the azure sky
claw the thick skin of longing.

The scratched barks of trees
are my rain-soaked letter,
its fragments surrendered to the wind
by a migrant bird.

It's a sweet temptation
the roar of my words
that cuts open the skin
of a sable searching for his lover.

My brand is a lion's sharp claw
in pursuit of a warm body
in the cold of the jungle.

Until the time my desire
is deciphered in the sable's furry dream,
I shall lend my song to the throat of a bird
twirling in the morning's milky mass;

Alive and mad with love
I have sung you my words;
Are you a snake that you do not hear?

Translated from the Persian by Sholeh Wolpé

BASSAM HAJJAR

Hatred

Had this heart been a tree trunk
it would have loved me
Had this tree trunk been a heart
it would have awaited the woodcutter

Translated from the Arabic by Sharif S. Elmusa

NADER NADERPOUR

The Sculptor

I am the old sculptor and with fancy's chisel
I created you one night from the marble of verse
Cutting facets of desire on the gemstones of your eyes
I paid for the soft glances of a thousand dark eyes

On your tall form, which tempts me to wash you,
I have sprinkled the moon's sparkling wine,
A potion to guard you from evil-eyed harm
From the jealous ones I have stolen you from

To refine the curves and curls of your form
I have reached out in need to beg from all sides
From each woman's body I carve something borrowed
From each I rob a dance, a glance, a nod

But you, an idol whose eyes avoid your maker
Cast me down in the dust at your feet
Drunk with pride and distant from my pain
You break faith, it seems, with your creator

Beware! Behind this curtain of need
I am that blind, capricious sculptor who shaped you
One night when your love's rage makes me insane
The shadows will also watch me break you.

Translated from the Persian by Zara Houshmand

ŌOKA MAKOTO

Rocking Horse

night after night a lone woman
is making her journey in secret

—Paul Éluard

Across the skies from which the sunlight falls
I saw a lonely rocking horse.
Floating almost like a phantom,
The rocking horse traversed the skies.

O kind companion—close the window,
Just run your fingers through my hair.
Take this rocking horse heart of mine
Just bind me
In that golden hoop of a palm
Like handcuffs.

Translated from the Japanese by Ry Beville

AGNES LAM

the red grapefruit

you cut open the grapefruit
cutting carefully
like tearing down my cocoon
the grapefruit is opened
into two red suns
I feel so free

flying out from the cocoon like the summer butterfly
flowers are full of my eyes
sweet as the grapefruit's red
the two pieces of the fruit stay firm together
plentiful like the smile of first love
it's thus I fall in love with red

you cut the grapefruit into eight pieces
red mouthful by mouthful
it's like eating my sweetest memories
I take up the last segment
and kissing this last piece of red
my heart becomes pale

the taste of grapefruit
like your love to me
surprisingly
sweet and plump to see
bitter to the taste
like sorrow

when there is no more flesh in the grapefruit
the inner skin of the fruit is
so pale as to make me cherish
that sugary smile of the red fruit that was

I hold the pale skin in my hand
mind and eye bringing back the original
it's like letting the cocoon wrap my body
and now I can see
the outer skin of the grapefruit
was never red at all

Translated from the Chinese by Christopher Kelen, Agnes Lam, and Agnes Vong

REETIKA VAZIRANI

Quiet Death in a Red Closet

Fourteen anniversaries.
Thirteen moons,
A baker's dozen.
Eleven moves.
Ten attempts.
Nine lives.
Eight spoons.
Seven of us.
Six survive.
Five children.
Four daughters.
Three stay.
Too far away.
In marriage,
Someone had to go.

DOROTHEA ROSA HERLIANY

Saint Rosa, 1

for the husband of my past, I write no history.
the old books in the library of my heart
only record a few sad stories of defeat.
a group of soldiers lined up like children.
returning home to snail shells on coral reefs.
abandoning vague scraps of hope, among
broken sharks' teeth.
for my lovers, I search for an anxious body
abandoned in a room filled with men
eager to set the world on fire. they offer
stacks of second-hand goods, wonderful
air-conditioning machines. I enjoy the heat,
it is brief, silent, while my thirst is endless.
my disappointment makes me mad. I have stayed too long.

I want to climb up into the Himalayas and stay there.
watch my lust grow cold, then explode
and destroy the world.
but I am tired of dreaming.
the house is narrow and covered with dirt.
if hope should ever arrive
it would be a useless lump of time.

Translated from the Indonesian by Harry Aveling

ZAHRAD

Who Struck First?

True. There wasn't the difference
of an eyelash's flicker.
Not a second. Still
I like to relive that moment
from that long-ago night
when the big city put out
all of its lights.
Was it me? Or did you first
lift your lips sweetly?
True. There wasn't a difference,
no flicker in time.

Translated from the Armenian by Diana Der-Hovanessian

NABILA AZZUBAIR

The Closed Game

And now
there are two boxes
we will throw to the sea

My box, the sea entered
because it was open
Your box, the beach buried
because you never got out

Translated from the Arabic by Najwan Darwish

HARRIS KHALIQUE

She and I

She and I would talk of wonder and dread,
of desires and disasters,
boys and girls pacing up and down
the sidewalk beside us,
milk she forgot to put back in the fridge,
writing tables, bookshelves, table lamps, kitchens,
plumbers and fixers.

She and I would talk of families, spouses and siblings,
pets in the neighborhood
who have the same faith as their keepers,
of lying to loved ones about sex and night outs,
travels,
friends found when traveling,
hat racks in aircrafts with defective latches,
unkempt interiors of slow-moving trains,
rivers, mountains, forests, deserts,
oceans and dreams.

She and I would talk of our country,
dust can hold it together for so long,
of Gog and Magog
licking up the walls of sanity,
of people and their struggle,
wounds unhealed and seasons we fear.

The sibilance of sorrow creeping behind us,
we wished to chat till the world ends
and the world always ended.

HSIA YÜ

Fusion Kitch

When did it all begin
This bucolic and pan-incestuous atmosphere
Was it not always there in the selfsame family album
Lovers fallen to the status of kin
Animals fallen to the condition of lovers
Nor let us forget the repressive inclinations
In the animistic discourse to which
All romances arrive in the end

Translated from the Chinese by Steve Bradbury

HỮU THỈNH

Poem Written by the Sea

When you're far away
The moon too is alone,
The sun alone,
The sea, proud of its vastness,
Is quick to be lonely
                    when briefly without sails.

The wind is not a whip, but still erodes the mountainside.
You are not an evening, but dye me violet.

A wave goes nowhere
                    if it isn't bringing you back.

Even so,
It staggers me
Because of you.

Translated from the Vietnamese by George Evans and Nguyen Qui Duc

NIZAR QABBANI

What Is Love?

What is love?
We have read a thousand treatises on it
and still do not know what we have read,
read works of interpretation, astrology and medicine
and do not know where we began
we have memorized the whole of folk literature
poetry and song
and remember not a single line
we have asked the sages of love about their state
and discovered that they knew no more than we do

What is love?
We asked after it in its secret hiding place, but
each time we came to grasp it, it broke loose from us
we followed it through the forests, for years and years,
    but we lost our way
we pursued it to Africa . . . to Bengal
Nepal, the Caribbean, Majorca
and the jungles of Brazil
but never arrived
we asked love's wise men about their news
and discovered that they knew no more than we did

What is love?
We asked the saints about it, we asked the heroes of tales
they spoke the most beautiful words, but we were
  not convinced
once we asked our schoolmates about it
and they answered that it was a dreamy child
who wrote poetry about a narcissus
collected ants, nuts, and berries in its pinafore
and comforted abused kittens
we asked the experts on love about their experience
and discovered that they knew no more than we did

What is love?
We asked the pious and the good about it . . . but in vain
we asked men of religion . . . but in vain
we asked lovers about it, and they said:
it left home as a child . . .
carrying a bird and a branch in its hand
and we asked all its contemporaries about its age
they answered mockingly:
since when did love have an age?

What is love?
We heard that it was a divine decree
we believed what we had heard
and we heard that it was a heavenly star
so we opened the windows each night . . . and sat waiting
we heard that it was lightning . . . that if we touched it
  we would be electrified
we heard that it was a well-honed sword
that if we were to unsheathe it we would be slain
we asked the ambassadors of love about their travels
and discovered that they knew no more than we did

What is love?
We saw its face in the orchid . . . but we did not
  understand
we heard its voice in the nightingale's cry . . . yet we
  did not understand
glimpsed it atop a wheat stalk, in the deer's gait
in the colors of April
in the works of Chopin
but we did not notice
we asked the prophets of love about their secrets
and discovered that they knew no more than we did

And we turned to the princes of love in our history
we consulted with Laila's demented lover
we consulted with Lubna's demented lover
and discovered that they were called princes of love
were never happier than we were in their love.

Translated from the Arabic by Lena Jayyusi and W. S. Merwin

AUTHOR BIOGRAPHIES

Gémino H. Abad is university professor emeritus at the University of the Philippines. Poet, fictionist, and literary critic, he has received many honors and awards, and is noted for his three-volume historical anthology of Filipino poetry in English since 1905. His other books include *Man of Earth* (1989), *A Native Clearing* (1993), and *A Habit of Shores* (1999).

Elmaz Abinader is a poet, author, and storyteller. Her works include a memoir, *Children of the Roojme: A Family's Journey from Lebanon*; a collection of poetry, *In the Country of my Dreams*; and four one-woman plays, which have been performed around the world.

Nazeeh Abu Afash was born in 1946 in Syria. He is the author of more than thirteen books of poetry and is the chief editor for the monthly magazine *Al-Mada*.

Fawziyya Abu Khalid was born in 1956 to a traditional Bedouin family in Riyadh, Saudi Arabia. She has published more than three poetry books and more than two hundred articles on social, political, and literary issues.

Muhammed al-Acha'ari was born in 1951 in Morocco. He is the author of numerous books of poetry, one novel, and a book of short stories. In 2000, he became the Moroccan Minister of Culture and Communications.

Shanta Acharya was born in India, educated at Oxford and Harvard, and is currently based in London. Her four poetry books are *Shringara* (Shoestring Press, UK, 2006), *Looking In, Looking Out* (Headland Publications, UK, 2005), *Numbering Our Days' Illusions* (Rockingham, UK, 1995), and *Not This, Not That* (Rupa, India, 1994).

Etel Adnan was born in 1925 in Beirut, Lebanon, of a Syrian Muslim father and

Greek mother. She is an essayist, visual artist, and the author of more than twelve books of poetry and prose. Adnan lives in Paris, Lebanon, and California.

Adonis was born in 1939 in Syria. For over fifty years, he has written poetry and literary criticism, translated widely, as well as edited anthologies. He has won numerous international poetry awards and was a finalist for the 2003 Nobel Prize in Literature.

Mamdouh Adwan was born in 1941 and died in 2004. Poet, playwright, scriptwriter for television, journalist, and translator, he was born in Hama, northern Syria. Author of more than twenty plays, ten collections of poetry, two novels, and numerous essays, he also translated English and Greek literature into Arabic, including Homer's *Iliad* and Nikos Kazantzakis's autobiography.

Muhammad 'Afifi Matar was born in 1935 in Egypt. He later moved to Baghdad as one of the editors of *Al-Aqlam* literary review. He is the author of many books, including *From the Notebook of Silence, Engraving on Nocturnal Crust,* and *The Silt Speaks.*

Fawzia Afzal-Khan is professor in the department of English at Montclair State University. Her most recent books include, *A Critical Stage: The Role of Secular Alternative Theatre in Pakistan* (Seagull, 2005) and *Shattering the Stereotypes: Muslim Women Speak Out* (Interlink, 2005). She has won several prestigious fellowships, including the W. E. B. Du Bois Fellowship at Harvard.

Vidhu Aggarwal teaches poetry and poetics and postcolonial studies at Rollins College. She has a forthcoming book of poems, *Playback Singer,* peopled with lip-synchers, karaoke addicts, silent movie comedians, and Bollywood playback singers.

Agyeya is the penname of S. H. Vatsyayan, who was born in 1911 and died in 1987. Considered the founder of modernism (*Navi kavita*) in Hindi poetry, he served as editor for numerous Hindi and English magazines and as commentator on All India Radio. His books include *Aangan ke paar dvaar* and *Kitni naavon mein kitni baar* and he received numerous honors, including the Sahitya Adademi Award, Jnanpith Award in 1978.

Ahmad Reza Ahmadi was born in 1940 in the City of Kerman. He was a central figure in a group of younger poets popularly known as the "New Wave." Ahmadi is the author of numerous books of poetry.

Aku Wuwu (Luo Qingchun) is a member of the Yi ethnic group in southwest China. He has been described as the creator of modern Yi poetry written in Yi. A native of Sichuan Province, he is a professor of Yi studies in the Southwest Nationalities University in Chengdu. His work has been included in *MĀNOA*. His other publications include *Tiger Traces: Selected Nuosu* and *Chinese Poetry of Aku Wuwu*.

Meena Alexander's poetry includes *Illiterate Heart* (2002), winner of a PEN Open Book Award, and *Raw Silk* (2004). She is the editor of *Indian Love Poems* (2005). Her memoir *Fault Lines* (1993/2003) was one of *Publishers Weekly*'s Best Books of 1993. She is Distinguished Professor of English at Hunter College CUNY.

Agha Shahid Ali was born in New Delhi in 1941 and grew up in Kashmir. He taught at the University of Utah and the University of Massachusetts–Amherst. His poetry collections include, *The Half-Inch Himalayas, A Nostalgist's Map of America, The Country Without a Post Office,* and *Rooms Are Never Finished* (finalist for the National Book Award, 2001). He passed away in 2001.

Kazim Ali is a poet and novelist whose books include *The Far Mosque, Quinn's Passage,* and *The Fortieth Day*. He is the founder and publisher of Nightboat Books, and has taught at various universities, including Shippensburg University, the Culinary Institute of America, New York University, and in the Stonecoast MFA Program of the University of Southern Maine.

Taha Muhammad Ali was born in 1931 in the Galilee village of Saffuriyya. He is the author of four books of poetry in Arabic and a book of short stories. *So What: New & Selected Poems, 1971–2005,* translated by Peter Cole, Yahya Hijazi, and Gabriel Levin, was published in 2006 by Copper Canyon Press.

Merlie M. Alunan is associate faculty of the University of the Philippines Institute of Creative Writing. Her works have been collected in *Hearthstone Sacred Tree* (1993), *Amina Among the Angels* (1997), *Selected Poems* (2004). Her new works are written in both English and her native Cebuano.

Moniza Alvi was born in Pakistan in 1954 and grew up in England. She has published five books of poetry: *The Country at My Shoulder* (Oxford University Press, 1993), *A Bowl of Warm Air* (Oxford University Press, 1996), *Carrying My Wife* (Bloodaxe, 2000), *Souls* (2002), and *How the Stone Found Its Voice* (2005).

Yehuda Amichai was born in Germany in 1924, and immigrated with his parents to Palestine in 1936. He is the recipient of many awards, including the Israel Prize for Poetry. He has published eleven books of poetry in Hebrew, two novels, and a book of short stories. He lived in Jerusalem until his death on September 25, 2000.

Indran Amirthanayagam won the Paterson Prize for *The Elephants of Reckoning,* a U.S./Mexico Fund for Culture fellowship for his translations, and received first place in the Juegos Florales of Guaymas, Mexico, for his poem "Juarez." He has published poetry collections in English and Spanish, including *El Infierno de los Pajaros, El Hombre que Recoge Nidos, Ceylon R.I.P.,* and *The Elephants of Reckoning.*

Melih Cevdet Anday was a poet, translator, and member of the prominent literary movement known as "Garip." He wrote the award-winning novels, *Mikado's Garba* and *Secret Order*. His first poem was published in the prominent *Varlik* journal in 1936, and he went on to publish several poetry books, three of which won awards from universities and nongovernmental organizations.

Nadia Anjuman was born in Herat, Afghanistan, in 1980. She graduated from Maleka-e-Jalali High School in Herat and attended Herat University. She majored in journalism at the School of Literature and published her first and last poetry book, *Gul-E-Doudi (Black Flower)*, in 2005. She died as a result of domestic violence on November 11, 2005, leaving behind a six-month-old son.

Cesar Ruiz Aquino has authored collections of poetry and short fiction and received a number of awards in the Philippines, as well as the 2004 SEA Write (Southeast Asian Writers) Award from Thai royalty for lifetime achievement. He lives in Dumaguete City and teaches at Silliman University where he obtained a doctoral degree in literature.

Jean Arasanayagam was born to a burgher family in the hill town of Kandy in Sri Lanka. She has served as International Writer-in-Residence in the Southwest (UK) and a Visiting Fellow at Exeter University. She has published many books, including *Kindura* (1973), *Apocalypse '83* (1983), and *A Colonial Inheritance and Other Poems* (1985).

Mammad Araz was born in 1933 in the village of ;Nurs in the Shahbuz region of Nakhchivan. His books of poetry include: *Love Song*; *Father of Three Sons*; *Araz River is Flowing*; *Life Caravan*; *The World is Yours, The World is Mine*; and *The Sound Written on the Rocks*. Araz has received numerous honors, including Honored Culture Worker, Laureate of Republican State Award, People's Poet, and Istiglal (Independence) Order.

Lisa Asagi is an internationally published writer and media artist who frequently collaborates on conceptual, live art, performance, and film projects. She is the author of two fold-out books, *Physics* and *Twelve Scenes from 12 A.M.*, published by Tinfish Press and designed by visual artist Gaye Chan. Asagi is based in Honolulu and San Francisco.

Atamurad Atabayev was born in the ancient city of Margian in 1948. He has translated the Quran as well as the works of numerous authors such as Pushkin and Lermontov into Turkmen. He is the author of more than twenty books.

David Avidan was born in Tel Aviv in 1934 and died in 1995. He has won numerous awards, namely, the Abraham Woursell Prize from the University of Vienna, the Bialik Award, and the Prime Minister Award. He has published nineteen books of poetry, as well as plays and children's books.

Muhammed Hasan 'Awwad was born in 1902 and died in 1980 in Jeddah. He gained prominent position among his country's poets writing mainly in the inherited two-hemistich verse. He has published several volumes of poetry.

Ayukawa Nobuo was born in 1920 and died in 1986. He is a founding member of the Arechi (Wasteland) group, a translator of T. S. Eliot, and respected literary and social critic. Ayukawa fought with the Japanese army in World War II and returned from the front to create a poetics of social responsibility and political awareness that influenced generations of writers.

Rafiq Azad is a prime rebel of the 1960s poetry in Bangladesh. He has published twenty-two anthologies, including *Ausomvober Paaye* (1973), *Simaboddho Joley Simito Sobuje* (1974), and *Sresttho Kobita* (1987). Azad has received the Bangla Academy Literary Award (1966) among other honors. He now edits a literary magazine and teaches literature.

Nabila Azzubair is a novelist and poet from Yemen. She is the author of five books of poetry and two novels, including *It's My Body*, which was awarded the Naguib Mahfouz Medal for Literature in 2002.

Peter Balakian's most recent book of poems is *June-tree: New and Selected Poems 1974–2000* (HarperCollins, 2001). His memoir, *Black Dog of Fate*, won the PEN/Martha Albrand Prize, and *The Burning Tigris: The Armenian Genocide and America's Response* won the Raphael Lemkin Prize.

'Abd-Allah al-Baraduni was born in 1929. He is a poet and literary historian from Baradun in North Yemen. He has published many books of criticism and more than eight collections of poetry, including *City of Tomorrow* and *A Time Without Quality*.

Salim Barakat is originally Kurdish, born in 1951 in Qamishli, Syria. He studied Arabic literature at Damascus University and traveled to Beirut, then to Nicosia where he was the associate editor of *Al Karmel* (where Mahmoud Darwish serves as the editor-in-chief) and then to Stockholm, Sweden. Barakat is the author of ten books of poetry, nine novels, two autobiographies, and a diary.

Mureed Barghouthy was born in 1944 in the village of Deir Ghassaneh, not far from Ramallah, and currently resides in Cairo. He is the author of thirteen books of poetry. Barghouthy won the American University of Cairo 1997 Naguib Mahfouz Medal for Literature for his autobiographical novel, *I Saw Ramallah,* and the 2000 Palestine Award in Poetry.

Rick Barot was born in the Philippines and grew up in the San Francisco Bay Area. *The Darker Fall* was published by Sarabande Books in 2002. He has received a Wallace E. Stegner Fellowship from Stanford University and a poetry fellowship from the National Endowment for the Arts. *Want* will be published by Sarabande in 2008.

Shiv Kumar Batalvi was born in Bara Pind Lohtian (Shakargarh tehsil), in Punjab (now Pakistan) in 1936. He was an acclaimed lyricist and author of a number of books, including *Peeran Da Paraga* (*A Handful of Pains,* 1960), *Atte Deean Shirian* (*The Sparrows of Kneaded Flour,* 1962), and *Loonan,* an epic verse play considered a Punjabi masterpiece. When it won the Sahitiya Academi Award in 1967, Shiv was the youngest person to have ever won the award. He passed away in 1973.

Abdul Wahab al-Bayati was born in Baghdad in 1926 and died in 1999. In 1953, he cofounded the magazine *Al-Thaqafa al-Jadidi* (*New Culture*). He translated different poets from the French into Arabic, including Louis Aragon and Paul Éluard. Al-Bayati is the author of more than twenty books of poetry.

Simin Behbahani was born in 1927 in Tehran. She was awarded the Human Rights Watch–Hellman/Hammett grant in 1998, the Carl von Ossietzky Medal in 1999 for her struggle for freedom of expression in Iran, and was nominated for the Nobel Prize in Literature in 1997. She is the author of more than ten books.

Bei Dao was born in Beijing in 1949. In 1978, he cofounded *Today* (*Jintian*), the first unofficial literary journal in China since 1949. His work has been translated into thirty languages, including English versions of five poetry volumes, a collection of stories, and two collections of essays.

Maya Bejerano was born in Israel in 1949. She has published eight volumes of poetry, a book of essays, and a collection of short stories. Among her awards are the Prime Minister Award, the Bernstein Award, and the Israel Prize. Bejerano lives in Tel Aviv where she works as a librarian and teaches poetry.

Sherko Bekes was born in Sulaymani, Iraq, in 1940. In the 1970s he led a new trend of Kurdish poetry representing new nationalist themes expressed in diverse forms and genres of prose poetry. Bekes spent many years in exile in Sweden. He is the author of more than twelve books of poetry.

Muhammed Bennis was born in 1948 in Fes, Morocco. He has published eleven books of poetry, four books of essays, and has translated books from French into

Arabic. He currently lectures at the College of Literature and Humanities in Rabat, and is the director of the House of Poetry in Morocco.

İlhan Berk was born in Manisa, Turkey, in 1918. His early poetry books of the 1940s owed much to the realist aesthetics of the Birinci Yeni, the First New Wave. However, from the 1950s onward, his voice grew more experimental. Berk's *Collected Poems* is more than three volumes long, spanning over half a century.

Mei-mei Berssenbrugge was born in Beijing and lives in rural New Mexico. Her book of selected poems, *I Love Artists,* was published by the University of California Press in 2006. A collaboration with artist Kiki Smith, *Concordance,* was published by the Rutgers Center for Innovative Paper and Print and in a trade edition from Kelsey Street Press.

Abbas Beydoun was born in 1945 in southern Lebanon. He is the author of one novel and more than eight books of poetry. Beydoun is the cultural editor of *Al-Safir,* a daily newspaper in Beirut.

Sujata Bhatt was born in Ahmedabad, India, and is a graduate of the Writers' Workshop at the University of Iowa. Her books include *Brunizem* (1988), which won the Alice Hunt Barlett prize and the Commonwealth Poetry Prize (Asia). *Monkey Shadows* (1991) was a Poetry Book Society recommendation. She received a Cholmondeley Award in 1991. She now lives in Bremen, Germany.

Buddhadhasa Bhikkhu was a Thai monk of the forest tradition, born in 1903, who founded the "Suan Mokh" (Garden of Liberation) reform movement. He received five honorary doctorates from Thai universities and published many books of poetry and prose, including *Extinction without Remainder* (1967), *Me and Mine* (1990), and *Heartwood of the Bodhi Tree* (1994). He passed away in 1993.

Walid Bitar was born in Beirut in 1961 and immigrated to Canada in 1969. He has taught English, most recently at Lebanese American University. His latest collection of poetry is *Bastardi Puri* (*The Porcupine's Quill,* 2005); his next collection, *The Empire's Missing Links,* will be published in 2008 (Signal Editions/ Vehicule Press).

Boey Kim Cheng was born in Singapore in 1965. He is now an Australian citizen and teaches creative writing at the University of Newcastle. He has published four collections of poetry: *Somewhere-Bound, Another Place, Days of No Name,* and *After the Fire: New* and *Selected Poems.*

Buddhadeva Bose was born in 1908 and became a prominent poet, translator, fiction writer, and dramatist. He was the founder and editor of *Kavita,* a platform for modernist poets and he introduced the academic discipline of comparative literature to India. His books include *The Book of Yudhisthir* (Sangam Books, 1986) and *Selected Poems of Buddhadeva Bose* (Oxford University Press, 2003).

Jenny Boully is the author of *[one love affair]** (Tarpaulin Sky Press, 2006) and *The Body* (Slope Editions, 2002). Her book *The Book of Beginnings and Endings* is forthcoming from Sarabande. Her work has been anthologized in *The Best American Poetry 2002, The Next American Essay,* and *Great American Prose Poems.*

Sargon Boulus is an Assyrian born in Iraq. He is a poet, short story writer, and translator. Boulus is the author of numerous books of poetry and has lived in many places, including Lebanon, Greece, Germany, England, and the United States.

Ravil Bukharaev was born in Kazan in 1951. He has published more than thirty books in Russian, English, his native Kazan Tatar, and Hungarian. Since 1992, he has been living in London. In 2005, he was awarded the M. Lomonosov Golden Medal for his contribution to Russian Arts, Science and Education and, in 2006, the State Prize of the Republic of Tatarstan for two of his latest collections of poetry.

Luis Cabalquinto was born in the Philippines and first came to the United States in 1968. He is the recipient of a poetry prize from the Academy of American Poets and a fellowship from The New York Foundation for the Arts, among others. His books include *Bridgeable Shores* (Kaya Press) and *Native Loam.* He divides his writing time between New York City and the Philippines.

Edip Cansever was born in Istanbul in 1928 and died in 1986. He opposed rigid forms and was a member of the İkinci Yeni movement. Cansever was the author of more than seventeen books of poetry.

Nick Carbó is the author of *El Grupo McDonald's* (1995), *Secret Asian Man* (2000), and *Andalusian Dawn* (2004) and the editor of *Returning a Borrowed Tongue* (1996), *Babaylan* (2000), and *Pinoy Poetics* (2004). Among his awards are fellowships from the New York Foundation for the Arts and the National Endowment for the Arts. He lives in Hollywood Beach, Florida, with his wife, the poet Denise Duhamel.

Priya Sarukkai Chabria is a poet and novelist. *Dialogue and Other Poems* (2005) was published by the Indian Academy of Literature. Her work is published or forthcoming in many journals, including *Alphabet City, Atlas,* and the *South Asian Review.*

G. S. Sharat Chandra was born in 1935 and died in 2000. *Family of Mirrors* was a 1993 Pulitzer Prize nominee for poetry. Author of ten books, including translations from Sanskrit and English into Kannada, he was a former Fulbright Fellow and recipient of an NEA Fellowship in Creative Writing.

Tina Chang is the author if *Half-Lit Houses*. Her poems have appeared in numerous journals and anthologies worldwide and she has received awards from the Academy of American Poets, the New York Foundation for the Arts, *Poets & Writers,* among many others. She teaches at Sarah Lawrence College and Hunter College.

Hayan Charara was born in Detroit, Michigan, in 1972. He is the author of *The Alchemist's Diary* (Hanging Loose Press, 2001) and *The Sadness of Others* (Carnegie Mellon, 2006). Charara currently lives in Austin, Texas.

Debjani Chatterjee, award-winning poet, translator, and children's writer, is a Royal Literary Fund Fellow, chair of the National Association of Writers in Education, and patron of Survivors' Poetry. Her many books include *Namaskar: New and Selected Poems* and *Masala: Poems from India, Bangladesh, Pakistan and Sri Lanka.*

Che Qianzi, a Chinese poet and ink wash painter, was originally named Gu Pan. Born in 1963 in Suzhou, he has settled in Beijing since 1998. Volumes in English translation include *Original: Chinese Language-Poetry Group* (1994), *Old Cultural Works* (2002), and *Vegetarian Hugging a Rooster* (Barque Press, 2002).

Andrée Chedid was born in 1921 in Cairo, of Syrian-Lebanese parents. Chedid has published more than nineteen collections of poetry, nine novels, five plays, and many other works. She has been awarded numerous prizes: The Royal Belgian Academy Grand Prize for French Literature (1975), the Mallarmé Award for Poetry (1976), and the Goncourt Prize (1979).

Chen Li was born in 1954 and raised in Hualian, on the east coast of Taiwan. He has published seven books of poetry. He is also a prolific translator who has translated the work of Neruda and Szymborska among other Latin American and eastern European poets into Chinese.

R. Cheran was born in 1958. His two early collections of poetry, together with an anthology of Sri Lankan Tamil resistance poems, *Maranatthul Valvom (Amidst Death We Live)*, are all landmarks of contemporary Tamil poetry. He is currently a professor of sociology at the University of Windsor, Canada.

Justin Chin is the author of *Harmless Medicine* and *Bite Hard* (Manic D Press) and two collections of essays, *Burden of Ashes* (Alyson Press) and *Mongrel: Essays, Diatribes + Pranks* (St. Martin's Press). *Harmless Medicine* was a poetry finalist at the 2002 Bay Area Book Reviewers Association Awards, the Lambda Literary Awards, the Publishing Triangle Award, and the Firecracker Alternative Book Awards.

Marilyn Chin is the author of *Dwarf Bamboo* and *The Phoenix Gone, The Terrace Empty. The Ballad of the Plain Yellow Girl* was published by Norton in 2002. She has won two NEA grants, the Stegner Fellowship, the PEN/Josephine Miles Award, four Pushcart Prizes, and a Fulbright Fellowship to Taiwan, among others.

She codirects the MFA program at San Diego State University. She is currently a Radcliffe Institute Fellow at Harvard.

Dilip Chitre was born in 1938 and he writes poetry in Marathi and English and translates both. He also paints, makes films, writes fiction and essays, and is the author of twenty-seven books. His work has been widely translated in and outside India. He has won many national and international awards and prizes.

Chuan Sha is a Chinese-Canadian writer, poet, and critic, and his work includes novels, short stories, poems, plays, essays, and literary reviews. A graduate of Sichuan University, he has lived in Toronto since 1999. Chuan Sha is now editor-in-chief of Canada's Poseidon Publishing House, director of the Chinese Canadian Poets Association, and a member of the Chinese Canadian PEN Society.

Fazil Hüsnü Dağlarca was born in 1914. He directed the Kitap publishing house and edited the journal *Türkçe* (1960–1964). He is the author of more than thirty-five books of poetry, plays, and children's books.

Ahmad Dahbour was born in Haifa in 1946. He has published more than eight collections of poetry, including *The Story of the Palestinian Boy, Mixing Night and Day*, and *Twenty-One Seas*.

Suresh Parshottamdas Dalal, born in 1932 in Mumbai, is a five-time recipient of the Gujarat Government Award for his contribution to Gujarati literature as well as many other important literary awards. In addition to directing a publishing house, he edits the Gujarati poetry journal *Kavita* and the literary quarterly *Vivecana*.

Sapardi Djoko Damono was born in Surakarta, Central Java, in 1940. He is a well-known poet, literary critic, and taught Indonesian language and literature at the University of Indonesia in Jakarta until his recent retirement. His poetry has been translated into numerous other languages.

Keki N. Daruwalla has published nine volumes of poetry and three collections of short stories. His *Collected Poems* has just been published by Penguin India. He is working on a novel. He retired as an Indian governmental secretary.

Mahmoud Darwish was born in 1941 in al-Birweh, Palestine. He is the author of twenty books of poetry and seven volumes of prose. His work has been translated into twenty-two languages. Darwish is the editor of the literary quarterly, *Al Karmel,* and divides his time between Ramallah and Amman. He received the 2001 Prize for Cultural Freedom from the Lannan Foundation.

Najwan Darwish was born in Jerusalem in 1978. Poet, writer, and editor, he studied law and works on different cultural projects. He published two books of poetry, parts of which were translated into French. He lives in Jerusalem.

Jibananda Das was born in 1899 and died in 1954. His volumes of poetry include *Jhara Palak* (*Fallen Feathers,* 1927), *Dhusar Pandulipi* (*Gray Manuscript,* 1936), *Banalata Sen* (1942), *Rupasi Bangla* (*Beautiful Bengal,* 1957), and *Bela Abela Kalbela* (1961). *Banalata Sen* received an award (1953) at the All Bengal Rabindra Literature Convention and he won the Sahitya Akademi Award in 1954.

Oliver de la Paz is the author of *Names Above Houses* (Southern Illinois University Press, 2001) and *Furious Lullaby* (Southern Illinois University Press, 2007). He is a cofounder of Kundiman, a not-for-profit organization committed to the discovery and cultivation of emerging Asian American poets. He teaches creative writing at Western Washington University.

Eunice de Souza was the head of the department of English at St. Xavier's College in Mumbai. She has written four books of poems and two novellas, as well as academic books and several books for children.

Brian Komei Dempster's poems have appeared in journals such as *New England Review, North American Review, Ploughshares, Prairie Schooner,* and *Quarterly West.* His work has been anthologized in *Asian American Poetry: The Next Generation* (2004) and *Screaming Monkeys: Critiques of Asian American Images* (2003).

Diana Der-Hovanessian is the author of twenty-two books of poetry and translations and the winner of numerous awards. She was a Fulbright Professor of American Poetry at Armenia's Yerevan State University in 1994 and 1999.

Tsering Wangmo Dhompa grew up in the Tibetan exile communities in Nepal and India and has studied at Delhi University, University of Massachusetts, and San Francisco State University. She lives and works in San Francisco. Tsering is the author of *Rules of the House* and *In the Absent Everyday* (Apogee Press).

K. Dhondup was born in Rupin Gang of upper Dromo, Tibet, in 1952 and died in 1995. After graduating from St. Joseph's College, Darjeeling, he joined the Library of Tibetan Works and Archives, Dharamshala. He was a poet, historian, and journalist. His works include *Songs of the 6th Dalai Lama, The Water-Bird and Other Years: A History of the 13th Dalai Lama and After,* and *Mystery of Tibetan Medicine.*

Farah Didi was born in the Maldives and now lives in the UK, where she completed her higher education. She has a PhD in politics and recently coedited the book *Women, Security, South Asia* under her maiden name, Faizal. Her poems have often appeared on the BBC.

Linh Dinh is the author of *Fake House* (2000), *Blood and Soap* (2004), *All Around What Empties Out* (2003), *American Tatts* (2005), and *Borderless Bodies* (2005). He is also the editor of *Night, Again: Contemporary Fiction from Vietnam* (1996) and *Three Vietnamese Poets* (2001), and translator of *Night, Fish, and Charlie Parker, the Poetry of Phan Nhiên Hạo* (Tupelo, 2006).

Chitra Banerjee Divakaruni's books include *Queen of Dreams, Sister of My Heart,* and *The Unknown Errors of Our Lives.* Her prizes include an American Book Award, a PEN/Josephine Miles Award, several Pushcart Prizes, and an Allen Ginsberg poetry award. She teaches in University of Houston's nationally ranked creative writing program.

Gregory Djanikian was born in Alexandria, Egypt, and immigrated to the United States when he was eight years old. He is the author of *The Man in the Middle, Falling Deeply into America,* and *About Distance,* among others. He directs the creative writing program at the University of Pennsylvania.

Jennifer Kwon Dobbs is the author of *Paper Pavilion,* which received the White Pine Press Poetry Prize (2007). Her work appears in *MiPOesias, The Cimarron Review, Crazyhorse, Poetry NZ,* among others and is anthologized in *Echoes Upon Echoes.* She is an Edwin Mem Fellow at the University of Southern California and lives in New York.

Dư Thị Hoàn was born in 1947 in Hai Phong into a family of Chinese origin. She is now the chief of the Poetry Committee of the Hai Phong Union of Literature and Art Associations. Her published works include *The Small Path, Genesis as Pre-School,* and *The Light Between.*

Rishma Dunlop's books include: *The Body of My Garden, Reading Like a Girl, Metropolis,* and the coedited *Red Silk: An Anthology of South Asian Canadian Women Poets.* She is a professor at York University, Toronto, and was poet-in-residence at the University of British Columbia, 2006–2007.

Amal Dunqul was born in 1940 and died in 1982. He was the author of six collections of poetry, including *The Coming of Testament* in 1975, which was one of his most important works.

Duo Duo, born as Li Shizheng in 1951 in Beijing, was one of the first to break Maoist poetic molds during the Cultural Revolution. His volumes in English include *The Boy Who Catches Wasps,* among others.

Ketaki Kushari Dyson was born in 1940, educated at Calcutta and Oxford, lives in England and has published thirty-three titles in Bengali and English in several different literary genres. She writes original poetry in both her languages and has published ten poetry collections as well as major works of poetry translation.

Noozar Elias (M. Azim) was born in 1958 in Herat, Afghanistan, where he graduated with a degree in law and political science from Kabul University in 1982.

During the early days of the Soviet occupation, he was active in the underground resistance. His Dari/Persian publications consist of three collections of poetry and a children's poetry book.

Gevorg Emin was born in 1919 and died in Yerevan, Armenia, in 1998. He is widely translated and the author of more than thirty books of poetry and prose.

Suyunbay Eraliev was born in 1921 and came from the Talkog region of Russia. He is the author of numerous books, and his best-known works include *Ak-Moor, To the Stars,* and *The Testament of Djalil Mirza.*

Ashur Etwebi was born in Libya in 1952. He has published four collections of poems, most recently *A Box of Old Laughs* (2005). His work is widely anthologized in the Arab-speaking world and Europe, including the *Anthology of Modern Arabic Poetry* (France).

Marjorie Evasco is originally from the island of Bohol in the Central Visayas of the Philippines and now resides and teaches in Manila. Her two collections of poetry, *Dreamweavers* and *Ochre Tones* have received the National Book Award for poetry for 1987 and 1999. She writes in English and in Cebuano-Visayan, her mother tongue.

Nissim Ezekiel was a poet, playwright, and art critic of Indian-Jewish descent. He published *The Unfinished Man* in 1960. He was the art critic of *The Times of India* (1964–1966) and was visiting professor at the University of Leeds and University of Chicago. His five books of poetry include *The Exact Name* (1965) and received awards, including the Sahitya Akademi Award in 1988 and the Padma Shri in 1988.

Gurbannazar Eziz is a Turkmen poet who was born in 1940 and died in 1975. He is considered one of Turkmenistan's leading poets, and English translations of his work have appeared in *World Literature Today.*

Muhammed al-Faituri was born in 1930. His father was a Sufi sheikh of Libyan Bedouin extraction and his mother was from a Gulf tribe that traced its lineage back to the Prophet Muhammad. The family moved to Alexandria, and later al-Faituri lived and worked as a journalist and writer in many countries, including Lebanon, Libya, and Sudan. He published numerous books of poetry.

Faiz Ahmed Faiz was born in pre-partition Punjab, in Sialkot, Pakistan. His first volume of poetry, *Naqsh-e-Faryadi,* came out in 1943, but his reputation was secured by the 1952 publication of *Dast-e Saba,* poems written during his imprisonment by the Pakistani government. Faiz was a nominee for the Nobel Prize in Literature and in 1963 was the first Asian poet to win the Lenin Peace Prize.

Saqi Farooqi is the pen name of Qazi Mohammad Shamshad Nabi Farooqi, born in 1936 in Gorakhpur, India. He emigrated to Pakistan in 1948 and to the UK in 1963. He has written six collections of Urdu poetry and one collection of English poetry.

Forugh Farrokhzad was born in 1935 in Tehran and died in 1967. Her poetry collections include *The Captive* (1955) and *Another Birth* (1963). She was also a filmmaker who directed the award-winning film, *The House in Black* (1962).

Yao Feng lectures in the Portuguese Department at the University of Macau. His books of poetry and poetry translation include *Selecta de Poetas Portugueses Contemporâneos* (1999) and *A Noite Deita-se Comigo* (2001). His poems have been selected for many poetry anthologies. He is also the editor of *Poesia Sino-Ocidental*.

Monica Ferrell is a former Wallace Stegner Fellow and a "Discovery"/*The Nation* contest prizewinner. She is an assistant professor in the creative writing program at SUNY Purchase. Her forthcoming books include a novel to be published by Dial Press in 2008 and a collection of poems, *Beasts for the Chase* (Sarabande Books, 2008).

Sesshu Foster grew up in East L.A., where he continues to teach literature and composition at Bravo Medical Magnet High School. He is the author of *City Terrace Field Manual* (Kaya, 1996) and other books.

Luis H. Francia is a poet, nonfiction writer, and teacher. His books include *Museum of Absences* (2004) and the semiautobiographical *Eye of the Fish: A Personal Archipelago* (2001), winner of the 2002 PEN Open Book and the 2002 Asian American Writers' Workshop Literary Award. He teaches at New York University.

Sylva Gaboudikian is the author of numerous books, including *With the Days, The Shores of the Ganges, This is My Country, My Intimates, Candid Conversation, Bon Voyage, Midway Meditations,* and *My Pages*.

Eric Gamalinda is the author of *Zero Gravity* (1999), which was awarded the Asian American Writers' Workshop Literary Award in 2000. He also coedited *Flippin': Filipinos on America* (1996). He has published fiction and poetry in the Philippines, including *My Sad Republic,* winner of the Philippine Centennial Award in 1998. He teaches at Columbia University. His new poetry collection is *Amigo Warfare*.

Sarah Gambito is the author of *Matadora* (Alice James Books). Her poems have appeared or are forthcoming in *The Iowa Review, The Antioch Review, Denver Quarterly, The New Republic, Field, Quarterly West, Fence,* and other journals.

Nujoum al-Ghanim's books of poetry include *The Evening of Paradise* and *Transgressions*.

Sankha Ghosh, born in 1932, is a Bengali poet who has published some sixty volumes, including sixteen volumes of poetry. He is a critic who has received many awards, including the Akademi Award and the Rabindra Puraskar. Besides English, his works have been translated into Hindi, Marathi, Punjabi, Asamiya, and Malayalam.

Muhammad al-Ghuzzi was born in 1949 in Qairwan, Tunisia. He has published three books of poetry and he is currently a professor at Tunis University.

Banira Giri, born in West Bengal in 1946, was the first woman to be awarded a PhD at Tribhuvan University, where she is currently associate professor. Her many books of poems and novels are widely popular in Nepal, and have been translated into several languages.

Eugene Gloria is the author of *Hoodlum Birds* (Penguin, 2006) and *Drivers at the Short-Time Motel* (Penguin, 2000), which was selected for the 1999 National Poetry Series and the 2001 Asian American Literary Award. He is an associate professor of English at DePauw University in Greencastle, Indiana.

Nirmalendu Goon was born in 1945 and is the author of more than thirty collections of poetry, twenty collections of prose, autobiographies, travelogues, and books for children and youth. Many of his awards include the Bangla Academy prize (1982) and the Ekushey Padak (2001), commemorating the martyrs of the Bengali Language Movement in 1952.

Yasmine Gooneratne, poet and critic, was born in Sri Lanka and educated there and at Cambridge (UK). She received the Order of Australia in 1990 for service to literature and education. Her twenty published books include four volumes of poetry, three novels, four literary biographies, essays, and a family memoir.

Abdullah Goran was born in 1904 in Halabja, in Kurdistan, and died in 1962. He spent many years in Iraqi state prisons because of his progressive ideas. He taught Kurdish language and literature at the College of Arts in Baghdad. He has published several books of poetry.

Gu Cheng was born in Beijing in 1956. He was a member of the Chinese Writers' Association and also lived as a swineherd and carpenter. He came to prominence during and after the 1978–79 liberalization. He is associated with a group of younger writers whose work has some affinities with Western modernism. Gu Cheng traveled a good deal in the West, returning to his adopted New Zealand shortly before his suicide on October 8, 1993.

Romesh Gunesekera was born in Sri Lanka and lives in London. His fourth novel, *The Match,* was published 2006; his first, *Reef,* was shortlisted for the Booker Prize. His other books are: *Heaven's Edge, The Sandglass,* and *Monkfish Moon.* He was recently elected a Fellow of the Royal Society of Literature and awarded a Sri Lankan national honor.

Toya Gurung, born in 1948 in Sindhupalchowk, Nepal, received her MA in Nepali at Tribhuvan University in Kathmandu. An award-winning poet with four published collections, she was one of the first women in Nepal's history to be elected a member of the Royal Nepal Academy, in 1999.

Gyalpo Tsering is an associate professor at the Tibet Academy of Social Sciences (TASS), where he is also vice director of the Institute of Religious Studies. He has also been a visiting professor at Vienna University, the University of Virginia (2000–01, 2004), and Harvard University (2003–04). He has many publications to his credit in Tibetan, Chinese, and English.

Asadullah Habib was born in 1941. He was a professor of literature in the Department of Language and Literature at the Kabul University, and also served as president of Kabul University for several years.

Qasim Haddad, born in 1948, is the head of the Union of Bahraini writers and has published more than seven collections of poetry, including *The Good Omen* and *Doomsday*.

Jessica Hagedorn is the author of *Dream Jungle, The Gangster of Love, Danger and Beauty,* and *Dogeaters,* a National Book Award finalist. She is also the editor of *Charlie Chan Is Dead: An Anthology of Contemporary Asian American Fiction,* volumes 1 and 2.

Kimiko Hahn's seven books of poems include *The Unbearable Heart,* which received an American Book Award, and *The Narrow Road to the Interior*. In the latter volume, she collects work inspired by the Japanese forms *tanka* and *zuihitsu;* the title comes from Bashō's famous poetic journal, *Okunohosomichi*. She is a Distinguished Professor at Queens College, City University of New York.

Unsi al-Haj was born in 1937 in Lebanon. He is the author of numerous books of poetry, including *Never* (1959), which established him as a well-known avant-garde poet. His other publications include *What Have You Made of the Gold, What Have You Done with the Rose* (1970).

Bassam Hajjar was born in Tyre, Lebanon. He is the author of more than ten books of poetry, and has translated numerous novels, poetry, and books of literary criticism from the French.

Jalal el-Hakmaoui is a poet and translator born in Casablanca in 1965 and currently living in Rabat. In the 1990s he cofounded the journal *Israft* (*Excess*), and currently edits the magazine *Electron Libre*. He is the author of two books of poetry.

Suheir Hammad is an original cast member of Russell Simmons Presents Def Poetry Jam. She is the author of three books, most recently *ZaatarDiva*.

Nathalie Handal is the author of numerous award-winning books and anthologies, including *The Lives of Rain* and *The Poetry of Arab Women: A Contemporary Anthology* (Academy of American Poets Bestseller and Winner of the PEN Oakland/Josephine Miles Award). She has been involved either as a writer, director, or producer in over twelve film and/or theatrical productions worldwide. She is currently working on the feature film *Gibran*.

Syed Shamsul Haq is a short story writer, playwright, novelist, and poet as well as film director, broadcaster, and journalist. He has published fifty books, including *Ekoda Ek Rajjey, Boishakhe Rochito Pongtimala,* and seventeen other anthologies. He has received the Bangla Academy Literary Award (1966) and the Ekushey Padok (1984).

Choman Hardi was born in Iraqi Kurdistan and grew up in Iraq and Iran before coming to the United Kindgom in 1993. She has published three collections of poetry in Kurdish, and *Life for Us* was her first English collection (Bloodaxe, 2004).

Cecep Syamsul Hari was born in Bandung, West Java, in 1967. His writing moves in a unique realm of fantasy and personal exploration. The poem translated here is from his anthology *Efrosina* (2002).

Anjum Hasan's first book of poems, *Street on the Hill,* appeared in 2006. Her poetry has been included in a number of of Indian anthologies and the American poetry journal *Fulcrum*. Her first novel appeared in 2007. She lives in Bangalore, India.

Alamgir Hashmi is a major Anglophone poet, scholar, and university professor. His eleven books of poetry include *The Poems of Alamgir Hashmi* (NBF, 1992) and *The Ramazan Libation* (Arc, 2003). Hashmi's work has won him many awards.

Samuel Hazo is the author of many books of poetry, fiction, essays, and plays. He is the director of the International Poetry Forum in Pittsburgh and McAnulty Distinguished Professor of English Emeritus at Duquesne University. He has been a National Book Award finalist.

Dorothea Rosa Herliany was born in Magelang, Central Java, in 1963. Her books include *Kill the Radio: Sebuah Radio Kumatikan* (2001) and her selected works, *Para Pembunuh Waktu* (2002). She is the director of IndonesiaTera, a nonprofit organization dedicated to social and cultural research, publication, and documentation, relating to culture, education, and social awareness.

Ahmad 'Abd al-Mu'ti Hijazi was born in 1935 in Egypt. He is the author of many books of poetry, including *City Without Heart* (1959).

Nâzim Hikmet was born in Salonika (now Thessaloniki, Greece). A political pris-
oner for eighteen years in Turkey, Hikmet was released in 1951 and spent the last
thirteen years of his life in exile, mainly in Eastern Europe. Many of his works
have been translated into English, including *Things I Didn't Know I Loved* (1975),
The Day Before Tomorrow (1972), *The Moscow Symphony* (1970), and *Selected
Poems* (1967).

Louise Ho is a Hong Kong English-language poet whose work has appeared in
anthologies and literary journals internationally. She has published two books of
poetry. A retired professor, she has taught Shakespeare and English/American poetry.

Cathy Park Hong's *Translating Mo'um* was published in 2002. Her second book,
Dance Dance Revolution, was chosen for the Barnard New Women Poets Prize and
was published by Norton in 2007. She's received a Fulbright Fellowship, an NEA
Fellowship, and a New York Foundation for the Arts Fellowship.

Hong Yun-suk was born in Chongju, Pyonganbuk-do (now North Korea) in 1925.
Since 1947 she has published many volumes of poetry and essays, as well as a col-
lection of poetic dramas. She has received many awards for her work. Her vision
of life is deeply affected by the suffering brought by the Korean War and the last-
ing division of Korea.

Garrett Hongo was born in Volcano, Hawai`i, and grew up in Los Angeles. His
work includes two books of poetry, three anthologies, *Volcano: A Memoir of Hawai`i*,
and a forthcoming volume of poems entitled *The North Shore*. He teaches at the
University of Oregon, where he is Distinguished Professor of Arts and Sciences.

Ranjit Hoskote is the author of four collections of poetry; most recently, of *Van-
ishing Acts: New & Selected Poems, 1985–2005* (Penguin, 2006). He has been a
fellow of the International Writing Program, University of Iowa (1995), and writer-
in-residence at Villa Waldberta, Munich (2003). His poems have appeared in Ger-
man translation as *Die Ankunft der Vögel* (Hanser, 2006).

Hsia Yü (sometimes spelled Xia Yu) was born and raised in Taiwan, but has spent
many years in France. She now lives in Taipei, where she makes her living as a lyri-
cist and translator. She is cofounder of the journal *On Time Poetry* and the author
of four volumes of verse.

Hung Hung (sometimes spelled Hong Hong) is a poet, translator, and director of
many plays, operas, and award-winning films. He lives in Taipei, where he coed-
its the avant-garde journal *On Time Poetry* and curates the Taipei International
Poetry Festival.

Adrian A. Husain was educated in Switzerland and England. Winner of the Guin-
ness Poetry (1st) Prize in 1968, he is the author of a book of verse, *Desert Album*

(Oxford University Press, Pakistan, 1997), and a critical work, *Politics and Genre in "Hamlet."*

Hữu Thỉnh was born in 1942 and currently lives in Hanoi, where he heads the Vietnam Writers' Association. During the war in Vietnam, he served as a tank driver and a journalist. He has also been editor of the literary journals of the army and the Writers' Association. His poems have been included in numerous anthologies and he has received several national prizes for his various collections of poetry.

Luisa A. Igloria (previously published as Maria Luisa Aguilar Carino) is associate professor on the faculty of the MFA Creative Writing Program at Old Dominion University. She has published nine books, including *In the Garden of the Three Islands* (1995) and the anthology *Not Home, But Here: Writing from the Filipino Diaspora* (2003). Her most recent publication is *Trill & Mordent* (2005).

Attilâ Ilhan was born in 1925 and died in 2005. He is the author of one short story book, eleven books of poetry, ten novels, twenty-one books of essays, and has also translated widely.

Ishigaki Rin was born in Akasaka in downtown Tokyo in 1920. From 1934 to 1975 she worked as a bank clerk and first became known as the "bank clerk poet." Her books of poetry include *In Front of Me the Pot* and *Ricepot and Burning Flames* (1959), *Nameplates etc.* (1968), *Brief CV* (1979), and *Soft Words* (1984), among others.

Kazi Nazrul Islam was born in 1899 and died in 1976. He was the "Rebel Poet" of Bengal and the National Poet of Bangladesh. He wrote twenty-five books of poetry, four thousand songs and ghazals, books of stories, translations, plays, operas, movie scripts, books of essays, and novels.

Abed Ismael was born in Lattakia, Syria, in 1963. He is a poet and translator, and teaches American literature at Damascus University. Ismael is the author of four books of poetry and thirteen books of translations from English into Arabic.

Jam Ismail was born and raised in the British crown colony of Hong Kong. Canadian publications include *sexions* (1984), 'from *diction air*' (1989), 'from *scared texts*' (1991), *jamelie-jamila project* (with Jamelie Hassan, 1992). Ismail currently lives in Hong Kong.

Hamid Ismailov was born in 1954 in Tokmak, Kyrgyzstan. He has published dozens of books in different languages. He was forced to flee Uzbekistan in 1992 and now lives and works in London.

Itō Hiromi was born in Tokyo in 1955. In the 1980s her distinctive poetic style created unprecedented interest in women's writing. She left Japan to live in the

United States in the early 1990s. In recent years she has established a strong reputation as a novelist.

Sally Ito has published two books of poetry, *Frogs in the Rain Barrel* and *Season of Mercy*, and a collection of short stories titled *Floating Shore*. She lives in Winnipeg, Canada.

'Enayat Jaber is a Lebanese poet, critic, film critic, and journalist, born in 1958. She works at the *Al-Safir* newspaper in Beirut. She has published more than six books of poetry and her work has appeared in many literary journals in the Arab world.

Hasab al-Shaikh Ja'far was born in 1942 in Iraq. He is the author of numerous collections of poetry, which include *Visit to the Sumerian Lady* (1974) and *In the Mirror Across the Wall* (1977).

Abdul Bari Jahani is a well-known Pashto poet and essayist, who has published three collections of poetry and essays, including *Da Sabawoon Pa Tama, Shpelai, Kohinoor*. He has also written a poem on which a version of the Afghanistan National Anthem is based. Many of Jahani's poems can be heard in song lyrics of contemporary Pashto music, including songs sung by the famous Pashto pop vocalist Nashenas.

Hatif Janabi was born in 1952 in Iraq, and in 1976 he left for Poland where he continues to live. He is the author of more than eight books of poetry, and numerous books of literary criticism. He is a member of Polish PEN.

Paolo Javier is the author of *60 lv bo(e)mbs* (O Books) and *the time at the end of this writing* (Ahadada), which received a Small Press Traffic Book Award. He lives in New York.

Salma Khadra Jayyusi is a poet, scholar, critic, and anthologist. She was born in 1926 in Salt, in East Jordan, of a Palestinian father and Lebanese mother. In 1980, she founded PROTA (Project of Translation from Arabic) in order to spread Arabic literature in the West. Through PROTA, she has edited more than thirty volumes, from single-author works to large anthologies.

Kadhim Jihad was born in the south of Iraq in 1955 and moved to Paris in 1976. He has translated numerous poets and writers into Arabic, including Jean Genet, Jacques Derrida, and Juan Goytisolo. He is the author of several collections of poetry.

Ha Jin grew up in Mainland China and came to the United States in 1985. He is currently a professor of English at Boston University. His books of poetry include *Between Silences* (1990), *Facing Shadows* (1996), and *Wreckage* (2001) as well as three volumes of short stories and five novels. *A Free Life* is his latest novel. Among his honors are the PEN/Hemingway Award, the National Book Award, the PEN/Faulkner Award, the Flannery O'Connor Award for Short Fiction, and others.

Lawrence Joseph's books of poetry include *Shouting at No One* (1982 winner of the Agnes Lynch Starrett Poetry Prize, University of Pittsburgh Press), *Curriculum Vitae,* and *Before Our Eyes.* He has also written a book of prose, *Lawyerland* (Farrar, Straus & Giroux).

Mohja Kahf is the author of *Emails from Scheherazad* (University of Central Florida Contemporary Poetry Series, 1999), which was nominated for the Paterson Prize, and the novel *Girl in the Tangerine Scarf* (Carroll & Graf, 2006).

Angkarn Kalayanaphong won the SEA Write Award for *A Poet's Pledge* in 1986 and was named Thailand's National Artist in Literature in 1989.

Sufia Kamal was born in 1911 and died in 1999. Kamal wrote twelve books of poetry as well as books of short stories, plays, novels, autobiographies, and travelogues. In addition to nearly fifty major awards in Bangladesh, Kamal received the Lenin Medal from the former Soviet Union and the Czechoslovakia Medal.

Amin Kamil was born in 1924 in Kaprin, a village in South Kashmir. He won the Sahitya Akademi Award in 1967 for his book of poems *Laveh Te Praveh.* His other collections include *Beyi Suy Paan* (*Again the Same Self,* 1967) and *Padis Pod Tshay* (*One Foot Shadowing the Other,* 1972).

Manju Kanchuli is the author of the short story collections *Some Love, Some Differences* and *Stories by Kanchuli,* and the poetry collections *My Life My World* and *Inside and Outside Eyelids.*

Fatma Kandil was born in 1958 in Cairo. She writes short stories and plays, and is the author of more than three books of poetry.

Bhanu Kapil teaches poetry and fiction at Naropa University's Jack Kerouac School of Disembodied Poetics in Boulder, Colorado. She is the author of *The Vertical Interrogation of Strangers* (Kelsey Street Press) and *Incubation: a space for monsters* (Leon Works). Currently, she is a British citizen of Punjabi heritage.

Dilawar Karadaghi was born in Sulaymani, Iraq, in 1963. He has published four books of poetry and a number of translations from Arabic. His last work is a book-length poem in collaboration with Nazand Begikhani, *The Colour of Land.*

Ziba Karbassi was born in 1974 in Tabriz, the capital of Iranian Azerbaijan. She now divides her time between London and Paris. Karbassi has published five volumes of poetry. She is the director of the Association of Iranian Writers in Exile.

Kyi May Kaung started writing poetry in 1992 when it became certain that she would never be returning to Burma. Kyi is the author of *Pelted with Petals: The Burmese Poems* and *Tibetan Tanka*, and has read poetry at universities, churches, libraries, and Burmese dissident meetings.

Suad al-Kawari is a Qatari poet born in 1965 in Bahrain. She is currently working in a cultural agency in Qatar. Her poetry collections include *Wrinkles* (1995), *It was not my soul* (2000), *A New Door to Enter* (2001).

Mohammad Kazem Kazemi was born in 1967 in Herat, Afghanistan, into a literary family. He moved with his family to Kabul at the age of seven, and then to Mashhad, Iran, in 1984. In 1988 he became active in refugee literary circles, and eventually took on a leading public role in literature and culture among Afghans in Iran. He has written and/or edited the following poetry books: *I Came on Foot, Morning in Chains*, and *A Tale of Stone and Brick*.

Yusuf al-Khal was born in Tripoli, Lebanon, in 1917. In 1948 he left for New York where he published a play in verse, *Herodias*. In 1955 he established *Shi'r*, a revolutionary poetry magazine in Lebanon. He is the author of many books, including *Poems at Forty*.

Ustad Khalilullah Khalili was born in 1905 and died in 1988. Khalili served as Afghan ambassador in a number of countries and held numerous official positions, including Secretary General and Minister of Information. As a key government official, Khalili used these opportunities to cultivate his relationships with poets and writers of Iran and Iraq. He published nearly fifty works of poetry, fiction, history, travel, and Sufism.

Harris Khalique was born in Karachi, Pakistan, in 1966 and started publishing in the 1990s. He writes poetry and nonfiction in both Urdu and English and has published seven collections of poetry, a book of essays, and many papers.

Masud Khan was born in Joypurhat, Bangladesh, in 1959. He emerged as an important poet of the 1980s, mainly through antiestablishment magazines. He has published three volumes of poetry including, *Pakhiteertha Dine* (1993), *Nadeekoole Kari Bas* (2001), and *Saraikhana o Kayekjan Harano Manush* (2006).

Waleed Khazindar was born in Gaza City in 1950. He was awarded the first Palestine Prize for Poetry in 1977, and in 1998–1999 he was Arab writer-in-residence at the Near Eastern Studies Program, Oxford University. Khazindar has published several collections of poetry.

Esmail Khoi is an Iranian poet living in exile. He is the author of numerous books, namely, *On the Galloping Stallion of Earth, On the Roof of Whirlwind, Of Those*

Seafarers, Beyond the Night of the Present, To Sit by the Seashore and Exist, and *We Who Existed.*

Vénus Khoury-Ghata was born in 1937 in Baabda, Lebanon, and has been living in France since 1973. She is the author of a dozen books of poetry and more than seven novels. She has won many prizes, namely, the Grand Prix de Poésie de la Ville de Paris, the Apollinaire Prize, the Mallarmé Prize, and the Grand Prix de la Poésie de la Société des gens de lettres de France (1993) for the totality of her poetic oeuvres.

Zareh Khrakhouni is an Armenian poet born in Turkey in 1926. He is considered one of the main proponents of modern literature in Western Armenian letters. He became director and editor of the literary and artistic supplement of the Armenian daily newspaper of Istanbul, *Marmara*. He is the author of twenty-six books that include poetry, prose essays, translations, and plays.

Marne L. Kilates is the author of *Children of the Snarl & Other Poems* (1987) and *Poems en Route* (1998), both of which have won the Manila Critics Circle National Book Awards. He has also won several Palanca Awards for his poetry and the 1998 SEA Write Award given by the Thai royalty. He has recently completed a new poetry collection, *Mostly in Monsoon Weather* (2006).

Kim Kwang-kyu was born in Seoul in 1941. He was professor in the German department at Hanyang University until he retired in 2006. In addition to publishing eight volumes of his own award-winning poems, he has translated many major German poems into Korean, including volumes by Heinrich Heine, Gunter Eich, and Bertolt Brecht.

Kim Nam-jo was born in Taegu, South Korea, in 1927. She has published numerous volumes of poetry and essays and has been awarded many major literary prizes. She served for a time as president of the Korean Poets' Association. For almost forty years, until her retirement in 1993, she was professor of Korean at Sukmyong Woman's University in Seoul.

Suji Kwock Kim was a prize winner in the "Discovery"/*The Nation* Contest. Her first book, *Notes from the Divided Country,* won the Walt Whitman Award from the Academy of American Poets, the Bay Area Book Reviewers Award, and was a finalist for the PEN/USA Award and the Griffin International Poetry Prize.

Kim Sŭng-hŭi was born in South Korea's South Cholla Province in 1952. His books include *Talgyal sok ui saeng* (*Life in the Egg,* 1989), among others, and a volume of fiction *Santa Fe ro kanun saram* (*People Going to Santa Fe,* 1997) as well as a book-length study of the work of Yi Sang in 1998.

Kim Su-yŏng was born in Seoul in 1921. His early poems were marked by modernism. In his lifetime, he only published one volume of poetry, in 1959. After his death in a car accident in 1968, further collections of poetry and his critical essays were published. His essays are particularly important manifestos arguing for a renewal of poetry and aesthetics.

Kitamura Tarō was born in Tokyo in 1922 and died in 1992. In 1951, he joined Ayukawa Nobuo and Tamura Ryuichi in founding the postwar poet group Arechi (Wasteland). His chief books of poems include *Poems of Kitamura Tarō* (1966) and *A Man of the Port* (1988).

Kitasono Katue was born in 1902 and died in 1978. Over a half century he experimented with a wide variety of visual poetry that he dubbed "Diagrammatical" (1929), "Concrete" (1957), and "Plastic" (1966). Leader of the VOU group of poets from 1936, he was the only Japanese poet known to the international avant-garde before World War II, and after the war he became the accepted theoretical leader of the emerging "concrete" poetry movement.

Joy Kogawa was born in 1935 and lives in Toronto and Vancouver, Canada. Her best-known work is the award-winning novel *Obasan* (Penguin Canada, 1983). She is also the author of *Itsuka* (Penguin Canada, 1993), *Naomi's Road* (Oxford University Press, 1986), and *The Rain Ascends* (Knopf Canada, 1995). A member of the Order of Canada, the City of Vancouver proclaimed November 6 as Joy Kogawa Day in 2004.

Koike Masayo was born in Tokyo in 1959. Her books of poetry include *I Began to Walk from the Water Town* (1988), *The Bus that Never Comes* (1997), which was awarded the 15th Gendaishi Hanatsubaki Prize (Modern Poetry Camellia Prize), and *The Most Sensuous Room* (2000), which was awarded the 30th Takami Jun Literary Prize. In 2003 Masayo's first selected poems appeared.

Mohan Koirālā was born in Nepal in 1928. Appointed in 1999 as the Upa Kulpati of the Royal Nepal Academy, Koirālā is the author of seven poetry collections, including *Lek, Sarangi Bokeko Samudra, Ritu Nimantran, Nilo Maha,* and *Euta Poplarko Paat* and one essay collection *Kabitabare Charcha.* Koirālā is also the recipient of the Madan Puraskar award and two Sajha Puraskar prizes.

Arun Kolatkar was born in 1932 and died in 2004. He wrote in Marathi and English, publishing collections, including *Jejuri* (1976), which won the Commonwealth Poetry Prize in 1977. He won the Kusumagraj Puraskar given by the Marathwada Sahitya Parishad in 1991 and the Bahinabai Puraskar given by Bahinabai Prathistan in 1995.

Ko Un was born in South Korea's North Cholla Province in 1933. Immensely prolific, he has published some 140 volumes. After years as a Buddhist monk he became known as a leading pro-democracy spokesman in the 1970s and 1980s. In recent years he has read his work in many countries to great acclaim and the poems in the *Maninbo* (*Ten Thousand Lives*) series have attracted special attention.

Ku Sang was born in Seoul in 1919. His first poems were written while he was a student in Japan, and he has steadily written and published volumes of poetry as well as essays on social, literary, and spiritual topics. He has also written a number of plays, and edited literary anthologies. Ku Sang's poems have been translated into French, English, German, and Japanese.

Abdellatif Laâbi founded the avant-garde journal *Souffles* (1966), which helped spark a literary renaissance in North Africa. He is the author of fourteen books of poetry, four novels, numerous plays, three children's books, and ten collections of essays. He is the recipient of many awards including the Albert Droin Prize from the Société des gens de lettres de France and the Freedom Prize from French PEN.

Agnes Lam teaches at the University of Macau and is the vice president of Macau PEN and a columnist on two dailies in Macao. Lam has published four books in Macao and mainland China; of these, two are collections of poems and two of nonfiction. Three of her poems won the Macao Literature Prize in the 1990s.

Agnes S. L. Lam was born in Hong Kong and later studied in Singapore and America. She is now an associate professor at the University of Hong Kong. Her two collections, *Woman to Woman and Other Poems* and *Water Wood Pure Splendour*, were published by Asia 2000.

Lâm Thị Mỹ Dạ lives in Hue, Vietnam. She has published five collections of poems and three books for children in Vietnam and has won several major prizes for poetry. *Green Rice,* a bilingual edition of her poems with translations by Martha Collins and Thuy Dinh, was published by Curbstone in 2005.

Wafaa' Lamrani was born in El Ksar El Kébir, a small city in the north of Morocco. She has participated in numerous festivals in Morocco, the Arab world, and Europe. She is the author of more than four collections of poetry.

Evelyn Lau is the author of *Runaway: Diary of a Street Kid* (1989), *Oedipal Dreams* (1992), nominated for a Governor General's Award, *In the House of Slaves* (1994), *Choose Me* (1999), and *Treble* (2005), among many other books. She currently lives in Vancouver.

Li-Young Lee is the author of four books of poems, the most recent of which is *Behind My Eyes* (Norton, 2008).

Joseph O. Legaspi's debut poetry collection, *Imago*, was published in 2007 by CavanKerry Press. A recipient of a 2001 poetry fellowship from the New York Foundation for the Arts, he is a founding member of Kundiman, a nonprofit organization serving Asian American poets.

Leong Liew Geok was born in 1947 and taught in the department of English language and literature, National University of Singapore. She edited *More Than Half the Sky: Creative Writings by Thirty Singaporean Women* (1998) and is the author of two volumes of poetry, *Love is Not Enough* (1991) and *Women Without Men* (2000).

Russell C. Leong, a poet, editor, and chen taichiquan practitioner, is the author of *The Country of Dreams and Dust* and a book of short fiction, *Phoenix Eyes and Other Stories* (University of Washington Press), which won the American Book Award and was translated and published in Taipei. He is the editor of *Amerasia Journal* and is an adjunct professor of English at UCLA.

Leung Ping-kwan is an essayist, novelist, poet, and cultural critic. He has published numerous poetry collections, including *City at the End of Time* and *Halfway—Selected Poems of Leung Ping-kwan*. He teaches comparative literature and film at the University of Hong Kong.

Shirley Geok-lin Lim's *Crossing the Peninsula* received the Commonwealth Poetry Prize. She has published four more poetry collections, two novels, three books of short stories, an award-winning memoir, two critical studies, and edited/coedited volumes, including *The Forbidden Stitch*, which received the 1990 American Book Award. She is currently professor of English at the University of California, Santa Barbara.

Tan Lin is an artist, writer, and cultural critic. He is the author of *Lotion Bullwhip Giraffe* and *BlipSoak01*. His video and artworks have been exhibited at the Marianne Boesky Gallery, the Drawing Center, the Yale Museum of Art, the Whitney Museum of American Art, and the Sophienholm Museum (Copenhagen). He is currently completing a novel entitled *ambience*.

Ling Yu was born in Taipei in 1952 and began writing poetry in the early 1980s. The author of four volumes of verse and a founding editor of *On Time Poetry*, she was a visiting scholar at Harvard University and an invitee to the Rotterdam 35th Poetry International Festival in 2004.

R. Zamora Linmark is the author of *Rolling The R's*, which he is currently adapting for the stage. He has just completed his first collection of poetry, *E.S.L.*, and a novel, *Leche*. He divides his time between Manila and San Francisco.

Liu Kexiang is a poet, nature writer, birder, historian, journalist, naturalist, and literary editor in Taiwan. In addition to several collections of poetry and novels, he is the author of dozens of books and articles on the natural history of Taiwan and Taiwan flora and fauna. He is the editor of the *China Times Literary Supplement* and is completing a wildlife survey of Ah-Li Mountain.

Timothy Liu is the author of six books of poems, most recently *Of Thee I Sing* and *For Dust Thou Art*. An associate professor of English at William Paterson University and a member of the core faculty in Bennington College's Graduate Writing Seminars, Liu lives in Manhattan.

Wing Tek Lum's first collection of poetry, *Expounding The Doubtful Points,* was published by Bamboo Ridge Press in 1987.

Luo Zhicheng was born in Taipei in 1955 and graduated from the Department of Philosophy of National Taiwan University. Active in Taiwanese media, including television and advertising, he is the publisher of the travel magazine *To Go* and an instructor at Soochow University. He has published five books of poetry, two books of prose, a volume of critical essays, and various translations.

Abdullah Habib al-Maaini is from Oman. His is the author of four collections of poetry and a book of short stories. His translations from English into Arabic of critical works on film, literature, and culture have appeared in many magazines. He also made five short films and is completing his PhD at UCLA's Film Critical Studies Program.

Rachida Madani was born in Tangier, Morocco, in 1951. She is the author of two books of poetry in French.

Muhammad al-Maghut was born in 1934 in al-Salamiyaa, Syria. He inspired many poets in the 1960s and 1970s with his vivid poetic vision. Al-Maghut along with Unsi al-Haj helped further modernize Arab poetics—putting forth new metrical expressions, new rhythms, and forms. He is the author of numerous books of poetry, plays, and satirical articles.

Jayanta Mahapatra was born in 1928. Physicist and poet, his honors include the Jacob Glatstein Prize for poetry (1975) and the Central Sahitya Akademi Award (1981) for his collection *Relationship*. He writes in English and Oriya, and edits the literary journal *Chandrabhaga*. He lives in Cuttack, India.

Fatima Mahmoud is a Libyan poet, writer, and journalist. She worked as a journalist in Libya from 1976 to 1987, and then moved to Cyprus and started a magazine focusing on Arab women's issues, for which she was the chief editor. In 1995, Mahmoud sought political asylum in Germany.

Al Mahmud was born in 1936. A Bengali poet, famed in both Bangladesh and India, he has published twenty-six books, including *Lok Lokantor* (1963), *Kaler*

Kalosh (1966), *Sonali Kabin* (1966), and *Mayabi Porda Dule Ottho* (1969). He has received eleven awards including the Bangla Academy Literary Award (1968).

Malathi Maitri was born in 1968. She has published three collections of poems. She is also a feminist activist and critic who belongs among the new wave of women poets. She lives in Pondicherry, India.

Lisa Suhair Majaj's poetry, creative prose, and academic articles have been published in a wide range of journals and anthologies. She has also published three collections of critical essays on Arab and third-world women. She now lives in Cyprus.

Issa Makhlouf is a poet and writer. He has published essays, criticism, and has translated the works of many Latin American and French writers into Arabic. He is the author of many books; *Mirages* is his first book published in France.

Nazik al-Mala'ika is a poet and critic, born in 1923 in Baghdad, Iraq. A pioneer in Arab literature, she broke away from the classical form of the Arabic *qasida*, leading the movement of modern Arabic verse. She is the author of seven volumes of verse and three volumes of criticism of Arabic poetry.

Firuza Mammadli was born in 1940 and graduated in philosophy at the Lenin Pedagogical Institute in Baku, Azerbaijan. She is the author of many books, including *Silver Drop, Spring Has Come My Way, Your Life,* and *A Span of Sublimity.*

Manjul was born in 1947 in Bhojpur district in the eastern hills of Nepal. He was a member of a folk-singing group protesting the feudal Panchayat regime. He is the author of a number of poetry collections, a work of fiction, and a travelogue.

Abd al-Aziz al-Maqalih is a poet and scholar who was born in 1939. He has published more than seven books of poetry and many books of literary criticism. He was the president of San'aa University, and he has been influencial in the literary and cultural movements in Yemen.

Edgar B. Maranan is a poet, essayist, fictionist, playwright, author of children's stories, translator, and former professor of Philippine Studies at the University of the Philippines Asian Center. He has won several first prizes in the Carlos Palanca Memorial Awards for Literature competition and a place in its Hall of Fame. He has also won major awards in other Philippine literary competitions.

B. S. Mardhekar was educated in Bombay and at King's College, London. He was the first "modernist" in Marathi, and his experimental poetry and fiction and theoretical work in aesthetics were influential for several decades. He published many collections, including *Shishiraagam.*

Monzer Masri is a poet and painter from Lattakia, Syria. He is the author of two books of poetry and two collections of short stories.

Khaled Mattawa was born in Libya in 1964. He is the author of *Ismailia Eclipse* and *Zodiac of Echoes*. He has also translated the works of many Arab poets into English. His awards include a Guggenheim Fellowship, an NEA translation grant, and the PEN American Center's 2003 Award for Poetry in Translation.

Bejan Matur was born to an Alevi Kurdish family in 1968 in the ancient Hittite city of Maraþin southeast Turkey. Her first book, *Rüzgar Dolu Konaklar* (1996), unrelated to the contemporary mainstream of Turkish poets and poetry, won several literary prizes. Matur went on to publish three more books of poetry.

Medaksé was born in Artig, Armenia, in 1929. She is the author of many books of poetry, and she is known as an extraordinary performance poet.

Saksiri Meesomsueb was born in 1957 in Chainat, Thailand, and studied poetry and philosophy before beginning to write poems in earnest. His books include *Tukta Roisai* (*Sand Trace Doll*) and *Mue Nan See Khao* (*That Hand is White*), which won the prestigious SEA Write Award in 1992.

Arvind Krishna Mehrotra was born in Lahore, Pakistan, in 1947. He is the author of four books of poems, the most recent of which is *The Transfiguring Places* (1998). His edited books include the *Oxford India Anthology of Twelve Modern Indian Poets* (1992) and *History of Indian Literature in English* (2003).

D. H. Melhem is the author of numerous books including *Stigma & The Cave, New York Poems, Blight,* and *Gwendolyn Brooks: Heroism in the New Black Poetry.* She has also edited two anthologies and published more than sixty essays. She is the recipient of many awards, including the American Book Award.

Meng Lang was founding editor of *Haishang,* an underground poetry journal in Shanghai during the 1980s. His books include *One Living in This Century, Even the Sunrise Is Stale,* and *A Child in the Sky.* In 1995 he came to America under the Freedom to Write Program at Brown University. He is the cofounder of the Independent Chinese PEN Center in New York. He now divides his time between Hong Kong and Boston.

Roy Miki is a writer, poet, and teacher who lives in Vancouver. His third book of poems, *Surrender* (Mercury Press, 2001), received the 2002 Governor General's Award for Poetry. *Redress: Inside the Japanese Canadian Call for Justice* (Raincoast, 2004) examines the Japanese Canadian redress movement. His latest book of poems, *There,* is available from New Star Books (2006).

Goenawan Mohamad was born in Central Java in 1941. He is a cofounder and former editor-in-chief of *Tempo,* Indonesia's most popular newsweekly and the author of several collections of essays and poems. He has been honored both at home and abroad for his support for freedom of speech.

Nacera Mohammadi was born in 1969. She is an Algerian poet, journalist, and radio broadcaster. Her work has been published in various Arabic magazines, and her poetry collections include *Gypsy* (2000) and *A Black Cup* (2002).

Mộng-Lan was born in Vietnam and left her native country on the last day of evacuation of Saigon in 1975. Her books include *Song of the Cicadas* and *Why Is the Edge Always Windy?* Honors include inclusion in Best American Poetry Anthology and Pushcart Prize anthology, a Stegner Fellowship at Stanford University, and a Fulbright grant to Vietnam. She lives in Tokyo, Japan.

Dom Moraes was born in Bombay in 1938. At Oxford, he received the Hawthornden Prize for *A Beginning* (1957) at the age of nineteen. He cowrote several books with Sarayu Srivatsa Ahuja, his companion and coauthor. He published three volumes of poetry in the years before he died in 2003.

Granaz Moussavi was born in 1974 in Tehran. She has made four short films, one of which won the Best Director Award at Flinders. Her second book, *Barefoot Till Morning,* was the winner of the literary journal *Karnameh*'s Best Poetry Book of the Year Award in 2001 and is currently in its third printing.

Sa'adyya Muffareh is a poet, critic, and journalist from Kuwait. She has published several books of poetry, namely *He Was the Last of Dreamers, When You Are Absent, I Saddle the Horses of My Suspicions, Book of Sins,* and *Only A Mirror Lying Back.*

Zakariyya Muhammad was born in Nablus, Palestine, in 1951. He studied in Baghdad, and then went to Jordan where he worked as a journalist. He is the author of several books.

Sarat Kumar Mukhopadhyay has published eleven books of poems as well as novels, short story collections, essays, and translations, and his work has received considerable acclaim. He lives in Calcutta with his wife, the poet Vijaya Mukhopadhyay.

Kamaran Mukri was born in Sulaymani, Iraq, in 1927 and died in 1986. He was a romantic revolutionary poet who took poetry to the streets. He spent years in Iraqi state prisons for his nationalist activities. He taught Kurdish language and literature at Sulaymani University and published five collections of poetry.

Lale Müldür was born in 1956. She is one of the central figures of the poetic movement of the 1990s in Turkey called the Poetry of Motion. Her books of poetry include *The Far Storm, Voyager II, The Book of Series, Notebooks of the North, Virgin Mary's Smile, The Turkish Book of Poems, Hours/Deer, Anemone: Collected Poems, 1988–1998,* and her latest, *ultra-sound in ultra-zone.*

Partaw Naderi was born in Badakhshan, Afghanistan, in 1953. He has published five poetry collections and several prose books on modern Afghan literature. Naderi has edited *Zhwandoon Quarterly Magazine,* directed the Art and Cultural Programs for Radio Afghanistan, and returned from exile to become president of Afghan PEN.

Nader Naderpour was born in 1929. He was educated in Tehran, Paris, and Rome. His later work, until his death in Los Angeles in 2000, focuses on the experience of exile.

Kishwar Naheed has written nine volumes of poetry, two memoirs, and a travel narrative; she has also translated poetry from other languages into Urdu and has edited essay collections about women's roles in literature and society. *The Distance of a Shout* is the latest translation of her work.

Rukmini Bhaya Nair is a professor at the Indian Institute of Technology, Delhi, and has taught at universities around the world from Singapore to Stanford. Nair says she writes poetry for the same reason that she does research in cognitive linguistics—to discover the limits of language. Her books of poetry include *The Hyoid Bone, The Ayodhya Cantos,* and *Yellow Hibiscus* (Penguin, 1992, 1999, and 2004).

Hassan Najmi was born in 1959 in Morocco. He cofounded the House of Poetry in Casablanca. He is the author of a collection of essays, two novels, and five books of poetry. Najmi currently lives in Rabat and is the president of the Moroccan Writers' Union.

Prathibha Nandakumar is a poet, translator, journalist, columnist, and activist who writes in Kannada and English. She has published seven collections of poems, two collections of short stories, two collections of essays, and two collections of column writings. She has won many awards and her work has appeared in several anthologies, including the *Chicago Review, Penguin Book of Contemporary Indian Writers,* and *Indian Literature.*

Kunwar Narain was born in Faizabad (Uttar Pradesh) in 1927. He has published six collections of poetry, short stories, literary criticism, plays, and translations of Cavafy and Borges into Hindi. He has been translated in many languages; his honors include the prestigious Hindustani Academy and the Sahitya Academy awards.

Vivek Narayanan's first book of poems, *Universal Beach,* was published by Harbour Line, Mumbai, in 2006. He was born in Ranchi, India, in 1972, grew up in

Zambia, and studied in the United States. He is currently based in Delhi, where he works at Sarai-CSDS, an organization that brings together visual artists, social scientists, writers, and others to reflect on new and old media forms and the city.

Taslima Nasrin, a Bangladeshi author of essays, poetry, and novels, fled her native country when religious fundamentalists arranged a fatwa for her having written *Lajja*. A fighter for women's rights, she, of necessity, lives in Sweden, the United States, and India.

Amjad Nasser was born in 1955. He is the author of more than eight books of poetry and one travel book. Nasser is the Arts and managing editor of *Al Quds Al-Arabi* in London.

Latif Nazemi was born in 1947 in Herat, Afghanistan, and he was one of the vanguard who helped modernize Persian poetry, publishing three collections and appearing in an important anthology of Persian poetry published in Kabul in 1962. He taught literature in many places, including Hambolt University in Germany.

Behçet Necatigil was born in 1916 and died in 1979. He published radio plays, essays, and fifteen books of poetry. His work combined local culture and Western traditions.

Aimee Nezhukumatathil is the author of *At the Drive-In Volcano* and *Miracle Fruit* (both from Tupelo Press). She is associate professor of English at State University of New York–Fredonia where she is the recipient of the Hagan Young Scholar Award and the Chancellor's Medal for Scholarship and Creative Activities.

Nguyễn Duy, born in 1948, now lives in Ho Chi Minh City. Among his published works are ten collections of poetry, three memoirs, and a novel. Among his awards are the *Van Nghe* poetry prize in 1973 and the poetry prize of the Vietnam Writers' Association in 1985.

Nguyễn Quang Thiều, born in 1957, is the poetry editor of *Van Nghe Weekly* in Vietnam. He has published seven books of poetry, five books of short stories, four novels, four books for children, three books of translations, and around two hundred articles and essays. His awards include The Poetry Award of The Writers Association of Vietnam.

Bimal Nibha was among the young poets opposing the Panchayat era, and is now one of the chroniclers of the ongoing struggle for democracy in Nepal. His first collection of poems was *Aagonira Ubhieko Machhe*; he was featured in *Himalayan Voices: An Introduction to Modern Nepali Literature*, edited by Michael James Hutt. He currently writes satire in the print media in Kathmandu.

Partow Nooriala, an Iranian poet, writer, and literary critic, was born in Tehran. She has published four books of poetry, a collection of critiques, a collection of short stories, and a play.

Naomi Shihab Nye was born in St. Louis, Missouri, in 1952, and currently lives in San Antonio, Texas. She is the author and/or editor of more than twenty volumes and has won numerous awards, including a Lavan Award from the Academy of American Poets and four Pushcart Prizes.

Michael Ondaatje was born in Sri Lanka, went to school in England, then moved to Canada. He is the author of four collections of poetry, works of nonfiction, and five novels, including *The English Patient*, which was later made into an Academy Award–winning film. He has won the Booker Prize, the Kiriyama Pacific Rim Book Prize, the Prix Medicis, the Governor General's Award, and the Giller Prize.

Ōoka Makoto was born in 1931. He has published more than two hundred books of poetry, art, and literary criticism, plays, movie screenplays, operas, and expository writing. His work has earned him awards, both in Japan and internationally, and his poetry has been translated into several languages. A translator of Paul Éluard, Ōoka sometimes infuses his work with the techniques of French symbolism, surrealism, and dadaism.

Amir Or was born in Tel Aviv in 1956. He is the cofounder and editor of the literary journal *Helikon*. He has won many awards and has published five volumes of poetry, two books of translations, and numerous papers, articles, and essays on literature, philosophy, and the classics.

Ouyang Yu, originally from China, now an Australian citizen, writes in both English and Chinese and has had thirty-six books published in the fields of fiction, poetry, literary translation, and literary criticism in both languages. He is now professor of English in the department of English at Wuhan University, China.

Bibhu Padhi, born in 1951, has published five books of poems and a chapbook of poems on D. H. Lawrence. His poems have appeared in distinguished magazines throughout the English-speaking world, such as *New Criterion, Poetry, TriQuarterly,* and *The Poetry Review,* and in several anthologies.

Dan Pagis was born in Bukovina, a German-speaking province of the Austro-Hungarian Empire in 1930. He published six volumes of poetry, a children's book, and studies on the aesthetics of medieval poetry.

Pak Chaesam was born in 1933 in Tokyo, Japan, and attended Korea University. His first book of poems, *The Mind of Chunhyang,* was published in 1962. His other books include *In the Sunshine* (1970), *A Thousand Year-old Wind* (1975), *Besides the Young*

Ones (1976), *The Autumn Tree Listening to the Rain* (1981), *My Love* (1985), *An Autumn River In Tears Afire* (1987), and *The Trace of the Sun and the Moon* (1990).

Rajinderpal S. Pal is the author of two collections of poetry: *pappaji wrote poetry in a language i cannot read* (TSAR, 1998) and *pulse* (Arsenal Pulp Press, 2002). He lives in Vancouver, British Columbia.

Ngodup Paljor, born in Tibet in 1948, was a refugee, monk, and student and was fluent in Tibetan, Hindi, Sanskrit, Pali, Thai, and English. He served as a translator for His Holiness the Dalai Lama and was an assistant professor of Tibetan studies at the University of Hawaìi. His poems are collected in *Muses in Exile—An Anthology of Tibetan Poetry,* edited by Bhuchung D. Sonam.

Rajendra Kishore Panda was born in 1944. He has published sixteen poetry collections, one novel, and has edited several anthologies and journals. He is the recipient of many awards, including the Sahitya Akademi Award (National Academy of Letters, India).

Alvin Pang is a poet and editor from Singapore. His writing has been featured in major publications, productions, and festivals around the world. A Fellow in Writing from the University of Iowa's International Writing Program, his latest volume is *City of Rain* (Ethos Books, Singapore, 2003).

Ishle Yi Park is a Korean American woman who is the poet laureate of Queens, New York. Her first book, *The Temperature of This Water,* was a winner of the PEN America Beyond Margins Award in 2005.

R. Parthasarathy is an Indian poet and translator whose works include *Rough Passage, Ten Twentieth-Century Indian Poets,* and *The Tale of an Anklet: An Epic of South India,* which received the National Academy of Letters Translation Prize in 1996. He teaches Indian literature at Skidmore College, Saratoga Springs, New York.

Gieve Patel has published three books of verse: *Poems* (1966), *How do you withstand, body* (1976), and *Mirrored, mirroring* (1991), the last published by Oxford University Press India. He has also written three plays. A volume of his collected plays published by Seagull Books, Calcutta, appeared in 2007.

Dorji Penjore studied literature in Sherubtse College, Bhutan, and anthropology in Australia. His compilation of Bhutanese folktales *Was it a Yeti or a Deity?* was published in 2005. He is a contributing editor to the Foundation of South Asian Association for Regional Cooperation (SAARC) Writers and Literature.

Phạm Tiến Duật, born in 1941, was seen by many as the poet of the war, as he traveled through the Truong Son mountains, living among the troops, following them into battle, hiding with them in caves during bombing raids, reading poems to them at night. He is the author of many books of poetry and is the deputy head of external relations of the Vietnam Writers' Association.

Phan Nhiên Hạo, born in 1967 in Kontum, Vietnam, immigrated to the United States in 1991, and now lives in Illinois. He is the author of *Paradise of Paper Bells* (1998) and *Manufacturing Poetry 99–04* (2004). His poems have been translated into English and published in *Of Vietnam: Identities in Dialogues* (2001) and in a bilingual collection, *Night, Fish and Charlie Parker, the Poetry of Phan Nhiên Hạo* (Tupelo 2006).

Jon Pineda is the author of *The Translator's Diary* (New Issues Poetry & Prose, 2008), winner of the 2007 Green Rose Prize in Poetry, and *Birthmark* (Southern Illinois University Press, 2004), winner of the 2003 Crab Orchard Award Series in Poetry Open Competition.

Chin Woon Ping, born in Malaysia, has published poetry, plays, critical essays, and translations and performed her work in the United States, Australia, Canada, and Southeast Asia. Her work has been anthologized in *Asian American Literature, Women's Inspirations, Westerly Looks to Asia, Women Write for the Singapore Stage, The City and You,* and *Literature.* She teaches at Dartmouth College and lives in Vermont.

Joko Pinurbo was born in West Java in 1962. He is a contributor of essays and poems to numerous national publications and is the recipient of several national literary awards. He is the author of *Trouser Doll: Selected Poems 1989–1998*, translated by Linda Owens and Harry Aveling.

H. S. Shiva Prakash was born in 1954. Kannada poet and playwright, he is the author of six books of poems, twelve plays, and is the winner of many state and national literary awards. Presently, he is an associate professor at the School of Arts and Aesthetics, Jawaharlal Nehru University, New Delhi.

Amrita Pritam was born in 1919 and died in 2005. A poet, novelist, and short story writer, she published *Nagmani*. She was the first woman recipient of the Sahitya Akademi Award and the first Punjabi woman to receive the Padma Shree from the president of India.

Nizar Qabbani was born in Damascus, Syria, in 1923. He has published more than fifty books of poetry and has won many awards. His work has been translated into Spanish, French, Russian, Persian, and Italian, among other languages.

Samih al-Qasim is the author of over thirty books of poetry. The first English collection of his work, *Sadder Than Water,* was published by Ibis Editions in 2006. He lives in the Galilee village of Rama.

Rafiq Raaz was born in Srinagar (Jammu and Kashmir) in 1950. He studied Urdu literature at Kashmir University. He has published two collections of poems in Kashmiri and one in Urdu. He is deputy director of All India Radio Srinagar. Rafiq won the Sahitya Academy Award for his first collection of poems.

Al-Saddiq al-Raddi is widely admired for the delicacy of his tone and his understated lyricism. He has published three books of poetry.

Taufiq Rafat was born in 1927 in Sialkot, Punjab, and died in 1998. Rafat's major work *Arrival of the Monsoon: Collected Poems 1947–1978*, which contains 150 poems, was published in Lahore in 1985.

Mohammad Rafiq was born in 1923 in a village near Bagerhat in East Bengal (now Bangladesh). The author of more than a dozen volumes of poetry and prose, Rafiq has earned major literary awards in his country, including the Bangla Academy Award. He has taught in the English Department at Jahangirnagar University in Savar, Bangladesh, for many years.

Saif al-Rahbi is a poet and journalist born in 1956 in Masqat, Oman. He is editor-in-chief of *Nizwa* and the author of numerous books of poetry, prose, and essays.

Rahman Rahi was born in Srinagar (Jammu and Kashmir) in 1925. He studied Persian and English Literature at Kashmir University where he later became professor of Kashmiri. He has published two collections of poems and two books of literary criticism. Rahi has received the Sahitya Academi and Padma Shree national awards.

Shamsur Rahman was born in 1929 and died in 2006. He published more than sixty volumes of poetry, in addition to collected essays, memoirs, translations, and juvenile literature. He received the nation's most prestigious awards, including the Bangla Academy prize and the Ekushey Padak.

Abd el-Monem Ramadan was born in 1951 in Cairo, where he continues to live. His work has appeared in English in *Jedat.com* and several anthologies. He is the author of more than three collections of poetry, including *Away from Beings*.

A. K. Ramanujan was born in Mysore, India, in 1929 and came to the United States in 1959, where he remained until his death in 1993. He taught at several American universities, including Harvard and the University of Chicago, where he was instrumental in shaping the South Asian Studies program. In 1976, the government of India awarded him the honorific title "Padma Sri," and in 1983, he was given a MacArthur Fellowship.

Eva Ranaweera is one of Sri Lanka's leading feminist poets and her most recent collection, *Blissfully*, came out with Hitech Prints in 2000. She is the founder of Voice of Women, a Sri Lankan women's rights organization.

Mani Rao's poetry is in seven collections, anthologies, and journals, including *Wasafiri, Meanjin, West Coast Line, The Iowa Review.* She has been featured at festivals, including PEN World Voices 2006, was a visiting fellow at the 2006 Iowa IWP and their 2006 writer-in-residence, and cofounded Hong Kong's OutLoud. She lives in Hong Kong and India.

Dahlia Ravikovitch was born in 1936. She published seven volumes of poetry, a collection of short stories, and two books of poetry for children. Some of her awards include the Prime Minister Award, the Shlonsky Award, the Brenner Award, and the Bialik Award.

Bino A. Realuyo was born and raised in Manila, the son of a survivor of the Bataan Death March and a World War II Japanese concentration camp in the Philippines. He is the author of the novel *The Umbrella Country* (Random House/BRC, 1999) and *The Gods We Worship Live Next Door,* winner of the 2005 Agha Shahid Ali Prize in Poetry (University of Utah Press, 2006).

Srikanth Reddy's first collection of poetry, *Facts for Visitors,* received the Asian American Literary Award for poetry in 2005. His work has appeared in various journals, including *APR, Fence, Grand Street, jubilat,* and *A Public Space.* Reddy is an assistant professor of English at the University of Chicago.

Oktay Rifat was born in 1914 and died in 1988. At the forefront of modern Turkish poetry since the late 1930s, he is the author of more than twenty books, including poetry, fiction, plays, and translated works.

Taher Riyad was born in Amman, Jordan. He is the author of several books of poetry and has translated numerous books from English into Arabic.

Fehmida Riyaz started the first women's publishing house in Pakistan. She launched a magazine, *Awaz,* and was exiled from Pakistan by Zia ul-Haq for her liberal views regarding Muslim women. She has published two collections of prose, *Pathar ki Zaban* and *Khatt-e Marmuz,* and a book of prose poems.

Patrick Rosal is the author of *My American Kundiman* (Persea Books, 2006) and *Uprock Headspin Scramble and Dive* (2003), winner of the Asian American Writers' Workshop Members' Choice Award. His chapbook, *Uncommon Denominators,* won the Palanquin Poetry Series Award from the University of South Carolina, Aiken.

Wadih Sa'adeh was born in the village of Shabtin, in northern Lebanon. He has lived in England, France, Cyprus, and Greece, and currently lives in Australia. He is the author of numerous volumes of poetry.

Salah 'Abd al-Sabur was born in 1931 and died in 1981. The author of many plays and poetry books, he was considered one of the most "modern" of the contemporary Arab poets.

Amina Saïd was born in Tunis in 1953, of a Tunisian father and French mother. She has published more than eight volumes of poetry, and two of them received prizes. She resides in Paris, where she works as a journalist.

Bashir Sakhawarz has written prose and poetry books in both Persian/Dari and English, and currently he lives in England. He has a PhD from Jamia Milia University, India.

Saniyya Saleh was born in Misyaf in northern Syria in 1935 and died in 1985. She is the author of two books of poetry: *al-Zaman al-Dayyeq* (*Straitened Times*; Beirut, 1964) and *Hibr al-l'dam* (*The Ink of Execution*; Damascus, 1970), which received the first prize for women's poetry from *al-Hasna'*, a woman's magazine.

Hilmy Salem was born in 1951. Poet, writer, and cultural journalist, he published fourteen collections of poetry and more than six books of literary criticism. He is the editorial director of the literary magazine *Adab wa Naqd,* in Cairo.

Muhammad Haji Salleh is a poet, critic, editor, and translator in Malay and English. He has published ten collections of poems and more than thirty books of criticism and translation, including *Beyond the Archipelago* and *Romance and Laughter in the Archipelago,* and has been awarded the Malaysian Literary Award and the Southeast Asian Literary Prize.

Sasaki Mikiro was born in 1947 in Nara Prefecture and brought up in Osaka. His first book of poems, *Whiplash of the Dead,* appeared in 1970. Since then he has published numerous other volumes of poetry, essays, and criticism.

K. Satchidanandan, the Indian poet, critic, and translator, was born in 1946. He headed the National Academy of Literature in India and has written in English and Malayalam twenty-one collections of poetry, fifteen collections of essays and travelogues, fifteen works of translations of world poetry, one full-length play, and one collection of short plays. His work has been translated into several languages.

Viswanatha Satyanarayana was born in 1895 and died in 1976. He was a prolific writer of epics, novels, poems, short stories, plays, and literary criticism. Satyanarayana wrote in a classical style, vigorously defended Brahminic ideology but powerfully depicted modern sensibilities.

Badr Shakir al-Sayyab was born in Iraq in 1924 and died in 1964. He, along with Nazik al-Malai'ka, started the free verse movement in Arabic poetry. Their revolutionary experiment in Arab poetics in the 1950s made them pioneers and changed

Arab poetry. Al-Sayyab published seven books of poetry.

Sudeep Sen's award-winning books include: *Postmarked India: New & Selected Poems* (HarperCollins, 1997), *Distracted Geographies, Prayer Flag,* and *Rain.* He has written for the *TLS, The Guardian, The Independent, The Observer, The Herald, The London Magazine, Literary Review,* and BBC. He has been a visiting scholar at Harvard University, and is an associate editor of the *Paris Review,* editor of *Atlas,* and editorial director of Aark Arts.

M. A. Sepanlu was born in Tehran in 1940. His fourth collection, *Sidewalks* (1968), snapshots of life as lived in Tehran's older quarters, marked him as a keen observer of everyday life.

Sohrab Sepehri was born in Kashan, Iran, in 1928. He is the author of two collections of poetry, *The Green Volume* and *The Sound of Water's Footstep.*

Vijay Seshadri was born in Bangalore in 1954 and came to America at the age of five. He grew up in the Midwest and has lived in many parts of the country. His poems and essays have been widely published and anthologized. He teaches at Sarah Lawrence College and resides in Brooklyn with his wife and son.

Rajee Seth was born in 1935 in Nowshehra, NWFP (now in Pakistan). She has five collections of short stories and two novels to her credit, and a "Collected Poems" is forthcoming. She is also well known for her translations of Rilke into Hindi.

Vikram Seth was born in India in 1952 and educated there and in England, California, and China. He has written six books in various genres: *The Golden Gate* (verse novel), *From Heaven Lake* (travel), *Beastly Tales* (fable), *A Suitable Boy* (epic), *An Equal Music* (novel), and *Two Lives* (family biography). He lives in London and Salisbury.

Barouyr Sevag was born in 1924, in the village of Sovedashen, Armenia. From 1963 to his death in 1972, he was senior researcher for the Literature Institute of the Academy of Sciences of Armenia. In 1966, he was elected secretary of the Writers Union of Armenia. Sevag's poems have appeared in many places, including the "Foreign Literatures" issue of the Arab Writers' Union in Damascus.

Aharon Shabtai, born in 1939, is regarded as the foremost Hebrew translator of Greek drama; he is also the author of some seventeen books of poetry. Two book-length selections of his work have appeared in English translations by Peter Cole: *Love & Selected Poems* (Sheep Meadow Press, 1997) and *J'Accuse* (New Directions, 2003), a collection of his recent political poetry.

Perveen Shakir was born in 1952 in Karachi, Pakistan. Her books of poetry include *Khushboo* (1976), *Sad-barg* (1980), *Khud-kalaami* (1990), *Inkaar* (1990), and *Maah-e-Tamaam* (1994). Her first book, *Khushboo,* won the Adamjee Award. Later she was awarded the Pride of Performance award, the highest award given by the Pakistan government.

Ahmad Shamlu was born in 1925 in Tehran. A follower of Nima Yushij (1897–1960), Iran's first modernist poet, he searched for new means to expand the metrical and verbal resources of poetry. He published over twenty volumes of poetry and translated Western poetry into Persian.

Shang Qin, born in 1930, pen name of Luo Yan, was forced to serve in the Nationalist army in Chengdu in 1945. From 1969 to 1971 he attended the International Writing Program at University of Iowa. He retired in 1992 and now lives in suburban Taipei. His collections include *Dreams or Dawn and Other Things* and *Thinking With One's Feet.*

Ravi Shankar is associate professor and poet-in-residence at Central Connecticut State University and the founding editor of the international online journal of the arts *Drunken Boat.* He has published a book of poems, *Instrumentality,* named a finalist for the 2005 Connecticut Book Awards. He has been a commentator for National Public Radio, read his work at such venues as the Asia Society, and serves on the advisory council for the Connecticut Center for the Book.

Sajjad Sharif was born in Dhaka, Bangladesh, in September 24, 1963. His first collection of poems, *Chhurichikitsha,* was published in 2006. He is also a critic and translator. He was involved with the literary journal *Gandiva,* which reshaped the recent scenario of Bangla poetry. He is a journalist by profession.

Prageeta Sharma is the author of *Bliss to Fill* (Subpress, 2000) and *The Opening Question* (Fence, 2004). She has taught at Cambridge College, University of Montana, and New York University. She currently teaches in the graduate creative writing program at The New School in New York City and in the low-residency BA program at Goddard College in Plainfield, Vermont.

Bhupi Sherchan was born in the lower Mustang region of Nepal and was the first poet to popularize free verse in Nepali literature. *Gumme Mechmathi Andho Manche (Blind Man on a Revolving Chair)* is his major collection and won the Sajha Puraskar, the highest literary prize in Nepal.

Manohar Shetty, born in 1953, is a graduate of Bombay University and has published three books of poems, including *Domestic Creatures* (Oxford University Press, New Delhi). In the United States, his poems have appeared in *Shenandoah, Chelsea, New Letters, Rattapallax,* and *Fulcrum.* He has edited *Ferry Crossing— Short Stories from Goa* (Penguin India). He lives in Goa.

Shin Kyŏng-nim was born in 1935 in Ch'ongju, North Ch'ungch'ong Province. His fame dates mainly from the publication of the collection *Nong-mu (Farmers' Dance)* in 1973, after spending over ten years working as a farmer, a miner, and a merchant.

Shiraishi Kazuko was born in Vancouver in 1931; her family then moved to Japan shortly before the war. She was involved in the surrealist VOU group, and later became known as a Beat poet. She has written over twenty books of poetry and has received every prestigious Japanese poetry award, including the Purple Ribbon Medal from the Emperor of Japan. Her books include *Seasons of Sacred Lust* (1975) and *Let Those Who Appear* (2002).

Shu Ting was born Gong Peiyu in 1952 in Fujian Province. In the early days of Mengleng poetry, she created a romantic and emotional atmosphere in her poetry that was no less revolutionary than more explicit political work of her male contemporaries. She lives in Xiamen.

Shukrulla was born in 1920. A poet, playwright, and fiction writer, he has published numerous books and has been honored with the Republic's State Hamza Award and the title of Uzbekistan People's Poet.

Eshqabil Shukur has published numerous books and was awarded the Usman Nasir Prize for his collection, *Flowers of Night*.

Kedarnath Singh was born in 1934 and was professor of Hindi at Jawaharlal Nehru University for two decades. Also a noted scholar and critic, he is widely regarded as one of the most influential living poets in Hindi, with half a dozen important collections in print. He was the featured Indian poet at the 34th Poetry International Festival, Rotterdam, in 2003.

Kirpal Singh is a renowned poet, fictionist, and scholar. He has performed at many major arts festivals, including Edinburgh, Cambridge, Adelaide, Toronto, and York, and his poems have been dramatized Off Broadway. In 1997, he was the Distinguished International Writer at the Iowa Writers' Workshop.

Sitor Situmorang, born in North Sumatra, Indonesia, in 1924, made his debut as an author in 1953 with the publication of *Green Paper Letter (Surat Kertas Hijau)*. Since that time, he has published more than a dozen volumes of poetry and other literary works.

S. Sivasegaram was born in 1942. Professor of mechanical engineering at the University of Peradeniya, Sri Lanka, his writings bridge the sciences and literature. He has been writing poetry since the 1970s and has published several collections of his poems. He also translates from English into Tamil.

Sŏ Chŏng-ju, also known by the pen name Midang, was born in South Korea's North Cholla Province in 1915 and died in 2000. *The Forest Books* volume contains the complete poems of his first four collections. In all he has published nine collections of poetry and has edited a number of anthologies and published works on literary history and criticism. He has been nominated for the Nobel Prize in Literature several times.

Bozor Sobir is the Tajikistani author of more than four major collections of verse.

Cathy Song was born in 1955. Her first collection of poetry, *Picture Bride* (1983), won the Yale Younger Poets prize. Her other volumes of poetry include *Frameless Windows, Squares of Light* (1988), *School Figures* (1994), and *The Land of Bliss* (2001). *Cloud Moving Hands* was published in 2007.

Carolyn Marie Souaid is a Montreal poet, book reviewer, and the author of four books, most recently *Satie's Sad Piano* (Signature Editions, 2005). She has appeared at many literary festivals across Canada and as a guest on CBC-Radio, Global TV, and TVOntario.

Brian Kim Stefans is the author of *Free Space Comix* (1998), *Gulf* (1998), *Angry Penguins* (2000), and *Fashionable Noise: On Digital Poetics*, a mixed-genre collection of poems, experimental essays, and an interview (Atelos). He edits arras.net and is a frequent critic for the *Boston Review* and other publications. A book of his prose, *Before Starting Over,* appeared in 2006 (Salt Publishing).

Arundhathi Subramaniam, awarded the Charles Wallace Fellowship at the University of Stirling in 2003, edits the India domain of *Poetry International*. Her books include *On Cleaning Bookshelves* (Allied, 2001) and *Where I Live* (Allied, 2005). She coedited *Confronting Love* (Penguin, 2001), an anthology of contemporary Indian love poems in English.

Pireeni Sundaralingam, born and raised in Sri Lanka, is a PEN USA Rosenthal Fellow. Her poetry has been published widely, from *The Progressive* (USA) to *The Guardian* (UK) to *Cyphers* (Eire) and university texts such as *Three Genres* (Prentice-Hall, 8th edition, 2006). Her work is featured in the International Museum of Women.

Arthur Sze is the author of eight books of poetry, including *Quipu* (2005), *The Redshifting Web: Poems 1970–1998* (1998), and *The Silk Dragon: Translations from the Chinese* (2001), all from Copper Canyon Press. He is a professor emeritus at the Institute of American Indian Arts and is the first poet laureate of Santa Fe.

Eileen Tabios has written eleven poetry collections, a collection of art essays, and a book of short stories. Recipient of the Philippines' National Book Award for

Poetry, she recently released *The Light That Left His Body Entered Thine Eyes* (Marsh Hawk, New York, 2007).

Tada Chimako was born in 1930 and died in 2003. She published fourteen anthologies of poetry during her life, two books of poetry that were published posthumously, more than a dozen books of essays, and just as many translations. Although she was part of a movement during the 1950s that brought surrealism into the poetic mainstream, her poetry is rarely inaccessible, even as it shows her erudition in the fields of mythology, ancient thought, and contemporary philosophy.

M. Athar Tahir, the 1974 Rhodes Scholar for Pakistan, has published twenty works on literature, calligraphy, art, etc., including four volumes of poems. He won Pakistan's highest national award, the Patras Bokhari Prize for literature in English. His poems have been published abroad, anthologized, and translated into Urdu and Chinese.

Takahashi Mutsuo was born in 1937 and came to international attention in the 1970s for his bold expressions of homoerotic desire. His most recent book of English translations is *On Two Shores: New and Selected Poems* (Dedalus Press, 2006).

Tamura Ryuichi, born in 1923 and died in 1998, founded the poetry journal *Arechi* (*Wasteland*) in 1947. From his wartime experiences, his poems reflect post-war Japan, in harsh intellectual terms, creating an aesthetic in his poems that straddles despair and hope and addresses civilization as a whole. He wrote thirty books of poetry and received Japan's highest honor, the 54th Japan Academy of Arts Award for Poetry in 1998.

Paul Tan has published *Curious Roads* (1994) and *Driving Into Rain* (1998), which won the Commendation and Merit Prizes at the Singapore Literature Prize competition respectively. *First Meeting of Hands* was published in fall 2006.

Tanikawa Shuntarō was born in 1931 in Tokyo, son of the distinguished philosopher Tetsuzo Tanikawa. By the age of eighteen he was writing poetry and with the imprimatur of Miyoshi Tatsuji (1900–1964), one of the leading poets of the day. *Twenty Billion Light Years of Loneliness*, was published to instant acclaim in 1952. Tanikawa's collections have been translated into English and many other languages.

Qian Xi Teng's first collection of poetry, *Eye and Tongue*, appeared in 2007. Her work has been published in softblow.com, *Slope,* and the *London Underground*. She freelances as a writer, translator, and publicist, and will be returning to Columbia University to finish her BA in comparative literature.

Habib Tengour was born in Mostaganem in the west of Algeria in 1947. He moved to France when he was only five years old. He is the author of many books of poetry and novels.

Hilary Tham is the author of nine books of poetry, including *Counting*, *The Tao of Mrs. Wei*, and *Bad Names for Women*; a collection of short fiction, *Tin Mines and Concubines*; and a memoir, *Lane With No Name*. She served as editor-in-chief for *The Word Works* and as poetry editor for the *Potomac Review*.

Thanh Thảo was born in 1946 in Quang Ngai and now lives in Hanoi. His books include *Those Who Reach the Sea* (1977), *Footprints Across the Grass* (1980), *The Rubik's Cube* (1985), *From One to a Hundred* (1988), and *The Sun's Waves* (1994). His awards include prizes from the Vietnam Writers' Association.

Jeet Thayil was born in Kerala, India, and educated in Bombay, Hong Kong, and New York. He is the author of *English* (Penguin/Rattapallax, 2004). He is the editor of the anthology *Give the Sea Change and It Shall Change: Fifty-Six Indian Poets* (1952–2005), published by the Boston-based poetry annual *Fulcrum*.

Edith L. Tiempo was declared a National Artist in Literature in 2001, the highest official recognition awarded to a writer by the Philippine government. She is a poet, fiction writer, essayist, critic, author of more than fifteen books, and editor of several textbooks on literature and creative writing. At eighty-seven, she continues to organize and direct the National Writers' Workshop, conducted every summer in Dumaguete City since its start in 1962.

Tố Hữu was born in 1920 to a poor Confucian family. He currently lives in Hanoi. A leader of the Union of Democratic Youths in Hué, he published his first poems in 1937. His poetry collections include *Since Then* (1946), *The Northernmost Base* (1954), *Strong Winds* (1961), *To the Front* (1972), *Blood and Flowers* (1977), and *A Single Note* (1992).

Tô Thùy Yên was born in 1938 in Gia Dinh, South Vietnam. He began his literary career in the late 1950s. He was detained for more than ten years in the so-called communist reeducation camp as a former South Vietnam officer. He came to the United States in 1993. He was awarded the Freedom of Expression Award from Human Rights Watch in 1994.

Hsien Min Toh has published two collections of poetry, *Iambus* (1994) and *The Enclosure of Love* (2001). His work has also been published in periodicals such as the *London Review of Books*. He is the founding editor of the *Quarterly Literary Review Singapore*, recipient of the Shell National Arts Council Scholarship, and the organizer for Singapore's first international poetry festival, Wordfeast.

Barbara Tran's poetry collection, *In the Mynah Bird's Own Words*, was selected as a PEN Open Book Award finalist. Barbara is the recipient of a Pushcart Prize, Bread Loaf scholarship, and Lannan Foundation writing residency.

Pimone Triplett is the author of *The Price of Light* (Four Way Books, 2005) and *Ruining the Picture* (TriQuarterly/Northwestern, 1998). She holds an MFA from the University of Iowa. Currently, she teaches at the University of Washington and the Warren Wilson MFA Program for Writers.

Chögyam Trungpa was born in Kham, in eastern Tibet, in 1939 and died in 1987. After the Chinese occupation of Tibet, he escaped into exile and became a spiritual guide to Westerners. Trungpa founded Naropa Institute in Boulder, Colorado, including the Jack Kerouac School of Disembodied Poetics. His numerous works include *Cutting Through Spiritual Materialism, Myth of Freedom, First Thought Best Thought,* and *Crazy Wisdom.*

Tsai Yim Pui was born in Guangdong and moved to Hong Kong. He studied at the University of Taiwan, later returning to serve editorial positions at local newspapers. His books include *Three Scrolls of Short Poems, Mutant Red Beans, Lantian Warmed in the Sun,* and *Book of Knotted Hair.*

Tsuji Yukio, born in 1939 in Asakusa, Tokyo, studied French literature at Meiji University. "Rum and Snow" has been taken from *In the Margin of Verlaine* (1990). His other books include *Recollections from School Days* (1962), *How to Catch a Cold* (1987), *Collected Poems* (1996), and *Selected Poems* (2003) among many others.

Tenzin Tsundue's books include *Crossing the Border* and *Kora,* currently in its third printing. His writings have been published in *International PEN, The Little Magazine, Outlook,* and the *Times of India.* He is the general secretary of the Friends of Tibet, Indian chapter, and is very active as a poet and Tibetan rights activist.

Nadia Tuéni was born in 1935 in Beirut, Lebanon, and died in 1983. She published nine collections of verse in French and was awarded prizes in France and Lebanon, including the Prix de l'Académie Française in 1973, the Order of La Pléiade, and the Gold Medal of Honor for Public Instruction.

Fadwa Tuqan was born in 1917 in Nablus, Palestine. She is the author of more than nine books, and in 1990 was awarded the Sultan Uweis Prize for Poetry and the Jerusalem Medal for Literary Achievement.

Suerkul Turgunbayev is a poet and translator born in 1940. He is the author of more than ten collections of poetry, including *The Evening Trolley, Two Cliffs,* and *A New Day.*

U Sam Oeur was born in rural Cambodia in 1936, received his BA and MFA in the United States, served as a member of Cambodia's Parliament and delegate to the UN, and survived the Pol Pot regime. A bilingual edition of his poetry, *Sacred Vows,* and his memoir, *Crossing Three Wildernesses,* were published by Coffee House Press.

U Tin Moe, a poet laureate of Burma, published over thirty books. Born in 1933, he began writing poetry and essays in 1959 and won numerous literary awards. He became involved in the pro-democracy movement in 1988, and as a result, he was imprisoned in Insein Jail from 1991 until 1995. All his published works are banned in Burma. He left the country in April of 1999. He died in his home in California in 2007 at the age of seventy-three.

Khalil Reza Uluturk was born in the Salyan region of Azerbaijan in 1932 and died in 1994 in Baku. He worked at the magazine *Azerbaijani Woman* and, from 1969 until his death, worked at the Institute of Literature. He published over thirty-five books, including *Poem of Love, Prestige, Where is this World Going?, 1937 Still Lives On, Between the Sun and Moon,* and *I am the East.*

Montri Umavijani was born in 1941 and died in 2006. He wrote twenty-seven books in English, several in Thai, and translated poetry, especially nineteenth-century classics, from a half-dozen languages into Thai. Praised by poet Kenneth Rexroth, Montri was featured in *New Directions Annual #41* (New York, 1980). Umavijani was twice nominated for the Nobel Prize in Literature.

Ricardo M. de Ungria had been a Fulbright Grantee at Washington University in St. Louis and a writing fellow at Hawthornden Castle, The International Retreat for Writers in Scotland and Bellagio Center in Italy. A poet and an artist, he has seven books of poetry and several anthologies to his name. He is chancellor at the University of the Philippines in Mindanao.

Bahtiyar Vahapzade is the author of numerous scholarly articles and plays, as well as books of poems, short stories, and travel journals.

Erkin Vahidov was born in 1936. He is the author of many books of poetry, including *Breath of Dawn* (1961), *Light Keeper* (1970), and *Living Planets* (1980).

Purna Bahadur Vaidya participated in the revival of Nepal Bhasa, the language of the Newars, the indigenous people of the Kathmandu Valley. His major work is *La la kha* (*Water Is Water*). Translations of his poetry have appeared in *MĀNOA* and *Nimrod.*

Michelle Yasmine Valladares, a poet, essayist, and filmmaker, is a lecturer in English at The City College of New York. *Nortada, The North Wind,* her first collection of poems, was published by Global City Press. She lived in Kuwait, India, Arizona, California, and Brazil, before finally settling down in Brooklyn.

Reetika Vazirani was born in India in 1962 and died in 2003. She was the recipient of a 2003 Anisfield-Wolf Book Award for *World Hotel* (Copper Canyon, 2002) and a Barnard New Women Poets Prize for *White Elephants* (1996). She received a "Discovery"/*The Nation* prize, a Pushcart Prize, and the Glenna Luschei/Prairie Schooner Award for her essay "The Art of Breathing."

José Garcia Villa was born in 1908 and died in 1997. He is the author of *Have Come, Am Here* (1942), *Volume Two* (1949), *Selected Poems and New* (1958), *Appassionata: Poems in Praise of Love* (1979), *The Parlement of Giraffes: Poems for Children—Eight to Eighty* (John Cowen and Larry Francia, eds., 1999). Other volumes include *The Anchored Angel: Selected Writings* (Eileen Tabios, ed.); *The Critical Villa: Essays in Literary Criticism* (Jonathan Chua, ed.). *The Collected Villa* is forthcoming.

Al-Munsif al-Wahaybi was born in Qairwan, Tunisia. He is the author of numerous books and has translated widely.

Yona Wallach was born in a suburb of Tel Aviv in 1944. She was active in the circle of "Tel Aviv Poets," and, after her death, became an icon of the feminist revolution. She published six volumes of poetry and a posthumous selection appeared in 1992.

Wang Ping was born in China and came to the United States in 1985. Her publications include *American Visa, Foreign Devil, Of Flesh and Spirit, New Generation: Poetry from China Today, Aching for Beauty: Footbinding in China,* and *The Magic Whip.* She won the Eugene Kayden Award for the Best Book in Humanities and is the recipient of an NEA and the Bush Artist Fellowship for poetry. She is associate professor of English at Macalester College.

Wang Xiaoni, born in 1955 in Northeast China, has over thirteen publications, including *Selected Poems by Wang Xiaoni*. She has been the recipient of many awards, including the 2002 Year Poetry Award of China and the Shanghai Literature Journal Award.

Ak Welsapar was born in 1956 in the former Soviet Republic of Turkmenistan. He fled to Sweden in 1993 and in 1996 was accepted into the Swedish Writers' Union. He is the author of twelve books of poetry.

Woeser (Weise) is a Tibetan poet from the western Tibetan area of Sichuan (Kham). She was born in 1966 and grew up among both Tibetan and Han Chinese cultures. She currently lives in Lhasa and writes about the religious and cultural struggles of modern Tibet in the Chinese language.

Sholeh Wolpé was born in Iran. She is the author of *The Scar Saloon* (Red Hen Press) and the translator of *Sin: Poems of Forugh Farrokhzad, Iran's Rebel Poet* (University of Arkansas Press). Her poems, translations, essays, and reviews have appeared in scores of literary journals, periodicals, and anthologies worldwide, and have been translated into several languages.

Cyril Wong is the author of five books of poetry in Singapore. He won the National Arts Council's Young Artist Award for Literature in 2005. His poems have appeared in *Atlanta Review, Poetry International*, and *Fulcrum 3,* among other journals and anthologies.

Laurence Wong is currently professor of translation in the department of translation at The Chinese University of Hong Kong. His publications include twelve collections of poems, six collections of lyrical essays, seven collections of critical essays, and a Chinese verse (terza rima) translation of Dante's *La Divina Commedia*.

Wong Phui Nam was born in 1935 in Kuala Lumpur. His poems first appeared in *Bunga Emas,* an anthology of Malaysian literature (1960). They subsequently appeared in book form as *How the Hills Are Distant* (1968). Other books include *Remembering Grandma and Other Rumours* (1989), *Ways of Exile* (1993), *Against the Wilderness* (2000), and *An Acre of Day's Glass—Collected Poems* (2006).

Bryan Thao Worra was born in Vientiane, Laos, in 1973; he has been actively engaged in Southeast Asian refugee resettlement and the arts. He currently resides in St. Paul, Minnesota, and received the 2005 Minnesota State Arts Board Cultural Collaboration Award. His e-book *Touching Detonations* is available with Sphinx House Press.

Xi Chuan's books include *A Fictitious Family Tree* (1997) and *Roughly Speaking* (1997), two books of essays, one book of critique, a play, and numerous translations. He is the winner of prizes, honors, and fellowships and was awarded one of the top ten winners of the Weimar International Essay Prize Contest (Germany, 1999). He is an associate professor at the Central Academy of Fine Arts in Beijing.

Xi Xi was born in 1938 in Shanghai, but moved with her family to Hong Kong in 1950. Often experimental, she is the author of poetry, fiction, essays, children's stories, screenplays, and translations. She taught primary school for two decades before taking early retirement in 1979.

Xie Ye was born in Shanghai and wrote stories, sketches, and poems. It is not possible, in these few words, to capture the tragedy of her death in New Zealand in 1993.

Xiong Hong also known as Hsiung Hung was born in 1940 in Taidong, in southeastern Taiwan. She began writing at the age of fifteen; much of her early work appeared in the *Blue Star Poetry Journal*. She has published three poetry collections since 1968. A Buddhist all her life, she has written many Buddhist *gathas*, or paeans, since the 1980s.

Xuân Quỳnh was born in 1942; her poems spoke for generations of women in Vietnam. Her books include *Loas Winds, White Sand; A Lullaby on the Ground; Singing Alone; The Co May Flower* among many others. After many years of committing her life to her marriage and poetry, an automobile accident took her life and the lives of her husband and two children.

Xue Di was born in Beijing in 1957. He is the author of three volumes of collected works and one book of criticism on contemporary Chinese poetry in Chinese. In English translation, he has published *Zone, Another Kind of Tenderness, An Ordinary Day, Heart into Soil,* and four chapbooks. Xue Di is a two-time recipient of the Hellman/Hammett Award, sponsored by Human Rights Watch.

Ý Nhi was born in Quang Nam in Central Vietnam in 1944. During the war she worked as an editor at the Liberation Literature and Arts Publishing House. An advocate for the work of women writers, her poems are included in bilingual translation in the collection *Six Vietnamese Poets* from Curbstone Press. She currently resides in Ho Chi Minh City.

Yan Li joined with Bei Dao in underground writing activities during the Cultural Revolution, and was a contributor to the original *Today* magazine. His poetry collections include *This Poem Is Probably Not Bad* and *Spinning Mirror*. Since 1997, Yan Li has lived in Shanghai with his wife and two daughters.

Yang Lian began publishing poetry in China in 1979. In 1989 he relocated to Auckland, and in 1991 to London. His poems, essays, and criticism were collected in two volumes as *Yang Lian zuopin* (1998) and his poetry has been published in more than thirty languages. In 1999 he won the Flaiano International Prize for Poetry.

Yang Mu, the pen name of Wang Ching-hsien, was born in Hualian on the east coast of Taiwan in 1940. He is a professor of comparative literature at University of Washington, Seattle. After a stint as dean of Humanities and Social Sciences at the National Dong Hwa University, Taiwan, he is the director of Literature and Philosophy Institute at Academia Sinica, Taiwan.

Arthur Yap was born in 1943 and died in 2006. *Only Lines,* published in 1971, received the National Book Development Council of Singapore's first award for poetry in 1976. In 1983, he was awarded the SEA Write Award in Bangkok and the Cultural Medallion for Literature in Singapore. He has taught at the National University of Singapore and his poems have been translated into Japanese, Mandarin, and Malay.

John Yau is the author of *Borrowed Love Poems* (Penguin, 2002), *Ing Grish* (Saturnalia, 2005), *Paradiso Diaspora* (Penguin, 2006), and *The Passionate Spectator* (University of Michigan, 2006), among others. His work is included in *The Oxford Book of American Poetry*. A Guggenheim Fellow (2006–07), he teaches at the Mason Gross School of the Arts (Rutgers University) and lives with his wife and daughter in New York.

Yeow Kai Chai has worked as an entertainment and arts editor, writer, and music critic in Singapore for more than a decade, including for the country's biggest newspaper, *The Straits Times*. His books include *Secret Manta* (2001) and *Pretend I'm Not Here* (2006).

Yi Sha graduated from Beijing Normal University (1989), where he studied under the critic/thinker Liu Xiaobo. Yi Sha fell under the influence of Bei Dao and other "Misty" poets, but he belongs squarely to the post-Misty generation. His first poetry collection, *Starve the Poets*, presents a rebellious, irreverent, and wryly humorous persona.

Yong Shu Hoong, born in 1966, has published three books of poetry: *Isaac* (1997), *dowhile* (2002), and *Frottage* (2005). He has also written for *The Straits Times* and *South China Morning Post* and participated in literary festivals in Malaysia, Hong Kong, Australia, and the United States.

Monica Youn's first book, *Barter,* was published by Graywolf Press in 2003. She has been awarded the Rhodes Scholarship and the Wallace Stegner Fellowship in Poetry at Stanford University, among other honors.

C. Dale Young practices medicine full-time, serves as poetry editor of the *New England Review,* and teaches in the Warren Wilson College MFA Program. He is the author of *The Day Underneath the Day* (TriQuarterly Books, 2001) and *The Second Person* (Four Way Books, 2007).

Saadi Youssef was born in Basra in 1934, left Iraq in 1979, and currently resides in London. He has translated Walt Whitman, George Orwell, and Wole Soyinka, among others, into Arabic; he is the author of more than thirty books of poetry and seven books of prose.

Yu Jian, born in 1954 in Kunming, China, is a poet, author, and documentary film director. A major participant among "The Third Generation Poets" after the "Misty Poetry" movement in the early 1980s, his work has been translated into English, French, German, Dutch, Spanish, Italian, Swedish, Danish, and Japanese. *Anthology of Works* is a five-volume collection of his poems and essays from 1975 to 2000.

Alfred A. Yuson was a 2003 fellow of the Rockefeller Foundation at the Bellagio

Center by Lago di Como in Italy. Born and based in Manila, Yuson has authored eighteen books, including novels, short stories, poetry and essay collections, children's books, and translation. He contributes regularly to the *Philippine Star,* a national daily broadsheet, and teaches poetry and fiction at the Ateneo de Manila University.

Nathan Zach was born in Berlin in 1930, and arrived in Haifa as a child. He has published seven volumes of poetry, a memoir, two books of essays, and a play. His awards include the Bialik Award and the Israel Prize.

Zahrad was born in 1924. He is the author of numerous books, including *The Big City* (1960), *Colored Boundaries* (1968), *Gigo Poems* (1969), and *Benevolent Heavens* (1971).

Baha Zain (Baharuddin Zainal)'s books include *Three Sketches from a Journey* (1980) and *The City's Exile* (2007), a collection of English translations from his Malay originals. He lives in Kuala Lumpur.

Katayoon Zandvakili is the author of *Deer Table Legs,* which won the University of Georgia Press's Contemporary Poetry Series Prize in 1998. She resides in Oakland, California, and is finishing a novel.

Ghassan Zaqtan was born in Beit Jala, Palestine, in 1954. He is the author of many books of poetry and a novel, and has made two documentary films. He currently lives in Ramallah, working at the Palestinian Ministry of Culture.

Nurit Zarhi was born in Jerusalem in 1941. Her poems have been widely translated and anthologized in Europe. She writes both poetry and prose for young readers. She has published seven volumes of poetry and has received every major Israeli award, including The Prime Minister Award.

Zhai Yongming was born in Chengdu, Sichuan Province, in 1955. Her poem cycle *Woman* (1986) received much attention for its forthright feminist point of view. Although she publishes in *Today* magazine (associated with the "Misty" poets), Zhai is known as a member of the "Newborn Generation."

Zhang Er was born in Beijing, China, and moved to the United States in 1986. Her writings of poetry, nonfiction, and essays have appeared in publications in Taiwan, China, the American émigré community, and in a number of American journals. Her books include *Cross River, Pick Lotus,* and *Carved Water.*

Zheng Danyi was born in Sichuan, China, in 1963. His six collections of poetry include *Wings of Summer: Selected Poems 1984–1997,* a bilingual edition with translations by Luo Hui (Hong Kong, 2003). Shortlisted for the 2003 Grand Chinese Media Prize in Literature, the book has spawned an updated Chinese-only edition. His poems have been translated into ten languages. Zheng has lived in Hong Kong since 1999.

Abdallah Zrika was born in Casablanca in 1953. He writes in French and Arabic and is the author of two novels and more than nine collections of poetry.

TRANSLATOR BIOGRAPHIES

Kamal Abu-Deeb is chair of Arabic at the University of London. He is the author of many books and articles, including *Al-Jurjani's Theory of Poetic Imagery* (1979) and *Imagination Unbound: (al-Adab al-'Aja'ibi) and the Literature of the Fantastic in the Arabic Tradition* (2007).

Fareda Ahmadi was born in Kandahar, Afghanistan, and immigrated to the United States in 1982 with her parents and siblings. She grew up in Philadelphia but currently lives in Northern Virginia where she works as a civil engineer.

Wali Ahmadi is an assistant professor of Persian literature at the University of California, Berkeley. He is the author of *Anomalous Visions: History and Form in the Modern Literature of Afghanistan* (forthcoming). He studied literature in Kabul and holds a PhD in comparative literature from UCLA.

Aytan Aliyeva works at *Azerbaijan International Magazine*.

Wayne Amtzis is a poet, photographer, and longtime resident of Nepal. He is the editor and cotranslator of *Two Sisters: The Poetry of Benju Sharma and Manju Kanchuli,* and of *From The Lake, Love: The Poetry of Banira Giri.*

Hil Anderson is a graduate of Brown University and Georgetown University's Law Center. He is currently pursuing a PhD at Harvard University's East Asian Languages and Civilizations Department focusing on Chinese poetry.

Jeffrey Angles is the head of the Japanese language program at Western Michigan University. His translations have appeared in *The Columbia Anthology of Modern Japanese Literature, Critical Asian Studies,* and numerous other journals. He is the coeditor of *Japan: A Traveler's Literary Companion* (Whereabouts Press, 2006).

Brother Anthony of Taizé was born in 1942 in England. He is a member of the Community of Taizé (France). Since 1980, he has been teaching English literature at Sogang University in Seoul (Korea). He has published twenty volumes of English translations of modern Korean literature, including six volumes of works by Ko Un.

S. V. Atallah was born in New York, went to school in Amman, and currently resides in California. Her poetry and translations have been published in many literary journals and magazines in the United States and Europe.

Harry Aveling is head of the Indonesian/Malay Program at La Trobe, University of Melbourne. His work includes *Secrets Need Words: Indonesian Poetry 1965–1998* (2001) and *Life Sentences: Selected Poetry of Dorothea Rosa Herliany* (2003). He has translated extensively from Indonesian and Malay literature, and was awarded the Anugerah Pengambangan Sastra in 1991 for his contributions to the international recognition of Malay literature.

Jjiepa Ayi is a recent graduate in Yi literature studies from Southwest Nationalities University, Chengdu, Sichuan Province, China.

Baidar Bakht teaches in the Department of Civil Engineering at the University of Toronto. He is a retired bridge engineer and a translator of Urdu poetry.

Jean-Pierre Balpe is the author of *101 poèmes du poète aveugle* and *La Toile*. Since 1985, he has taken part or initiated numerous exhibitions on art and new technologies. He is a founding member of ALAMO, the worldwide first artist group for digital literature (since 1981). His latest text-generative work is the e-novel *Trajectoire*.

Ron D. K. Banerjee, born in India, is a poet, translator, and literary scholar who translates poetry from Sanskrit, Bengali, French, Italian, Russian, and Czech (the last two with Maria Banerjee). His publications include *Far From You* (Toronto, 1981); *Poetry From Bengal* (UNESCO, 1989); *L'Antica Fiamma* (Lucca, 1995), a prose narrative framing his Italian poems; and a bilingual selection, *The Milan Pieta and Other Poems* (Milano, 2006).

The Beloit/Fudan Translation Workshop, in existence since 1987, has made available in English work by leading contemporary Chinese poets. Begun by John Rosenwald, Sun Li, and Ann Arbor, its work continues through students and colleagues at Beloit College in Wisconsin and Fudan University in Shanghai, particularly Chu Mengdan and Chen Yanbing.

Mark Bender teaches courses on Chinese oral and oral-connected literature at the Ohio State University. His recent publications include *Plum and Bamboo: China's Suzhou Chantefable Tradition*, a book introducing a style of traditional Chinese storytelling, and a translation of oral poetry entitled *Butterfly Mother:*

Miao (Hmong) Creation Epics from Guizhou, China. He has worked with poet Aku Wuwu on a number of translation projects.

Ry Beville was born and raised in Richmond, Virginia, and was educated at the University of Notre Dame (BA) and the University of California, Berkeley (MA). He has previously published two translated volumes of poetry by Nakahara Chuya.

Kamal Boullata is a Palestinian artist and writer, born in Jerusalem in 1942. He has translated the work of numerous Arab poets, including the Palestinian poet Rashad Hussein, and many Arab women poets. Boullata currently lives in the South of France.

Sargon Boulus is an Assyrian born in Iraq. He is a poet, short story writer, and translator. Boulus is the author of numerous books of poetry and has lived in many places, including Lebanon, Greece, Germany, England, and the United States.

Kevin Bowen is director of the William Joiner Center for the Study of War and Social Consequences at the University of Massachusetts, Boston. His most recent collections are *Eight True Maps of the West* (Dedalus Press, Dublin) and, with Nguyen Ba Chung, *Six Vietnamese Poets* (Curbstone).

Steve Bradbury has published poems, essays, and three volumes of poetry in translation, notably *Fusion Kitsch: Poems from the Chinese of Hsia Yü* (Zephyr Press, 2001). He is associate professor of English at National Central University in Taiwan.

Carolyn B. Brown's translations of poems by Mohammad Rafiq have appeared in *Modern Poetry in Translation, Exchanges, 100 Words, 91st Meridian,* and *Parabaas.* A volume of selected poems by Amiya Chakravarty, *Another Shore,* and *Tagore Tales* (both cotranslated with Bengali poet Sarat Kumar Mukhopadhay) have been published in India.

Alan Brownjohn is an English poet, novelist, children's book writer, broadcaster, reviewer, and contributor to journals. He was a critic for the *New Statesman* and chairman of Poetry Society between 1982 and 1988. His latest poetry book is *The Men Around Her Bed.*

Ravil Bukharaev was born in Kazan, Russia, in 1951. He has published more than thirty books in Russian, English, his native Kazan Tatar, and Hungarian. Since 1992, he has been living in London. In 2005, he was awarded the M. Lomonosov Golden Medal for his contribution to Russian Arts, Science and Education and, in 2006, the State Prize of the Republic of Tatarstan for two of his latest collections of poetry.

Clarissa Burt has taught Arabic poetry at different universities, and has lived and traveled all over Egypt. Her translations and critical essays have been published in numerous journals, and she has given many talks in the United States and the Arab world.

John Cayley is a London-based Anglo-Canadian poet as well as a translator, bookseller, and the founding editor of Wellsweep Press. He is known internationally for his writing in networked and programmable media.

Martha P. Y. Cheung teaches translation at Hong Kong Baptist University. Her works of translation include novels by Han Shaogong and Liu Sola and poetry collections by Leung Ping-kwan. The first volume of her new work, *An Anthology of Chinese Discourse on Translation,* was published in 2006.

Ruth Christie was born and educated in Scotland, and then studied Turkish language and literature at the School of Oriental and African Studies, London University. She has translated numerous novels, short stories, and poetry from Turkish.

Peter Cole's most recent collection of poems is *What Is Doubled: Poems 1981–1998.* He has published many volumes of translation from medieval and contemporary Hebrew and Arabic, and has received numerous awards for his work, including the PEN Translation Prize and fellowships from the NEA, the NEH, and the Guggenheim Foundation.

Martha Collins is the author of the recent book-length poem *Blue Front,* as well as four earlier collections of poems. She has also cotranslated two collections of poetry from the Vietnamese, *Green Rice* by Lâm Thị Mỹ Dạ and *The Women Carry River Water* by Nguyễn Quang Thiều.

d dalton is a translator and researcher of Chinese minority poetry. He currently lives in Hangzhou, China, and teaches at the Long Island University China Center.

Robert Abdul Hayy Darr is the director of the Afghan Cultural Assistance Foundation. He attended the Ali Akbar Khan School of North Indian Music, studied Persian poetry with Ali Zulanvar, and published translations of Ustad Khalilullah Khalili in the *Garden of Mystery,* edited by Mahmud Shabistari. He has presented his scholarly work at the Asian Art Museum in San Francisco and at the Ismaili Institute in London.

Najwan Darwish was born in Jerusalem in 1978. Poet, writer, and editor, he studied law and works on different cultural projects. He has published two books of poetry; parts of which were translated into French. He lives in Jerusalem.

Theodore Deppe's books include *Children of the Air* (Alice James, 1990), *The*

Wanderer King (Alice James, 1996), and *Cape Clear: New and Selected Poems* (Salmon Books, Ireland, 2002). He has received two fellowships from the National Endowment for the Arts and a Pushcart Prize.

Diana Der-Hovanessian is the author of twenty-two books of poetry and translations and the winner of numerous awards. She was a Fulbright Professor of American Poetry at Yerevan State University in 1994 and 1999.

Vinay Dharwadker was born in Pune, India, in 1954. He is the author of *Sunday at the Lodi Gardens* (1994), an editor of *The Oxford Anthology of Modern Indian Poetry* (1994), and a coeditor of *The Collected Poems of A. K. Ramanujan* (1995). He has published translations of modern Hindi, Marathi, Urdu, and Punjabi poetry, as well as essays on literary theory and Indian English literature. He teaches at the University of Wisconsin–Madison.

Linh Dinh is the author of *Fake House* (2000), *Blood and Soap* (2004), *All Around What Empties Out* (2003), *American Tatts* (2005), and *Borderless Bodies* (2005). He is also the editor of *Night, Again: Contemporary Fiction from Vietnam* (1996) and *Three Vietnamese Poets* (2001), and translator of *Night, Fish and Charlie Parker, the Poetry of Phan Nhiên Hạo* (Tupelo, 2005).

Thuy Dinh cotranslated with Martha Collins *Green Rice*, an anthology of poetry by the Vietnamese poet Lâm Thị Mỹ Dạ, which was named Kiriyama Notable Book of 2006. Other translations and writing have appeared in *MĀNOA, Asian American Writers* (2001), *Once Upon A Dream: Twenty Years of Vietnamese-American Experience* (1995), and *Amerasia Journal,* among others.

William M. Dirks has translated many Uzbek and Turkmen poets. He was the recipient of the International Research and Exchanges Board (IREX) Special Projects Grant for completion of an Uzbek Language Textbook in 1993, and the Foreign Language and Area Studies Fellowship (FLAS), 1986–1987.

Charles Doria is an American poet and translator. He has published many books of poetry including *The Game of Europe* and *Short and Shorter*. Some of his translations include *Origins: Creation Texts from the Ancient Mediterranean* and *The Tenth Music: Classical Drama in Translation.*

Ketaki Kushari Dyson was born in 1940 and educated at Calcutta and Oxford; she lives in England and has published thirty-three titles in Bengali and English in several different literary genres. She writes original poetry in both her languages and has published ten poetry collections as well as major works of poetry translation.

William I. Elliott, Kawamura's colleague at Kanto Gakuin University, is himself a poet. He and Kawamura together have published fifteen Tanikawa Shuntarō poetry volumes in English translation and have won translation prizes both in the United States and England.

Sharif S. Elmusa was born near Jaffa and grew up in the al-Nuwayima refugee camp, not far from Jericho. He is currently the director of the Middle East Studies Program and an associate professor of political science at the American University of Cairo. His poetry and translations have been published in numerous magazines and literary journals.

George Evans is the author of five books of poetry, including *The New World* and *Sudden Dreams*. He has received writing fellowships from the National Endowment for the Arts, the California Arts Council, the Lannan Foundation, and a Japanese government *Monbusho* Fellowship for the study of Japanese literature. He also translated *The Violent Foam: New and Selected Poems* by Nicaraguan poet Daisy Zamora.

Thomas G. Ezzy was born to a Lebanese American father and a French Canadian mother. He is a writer and translator whose work has been published in many journals and anthologies. He has worked closely with PROTA.

Mona Fayad graduated from the University of Illinois with a PhD in comparative literature. She has taught Arabic and English literature at a number of universities, including UCLA, Colorado College, and Oregon State University.

Annie Finch is the author of four books of poetry, including *Calendars* (2003), shortlisted for the Foreword Poetry Book of the Year award, and a translation of the *Complete Poems* of Louise Labé (2006).

Carolyn Forché is the author of *Gathering the Tribes*, *The Country Between Us*, *The Angel of History*, and *Blue Hour: Poems*. Her honors include fellowships from the Guggenheim Foundation, the Lannan Foundation, and the National Endowment for the Arts. She teaches in the MFA Program at George Mason University in Fairfax, Virginia. Forché is also the editor of *Against Forgetting: Twentieth Century Poetry of Witness* (Norton).

Bassam K. Frangieh, born in Lebanon in 1950, is a scholar of contemporary Arabic literature and culture best known for his pedagogical innovations in the study of the Arabic language, as well as his translations of modern Arabic poets and novelists. His translations include *Arabian Love Poems* (1993), selected poems by Nizar Quabbani, and *Anthology of Arabic Literature, Culture and Thought* (2004).

Gary Gach is editor of *What Book!—Buddha Poems from Beat to Hiphop* (American Book Award) and author of *The Complete Idiot's Guide to Understanding Buddhism*. He was C. H. Kwock's cotranslator on *Searching for Plum Blossoms in the Snow*, an anthology of several thousand years of Chinese song. He won the Northern California Book Award for Translation in 2007.

Ferial Ghazoul was born in Iraq and studied in Lebanon, Europe, and the United States. She is the author of several books including *The Arabian Nights: A Structured Analysis.*

Kuldip Gill, author of *Dharma Rasa* (Nightwood Editions), also writes short fiction, nonfiction, and translates poetry from Punjabi to English. She is writer-in-residence (2006) at the University College of the Fraser Valley, Abbotsford, BC, Canada, where she is working on a memoir and a novel.

Subrata Augustine Gomes was born in Dhaka, Bangladesh, in 1965. He studied English literature at Dhaka University. His publications include: *Tanumadhya, Pulipolao, Kabitasangraha,* and *Digambar Champu* (poems); *Kalketu O Phullara* (novel); *Matrimurti Cathedral* (short stories); and translations of W. B. Yeats, T. S. Eliot, Emily Dickinson, and others. He now resides in Sydney, Australia.

Samuel Grolmes was born 1931 and died in 2004. He was a poet and a Fulbright professor of English in Japan. He wrote book reviews on modern Japanese literature for the *Japan Times.* His translations include *Tamura Ryuichi Poems 1946–1998* (CCC Books, 2000) and Kazuko Shiraishi's *Let Those Who Appear* (New Directions, 2002) in collaboration with Yumiko Tsumura.

Nandini Gupta is an assistant professor of electrical engineering at the Indian Institute of Technology, Kanpur, India. She has published translations of modern Bengali poetry in many national and international journals.

Marilyn Hacker has published numerous books of poetry, including *Desesperanto Poems 1999–2002,* and has been awarded many prizes, such as the National Book Award. She divides her time between Paris and New York.

Talât Sait Halman is one of the leading experts on Turkish literature. He was professor of Turkish Literature at Princeton, and currently teaches at Bilkent University, Ankara.

Choman Hardi was born in Iraqi Kurdistan and grew up in Iraq and Iran before coming to the United Kingdom in 1993. She has published three collections of poetry in Kurdish, and *Life for Us* was her first English collection (Bloodaxe, 2004).

Samuel Hazo is the author of many books of poetry, fiction, essays, and plays. He is the director of the International Poetry Forum in Pittsburgh and McAnulty Distinguished Professor of English Emeritus at Duquesne University. He has been a National Book Award finalist.

John Heath-Stubbs is an English poet, critic, and translator. He is the author of many books of poetry, namely, *Artorius,* his long poem that won the Queen's Gold

Medal for poetry in 1972. In 1978, he won the Oscar Williams–Gene Durwood Award. He has also published many plays and books of criticism, and has translated poetry and prose from Arabic, Persian, and Italian into English. He resides in Oxford.

Khaled Hegazzi is an Egyptian poet living in New Orleans. He has published two poetry collections and is the coeditor of *Khamaseen* and of *Meena,* a bilingual Arabic/English literary journal.

Dima Hilal is a poet and writer, born in Beirut and raised in California. Her work has appeared in publications such as the *San Francisco Chronicle, Orion,* and *The Poetry of Arab Women: A Contemporary Anthology.*

Yahya Hijazi was raised in Jerusalem's Old City. A project consultant at the Palestinian Counseling Center and lecturer in the Department of Education at the David Yellin College, he has also worked as a teacher of Arabic and as a facilitator on projects bringing together Arab and Jewish communities in Israel and Palestine.

Hassan Hilmy is a Moroccan translator and professor of English at the Shiq al-Ayn College of Literature in Casablanca. He has published countless English translations of contemporary Moroccan writers, and Arabic translations of European and American poetry.

Ho Anh Thai was born in 1960. He graduated from the Hanoi College of Diplomacy, and then earned a PhD in Oriental culture. He is on the executive committee of the Vietnam's Writers' Association.

Lakshmi Holmström has been translating Tamil fiction and poetry for the past twenty years. Recently she held a Royal Literary Fund Writing Fellowship at the University of East Anglia, Norwich. She lives in England and is currently preparing an anthology of Tamil poetry in English translation.

Brian Holton studied Chinese at the universities of Edinburgh and Durham, and later taught Chinese in both these institutions. He currently teaches translation at the Hong Kong Polytechnic University. He has translated several books of poetry by Yang Lian, and has published many translations of ancient and modern Chinese literature in both English and his native Scots.

Soraj Hongladarom is director of the Center for Ethics of Science and Technology and an associate professor of philosophy at Faculty of Arts, Chulalongkorn University, Thailand. His research interests include epistemology, philosophy of language, logic, and literature. At present, he is most interested in the interplay between modern science and Thai culture.

Zara Houshmand is an Iranian American writer and theater artist who has been involved in pioneering the development of virtual reality as an art form and has also served as editor for the Mind and Life Institute, facilitating a long-term dialogue between Buddhism and Western science. She is a contributing editor for *Words Without Borders*.

Mohammad Nurul Huda was born in 1949. He has published over three dozen volumes of poetry, fiction, essays and criticism, and anthologies of Bengali poetry. He is the director for Planning and Training of the Bangla Academy. With Carolyne Wright, he prepared initial English versions of work by several Bangladeshi women poets, including many of the poems of Taslima Nasrin. His awards include the Abul Hasan Poetry Prize (1983) and the Bangla Academy Award (1988).

Ann Hunkins is an award-winning poet, photographer, and translator of Nepali. A former Fulbright grantee with an MA in poetry from the University of California, Davis, her poems and translations have appeared in *MĀNOA*, the *North American Review*, and various publications in Nepal. She worked most recently as an interpreter for the United Nations.

Laith al-Husain is a translator of poetry and prose, and a specialist in comparative literature.

Michael James Hutt is a lecturer in Nepali Studies at the School of Oriental and African Studies at the University of London. His books include *Himalayan Voices: An Introduction to Modern Nepali Literature* (1991).

Aynur H. Imecer works at *Azerbaijan International Magazine*. She currently teaches English in Turkey.

Hamid Ismailov was born in 1954 in Tokmak, Kyrgyzstan. He has published dozens of books in different languages. He was forced to flee Uzbekistan in 1992 and now lives and works in London.

Lena Jayyusi has translated numerous poems, short stories, and novels into English, namely, *Songs of Life* by Abu 'l-Qasm al Shabbi and the epic folk romance, *Sayf ibn Dhi Yazan*.

May Jayyusi's translations have appeared in many journals and anthologies; some of the books she translated include Ghassan Kanafani's *All That's Left to You and Other Stories* and Ibrahim Nasrallah's novel, *Prairies of Fever*. She currently works as the executive director of Muwatin, the Palestinian Institute for the Study of Democracy.

Salma Khadra Jayyusi is a poet, scholar, critic, and anthologist. She was born in 1926 in Salt, in East Jordan, of a Palestinian father and Lebanese mother. In 1980, she founded PROTA (Project of Translation from Arabic) in order to spread Arabic literature in the West. Under PROTA, she has edited over thirty volumes, from single-author works to large anthologies.

Pierre Joris is an award-winning translator from Luxembourg. He has written many books of poetry, edited numerous anthologies, and translated widely from French. Joris teaches at the University at Albany, State University of New York.

Fady Joudah's poetry has appeared in the *Kenyon Review, Prairie Schooner, Bellingham Review,* and *Crab Orchard Review,* among many others. His translation of Mahmoud Darwish's most recent poetry collection, *The Butterfly's Burden,* was published by Copper Canyon Press, 2006.

Ayesha Kabir was the editor of the Dhaka-based *PROBE News Magazine* and is a translator of Bengali literature.

Pauline Kaldas is the author of *Egyptian Compass,* a collection of poetry; *Letters from Cairo,* a travel memoir; and the coeditor of *Dinarzad's Children: An Anthology of Contemporary Arab American Fiction.* She currently teaches at Hollins University in Roanoke, Virginia.

Nicholas A. Kaldis is an assistant professor at Binghamton University, State University of New York, where he teaches courses in Chinese literature, film, and language.

Sajed Kamal is a bilingual poet, artist, educational consultant, solar energy expert, Brandeis University professor, and translator of *Kazi Nazrul Islam: Selected Works; Mother of Pearls and Other Poems of Sufia Kamal; Why Mustn't I Flare Up?* (poetry of Kabita Chakma); and *Awake Beautiful Eternal Youth!* (a play by Nazrul Islam).

Yuri Vidov Karageorge is a writer and translator of numerous Central Asian and Eastern European authors. He has taught comparative literature in various colleges and universities and has published many scholarly works during the past thirty years.

Ahmad Karimi-Hakkak was born in Mashhad, Iran. He has published numerous articles, translated many literary works, and is the author of sixteen books. He is currently professor and founding director of the Center for Persian Studies at the University of Maryland.

Wayne Karlin, a novelist, coedited the anthologies *The Other Side of Heaven: Postwar Fiction by Vietnamese and American Writers* and *Love After War: Contemporary Fiction from Vietnam.* He is American editor for Curbstone Press's *Voices from Vietnam* series, which has to date published work by five modern Vietnamese authors.

Suman Kashyap received her MA in English literature from Bombay University. She translates poetry from Punjabi into English with the focus, at present, being on Shiv Kumar Batalvi, Shah Hussein, Bulhe Shah, Mohan Singh, and the folk and marriage songs of Punjab.

Nazih Kassis is a lexicographer and translator from and into contemporary Arabic poetry and prose. Born in the Palestinian village of Iqrit in 1944, he received his PhD from the University of Exeter and currently teaches at the University of Haifa. He lives in Rama.

Kyi May Kaung started writing poetry in 1992 when it became certain that she would never be returning to Burma. Kyi is the author of *Pelted with Petals: The Burmese Poems* and *Tibetan Tanka* and has read poetry at universities, churches, libraries, and Burmese dissident meetings.

Kazuo Kawamura formerly taught at Kanto Gakuin University in Yokohama. He has devoted his life to the study and teaching of poetry; in particular, that of the English Romantics (Shelley above all), on whose work he has published many scholarly articles.

Samira Kawar has translated extensively from Arabic into English, including Liana Badr's novel *The Eye of the Mirror* (Garnet Press, United Kingdom); the film script *Suspended Dreams*, directed by Jean Chamoun and aired by the BBC; and the childhood autobiography of Abdul Rahman Munif, *Sirat Madina* (Quartet Books, UK).

Christopher Kelen is an Australian poet and has taught creative writing and literature at the University of Macau over the last six years. His sixth and latest volume of poetry, *Eight Days in Lhasa*, was published by VAC in Chicago. A seventh volume, *Dredging the Delta*, is forthcoming from Cinnamon Press in the UK.

Tsipi Keller is the recipient of a National Endowment for the Arts Translation Fellowship, of an Armand G. Erpf Award from the Translation Center at Columbia University, and of CAPS and NYFA awards in fiction. Her translations include Dan Pagis's collection *Last Poem* and Irit Katzir's collection *And I Wrote Poems*. Her novels include *The Prophet of Tenth Street* and *Leverage*.

Hafiz Kheir was born 1968 in Khartoum, Sudan. He is a writer, translator, and filmmaker. He has written and published poems, short stories, and articles on media, the arts, and language in various Arabic newspapers and magazines and Sudanese publications.

Young-moo Kim was born in 1944 and died in 2001. With Brother Anthony of Taizé, he translated books of poems by Ko Un, Ch'on Sang-Pyong, Kim Kwang-kyu, Sŏ Chŏng-ju, as well as Kim Sŭ-yong, Shin Kyŏng-nim, and Lee Si-Young. Their volume by Kim Kwang-kyu was awarded the Grand Prize for Translation in

1991 by the Republic of Korea Literary Awards, and their Ch'on Sang-Pyong volume was awarded the 1996 Korean PEN Translation Award.

Jane Lai taught translation at the University of Hong Kong and Hong Kong Baptist University for many years up till her retirement in 2004. She has translated many playscripts into Chinese for performance, most of which are collected in her recently published eighteen-volume *Jane Lai Drama Translation Series*.

Leslie Lavigne has an MA from Concordia University, Montreal, with a concentration on the modern and contemporary periods in English literature. A poet in her own right, she has translated works of several Urdu poets in collaboration with Baidar Bakht. She makes her home in Montreal.

Naomi Lazard is known for her translations of Faiz Ahmed Faiz. Her own poems have appeared in the *American Poetry Review, The Nation, Haroers,* and *The New Yorker*. She is author of *The Moonlight Upper Deckerina* (Sheepmeadow Press, 1977), *Cry of the Peacocks* (Harcourt Brace, 1975), and *Ordinances* (Ardis).

Alex Lemon's first collection of poems is *Mosquito* (Tin House Books). Among his awards are a 2005 Literature Fellowship in Poetry from the National Endowment for the Arts and a 2006 Minnesota State Arts Board Grant.

Gabriel Levin's books include two collections of poems, *Sleepers of Beulah* and *Ostraca*; a prose work, *Hezekiah's Tunnel*; and translations from the Hebrew of Yehuda Halevi and S.Y. Agnon, and from the French of Ahmed Rassim. His work has appeared in the *TLS, PN Review, Prooftexts, Parnassus,* and many other journals.

Andrea Lingenfelter is a poet and translator of poetry, fiction, and occasional film subtitles. Her translations of Ling Yu, Zhai Yongming, and others have appeared in a number of anthologies and journals. She translated the novels *Candy*, by Mian Mian, and *Farewell My Concubine*, by Lilian Lee.

Liu Hong is a Canadian freelance translator whose major translations include a poetry anthology by Liu Zhan-qiu, *Untitled Lyrics* (Literature Press of Hong Kong, 1994), and a poetry anthology by Chuan Sha, *Spring Night* (Guangxi Normal University Press, 2006). He lives in Toronto with his wife and daughter.

Timothy Liu is the author of six books of poems, most recently *Of Thee I Sing* and *For Dust Thou Art*. An associate professor of English at William Paterson University and a member of the core faculty in Bennington College's Graduate Writing Seminars, Liu lives in Manhattan.

Leza Lowitz is an award-winning writer and editor who has published over a dozen books on Japan, including *Other Side River* (Stone Bridge). Together with Shogo

Oketani, she received a fellowship in translation from the NEA and the Japan–U.S. Friendship Commission Award for the Translation of Japanese Literature.

Luo Hui's translations have appeared in two books of poetry and various literary journals in North America and Asia. He is currently a PhD candidate at University of Toronto.

Sarah Maguire is the founder and director of The Poetry Translation Centre at the School of Oriental and African Studies. Her fourth collection of poems, *The Pomegranates of Kandahar,* was published in 2007. Her selected poems, *Haleeb Murag,* translated into Arabic by the distinguished Iraqi poet Saadi Yousef, was published in Damascus in 2003.

Quader Mahmud was born in Bangladesh in 1943 and has lived in Britain since 1973. He has published in Dhaka eleven Bengali books, including three anthologies (*Ek Dhoroner Slok,* 1999; *Baashor Aalper Naandipaath,* 2001; *Kaaler Modr,* 2005), four novels, and two short story collections. He has been a journalist, translator, broadcaster, and UK immigration law adviser.

Denis C. Mair's translations include memoirs of the monk Shih Chenhua (SUNY Albany), the autobiography of Feng Youlan (Hawai`i University), and fiction by Wang Meng (Foreign Languages Press). His book of poetry, *Man Cut in Wood,* was published by Valley Contemporary Poets (Los Angeles). He has lectured on the *I Ching* at the Temple School of Poetry (Walla Walla).

Khaled Mattawa was born in Libya in 1964. He is the author of *Ismailia Eclipse* and *Zodiac of Echoes.* He has also translated the works of many Arab poets into English. Some of his awards include a Guggenheim Fellowship, an NEA translation grant, and the PEN/USA Center's 2003 Award for Poetry in Translation.

John T. Mattioli is working on his PhD in comparative literature at the University of Wisconsin–Madison. These translations come out of research conducted under the Thailand Research Fund's Senior Researcher's Program on Spiritual and Intellectual Force in Contemporary Thai Poetry and a Fulbright Institute of International Education research grant at Chulalongkorn University, Thailand.

David R. McCann has published *Enough to Say It's Far,* selected poems by Pak Chaesam, cotranslated with Jiwon Shin, in the Princeton University Press Lockert Library of Poetry in Translation. New books include *Azaleas,* poems by Kim Sowol (Columbia University Press), and his own poetry collection, *The Way I Wait for You* (Codhill Press). He is the Korea Foundation Professor of Korean Literature at Harvard University.

Ken McCullough's most recent poetry books are *Obsidian Point* and *Walking*

Backwards, as well as a book of short stories, *Left Hand.* He has received numerous awards for his poetry. McCullough cotranslated the bilingual edition of U Sam Oeur's *Sacred Vows* and collaborated on U's memoir, *Crossing Three Wildernesses.*

Richard McKane is a British poet, translator, human rights interpreter, and a member of English PEN's Writers in Prison Committee. He has translated more than twenty books from Russian and Turkish into English, including works by Anna Akhmatova, Osip Mandelstam, Leonid Aronzon, and Nâzim Hikmet.

John H. McGlynn, from Wisconsin, is a long-term resident of Indonesia. Founder of the Lontar Foundation, McGlynn has brought into print more than sixty books on Indonesian language, literature, and culture. A translator of more than three dozen full-length books, he has also produced two dozen films on Indonesian writers.

Robert McNamara has published two collections of poetry, *Second Messengers* (Wesleyan University Press) and *The Body & the Day* (David Robert Books). The recipient of fellowships from the National Endowment for the Arts and the Fulbright Commission, he currently lives in Seattle and teaches at the University of Washington.

W. S. Merwin is the author of more than fifteen books of poetry and nearly twenty books of translations. His awards include the Pulitzer Prize, the Tanning Prize, the Bollingen Prize, and the 2004 Lannan Lifetime Achievement Award. His latest book, *Migrations,* won the 2005 National Book Award for Poetry, and was also named winner of the 2006 Ambassador Book Award for Poetry.

Farzaneh Milani is the author of *Veils and Words: The Emerging Voice of Iranian Women Writers* and *A Cup of Sin: Selected Poems of Simin Behbahani* (with Kaveh Safa). She has written over sixty articles, book chapters, introductions, and afterwords in Persian and English, and has lectured at more than one hundred colleges and universities internationally.

Kamal Mirawdeli was born in South Kurdistan in 1951 and went into exile in England in 1981. He emerged as a writer, literary critic, and poet in the 1970s and since then has written on the subjects of literature, history, politics, and philosophy in Kurdish, Arabic, and English, and has published two volumes of poems.

Leith Morton teaches English at the Tokyo Institute of Technology. He taught at Sydney University and Newcastle University, where he held the Foundation Chair in Japanese. He has written six books of poetry, translated five volumes of contemporary Japanese poetry, and written several scholarly works on Japanese literature and poetry.

Sulochana Musyaju, along with Wayne Amtzis, had translated many works of contemporary Nepali poetry into English. She received her MA in international economics from Brandeis University and is currently working as an entrepreneurship consultant in the Greater Boston area.

C. M. Naim is professor emeritus, Department of South Asian Languages and Civilizations, University of Chicago.

Najwa Nasr teaches at Lebanese University. She has translated numerous Lebanese poets.

Marilyn Nelson, the author or translator of twelve books and three chapbooks, has held fellowships from the NEA, A.C.L.S., Fulbright Foundation, and John Simon Guggenheim Memorial Foundation. She was the third poet laureate of the state of Connecticut, and is founder/director of Soul Mountain Retreat.

Murat Nemet-Nejat is a poet, essayist, and translator. His recent work includes: *New Translations, Eleven Septembers Later: Benjamin Hollander's Vigilance,* and *Eda: An Anthology of Contemporary Turkish Poetry.*

Nguyễn Bá Chung is cotranslator of Lê Lựu's *A Time Far Past* and the author of three collections of poetry in Vietnamese: *Distant Rain, Gate of Kindness, A Thousand Years of Old At Birth.* He lives in Boston, where he works at the Joiner Center for the Study of War and Social Consequences of the University of Massachusetts.

Nguyễn Quang Thiều, born in 1957, is the poetry editor of *Van Nghe Weekly* in Vietnam. He has published seven books of poetry, five books of short stories, four novels, four books for children, three books of translations, around two hundred articles and essays. His awards include The Poetry Award of The Writers Association of Vietnam.

Nguyen Qui Duc is the author of *Where the Ashes Are* and coeditor of *Vietnam, A Traveler's Literary Companion.* He is the translator of the novella *Behind the Red Mist,* by Ho Anh Thai, and numerous short stories. His short stories and essays have been published in *MĀNOA, Salamander, Zyzzyva,* and several anthologies. After thirty years in the United States, Indonesia, the United Kingdom, and Morocco, he returned to live in Vietnam.

Idra Novey is the author of *The Next Country,* winner of the 2005 Poetry Society of America Chapbook Fellowship. Her selected translations of Brazilian poet Paulo Henriques Britto was published by BOA Editions.

Naomi Shihab Nye was born in St. Louis, Missouri, in 1952, and currently lives in San Antonio, Texas. She is the author and/or editor of more than twenty volumes and has won numerous awards, including a Lavan Award from the Academy of American Poets and four Pushcart Prizes.

Desmond O'Grady was born in Limerick, Ireland in 1935. In 1975–1976 he was poet-in-residence at the American University in Cairo, and in 1978 he became a lecturer in English literature there. He has published several collections of poetry and translations.

Shogo Oketani is a freelance translator, poet and, fiction writer. With Leza Lowitz, he received a fellowship in translation from the NEA, and the Japan–U.S. Friendship Commission Award for the Translation of Japanese Literature from the Donald Keene Center at Columbia University for their translations of the poetry of Ayukawa Nobuo.

Zuzanna Olszewska is a PhD candidate in social anthropology at Oxford University, working on a dissertation titled *Poetry and Its Social Contexts Among Afghan Refugees in Iran*. A native of Poland, she has been studying Persian for the past five years.

Wen Chen Ouyang was born in Taiwan, raised in Libya, and educated in the United States. She has published numerous articles and given many talks on Arabic literature in the United States and Europe. She is the author of *Literary Criticism in Medieval Islamic Culture: The Making of a Tradition*.

Linda Owens lived from 1991 to 1997 in Indonesia, where she took advanced Indonesian language studies at the University of Indonesia, Jakarta. She has translated from Indonesian since 1993.

Ron Padgett's books include a collection of poems, *You Never Know,* and two memoirs, *Oklahoma Tough: My Father, King of the Tulsa Bootleggers* and *Joe: A Memoir of Joe Brainard.* He is also the translator of Blaise Cendrars's *Complete Poems.*

Bhadra Patel-Vadgama was born and educated in East Africa. She got her first arts degree at Makerere University, Uganda, and a postgradute Diploma in Library & Information Science from the Polytechnic of North London. In 1998, she won the Library Association's Royal Charter Centenary Award for her contribution to the profession.

Simon Patton teaches Chinese and translation at the University of Queensland (Australia). Since 2002, he has been editing the China domain of Poetry International Web with the mainland Chinese poet Yu Jian.

The Poetry Translation Centre was founded by the British poet Sarah Maguire in 2004. Based at the School of Oriental and African Studies in London, the PTC translates leading contemporary poets from non-European countries through translators collaborating with distinguished British poets.

Peter Porter was born in Brisbane, Australia, in 1929 and moved to London in 1951. He is the author of *The Cost of Seriousness* (1978), and his latest book, *Afterburner*, was shortlisted for the 2004 T. S. Eliot Prize. Porter was awarded the Gold Medal for Australian Literature in 1990 and the 2002 Queen's Gold Medal for Poetry.

H. S. Shiva Prakash was born in 1954. A Kannada poet and playwright, he is the author of six books of poems and twelve plays, and is the winner of many state and national literary awards. Currently, he is an associate professor, School of Arts and Aesthetics, Jawaharlal Nehru University, New Delhi.

Frances W. Pritchett is a professor in the Department of Middle East and Asian Languages at Columbia University. Her research interests include Urdu and Hindi poetic and narrative literature. She maintains a Web site of South Asian study materials.

Muneebur Rahman was born in Srinagar (Jammu and Kashmir) in 1956. He studied and taught linguistics at Aligarh Muslim University. He is currently director of BLI Translations in Boston. Rahman edits a Kashmiri literary magazine *Neab*.

Velcheru Narayana Rao is Krishnadevaraya Professor of Languages and Cultures of Asia at University of Wisconsin–Madison. One of the world's foremost scholars of Telugu and Indian Literature, he has extensively translated Telugu literature into English.

Jeremy Reed is a poet, novelist, translator, and critic. He has published more than three novels and many volumes of poetry, as well as a *Selected Poems* (Penguin). He received the Eric Gregory and Somerset Maugham Award in 1985. Reed has translated widely, namely, Montale, Novalis, and Cocteau.

Lucy Rosenstein grew up in Sofia, Bulgaria. She received her MA and PhD in Hindi from the School of Oriental and African Studies, University of London, where she currently teaches. She has published two books, *The Devotional Poetry of Svami Haridas: A Study of Braj Bhasha Verse* and *New Poetry in Hindi (Nayi Kavita): An Anthology*, and numerous articles on and translations of contemporary Hindi poetry.

John Rosenwald travels between China, Beloit College, and Farmington, Maine. He coedits the English-language version of Bei Dao's magazine *Jintian* and the venerable *Beloit Poetry Journal*.

Kaveh Safa has taught Persian language and literature at the Universities of Virginia and Chicago. With Farzanah Milani, he translated *A Cup of Sin* by Simin Behbahani (Syracuse University Press, 1999).

Bashir Sakhawarz has written prose and poetry books in both Persian/Dari and English, and currently he lives in England. He has a PhD from Jamia Milia University, India.

Muhammad Haji Salleh is a poet, critic, editor, and translator in Malay and English. He has published ten collections of poems and over thirty books of criticism and translation, including *Beyond the Archipelago* and *Romance and Laughter in the Archipelago*, and has been awarded the Malaysian Literary Award and the Southeast Asian Literary Prize.

K. Satchidanandan, the Indian poet, critic, and translator, was born in 1946. He headed the national Academy of Literature in India and has written in English and Malayalam twenty-one collections of poetry, fifteen collections of essays and travelogues, fifteen works of translations of world poetry, one full-length play, and one collection of short plays. His work has been translated into several languages.

Rajee Seth was born in 1935 in Nowshehra, NWFP (now in Pakistan). She has five collections of short stories and two novels to her credit, and a "Collected Poems" is forthcoming. She is also well known for her translations of Rilke into Hindi.

Shafi Shauq was born in 1950. He is a notable critic, translator, and poet of Kashmiri language. Currently he is the professor and head of the Postgraduate Department of Kashmiri at the University of Kashmir, Srinagar. He is the author of many books written in Kashmiri.

Abdul Salam Shayek's father was the president of the Literary Society of Heart for a decade and Abdul himself has written and translated poems into and from Persian. His translations were recently published in the English folio of the Iranian monthly paper *Pezhvak*. He has published *Naweed Monthly* for the Afghan American community in California.

Jiwon Shin completed her PhD in Korean literature at Harvard and is assistant professor of Korean Literature at the University of California, Berkeley.

Mahwash Shoaib is a poet, translator, and scholar. Her work has appeared most recently in *Encyclopedia* (volume 1 A–E), *Chain*, and *Shattering the Stereotypes: Muslim Women Speak Out*. She is currently working on her dissertation on the transnational poetics of American and Asian poets.

John Solt is a poet and independent scholar who was awarded the 1996 Japan–U.S. Friendship Commission Prize for the Translation of Modern Japanese Literature for *Glass Beret: The Selected Poems of Kitasono Katue*. Solt's critical biography, *Shredding the Tapestry of Meaning: The Poetry and Poetics of Kitasono Katue*, was published by Harvard University Asia Press in 1999. Solt is associate-in-research at the Edwin O. Reischauer Institute of Japanese Studies at Harvard University.

Manjushree Thapa was born in 1968. Thapa is a fiction and nonfiction writer and the author of *Mustang Bhot in Fragments, The Tutor of History,* and *Forget Kathmandu: An Elegy for Democracy.* The last was a Lettre Ulysses Award finalist in 2006. Her translations of the short stories of Ramesh Vikal was published in 2000 as *A Leaf in a Begging Bowl.* She has appeared in leading journals of Nepal, India, and the United States.

Yumiko Tsumura is a poet, translator of Modern Japanese literature, and professor of Japanese at Foothill College. Her translations include *Tamura Ryuichi Poems 1946–1998* (CCC Books, 2000) and Shiraishi Kazuko's *Let Those Who Appear* (2002). Shiraishi's *My Floating Mother, City,* translated in collaboration with Samuel Grolmes, is forthcoming in 2008 (New Directions).

Jeffrey Twitchell-Waas is the academic dean of Overseas Family College, Singapore. His recent translation-related publications include a chapbook of poems by Che Qianzi, *Vegetarian Hugging a Rooster* (Barque Press), and an article on Yang Lian's *Yi* in the *Chicago Review.*

Shouleh Vatanabadi was born in Iran in 1955 and came to the United States in 1978. Her books include *A Feast in the Mirror: A Collection of Short Stories by Iranian Women* (coedited and cotranslated with Mohammad Mehdi Khorrami), and *Another Sea, Another Shore: Persian Stories of Migration* (coedited and cotranslated with Mohammad Mehdi Khorrami).

Agnes Vong graduated from the University of Macau in 2002 and is currently writing her MA thesis on the topic, "Macao Poetry Today—A Study of Contemporary Writing Across Cultures."

Aimee Walker is a poet and translator. Her work has been published in the *Paris Review, Heliotrope,* and the *Grolier Poetry Prize Anthology.* She received a grant from the Astraea Lesbian Writers Fund and a scholarship to attend the Provincetown Fine Arts Work Center.

Wang Ping was born in China and came to the United States in 1985. Her publications include *American Visa, Foreign Devil, Of Flesh and Spirit, New Generation: Poetry from China Today, Aching for Beauty: Footbinding in China,* and *The Magic Whip.* She won the Eugene Kayden Award for the Best Book in Humanities and is the recipient of an NEA and the Bush Artist Fellowship for poetry. She is associate professor of English at Macalester College.

Stephen Watts is a poet, editor, and translator. He is the author of *The Blue Bag* and *Gramsci & Caruso,* and the coeditor of *Voices of Conscience, Mother Tongues,* and *Music While Drowning*. He has cotranslated contemporary Iranian, Kurdish, and Slovenian poets, and has compiled an impressive bibliography of modern poetry in English translation.

Eliot Weinberger's books of literary and political essays include *Karmic Traces, What Happened Here: Bush Chronicles,* and *An Elemental Thing*. He is the editor of the *New Directions Anthology of Classical Chinese Poetry,* and the editor and translator of the *Collected Poems of Octavio Paz* and the *Selected Non-Fictions of Jorge Luis Borges*.

Eric Welsapar is the brother of the poet Ak Welsapar. He has translated several Turkmen poets. He currently resides in Sweden.

Judith M. Wilks is a translator and coordinator of Persian at Northwestern University. Her research interests include Turkish and Persian literature, especially heroic traditions, folk literature, and mystical poetry. She has also done various projects in Tajik, Azeri, and other languages of the former Soviet Union.

Sholeh Wolpé was born in Iran. She is the author of *The Scar Saloon* (Red Hen Press) and the translator of *Sin: Poems of Forugh Farrokhzad, Iran's Rebel Poet* (University of Arkansas Press). Her poems, translations, essays, and reviews have appeared in scores of literary journals, periodicals, and anthologies worldwide, and have been translated into several languages.

Carolyne Wright has received a Witter Bynner Foundation Grant, an NEA Grant in Translation, and a Fellowship from the Bunting Institute of Radcliffe College for her translations. She spent five years (1986–1991) on a Fulbright Fellowship in Calcutta and Dhaka, Bangladesh, collecting and translating Bengali women writers for *A Bouquet of Roses on the Burning Ground*. She has been Taslima Nasrin's chief translator and serves on the faculty of the Whidbey MFA Program and on the AWP Board of Directors.

Yang Liping is a graduate of Shandong University, a translator for the Central Compilation and Translation Bureau in Beijing, and is currently completing his doctorate at the National University of Singapore. He has translated many works of fiction and nonfiction into Chinese, as well as works on Chinese drama and art into English.

Yama Yari was born in Herat, Afghanistan, in 1980 and came to the United Kingdom in 1999. With Sarah Maguire, he translated the second novel by Atiq Rahimi, Afghanistan's most important living novelist; it was published by Chatto & Windus in 2006.

Michelle Yeh's major publications include *Modern Chinese Poetry: Theory and Practice since 1917; Anthology of Modern Chinese Poetry* (edited and translated);

Essays on Modern Chinese Poetry (in Chinese); *From the Margin: An Alternative Tradition of Modern Chinese Poetry* (in Chinese); *Frontier Taiwan: An Anthology of Modern Chinese Poetry* (coedited with Göran Malmqvist); and *Iconography of the Sea: Poems of Derek Walcott* (edited, translated, and introduced in Chinese) among others.

Andy Young is a poet and translator. Her work has been published in the United States, Ireland, Mexico, and Egypt. She is the coeditor of *Meena,* a bilingual Arabic/English literary journal, and she teaches at the New Orleans Center for Creative Arts.

Arlene Zide's poetry has been published in *Meridians* (Smith College), *Xanadu, Rattapallax, Primavera,* and *Colorado Review* among others. Her translations from Hindi have appeared in *Manushi, Salt Hill, The Malahat Review,* and the *Oxford Anthology of Indian Poets.* She has edited *In Their Own Voice,* an anthology of contemporary Indian women poets (Penguin India, 1993).

COUNTRY INDEX

Dom Moraes (Goan-Indian)
Rukmini Bhaya Nair (Indian)
Sudeep Sen (Indian/American)

United States
Elmaz Abinader (Lebanese)
Etel Adnan (Lebanese)
Vidhu Aggarwal (Indian)
Meena Alexander (Indian)
Kazim Ali (Indian/Pakistani)
Indran Amirthanayagam (Sri Lankan)
Peter Balakian (Armenian)
Rick Barot (Filipino)
Mei-mei Berssenbrugge (Chinese)
Jenny Boully (Thai)
Luis Cabalquinto (Filipino)
G. S. Sharat Chandra (Indian)
Tina Chang (Chinese)
Hayan Charara (Lebanese)
Justin Chin (Chinese-Malaysian/
    Singaporean)
Chin Woon Ping (Hakka Chinese/
    Malaysian)
Oliver de la Paz (Filipino)
Brian Komei Dempster (European/
    Japanese)
Diana Der-Hovanessian (Armenian)
Linh Dinh (Vietnamese)
Chitra Banerjee Divakaruni (Indian)
Gregory Djanikian (Armenian)
Jennifer Kwon Dobbs (Korean)
Monica Ferrell
Sesshu Foster
Eric Gamalinda (Filipino)
Sarah Gambito (Filipina)
Eugene Gloria (Filipino)
Jessica Hagedorn (Filipina)
Kimiko Hahn (Japanese/European)
Suheir Hammad (Palestinian)
Nathalie Handal (Palestinian/French)
Samuel Hazo (Lebanese)
Cathy Park Hong (Korean)
Garrett Hongo (Japanese)
Luisa A. Igloria (Filipina)
Paolo Javier (Filipino)
Ha Jin (Chinese)
Lawrence Joseph (Lebanese)
Mohja Kahf (Syrian)

Kyi May Kaung (Burmese)
Suji Kwock Kim (Korean)
Joseph O. Legaspi (Filipino)
Russell C. Leong (Chinese)
Tan Lin
R. Zamora Linmark (Filipino)
Timothy Liu (Chinese)
Wing Tek Lum
Lisa Suhair Majaj (Palestinian)
Khaled Mattawa (Libyan)
D. H. Melhem (Lebanese)
Aimee Nezhukumatathil (Indian)
Partow Nooriala (Iranian)
Naomi Shihab Nye (Palestinian)
R. Parthasarathy (Indian)
Jon Pineda (Filipino)
Bino A. Realuyo (Filipino)
Srikanth Reddy (Indian)
Patrick Rosal (Filipino)
Vijay Seshadri (Indian)
Ravi Shankar (Indian)
Prageeta Sharma (Indian)
Cathy Song (Chinese/Korean)
Brian Kim Stefans (Korean)
Arthur Sze (Chinese)
Eileen Tabios (Filipina)
Barbara Tran (Vietnamese)
Pimone Triplett (Thai)
Michelle Yasmine Valladares (Indian)
Reetika Vazirani (Indian)
José Garcia Villa (Filipino)
Sholeh Wolpé (Iranian)
Xue Di (Chinese)
John Yau
Monica Youn (Korean)
C. Dale Young (Chinese/Indian)
Katayoon Zandvakili (Iranian)

Uzbekistan
Hamid Ismailov
Shukrulla
Eshqabil Shukur
Erkin Vahidov

Vietnam
Dư Thị Hoàn
Hữu Thỉnh
Lâm Thị Mỹ Dạ

LANGUAGE LIST

Arabic
Armenian
Assamese
Azeri
Bengali
Burmese
Chinese
Dari
Dhivehi
French
Gujarati
Hebrew
Hindi
Indonesian
Japanese
Kannada
Kashmiri
Khmer
Korean
Kurdish
Malay

Malayalam
Marathi
Nepal Bhasa (Newari)
Nepali
Oriya
Pashto
Persian
Punjabi
Russian
Tajik
Tamil
Tartar
Telugu
Thai
Tibetan
Turkish
Turkmen
Urdu
Uzbek
Vietnamese
Yi

EDITOR BIOGRAPHIES

Tina Chang is the author of *Half-Lit Houses* (Four Way Books, 2004). Her poems have appeared in *American Poet, Indiana Review, McSweeney's, Missouri Review, Ploughshares, Quarterly West, Sonora Review*, among others. Her poems have been anthologized in *Identity Lessons, Poetry Nation, Asian American Literature, Asian American Poetry: The Next Generation*, and in *Poetry 30: Poets in Their Thirties*. She has received awards from the Academy of American Poets, the Barbara Deming Memorial Fund, the Ludwig Vogelstein Foundation, the New York Foundation for the Arts, *Poets & Writers*, the Van Lier Foundation, among others. She teaches at Sarah Lawrence College and Hunter College.

Nathalie Handal's work has appeared in numerous anthologies and magazines, such as *Poetrywales, Ploughshares, Poetry New Zealand, Stand Magazine, Crab Orchard Review, Perihelion*, and *The Literary Review*. Her work has been translated into more than fifteen languages, she has been featured on NPR, KPFK, and PBS radio, and she teaches in the U.S. and abroad. Handal has been involved either as a writer, director, or producer in over twelve film and/or theatrical productions worldwide, and most recently she has worked with New York Theater Workshop and The Public Theater. She is the author of numerous award-winning books, including *The Lives of Rain* and *The Poetry of Arab Women: A Contemporary Anthology* (an Academy of American Poets bestseller and winner of the PEN Oakland/Josephine Miles Award). Handal is the poetry books review editor for *Sable* (UK) and an advisory board member for the Center for Literary Translation at Columbia University. She is currently working on the feature film *Gibran*.

Ravi Shankar is associate professor and poet-in-residence at Central Connecticut State University and the founding editor of the international online journal of the arts, *Drunken Boat* (drunkenboat.com). He has published a book of poems, *Instrumentality* (Cherry Grove, 2004), was named a finalist for the 2005 Connecticut Book Awards, and coauthored a chapbook, *Wanton Textiles* (No Tell Books). His creative and critical work has previously appeared in such publications as the *Paris Review, Poets & Writers, Fulcrum, McSweeney's,* and the *AWP Writer's Chronicle,* among many others. He has appeared as a commentator on NPR and Wesleyan Radio and read his work in many places, including the Asia Society, St. Mark's Poetry Project, and the National Arts Club. He currently reviews poetry for the *Contemporary Poetry Review* and serves on the Advisory Council for the Connecticut Center for the Book.

PERMISSIONS ACKNOWLEDGMENTS

Mammad Araz, "If There Were No War," from *Azerbaijan International,* AI 12.1., edited by Betty Blair, and translated by Aytan Aliyeva. Translation Copyright © 2004 by Betty Blair. Reprinted by permission of editor.

Lisa Asagi, "Physics," from *Physics* (Tin Fish Press). Copyright © 2006 by Lisa Asagi. Reprinted by permission of author.

Atamurad Atabayev, "Depth: A Sonnet," from *World Literature Today,* vol. 70, no. 3, translated by William M. Dirks. Translation Copyright © 1996 by WLT/David D. Clark. Reprinted by permission of WLT/David D. Clark.

David Avidan, "Dance Music," translated by Tsipi Keller. Printed by permission of translator.

Muhammed Hasan 'Awwad, "Secret of Life and Nature," from *Beyond the Dunes* (London: I.B. Tauris Press), edited by Mansour I. Al-Hazimi and Ezzat A. Khattab, English edition edited by Salma Khadra Jayyusi, and translated by Laith al-Husain and Alan Brownjohn. Translation Copyright © 2006 by I.B. Tauris Press. Reprinted by permission of I.B. Tauris Press.

Ayukawa Nobuo, "In a Dilapidated House," from *Ayukawa Nobuo: Collected Works, Volume I,* translated by Leza Lowitz and Shogo Oketani. Translation Copyright © 1989 by Leza Lowitz and Shogo Oketani. Reprinted by permission of Kaya Press.

Rafiq Azad, "Give me *Bhaat,* Bastard," translated by Quader Mahmud. Printed by permission of translator.

Nabila Azzubair, "The Closed Game," translated by Najwan Darwish. Printed by permission of translator.

Peter Balakian, "Mandelstam in Armenia, 1930," from *June-tree: New and Selected Poems, 1974–2000.* Copyright © 2001 by Peter Balakian. Reprinted by permission of HarperCollins Publishers.

'Abd-Allah al-Baraduni, "From Exile to Exile," from *Modern Arabic,* edited by Salma Khadra Jayyusi, and translated by Diana Der-Hovanessian with Sharif S. Elmusa. Translation Copyright © 1987 by Columbia University Press. Reprinted by permission of Columbia University Press.

Salim Barakat, "Index of Creatures," translated by Fady Joudah. Printed by permission of author and translator.

Mureed Barghouthy, "Desire," from *Modern Palestinian Literature,* edited by Salma Khadra Jayyusi, and translated by Lena Jayyusi and W. S. Merwin. Translation Copyright © 1992 by Columbia University Press. Reprinted by permission of Columbia University Press.

Rick Barot, "Many Are Called," from *Want* (Sarabande Books). Copyright © 2007 by Rick Barot. Printed by permission of author.

Shiv Kumar Batalvi, "Turbaned One," from apnaorg.com/suman/, translated by Suman Kashyap. Translation Copyright © 1995 by Suman Kashyap. Reprinted by permission of translator.

Abdul Wahab al-Bayati, "Aisha's Profile," from *Love, Death and Exile* (Georgetown

Edip Cansever, "Bedouin," from *Cave*, vol. 9, no. 1, translated by Talât Sait Halman. Translation Copyright © 1976 by Talât Sait Halman. Reprinted by permission of translator.

Nick Carbó, "Directions to My Imaginary Childhood," from *Andalusian Dawn* (Cherry Grove). Copyright © 2004 by Nick Carbó. Reprinted by permission of author.

Priya Sarukkai Chabria, "Flight: In Silver, Red and Black," from *Dialogue and Other Poems* (Sahitya Akademi). Copyright © 2005 by Priya Sarukkai Chabria. Reprinted by permission of author.

G. S. Sharat Chandra, "In the Third Country," from *Heirloom* (Delhi: Oxford University Press). Copyright © 1982 by Oxford University Press. Reprinted by permission of Jane Chandra.

Tina Chang, "Origin & Ash," from *Half-Lit Houses*. Copyright © 2004 by Tina Chang. Reprinted by permission of Four Way Books.

Hayan Charara, "Thinking American," from *The Alchemist's Diary* (Hanging Loose Press). Copyright © 2001 by Hayan Charara. Reprinted by permission of author.

Debjani Chatterjee, "Swanning In," from *Namaskar: New and Selected Poems by Debjani Chatterjee* (Bradford: Redbeck Press). Copyright © 2004 by Debjani Chatterjee. Reprinted by permission of author.

Che Qianzi, "Sentences," translated by Jeffrey Twitchell-Waas and Yang Liping. Copyright © 2006 by Che Qianzi. Reprinted by permission of author and Jeffrey Twitchell-Waas.

Andrée Chedid, "To Each of the Dead," from *Rattapallax 7*, translated by Annie Finch. Translation Copyright © 2002 by Annie Finch. Reprinted by permission of translator and *Rattapallax*.

Chen Li, "War Symphony," from *Frontier Taiwan: An Anthology of Modern Chinese Poetry*, edited by Michelle Yeh and N. G. D. Malmqvist. Copyright © 2001 by Columbia University Press. Reprinted by permission of Columbia University Press.

R. Cheran, "I Could Forget All This," from *Modern Poetry in Translation*, edited by D. & H. Constantine, translated by Lakshmi Holmström. Translation Copyright © 2006 by Lakshmi Holmström. Reprinted by permission of translator.

Justin Chin, "Eros in Boystown," from *Harmless Medicine*. Copyright © 2001 by Justin Chin. Reprinted by permission of Manic D Press.

Marilyn Chin, "Tonight While the Stars Are Shimmering," from *Rhapsody in Plain Yellow*. Copyright © 2002 by Marilyn Chin. Reprinted by permission of W. W. Norton & Co., Inc.

Dilip Chitre, "Ode to Bombay," from *Traveling in a Cage* (Clearing House). Copyright © 1980 by Dilip Chitre. Reprinted by permission of author.

Chuan Sha, "The Wolves Are Roaring." Copyright © 2006 by Chuan Sha, translated by Liu Hong. Printed by permission of author.

Fazil Hüsnü Dağlarca, "Dead," from *the new renaissance*, vol. VI, no. 1, translated by Talât Sait Halman. Translation Copyright © 1984 by Talât Sait Halman. Reprinted by permission of translator.

right © 1987 by Columbia University Press. Reprinted by permission of Columbia University Press.

Faiz Ahmed Faiz, "Once Again the Mind," from *The True Subject: Selected Poems of Faiz Ahmed Faiz*, translated by Naomi Lazard (Princeton University Press). Copyright © 1987 by Naomi Lazard. Reprinted by permission of author.

Saqi Farooqi, "An Injured Tomcat in Love," from *A Listening Game: Poems by Saqi Farooqi*, translated by Frances W. Pritchett (London: Lokamaya Press, 1987/London: Highgate Poets, 2001). Translation Copyright © 1987 by Frances W. Pritchett. Reprinted by permission of translator.

Forugh Farrokhzad, "Sin," from *Sin, Selected Poems of Forugh Farrokhzad* (University of Arkansas Press), translated by Sholeh Wolpé. Translation Copyright © 2007 by Sholeh Wolpé. Reprinted by permission of translator.

Yao Feng, "The Poet's Lunch," from *University of Macau Poets' Jubilee Anthology*, translated by Agnes Vong and Christopher Kelen (The University of Macau). Translation Copyright © 2006 by Christopher Kelen. Reprinted by permission of translator.

Monica Ferrell, "Mohn Des Gedächtnis," from *PN Review*, no. 30.1 (UK, 2003). Copyright © 2003 by Monica Ferrell. Reprinted by permission of author.

Sesshu Foster, "Gigante." Copyright © 2006 by Sesshu Foster. Printed by permission of author.

Luis H. Francia, "Gathering Storm." Copyright © 2006 by Luis H. Francia. Printed by permission of author.

Sylva Gaboudikian, "What I Notice," from *The Other Voice: Armenian Women's Poetry Through the Ages* (Aiwa Press), translated by Diana Der-Hovanessian. Translation Copyright © 2005 by Diana Der-Hovanessian. Reprinted by permission of translator.

Eric Gamalinda, "Valley of Marvels," from *Amigo Warfare* (WordTech Communications). Copyright © 2007 by Eric Gamalinda. Reprinted by permission of author.

Sarah Gambito, "Scene: a Loom," from *Matadora* (Alice James Books). Copyright © 2004 by Sarah Gambito. Reprinted by permission of author.

Nujoum al-Ghanim, "Sand in Flames," from *The Poetry of Arab Women* (Interlink Press), edited by Nathalie Handal, and translated by Clarissa Burt. Translator Copyright © 2001 by Nathalie Handal. Reprinted by permission of editor.

Sankha Ghosh, "Four Poems from Panjore DanRer Shabda," from *Parabaas Translations* (2002), translated by Nandini Gupta. Translation Copyright © 2002 by Nandini Gupta. Reprinted by permission of translator.

Muhammad al-Ghuzzi, "A Dream," from *Modern Arabic Poetry*, edited by Salma Khadra Jayyusi, and translated by May Jayyusi and John Heath-Stubbs. Translation Copyright © 1987 by Columbia University Press. Reprinted by permission of Columbia University Press.

Banira Giri, "Kathmandu," from *From the Lake, Love* (Himshikhar Publications), translated by Ann Hunkins. Translation Copyright © 2000 by Ann Hunkins. Reprinted by permission of translator.

Eugene Gloria, "Allegra with Spirit," from *Hoodlum Birds*. Copyright © 2006 by

Syed Shamsul Haq, "Poem 240," translated by Quader Mahmud. Printed by permission of translator.

Choman Hardi, "Summer Roof," from *Life For Us* (Bloodaxe Books). Copyright © 2004 by Choman Hardi. Reprinted by permission of author.

Cecep Syamsul Hari, "Wooden Table," from *Efrosina,* translated by Harry Aveling. Copyright © 2002 by Cecep Syamsul Hari. Reprinted by permission of author and translator.

Anjum Hasan, "A Place Like Water," from *Street on the Hill* (New Delhi: Sahitya Akademi). Copyright © 2006 by Anjum Hasan. Reprinted by permission of author.

Alamgir Hashmi, "Snow," from *This Time in Lahore: New Poems* (London and Lahore: Vision Press, 1983). Copyright © 1983 by Alamgir Hashmi. Reprinted by permission of author.

Samuel Hazo, "Just Words," from *Just Once: New and Precious Poems* (Autumn House Press). Copyright © 2002 by Samuel Hazo. Reprinted by permission of author.

Dorothea Rosa Herliany, "Saint Rosa, 1," from *Santa Rosa,* translated by Harry Aveling. Copyright © 2005 by Dorothea Rosa Herliany. Reprinted by permission of author and translator.

Ahmad 'Abd al-Mu'ti Hijazi, "The Lonely Woman's Room," from *Modern Arabic Poetry,* edited by Salma Khadra Jayyusi, and translated by Sargon Boulus and Peter Porter. Translation Copyright © 1987 by Columbia University Press. Reprinted by permission of Columbia University Press.

Nâzim Hikmet, "Angina Pectoris," from *Beyond the Walls: Selected Poems* (Anvil Press Poetry), translated by Richard McKane. Translation Copyright © 2002 by Ruth Christie, Richard McKane, and Talât Sait Halman. Reprinted by permission of translators.

Louise Ho, "POP SONG 1 'At Home in Hong Kong' 1964," from *Local Habitation.* Copyright © 1994 by Louse Ho. Reprinted by permission of author.

Cathy Park Hong, "Ontology of Chang and Eng, the Original Siamese Twins," from *Translating Mo'um.* Copyright © 2002 by Cathy Park Hong. Reprinted by permission of Hanging Loose Press.

Hong Yun-suk, "Ways of Living 4," from *Korean Literature Today,* vol. 1, no. 3, translated by Brother Anthony of Taizé. Translation Copyright © 1996 by Brother Anthony of Taizé. Reprinted by permission of translator.

Garrett Hongo, *"Chikin Hekka,"* from *Amerasia Journal.* Copyright © 2006 by Garrett Hongo. Reprinted by permission of author.

Ranjit Hoskote, "Moth," from *Vanishing Acts: New & Selected Poems, 1985–2005* (New Delhi: Penguin Books). Copyright © 2006 by Ranjit Hoskoté. Reprinted by permission of author.

Hsia Yü, "Fusion Kitsch," from *Fusion Kitsch: Poems from the Chinese of Hsia Yü,* (Zephyr Press), translated by Steve Bradbury. Translation Copyright © 2001 by Steve Bradbury. Reprinted by permission of translator.

Hung Hung, "Woman Translating, or La Belle Infidèle," from *Joseph Keene Chadwick:*

695

Yusuf al-Khal, "Retaliation," from *Mundus Artium,* International Poetry Forum, PA, vol. X, no. 1, translated by Sargon Boulus. Translation Copyright © 1977 by Sargon Boulus. Reprinted by permission of translator.

Ustad Khalilullah Khalili, "Quatrains," translated by Robert Abdul Hayy Darr from *Quatrains* (Afghan Cultural Assistance Foundation, 1989). Translation Copyright © 1989 by Robert Darr. Reprinted by permission of translator.

Harris Khalique, "She and I," from *Between You and Your Love* (Fazleesons). Copyright © 2004 by Harris Khalique. Reprinted by permission of author.

Masud Khan, "The Age of Commerce," from *Pakhi Teertha Dine* (Nadi Publishers), translated by Subarta Augustine Gomes. Copyright © 1993 by Masud Khan. Reprinted by permission of author.

Waleed Khazindar, "At Least," from *Modern Palestinian Literature,* edited by Salma Khadra Jayyusi, and translated by Lena Jayyusi and W. S. Merwin. Translation Copyright © 1992 by Columbia University Press. Reprinted by permission of Columbia University Press.

Esmail Khoi, "Of Sea Wayfarers," translated by Sholeh Wolpé. Printed by permission of translator.

Vénus Khoury-Ghata, "Our cries, she used to say," from *Here There Was Once a Country* (Oberlin College Press, FIELD Translation Series), translated by Marilyn Hacker. Translation Copyright © 2000 by Marilyn Hacker. Reprinted by permission of Frances Collin, Literary Agent.

Zareh Khrakhouni, "Measure," translated by Diana Der-Hovanessian. Printed by permission of translator.

Marne L. Kilates, "Python in the Mall," from *Poems en Route* (University of Santo Tomas Publishing House). Copyright © 1998 by Marne L. Kilates. Reprinted by permission of author.

Kim Kwang-kyu, "North South East West," from *The Depths of a Clam* (White Pine Press), translated by Brother Anthony of Taizé. Translation Copyright © 2005 by Brother Anthony of Taizé and Young-moo Kim. Reprinted by permission of translators.

Kim Nam-jo, "Foreign Flags," from *Korean Literature Today,* vol. 3, no. 4, translated by Brother Anthony of Taizé. Translation Copyright © 1998 by Brother Anthony of Taizé. Reprinted by permission of translator.

Suji Kwock Kim, "The Korean Community Garden," from *Notes from the Divided Country.* Copyright © 2003 by Suji Kwock Kim. Reprinted with permission of Louisiana State University Press.

Kim Su-yŏng, "Variations on the Theme of Love," from *Variations: Three Korean Poets,* Cornell East Asia Series 110, translated by Brother Anthony of Taizé. Translation Copyright © 2001 by Brother Anthony of Taizé. Reprinted by permission of translator.

Kim Sŭng-hŭi, "Sun Mass," from *The Columbia Anthology of Modern Korean Poetry,* edited by David R. McCann, translated by Brother Anthony of Taizé. Copyright © 2004 by Columbia University Press. Reprinted by permission of Columbia University Press.

Lale Müldür, "311, series 2 (turkish red)*," from *EDA: An Anthology of Contemporary Turkish Poetry* (Talisman House), edited and translated by Murat Nemet-Nejat. Translation Copyright © 2004 by Murat Nemet-Nejat. Reprinted by permission of translator.

Partaw Naderi, "Lucky Men," translated by Sarah Maguire and Yama Yari. Translation Copyright © 2002 by The Poetry Translation Centre Workshop. Reprinted by permission of Sarah Maguire, Director of PTC.

Nader Naderpour, "The Sculptor," translated by Zara Houshmand. Reprinted by permission of translator.

Kishwar Naheed, "Non-Communication," translated by Mahwash Shoaib, from *Siyah Hashiay Mei Gulabi Rang (Pink in a Black Boundary)* (Sang-e-meel Publications). Copyright © 1986 by Mahwash Shoaib. Reprinted by permission of author and translator.

Rukmini Bhaya Nair, "Genderole," from *The Hyoid Bone: Poems by Rukmini Bhaya Nair* (Viking Penguin India). Copyright © 1992 by Rukmini Bhaya Nair. Reprinted by permission of author.

Hassan Najmi, "Train Station," translated by Fady Joudah. Printed permission of translator.

Prathibha Nandakumar, "At the Staircase," from *Poetry International Web* (India, March 2007). Copyright © 2007 by Prathibha Nandakumar. Reprinted by permission of author.

Kunwar Narain, "The Rest of the Poem," translated by Lucy Rosenstein, from *New Poetry in Hindi, Nayi Kavita: An Anthology* (London: Anthem Press, 2004/Permanent Black, 2002). Copyright © 2002 by Lucy Rosenstein. Reprinted by permission of translator and Anthem Press.

Vivek Narayanan, "The Dump," from *Universal Beach: Poems by Vivek Narayanan* (Harbour Line). Copyright © 2006 by Vivek Narayanan. Reprinted by permission of author.

Taslima Nasrin, "At the Back of Progress . . . ," from *The Game in Reverse: Poems by Taslima Nasrin* (George Braziller), translated by Carolyne Wright and Mohammad Nurul Huda. Translation Copyright © 1995 by Carolyne Wright. Reprinted by permission of translator.

Amjad Nasser, "One Evening in a Café," from *Rattapallax 7,* translated by S. V. Atallah. Translation Copyright © 2002 by Seema Atallah and *Rattapallax*. Reprinted by permission of translator and *Rattapallax*.

Latif Nazemi, "A Word for Freedom," translated by Bashir Sakhawarz. Printed by permission of author and translator.

Behçet Necatigil, "Phosphorus," from *Cave,* vol. I, no. 1, translated by Talât Sait Halman. Translation Copyright © 1976 by Talât Sait Halman. Reprinted by permission of translator.

Aimee Nezhukumatathil, "By the Light of a Single Worm," from *At the Drive-In Volcano* (Tupelo Press). Copyright © 2003 by Aimee Nezhukumatathil. Reprinted by permission of author.

Taufiq Rafat, "Lights," from *Arrival of the Monsoon: Collected Poems 1947–1978* (Lahore: Vanguard). Copyright © 1985 by Vanguard. Reprinted by permission of Vanguard.

Mohammad Rafiq, "No One Belonging to Me," translated by Carolyn B. Brown, from *91st Meridian* (May 2005). Copyright © 2005 by Carolyn B. Brown. Reprinted by permission of translator.

Saif al-Rahbi, "Clump of Grass," translated by Khaled Hegazzi and Andy Young. Printed by permission of translators.

Rahman Rahi, "Redemption," translated by Shafi Shauq. Printed by permission of translator.

Shamsur Rahman, "Into Olive Leaves," translated by Sajed Kamal. Printed by permission of translator.

Abd el-Monem Ramadan, "Preparation for Our Desires," translated by Khaled Hegazzi and Andy Young. Printed by permission of author and translator.

A. K. Ramanujan, "The Black Hen," from *The Oxford India Ramanujan*. Copyright © 2004 by Oxford University Press. Reprinted by permission of Oxford University Press.

Eva Ranaweera, "The Poson Moon." Printed by permission of author.

Mani Rao, "§," from *Echolocation* (Chameleon Press). Copyright © 2003 by Mani Rao. Reprinted by permission of author.

Dahlia Ravikovitch, "Grand Days Have Gone By Her," from *Partisan Review*, vol. LXV, no. 2, translated by Tsipi Keller. Translation Copyright © 1998 by Tsipi Keller. Reprinted by permission of translator.

Bino A. Realuyo, "Filipineza," from *The Gods We Worship Live Next Door*. Copyright © 2006 by Bino A. Realuyo. Reprinted by permission of University of Utah Press.

Srikanth Reddy, "Loose Strife with Apiary," from *Facts for Visitors: Poems*. Copyright © 2004 by The Regents of the University of California. Reprinted by permission of University of California Press.

Oktay Rifat, "Beyond the Seven Hills," translated by Ruth Christie and Richard McKane. Printed by permission of translators.

Taher Riyad, excerpt from "Signs," from *Modern Palestinian Literature*, edited by Salma Khadra Jayyusi, and translated by May Jayyusi and Jeremy Reed. Translation Copyright © 1992 by Columbia University Press. Reprinted by permission of Columbia University Press.

Fehmida Riyaz, "Iqleema," translated by C. M. Naim. Printed by permission of author and translator.

Patrick Rosal, "About the White Boys Who Drove By a Second Time to Throw a Bucket of Water on Me," from *My American Kundiman*. Copyright © 2006 by Patrick Rosal. Reprinted by permission of Persea Books, Inc.

Wadih Sa'adeh, "Genesis," from http://www.geocities.com/wadih2/english2.html, translated by Sargon Boulus. Printed by permission of author and translator.

Eshqabil Shukur, "The Corpse of a Sufi," from *World Literature Today*, vol. 70, no. 3, translated by William M. Dirks. Translation Copyright © 1996 by WLT/ David D. Clark. Reprinted by permission of WLT/David D. Clark.

Kedarnath Singh, "An Argument About Horses," translated by Vinay Dharwadker, from *TriQuarterly* 77 (1989–90). Copyright © 1989 and renewed 2006 by Vinay Dharwadker. Reprinted by permission of translator.

Kirpal Singh, "Two Voices," from *Palm Readings* (Singapore: Graham Brash Ltd). Copyright © 1986 by Kirpal Singh. Reprinted by permission of author.

Sitor Situmorang, "In Answer to Father's Letter," from *To Love, To Wander* (The Lontar Foundation), translated by John H. McGlynn. Translation Copyright © 1996 by John H. McGlynn. Reprinted by permission of translator.

S. Sivasegaram, "Ahalya," from *Lutesong and Lament*, edited by Chelva Kanaganayakam, translated by Lakshmi Holmström. Translation Copyright © 2001 by Lakshmi Holmström. Reprinted by permission of translator.

Sŏ Chŏng-ju, "Barley-Time Summer," from *The Early Lyrics 1941–1960*, Cornell East Asia Series 90, translated by Brother Anthony of Taizé. Translation Copyright © 1996 by Brother Anthony of Taizé. Reprinted by permission of translator.

Bozor Sobir, "Letters," from *World Literature Today*, vol. 70, no. 3, translated by Judith M. Wilks. Translation Copyright © 1996 by WLT/ David D. Clark. Reprinted by permission of WLT/David D. Clark.

Cathy Song, "Breaking Karma," from *Cloud Moving Hands*. Copyright © 2007 by Cathy Song. Reprinted with permission of University of Pittsburgh Press.

Carolyn Marie Souaid, "Apology to Orhan Pamuk." Printed by permission of author.

Brian Kim Stefans, excerpt from "The Screens," from *Kluge: A Meditation, and Other Poems* (Roof Books). Copyright © 2007 by Brian Kim Stefans. Reprinted by permission of author.

Arundhathi Subramaniam, "Strategist," from *How2*, vol. 2, Issue 4, Spring–Summer 2006, edited by Mani Rao. Copyright © 2006 by Arundhathi Subramaniam. Reprinted by permission of author.

Pireeni Sundaralingam, "Letters from Exile," from *Cyphers*. Copyright © 2002 by Pireeni Sundaralingam. Reprinted by permission of author.

Arthur Sze, "Labrador Tea." Copyright © 2005 by Arthur Sze. Printed by permission of author.

Eileen Tabios, "Tercets from The Book of Revelation," from *I Take Thee, English, for My Beloved*. Copyright © 2005 by Eileen Tabios. Reprinted by permission of Eileen Tabios and Marsh Hawk Press.

Tada Chimako, "Haiku," translated by Jeffrey Angles. Translation Copyright © by Jeffrey Angles. Reprinted by permission of translator and Maya Suzuki, daughter of Tada Chimako and executor of estate.

M. Athar Tahir, "Carpet Weaver," from *A Dragonfly in the Sun: An Anthology of Pakistani Writing in English*, edited by Muneeza Shamsie (Oxford University Press).

Reetika Vazirani, "Quiet Death in a Red Closet," from *World Hotel*. Copyright © 2003 by Reetika Vazirani. Reprinted by permission of Copper Canyon Press.

José Garcia Villa, "The Anchored Angel," from *Selected Poems and New* (McDowell, Obolensky). Copyright © 1942, 1949, 1958 by José Garcia Villa. Reprinted by permission of John Edwin Cowen, Literary Trustee for the José Garcia Villa Estate.

Al-Munsif al-Wahaybi, "In the Arab House," from *Modern Arabic Poetry*, edited by Salma Khadra Jayyusi, translated by Salma Khadra Jayyusi and Naomi Shihab Nye. Copyright © 1987 by Columbia University Press. Reprinted by permission of Columbia University Press.

Yona Wallach, "Tuvia," translated by Tsipi Keller. Printed by permission of translator.

Wang Ping, "Wild Pheasant," from *MĀNOA: A Pacific Journal of International Writing*. Copyright © 2005 by Wang Ping. Printed by permission of author.

Wang Xiaoni, "White Moon," translated by Wang Ping and Alex Lemon. Translation Copyright © 2006 by Wang Ping. Printed by permission of Wang Ping.

Ak Welsapar, "Midday," translated by Eric Welsapar and Idra Novey. Printed by permission of author and translators.

Woeser, "Midnight, on the Fifth Day of the Fourth Month in the Tibetan Calendar," translated by d dalton. Copyright © 1999 D. Dalton. Reprinted by permission of translator.

Sholeh Wolpé, "One Morning, in the *LA Times*," from *The Scar Salon* (Red Hen Press). Copyright © 2004 by Sholeh Wolpé. Reprinted by permission of author.

Cyril Wong, "Practical Aim," from *The Cortland Review* (issue 31, Spring 2006). Copyright © 2006 by Cyril Wong. Reprinted by permission of author.

Laurence Wong, "Dawn in the Mid-Levels," from *First Hong Kong International Poetry Festival: A Collection of Poems* (Hong Kong Arts Center). Copyright © 1997 by Laurence Wong, translated by the author. Reprinted by permission of author.

Wong Phui Nam, excerpts from *Against the Wilderness* (Kuala Lumpur: Blackwater Books). Copyright © 2000 by Wong Pui Nam. Reprinted by permission of author.

Bryan Thao Worra, "Burning Eden One Branch at a Time," Copyright © 2005 by Bryan Thao Worra. Reprinted by permission of author.

Xi Chuan, excerpts from "Misfortune," translated by Wang Ping and Alex Lemon. Translation Copyright © 2006 by Wang Ping. Reprinted by permission of Wang Ping.

Xi Xi, "Sonnet," from *A Marked Category: Nine Women of Modern Chinese Poetry 1920–1997*, translated by Andrea Lingenfelter. Translation Copyright © 1997 by Andrea Lingenfelter. Reprinted by permission of translator.

Xie Ye, "At Last I Turn My Back," from *Smoking People, Beloit Poetry Journal*, translated by John Rosenwald and The Beloit/Fudan Translation Workshop. Translation Copyright © 1989 by The Beloit/Fudan Translation Workshop. Reprinted by permission of by John Rosenwald.

Xiong Hong, "Dark Associations," from *Frontier Taiwan, An Anthology of Chinese*

INDEX